R. Gupta's®

SBI
State Bank of India

Clerical Cadre
Junior Associates

Phase-I : Preliminary Exam

Practice Papers
(Solved)

2021
EDITION

Ramesh Publishing House, New Delhi

Published by
O.P. Gupta *for* Ramesh Publishing House

Admin. Office
12-H, New Daryaganj Road, Opp. Officers' Mess,
New Delhi-110002 ① 23261567, 23275224, 23275124

E-mail: info@rameshpublishinghouse.com
Website: www.rameshpublishinghouse.com

Showroom
● Balaji Market, Nai Sarak, Delhi-6 ① 23253720, 23282525
● 4457, Nai Sarak, Delhi-6, ① 23918938

© *Reserved with the Publisher*

No Part of this book may be reproduced or transmitted in any form or by any means, electronic or mechanical including photocopying, recording or by any transformation storage and retrieval system without written permission from the Publisher.

Indemnification Clause: This book is being sold/distributed subject to the exclusive condition that neither the author nor the publishers, individually or collectively, shall be responsible to indemnify the buyer/user/possessor of this book beyond the selling price of this book for any reason under any circumstances. If you do not agree to it, please do not buy/accept/use/possess this book.

Book Code: R-1818

ISBN: 978-93-87604-36-0

HSN Code: 49011010

Scheme of Phase-I (Preliminary) Exam

PHASE-I : PRELIMINARY EXAMINATION

- Preliminary Examination (online) consisting of Objective Tests for 100 marks will be conducted online. This test would be of 1 hour duration consisting of 3 Sections as follows:

S.No.	Name of Test	No. of Questions	Marks	Duration
1.	English Language	30	30	20 Minutes
2.	Numerical Ability	35	35	20 Minutes
3.	Reasoning Ability	35	35	20 Minutes
	Total	**100**	**100**	**1 Hour**

- Each test will have a separate timing as mentioned above.

- There will be negative marks for wrong answers in the Objective tests. 1/4th of mark assigned for question will be deducted for each wrong answer.

- No minimum qualifying marks for individual subject as well as for aggregate (overall) are prescribed.

- Adequate number of candidates in each category as decided by the Bank (approximately 10 times the numbers of vacancies, subject to availability) will be short listed for the Main Examination from the list of all candidates arranged in descending order of aggregate marks scored.

CONTENTS

15 PRACTICE SETS

SBI

State Bank of India

Junior Associates
(Customer Support & Sales)

Junior Agricultural Associates

Clerical Cadre

PRACTICE PAPERS
(With Explanatory Answers)

SBI Junior Associates & Junior Agricultural Associates
(Clerical Cadre Exam)

General English

Directions (Qs. 1–15): *Read the following passage carefully and answer the questions given below it. Certain words/phrases have been printed in **bold** to help you locate them while answering some of the questions.*

Born in a small town in Switzerland, Louis Agassiz was determined from childhood to become a scientist. As a youngster, he and his brother had collected all kinds of living animals and plants and had learned their Latin names. He attended the University, at Lausanne, the medical school at Zurich, and the universities at Heidelberg and Munich. His father, a clergyman, **annoyed** by Louis's ambition to become a naturalist, **urged** him to **study** medicine instead so that he might **earn a** comfortable living. Louis obediently enrolled in medical school, but at night he continued his study of living and fossil fishes.

Fortune helped Agassiz to enter his chosen field. On the recommendation of one of his instructors, he was asked by C.P. Von Maritius, who had returned from Brazil with a cargo of rare Amazon fishes, to collaborate with him in studying and classifying the specimens for future publication. When Louis was twenty-one years old, his book was published and was greeted with acclaim. Agassiz was **recognised as** a young prodigy.

The success of this book had several important consequences. It **persuaded** his father to accept the fact that he was determined to be a naturalist. It also brought Louis to the attention of great French scientist, Curvier. The old scientist invited Louis to his home in Paris, encouraged him to write a book and handed over to him his notes, specimens and fossils.

1. Which of the following was not willingly undertaken by Louis?
   A. Collecting living animals and plants
   B. Studies to become a physician
   C. Writing a book in collaboration with Maritius
   D. Visit to Paris at the behest of Mr. Cuvier
   E. Laming Latin names of plants and animals

2. Louis's father was keen that his son should
   A. follow his profession
   B. study in Paris
   C. study along with his brother
   D. at least accept job in a medical college
   E. lead a comfortable life

3. Why did Louis accept the invitation of Cuvier?
   A. He longed to study under the guidance of Cuvier
   B. At the behest of one of his instructors
   C. One the advice of C.P. Von Maritius
   D. Not mentioned in the passage
   E. None of these

4. Why did Louis accept the offer of Von Martius?
   A. He was very keen to write a book on voyage to Brazil
   B. He was recommended by his instructors and it was obligatory for him
   C. He had an opportunity to work in the area of his interest

D. He had an opportunity to earn a good amount of money
E. None of these

5. Which of the following incidents proved decisive in Louis's pursuit of studying natural sciences?
   A. His study of plants and animals with his brother
   B. Invitation from the French scientist Cuvier
   C. His pursuit of study of living beings during his medical course
   D. His determination from the childhood days
   E. None of these

6. Louis's father wanted Louis to pursue the career because
   A. that was the family profession
   B. doctors were badly needed in the society
   C. Louis's brother had pursued the career in the same field
   D. Munich University was famous for medical education
   E. it was lucrative

7. Which of the following is not true about the publication of Louis's first book?
   A. Louis came to be known as a 'rising star' after publication of the book
   B. The book was held in high esteem
   C. The book was written with the help of Cuvier
   D. Cuvier came to know about Louis through this book
   E. C.P. Von Martius wanted to study Amazon fishes with Louis

8. Which of the following staements is true in the context of the passage?
   A. Louis's visit to Brazil proved a turning point in his life
   B. The book written by Louis at Paris received good response
   C. Louis's father never accepted him as naturalist
   D. Though Louis was unconvince, he took admission in medical college
   E. As young student, Louis was fond of Latin language

9. It appears from the passage that Louis studied at all the following places except
   A. Paris   B. Munich
   C. Heidelberg   D. Zurich
   E. Lausanne

Directions (Qs. 10–12): *Choose the word which is most OPPOSITE in meaning of the word given in bold as used in the passage.*

10. URGED
   A. distracted   B. displeased
   C. ignored   D. prevailed
   E. dissuaded

11. ANNOYED
   A. comforted   B. pleased
   C. complied   D. irked
   E.

12. RECOGNISED
   A. replaced   B. unnoticed
   C. forgotten   D. honoured
   E. unpadoned

Directions (Qs.13–15): *Choose the word which is most nearly the SAME in meaning as the word given in bold as used in the passage.*

13. PERSUADED
   A. requested   B. forced
   C. advocated   D. convinced
   E. projected

14. EARN
   A. have   B. merit
   C. realise   D. collect
   E. aspire

15. STUDY
   A. examine   B. observe
   C. learn   D. research
   E. analyse

Directions (Qs. 16–20): *Read each sentence to find out whether there is any grammatical error or idiomatic error in it. The error, if any, will be in one part of the sentence. The number of that part is the answer. If there is "No Error" the answer is 'E'. (Ignore errors of punctuation if any.)*

16. (A) If you would have/(B) gone to his house/(C) before 10 a.m., you would have/(D) got his autograph./(E) No error.

17. (A) His speech was/(B) judged by many/(C) as one of the most important speech/(D) given in the function./(E) No error.

18. (A) I am contacting you/(B) sometime in next week/(C) to explain to you/(D) my problem in detail./(E) No error.

19. (A) Whatever he was/(B) today is only because/(C) of his mother who/(D) was a renowned scientist./(E) No error.

20. (A) The Head of the Department along with his colleagues/(B) are coming to attend/(C) the conference which is/(D) scheduled this afternoon./(E) No error.

Directions (Qs. 21–30) : *In the following passage there are blanks, each of which has been numbered. These numbers are printed below the passage, against each, five words are suggested, one of which fits the blank appropriately. Find out the appropriate word in each case.*

Architecture is a unique ..... **(21)** ..... of art and science that has ..... **(22)** ..... out of man's primary need for shelter. It is concerned with the design and ..... **(23)** ..... of buildings in their sociological, technological and environmental context. This field is not only ..... **(24)** ..... but also provides the ..... **(25)** ..... of designing and building pleasing and ..... **(26)** ..... refined structures to serve various needs. ..... **(27)** ..... the fairly large number of practising architects, the countrywide ..... **(28)** ..... in building activity offers scope for more. And though the initial earnings in the field are relatively ..... **(29)** ..... what you make thereafter will depend entirely on your ..... **(30)** .....

21. A. procedure   B. process
C. portion   D. blend
E. subject

22. A. drifted   B. fizzled
C. contrived   D. earned
E. arisen

23. A. painting   B. construction
C. decoration   D. repairing
E. appearance

24. A. fatiguing   B. strenuous
C. encouraging   D. vast
E. rewarding

25. A. satisfaction   B. facility
C. infrastructure   D. amenities
E. decorum

26. A. practically   B. ideologically
C. aesthetically   D. principally
E. readily

27. A. Considering   B. Having
C. Assuming   D. Regarding
E. Despite

28. A. variation   B. slack
C. lethargy   D. spurt
E. deterioration

29. A. escalating   B. modest
C. unpredictable   D. negligible
E. exorbitant

30. A. ambition   B. appearance
C. expectation   D. experience
E. need

Reasoning Ability

Directions (Qs. 31-35): *In each question below is given a group of letters followed by five combinations of number/symbol codes letters (A), (B), (C) (D) and (E). You have to find out which of the combinations correctly represents the group of letters based on the following coding system and the conditions and mark the number of that combination as your answer.*

Letters : H U I F M T C W E B Q K R P A

Number/Symbol Code : 6 # 7 © $ 5 3 ★ @ 2 4 % β 8 9

Conditions :

(i) If both the first and the last elements are consonants, both these are to be coded as the code for the fifth element.

(ii) If the third element is a consonant and the fourth a vowel, the codes for both these are to be interchanged.

(iii) If both the second and the fifth elements are vowels, the second element is to be coded as the code for the last element.

31. WUTABE
- A. ★#295@
- B. ★#952@
- C. ★#592@
- D. ★#992@
- E. @#952★

32. MACBEU
- A. $932@9
- B. $#@32#
- C. $#32##
- D. $#32@#
- E. $#3@2#

33. HEITQK
- A. 4@5744
- B. 6@7544
- C. 6@754%
- D. 4@7546
- E. 4@7544

34. QEPMUA
- A. 4@8$#9
- B. 498$#@
- C. 498$#9
- D. 49#8$9
- E. 4@8$#@

35. IREPAH
- A. 9β@899
- B. 7β8@96
- C. 7β@896
- D. 76@896
- E. 7β89@6

36. Town D is 12 Km. towards the North of town A. Town C is 15 Km. towards the West of town D. Town B is 15 Km. towards the West of town A. How far and in which direction is town B from town C?
- A. 15 Km. towards North
- B. 12 Km. towards North
- C. 3 Km. towards South
- D. 12 Km. towards South
- E. Cannot be determined

37. '1' is subtracted from each odd digit and '1' is added to each even digit in the number 4873529. Which of the following will be the difference between the second digit from the left and the third digit from the right of the new number thus formed?
- A. 4
- B. 3
- C. 5
- D. 2
- E. 6

Directions (Qs. 38 to 42): *In the following questions, the symbols @, ©, $, ★ and % are used with the following meaning as illustrated below:*

'P © Q' means 'P is smaller than Q'.

'P @ Q' means 'P is greater than Q'.

'P ★ Q' means 'P is either smaller than or equal to Q'.

'P % Q' means 'P is either greater than or equal to Q'.

'P $ Q' means 'P is neither smaller than nor greater than Q'.

Now in each of the following questions assuming the given statements to be true, find which of the two conclusions I and II given below them is/are **definitely true**.

Give answer
- A. if only Conclusion I is true.
- B. if only Conclusion II is true.
- C. if either Conclusion I or II is true.
- D. if neither Conclusion I nor II is true.
- E. if both Conclusions I and II are true.

38. Statements : M % T, T $ K, K © N
Conclusions : I. K $ M
II. K © M

39. Statements : J @ T, T © D, D % R
Conclusions : I. R © T
II. D @ J

40. Statements : W $ M, M @ B, B © K
Conclusions : I. B © W
II. K @ W

41. Statements : R ★ B, B © D, D $ F
Conclusions : I. F @ B
II. D @ R

42. Statements : ★ © K, K ★ M, M @ J
Conclusions : I. J © K
II. M @ H

Directions (Qs. 43-47): *In each of the questions below are given three statements followed by three conclusions numbered I, II & III. You have to take the given statements to be true even if they seem to be at variance from commonly known facts. Read all the conclusions and then decide which of the given conclusions logically follows from the given statements disregarding commonly known facts.*

43. Statements : All keys are locks.
No lock is toy.
All bags are toys
Conclusions : I. No bag is key.
II. Some bags are keys.
III. Some toys are keys.
- A. None follows
- B. Only I follows
- C. Only II follows
- D. Only III follows
- E. Only I and II follow

44. Statements : Some days are nights.
Some nights are months.
Some months are years.
Conclusions : I. Some years are nights.
II. Some months are days.
III. No year is night.
A. Only I follows
B. Only II follows
C. Only III follows
D. Only either I or III follows
E. None of these

45. Statements : All cycles are tyres.
Some tyres are wheels.
All wheels are buses.
Conclusions : I. Some buses are tyres.
II. Some wheels are tyres.
III. Some buses are cycles
A. Only I and II follow
B. Only I and III follow
C. Only II and III follow
D. All I, II and III follow
E. None of these

46. Statements : Some dogs are cats.
Some cats are horses.
All horses are tigers.
Conclusions : I. Some tigers are cats.
II. Some horses are dogs.
III. Some tigers are dogs.
A. None follows   B. Only I follows
C. Only II follows   D. Only III follows
E. Only II and III follow

47. Statements : All ropes are sticks.
Some sticks are hammers.
Some hammers are lakes.
Conclusions : I. Some lakes are ropes.
II. Some hammers are ropes.
III. Some lakes are sticks.
A. None follows   B. Only I follows
C. Only II follows   D. Only III follows
E. Only I and III follow

Directions (Qs. 48–52): *Study the following information carefully and answer the given questions.*
A, B, C, D, E and F are sitting in a straight line facing North.
A. A sits third to the right of D.
B. Neither A nor D sits at any of the extreme ends of the line.

C. C sits second to left of E.
D. B sits second to right of F.
E. B does not sit at an extreme end of the line.

48. If all the persons are made to sit in alphabetical order from **right to left,** the positions of how many will remain unchanged as compared to the original seating positions?
A. None   B. One
C. Two   D. Three
E. Four

49. Who sits at the extreme right hand corner of the line?
A. C   B. E
C. F   D. Either C or E
E. None of these

50. What is the position of B with respect to E?
A. Third to the left
B. Third to the right
C. Immediately to the rigth
D. Second to the left
E. Immediately to the left

51. Four of the following five are alike in a certain way basded on their seating positions in the above arrangement and so form a group. Which is the one that **does not** belong to that group?
A. CB   B. EA
C. DF   D. BC
E. AC

52. How many persons sit between C and F?
A. None   B. One
C. Two   D. Three
E. Four

53. Pointing to a girl, Samir said "She is the daughter of my grandfather's only son". How is the girl related to Samir?
A. Sister
B. Cousin
C. Daughter
D. Cannot be determined
E. None of these

54. How many such pairs of digits are there in the number 49316872 each of which has as many digits between them in the number as when the digits are arranged in ascending order within the number?
A. None   B. One

C. Two   D. Three
E. More than three

55. Village D is towards South of village A. Village K is towards East of village D. Village R is towards North of village N. Village A is towards which direction of village N?
A. West   B. North-West
C. South-West   D. Data inadequate
E. None of these

56. 'DIVE' is related to 'EIVD' and 'SOUL' is related to 'LOUS' in the same way as 'FEAR' is related to—
A. AERF   B. AFRE
C. RFAE   D. REAF
E. None of these

57. In a certain code language 'many red flowers' is written as 'ho na ti' and 'flowers are fresh' is written as 'ka pa na'. How is 'red' written in that code language?
A. ho   B. ti
C. ho or ti   D. Data inadequate
E. None of these

58. The positions of how many digits in the number 8394265 will remain unchanged if the digits are rearranged in descending order within the number?
A. None   B. One
C. Two   D. Three
E. More than three

59. It is Thursday on 25th of September. What day will it be on the 25th of October in the same year?
A. Monday   B. Sunday
C. Friday   D. Saturday
E. None of these

60. If 'A' is called '2', 'B' is called '3', 'C' is called '5', 'D' is called '8' and so on, then what will be the numerical value of 'F' ?
A. 18   B. 16
C. 17   D. 20
E. None of these

Directions (Qs. 61–65): *Study the following information carefully and answer the questions given below:*

Ten people are sitting in two parallel rows having five people each, in such a way that there is an equal distance between adjacent persons. In row 1—V, W, X, Y and Z are seated (but not necessarily in the same order) and all of them are facing North. In row 2—F, G, H, I and J are seated (but not necessarily in the same order) and all of them are facing south. Therefore, in the given seating arrangement, each member seated in a row faces another member of the other row.

- Y sits third to the left of W. The one who faces Y sits second to the right of F.
- Only one person sits between F and I.
- H and J are immediate neighbours of each other. J does not sit at any of the extreme ends of the line.
- The one who faces G sits to the immediate Right of Z.
- X is not an immediate neighbour of Z.

61. Who amongst the following faces H?
A. Y   B. V
C. Z   D. W
E. X

62. Who amongst the following sits to the immediate left of the person who sits exactly in the middle of row—2?
A. J   B. H
C. I   D. G
E. F

63. Four of the following five are alike in a certain way based on the given seating arrangement and thus form a group. Which is the one that does not belong to that group?
A. H   B. I
C. W   D. Y
E. X

64. Who amongst the following sits third to the right of the person who faces X?
A. G   B. F
C. J   D. I
E. H

65. Which of the following is true regarding V?
A. None of the given option is true
B. An immediate neighbour of V faces F
C. X is an immediate neighbour of V
D. W sits to immediate right of V
E. V faces I.

Quantitative Aptitude

66. The value of $51 \div 7 \div 3 = ?$
A. 9
B. 4
C. 3
D. 1
E. None of these

67. What will be the value of $40 \times 2 \div 10 + 5 - 4$?
A. 5
B. 8
C. 11
D. 9
E. 6

68. The value of $28 \times 104 \div (18 + 6) + 3 = ?$
A. $124\dfrac{1}{3}$
B. $104\dfrac{1}{3}$
C. $125\dfrac{1}{3}$
D. 128
E. 120

69. What is the value of $35 \times .07 - 21 \times .03$?
A. 2.75
B. 1.72
C. 1.82
D. 2.13
E. 2.25

70. $\dfrac{(6+6+6+6) \div 6}{4+4+4+4 \div 4} = ?$
A. 1
B. $\dfrac{3}{2}$
C. $3\dfrac{6}{13}$
D. $\dfrac{4}{13}$
E. None of these

71. Find the value of $\sqrt{17+\sqrt{51+\sqrt{152+\sqrt{289}}}}$
A. 11
B. 5
C. 10
D. 8
E. 9

72. If $\sqrt{12 \times 16 \times x} = 196$, then what is the value of x ?
A. 52
B. 48
C. 44
D. 56
E. 54

73. In a class of 52 students, the number of boys is 2 less than the number of girls. Average weight of the boys is 42 kg, while the average weight of all the 52 students is 40 kg. What is the approx, average weight of the girls?
A. 38 kg
B. 42 kg
C. 40 kg
D. 39 kg
E. 38 kg

74. A person travels 120 km in 6 hrs, 130 km in 5 hrs and 200 km in 4 hrs. Find his average speed during the whole journey.
A. 25 km/hr
B. 28 km/hr
C. 30 km/hr
D. 32 km/hr
E. 35 km/hr

75. 40% of the number is equal to three fourth of the another number. What is the ratio between first number and second number?
A. 15 : 16
B. 15 : 8
C. 9 : 15
D. 8 : 17
E. 17 : 8

76. The ratio between boys and girls in a school is 4 : 6 respectively. If the number of the boys is increased by 200 the ratio becomes 5 : 6 respectively. How many girls are there in the school?
A. 1200
B. 800
C. 900
D. 860
E. 980

77. The difference of two numbers is 20% of the larger number. If the smaller number is 20, the larger number = ?
A. 28
B. 32
C. 48
D. 25
E. 30

78. 720 sweets were distributed equally among children, in such a way that number of sweets received by each child is 20% of the total number of children. How many sweets did each child received?
A. 10
B. 13
C. 12
D. 11
E. 9

79. On what sum of money lent out at 9% per annum simple interest for 6 years does the simple interest amount to ₹ 810?
A. ₹ 1600   B. ₹ 1500
C. ₹ 1000   D. ₹ 1200
E. ₹ 1100

80. At simple interest of 5%, 6% and 8% for three consecutive year, the interest earned ₹ 760. Find the principal.
A. ₹ 4000   B. ₹ 4800
C. ₹ 3500   D. ₹ 3000
E. ₹ 4200

Directions (Qs. 81–85): *What will come in place of the question mark (?) in the following number series?*

81. 4, 27, 256, 3125, 46656, ?
A. 823543   B. 876811
C. 876801   D. 867801
E. 868000

82. ?, 23, 34, 45, 56, 78
A. 15   B. 18
C. 32   D. 31
E. 12

83. 512, 128, 32, 8, 2, ?

A. $\dfrac{1}{4}$ B. $\dfrac{1}{2}$

C. $\dfrac{1}{8}$ D. $\dfrac{1}{16}$

E. $\dfrac{1}{32}$

84. 12, 21, 24, 42, 36, ?
A. 65   B. 64
C. 163   D. 70
E. 63

85. 8, 11, 16, 23, ?
A. 35   B. 38
C. 40   D. 36
E. 32

86. If $\sqrt{1+\dfrac{x}{144}} = \dfrac{13}{12}$, then what will be the value of x?

A. 25   B. 24
C. 36   D. 28
E. 32

87. If 50% of $\sqrt{?}$ = 20% of 10, then which of the following will replace the question mark (?)?
A. 16   B. 12
C. 13   D. 18
E. 14

88. By what smaller number 270 be multiplied so that the resulting number becomes a perfect cube?
A. 121   B. 109
C. 100   D. 99
E. 105

89. One-fifth of a number is equal to $\dfrac{5}{8}$ of another number. If 35 is added to the first, it becomes four times of the second number. What is the second number?
A. 125   B. 70
C. 40   D. 25
E. 80

90. The sum of three numbers is 264. If the first number be twice the second and third number be one-third of the first, find the second number.
A. 84   B. 72
C. 54   D. 48
E. 64

91. The present age of Deepak is 3 times the present age of his son. Five years hence, the ratio of their ages will be 34 : 13 respectively. The present age of Deepak is:
A. 54 years   B. 65 years
C. 62 years   D. 63 years
E. 60 years

92. The present age of a father is three tiems the age of his son. Five years ago, father's age was four times the age of the son. What is the present age of son?
A. 20 years   B. 18 years
C. 15 years   D. 12 years
E. 16 years

93. A fort has provision for 50 days. After 15 days a reinforcement of 150 men arrives and the provision now lasts 25 days. How many men were there in the fort?
A. 300   B. 225
C. 275   D. 200
E. 250

94. The price per kg of sugar decreases by 20%. By what percentage should be the consumption be increased such that the expenditure remain the same?
A. 12%   B. 20%
C. 15%   D. 25%
E. 18%

95. A sum of ₹ 5000 amounts to ₹ 6050 in two years. What is the rate of interest?
A. 15%   B. 13%
C. 11%   D. 10%
E. 14%

Directions (Qs. 96–100): *These questions refer to the following circle graph showing the expenditure distribution of a certain family. The family spends ₹ 6500 per month.*

Expenditure Distribution of a Certain Family

96. How much it spends on Food per month?
A. ₹ 1950
B. ₹ 950
C. ₹ 1850
D. ₹ 850
E. ₹ 1000

97. How much are its annual taxes?
A. ₹ 7800   B. ₹ 9360
C. ₹ 9800   D. ₹ 10080
E. ₹ 9500

98. How many degrees should there be in the central angle showing clothing, taxes and transportation combined?
A. 100   B. 110
C. 120   D. 126
E. 115

99. How much more money per month is spent by the family on food as compared to the rent?
A. ₹ 650   B. ₹ 700
C. ₹ 750   D. ₹ 800
E. ₹ 850

100. If the expenditure budget of the family is raised to ₹ 8000 per month and distribution on various items remain the same, then the monthly expenses on both the intertainment and the transport will be:
A. ₹ 1800
B. ₹ 1600
C. ₹ 1440
D. ₹ 1220
E. ₹ 1250

ANSWERS

1	2	3	4	5	6	7	8	9	10
B	E	D	C	D	E	C	B	A	E

11	12	13	14	15	16	17	18	19	20
B	B	D	A	C	A	C	B	A	B

21	22	23	24	25	26	27	28	29	30
D	E	B	D	C	C	E	D	B	D

31	32	33	34	35	36	37	38	39	40
B	D	E	C	C	D	C	C	D	A

41	42	43	44	45	46	47	48	49	50
E	B	B	D	A	B	A	C	B	A

51	52	53	54	55	56	57	58	59	60
D	C	A	E	D	D	C	A	D	E
61	**62**	**63**	**64**	**65**	**66**	**67**	**68**	**69**	**70**
A	D	C	C	B	D	D	A	C	D
71	**72**	**73**	**74**	**75**	**76**	**77**	**78**	**79**	**80**
B	B	A	C	B	A	D	C	B	A
81	**82**	**83**	**84**	**85**	**86**	**87**	**88**	**89**	**90**
A	E	B	E	E	A	A	C	C	B
91	**92**	**93**	**94**	**95**	**96**	**97**	**98**	**99**	**100**
E	C	B	E	D	A	B	D	A	C

Some Selected Explanatory Answers

31. Condition (ii) applies.

32. Condition (iii) applies.

33. Condition (i) applies.

34. Condition (iii) applies.

35. No condition applies.

36.

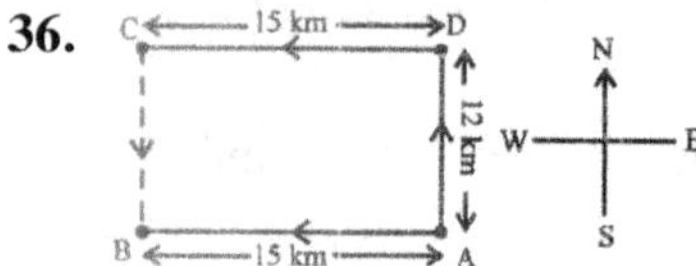

Obviously, CB = AD = 12 km and B is south of C.

37. 4873529 → 5962438

Now, 9 - 4 = 5

38. M % T → M ≥ T,   T \$ K → T = K;

K © N → K < N.

From these three, we get,

   M ≥ T = K < N

(i) K \$ M → K = M

(ii) K © M → K < M

From these two, K ≤ M

39. J @ T → J > T,   T © D → T < D;

D % R → D ≥ R.

From these three, we get

   J > T < D ≥ R

(i) R © T → R < T (False)

(ii) D @ J → D > J (False)

48.   First Condition : F D B C A E

Second Condition : F E D C B A

57. many red flowers → ho na ti

flowers are fresh → ka pa na

Thus, red → ho or ti

58. 8 3 9 4 2 6 5

9 8 6 5 4 3 2 ; *i.e.* none.

59. 25th September → Thursday

Number of days between 25th September to

25 October = 30 days = $\dfrac{30}{7} = 4\dfrac{2}{7}$

Thus we get 2 odd days.

Since, 25th October → Thursday + 2days = Saturday

60. Here,   A = 2

B = 2 + 1 = 3

C = 3 + 2 = 5

D = 5 + 3 = 8

E = 8 + 5 = 13

Thus,   F = 13 + 8 = 21

61-65.

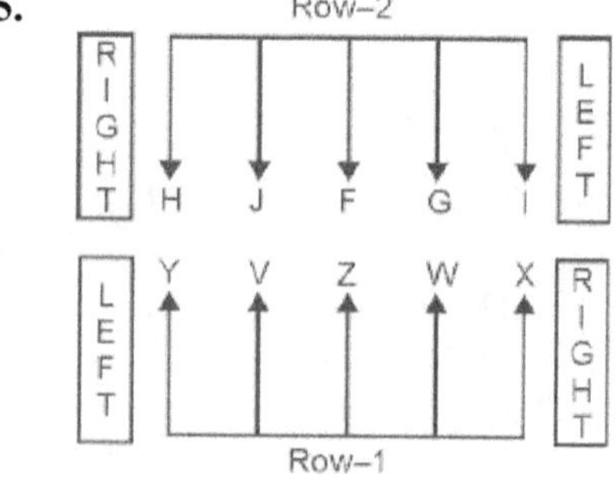

61. Y faces H.

62. F sits exactly in the middle of the row–2. G sits to the immediate left of F.

63. Except W, all others sit at ends of the lines.

64. I faces X. J sits third to the right of I.

65. Z faces F. Z is an immediate neighbour of V.

X is sitting at the extreme right end.

W sits second to the right of V. V faces J.

66. $51 \div 17 \div 3 = 3 \div 3 = 1$

67. $40 \times 2 \div 10 + 5 - 4$

$$= 40 \times \frac{2}{10} + 5 - 4$$

$$= 8 + 5 - 4 = 9$$

68. $28 \times 104 \div 24 + 3 = 28 \times \dfrac{104}{24} + 3$

$$= 28 \times \frac{26}{6} + 3 \ = \ \frac{14 \times 26}{3} + 3$$

$$= \frac{364}{3} + 3 \ = \ \frac{364 + 9}{3}$$

$$= \frac{373}{3} \ = \ 124\frac{1}{3}$$

69. $35 \times .07 - 21 \times .03 = 2.45 - .63 = 1.82$

70. $\dfrac{(6+6+6+6) \div 6}{4+4+4+4 \div 4} \ = \ \dfrac{24 \div 6}{12+1} \ = \ \dfrac{4}{13}$

71. $\sqrt{17 + \sqrt{51 + \sqrt{152 + \sqrt{289}}}}$

$$= \sqrt{17 + \sqrt{51 + \sqrt{169}}} \ = \ \sqrt{17 + \sqrt{64}}$$

$$= \sqrt{17 + 8} \ = \ \sqrt{25} \ = 5$$

72. $\sqrt{12 \times 16 \times x} = 96$

Squaring both sides

$12 \times 16 \times x = 96 \times 96$

$$x = \frac{96 \times 96}{12 \times 16}$$

$$= \frac{96 \times 96}{192} = 48$$

73. Let the number of girls be x, then the number of boys is $(x - 2)$

$$x + (x - 2) = 52$$

$$\Rightarrow \quad x + x - 2 = 52$$

$$\Rightarrow \quad 2x - 2 = 52$$

$$\Rightarrow \quad 2x = 54$$

$$\Rightarrow \quad x = \frac{54}{2} = 27$$

$\therefore$ There are 27 girls and 25 boys in the class.

Average weight of boys = 42 kg

Sum of boys weights = 25 × 42 = 1050 kg

Similarly, sum of the weights of the class

$$= 52 \times 40 = 2080 \text{ kg}$$

Sum of weight of the girls

$$= 2080 - 1050 = 1030 \text{ kg}$$

Average weight of the girls

$$= \frac{1030}{27} = 38.14 \text{ kg}$$

$$= 38 \text{ kg (approx)}$$

74. Average speed $= \dfrac{\text{total distance}}{\text{total time}}$

$$= \frac{(120 + 200 + 130) \text{ km}}{(6 + 4 + 5) \text{ hrs}}$$

$$= \frac{450}{15} = 30 \text{ km/hr}$$

75. According to the question,

$$40\% \text{ of } x = \frac{3}{4} \text{ of } y$$

$$\frac{40}{100} \times x = \frac{3}{4} \times y$$

$$160x = 300y$$

$$\frac{x}{y} = \frac{300}{160} = \frac{15}{8}$$

Hence, ratio of first number : 2nd number

$$= 15 : 8.$$

76. Let, the number of boys = $4x$ and

number of girls = $6x$

According to the question,

$$\frac{4x+200}{6x} = \frac{5}{6}$$

$\Rightarrow \quad 30x = 24x + 1200$

$\Rightarrow \quad 6x = 1200$

$\Rightarrow \quad x = 200$

$\therefore$ number of boys = $4 \times 200 = 800$

and number of girls = $6 \times 200 = 1200$

77. Let, the larger number be x

According to the question,

$(x - 20) = 20\%$ of x

$\Rightarrow \quad x - 20 = \dfrac{20x}{100} = \dfrac{x}{5}$

$\Rightarrow \quad 5x - 100 = x$

$\Rightarrow \quad 5x - x = 100$

$\Rightarrow \quad 4x = 100 \Rightarrow x = 25$

Hence, larger number = 25

78. Let, the total number of children = x

$\therefore \quad x \times \dfrac{20x}{100} = 720$

$\Rightarrow \quad \dfrac{x^2}{5} = 720$

$\Rightarrow \quad x^2 = 720 \times 5 = 3600$

$\Rightarrow \quad x = \sqrt{3600}$

$\qquad\quad x = 60$

Hence, number of sweets received by each

child = $\dfrac{20}{100} \times 60 = 12$

79. $\text{P} = \dfrac{\text{SI} \times 100}{r \times t} = \dfrac{810 \times 100}{9 \times 6}$

$= 15 \times 100 = 1500$

Hence, Principal = ₹ 1500

80. Let, the principal be ₹ x

Then,

$$\text{S.I.} = \left(\frac{x \times 1 \times 5}{100}\right) + \left(\frac{x \times 1 \times 6}{100}\right) + \left(\frac{x \times 1 \times 8}{100}\right)$$

$$760 = \frac{5x + 6x + 8x}{100}$$

$\Rightarrow \ 19x = 760 \times 100$

$\Rightarrow \quad x = \dfrac{760 \times 100}{19} = 4000$

Hence, principal = ₹ 4000

81. 4, 27, 256, 3125, 46656, $\boxed{823543}$

$\quad\ \downarrow \quad \downarrow \quad\ \downarrow \quad\ \ \downarrow \quad\ \ \downarrow \qquad \downarrow$

$\quad 2^2 \quad 3^3 \quad 4^4 \quad\ 5^5 \quad\ 6^6 \qquad 7^7$

82. $\boxed{12,}$ 23, 34, 45, 56, 78

$\qquad -11 \quad -11 \quad -11 \quad -11 \quad -11$

83. 512, 128, 32, 8, 2, $\boxed{\dfrac{1}{2}}$

$\qquad \div 4 \quad\ \div 4 \quad\ \div 4 \quad\ \div 4 \quad\ \div 4$

84. 12   21   24   42   36   63

Here there are two types of series

(*i*)   12,   24,   36

(*ii*)   21,   42,   63

85. 8   11   16   23 $\boxed{32}$

$\quad\ +3 \quad +5 \quad +7 \quad +9$

86. $\sqrt{1 + \dfrac{x}{144}} = \dfrac{13}{12}$

Squaring both sides,

$\Rightarrow \left(\sqrt{1 + \dfrac{x}{144}}\right)^2 = \left(\dfrac{13}{12}\right)^2$

$\Rightarrow \quad 1 + \dfrac{x}{144} = \dfrac{13}{12}$

$\Rightarrow \quad \dfrac{x}{144} = \dfrac{13}{12} - 1$

$$= \frac{13-12}{12} = \frac{1}{12}$$

$$\Rightarrow \quad 12x = 144$$

$$\Rightarrow \quad x = \frac{144}{12} = 12$$

Hence, value of $x = 12$

87. 50% of $\sqrt{x}$ = 20% of 10

$$\Rightarrow \frac{50}{100} \times \sqrt{x} = \frac{20}{100} \times 10$$

$$\Rightarrow \quad \frac{\sqrt{x}}{2} = 2$$

$$\Rightarrow \quad \sqrt{x} = 4$$

Squaring both sides,

$$\left(\sqrt{x}\right)^2 = (4)^2$$

$$\Rightarrow \quad x = 16$$

88. $\quad 270 = 2 \times 5 \times 3 \times 3 \times 3$

$$= 10 \times \underline{3 \times 3 \times 3}$$

From the above, we find that the number 10 does not make a group of three.

$\therefore$ If we multiply 270 by ($10 \times 10 = 100$), the product would be $\underline{10 \times 10 \times 10} \times \underline{3 \times 3 \times 3}$ which is a perfect cube.

89. Let, the two numbers be x and y

then, $\quad \dfrac{1}{5}x = \dfrac{5}{8}y$

$$\Rightarrow \quad x = \frac{25}{8}y \qquad\qquad ...(i)$$

And, $x + 35 = 4y$

$$\Rightarrow 4y - \frac{25}{8}y = 35$$

$$\Rightarrow \quad \frac{7y}{8} = 35$$

$$\Rightarrow \quad y = \frac{8 \times 35}{7} = 40$$

Hence, second number = 40

90. Let, the second number be x, then first and third will be $2x$ and $\dfrac{2x}{3}$.

According to the question,

$$2x + x + \frac{2x}{3} = 264$$

$$\Rightarrow \quad \frac{6x + 3x + 2x}{3} = 264$$

$$\Rightarrow \quad 11x = 3 \times 264$$

$$\Rightarrow \quad x = \frac{3 \times 264}{11}$$

$$= 3 \times 24 = 72$$

91. Let, present age of Deepak and his son be $3x$ and x years respectively; then

$$\frac{3x+5}{x+5} = \frac{34}{13}$$

$$\Rightarrow 39x + 65 = 34x + 170$$

$$\Rightarrow \quad 5x = 105 \Rightarrow x = 21$$

Hence, present age of Deepak

$$= 3 \times 21 = 63 \text{ years.}$$

92. Let, present age of father and his son are $3x$ and x years respectively.

According to the question,

$$4(x - 5) = 3x - 5$$

$$\Rightarrow 4x - 20 = 3x - 5$$

$$\Rightarrow \quad x = 15$$

Hence, son's age = 15 years

93. Days $\qquad$ Men

$$35 \uparrow \qquad\qquad x \downarrow$$
$$25 \qquad\quad x + 150$$

$$\Rightarrow \quad \frac{x+150}{x} = \frac{35}{25}$$

$$\Rightarrow \quad 35x = 25x + 25 \times 100$$

$$\Rightarrow \quad 10x = 25 \times 150$$

$$\Rightarrow \quad x = \frac{25 \times 150}{10} = 375$$

Required number of men = 375 – 150 = 225

94.
$$\text{Increase}\% = \left\{ \frac{r}{100-r} \times 100 \right\}\%$$

$$= \left(\frac{20}{100-20} \times 100 \right)\%$$

$$= \frac{20}{80} \times 100 = 25\%$$

95.
$$A = P\left(1 + \frac{r}{100}\right)^{t}$$

$$6050 = 5000\left(1 + \frac{r}{100}\right)^{2}$$

$$\Rightarrow \quad \frac{6050}{5000} = \left(1 + \frac{r}{100}\right)^{2}$$

$$\Rightarrow \quad \frac{121}{100} = \left(1 + \frac{r}{100}\right)^{2}$$

$$\Rightarrow \quad \left(\frac{11}{10}\right)^{2} = \left(1 + \frac{r}{100}\right)^{2}$$

$$\Rightarrow \quad \frac{11}{10} = 1 + \frac{r}{100}$$

$$\Rightarrow \quad \frac{11-10}{10} = \frac{r}{100}$$

$$\Rightarrow \quad \frac{1}{10} = \frac{r}{100}$$

$$\Rightarrow \quad r = 10\%$$

96. Food = 30% of ₹ 6500

$$= \frac{30}{100} \times 6500 = ₹\ 1950$$

97. Taxes = 12% of ₹ 6500

$$= \frac{12}{100} \times 6500 = ₹\ 780 \text{ per month}$$

$$= 780 \times 12 = ₹\ 9360 \text{ per year}$$

98. Clothing, taxes and transportation combined are 35%

Now, 100% = 360

$$\Rightarrow \quad 35\% = \frac{360}{100} \times 35 = 126$$

99.
$$10\% \text{ of } ₹\ 6500 = \frac{10}{100} \times 6500$$

$$= ₹\ 650 \text{ per month}$$

100.
$$18\% \text{ of } ₹\ 8000 = \frac{18}{100} \times 8000 = ₹\ 1440$$

SBI Junior Associates & Junior Agricultural Associates
(Clerical Cadre Exam)

General English

Directions (Qs. 1–15): *Read the following passage carefully and answer the questions given below it. Certain words/phrases have been printed in **bold** to help you locate them while answering some of the questions.*

Mahatma Gandhi has repeatedly called himself a truthseeker and has learned, in the course of his search, that truth is a condition of being, not a quality outside of oneself or a moral acquisition, that it is of the very essence of the divine in man. Though he saw deceit and falsehood all around him and knew that it was accepted as the standard of life by people occupying positions of authority and influence, he was never afterwards tempted to **yield to** it even when to have done so would have brought advantage and no condemnation.

For healing he always had a great love and some aptitude and when at the age of seventeen **his family in conclave** suggested his going to England to study law, he **begged** to be allowed to study medicine instead. This, however, was not permitted and law was chosen for him. But, the love of healing remained, and though he could not study in the **orthodox** schools of medicine, he **gratified** his desire by studying various forms of nature-cure treatment and by experimenting with these on his person and on his friends and relatives. Some of these experiments produced remarkable results possibly not only due to the treatment but also to his devoted and instinctive nursing.

1. On whom did Gandhiji practice nature-cure?
   A. On sick patients in hospitals
   B. On people occupying positions of authority and influence
   C. Those who were in great need of the treatment
   D. Those who were not cured by other medicines
   E. None of these

2. Gandhiji studied law mainly because
   A. he wanted to be an eminent lawyer
   B. he wanted to go to England
   C. his family thrust upon him the study of law
   D. he knew he can make a good career in legal profession
   E. he wanted to serve people by solving their legal problems

3. What was Gandhiji's idea of truth?
   A. It should be assimilated as a personal quality
   B. It should be observed with a healing touch
   C. It should not be followed with an idea of sacrifice
   D. It should be searched in the world around you
   E. None of these

4. Mahatma Gandhi described himself as a man:
   A. in search of divine qualities
   B. who would like to serve people
   C. who would like to set standard of life
   D. who would not compromise on his principles
   E. None of these

5. Choose the word that is MOST OPPOSITE in meaning of the word 'begged' as used in the passage.
   A. Demanded   B. Appealed
   C. Suggested   D. Requested
   E. Protested

6. Choose the word which is MOST OPPOSITE in meaning of the word 'orthodox' as used in the passage.
   A. Backward   B. Non-conventional
   C. Unpopular   D. Modern
   E. Customary

7. What temptation did Gandhiji always resist?
   A. Getting attracted towards wordly comforts
   B. Ignoring the dictates of elderly people
   C. Healing the wound of other
   D. Following deceit and falsehood
   E. None of these

8. What was probably the real cause of Gandhiji's success in nature-cure?
   A. His detailed study of various medicinal systems
   B. His confidence and desire to help people
   C. His skills and aptitude in nursing
   D. His experiments in search of truth
   E. None of these

9. What did Mahatma Gandhi learn in the course of his search?
   A. Being truthful is a divine blessing
   B. Truth is synonymous with one's existence
   C. People are full of deceit and falsehood
   D. Truth is a quality outside of oneself
   E. None of these

10. What did Gandhiji see around him?
   A. Sick and unhealthy people
   B. People accepting proper standard of life
   C. People suffering from poverty and disease
   D. People not having love and aptitude for healing
   E. Dishonesty and untruthfulness

11. Explain the meaning of expression 'his family in conclave' as used in the passage.
   A. Members of the family and relatives
   B. Figurehead of the family

C. Private meeting of the family
   D. Family meeting for celebrating Gandhiji's seventeenth birthday
   E. None of these

12. Choose the word that is most nearly the SAME in meaning as the word 'gratified' as used in the passage.
   A. Purified   B. Satisfied
   C. Nurtured   D. Glorified
   E. Projectd

13. Choose the word which is most nearly the SAME in meaning as the word 'yield' as used in the passage.
   A. Surrender   B. Provoke
   C. Confine   D. Adapt
   E. Adhere

14. Which of the following statements is NOT TRUE in the context of the passage?
   A. Gandhiji did many experiments in the area of nature-cure
   B. Gandhiji did not study medicine in the orthodox school
   C. Studying law was Gandhiji's first love
   D. Truthfulness is the condition of being
   E. Gandhiji was always a truthseeker

15. Which of the following statement(s) is/are true in the context of the passage?
   (1) Gandhiji had a love and aptitude for nursing
   (2) Gandhiji experimented nature-cure on himself
   (3) Gandhiji encouraged deceit and psychofancy
   A. Only (1)   B. (1) and (3)
   C. Only (3)   D. (1) and (2)
   E. Only (2)

Directions (Qs. 16–20) : *Each sentence below has a blank, indicating that something has been omitted. Choose the word for each blank which best fits the meaning of the sentence as a whole.*

16. There is no doubt that one has to keep ..... with the changing times.
   A. himself   B. tuning
   C. pace   D. oneself
   E. aside

17. The poor ones continue to ..... out a living inspite of economic liberalisation in that country.
    A. eke B. go
    C. manage D. bring
    E. find

18. ..... eye witnesses, the news reporter gave a graphic description of how the fire broke.
    A. Reporting B. Seeing
    C. Examining D. Quoting
    E. Observing

19. Before getting elected, he was ..... to the welfare of the people.
    A. devoted
    B. attended
    C. focussed
    D. neglected
    E. concentrated

20 The union leader was very critical ..... the attitude of the management.
    A. for B. at
    C. on D. against
    E. of

Directions (Qs. 21–25): *Read each sentence to find out whether there is any grammatical error or idiomatic error in it. The error, if any, will be in one part of the sentence. The number of that part is the answer. If there is "No Error" the answer is 'E'. (Ignore errors of punctuation if any.)*

21. (A) There is just not enough/(B) timing in my job to sit around/(C) talking about how we feel/(D) about each other./(E) No error.

22. (A) Reasonable ambition, if supported/(B) at persistent efforts,/(C) is likely to yield/(D) the desired results./(E) No error.

23. (A) Even after worked in the office/(B) for as many as fifteen years,/(C) he still does not understand/(D) the basic objectives of the work./(E) No error.

24. (A) Why some people don't get/(B) what they deserve/(C) and why others get what they don't deserve/(D) is a matter decided by luck./(E) No error.

25. (A) The five-member committee were/(B) of the view that the present service conditions/(C) of the employees of this company/(D) are quite good./(E) No error.

Directions (Qs. 26–30): *Which of the phrases A, B, C and D given below should replace the phrase given in* **bold** *in the following sentence to make the sentence grammatically meaningful and correct? If the sentence is correct as it is and 'No correction is required', mark E as the answer.*

26. If he has to spend five hours in the queue, it **was really a wastage.**
    A. is a really wastage
    B. is real a wastage
    C. has really a wastage
    D. is really a wastage
    E. No correction required

27. Why **did you not threw** the bag away?
    A. did you not throw
    B. had you not threw
    C. did you not thrown
    D. you did not thrown
    E. No correction required

28. They **are not beware of** all the facts
    A. are not aware for
    B. are not aware of
    C. are not to be aware
    D. must not to be aware for
    E. No correction required

29. **If I would have** realised the nature of the job earlier, I would not have accepted it.
    A. If I have had
    B. In case I would have
    C. Had I been
    D. Had I
    E. No correction required

30. The moment they saw me, they **were delight**
    A. had delighted
    B. were delighted
    C. are delighted
    D. have been delighted
    E. No correction required

Reasoning Ability

Directions (Qs. 31–33): *Following questions are based on the five three-digit numbers given below:*

| 519 | 364 | 287 | 158 | 835 |

31. If the positions of the first and the third digits within each number are interchanged, which of the following will be the third digit of the second lowest number?
A. 9
B. 4
C. 7
D. 8
E. 5

32. If the positions of the first and the third digits within each number are interchanged, which of the following will be the middle digit of the second highest number?
A. 1
B. 6
C. 8
D. 5
E. 3

33. Which of the following is the difference between the second digits of the highest and the lowest of these numbers?
A. 3
B. 1
C. 2
D. 0
E. None of these

Directions (34 & 35): *Read the following information carefully and answer the questions which follow:*

If 'A × B' means 'A is wife of B'.
If 'A + B' means 'A is brother of B'.
If 'A ، B' means 'A is daughter of B'.
If 'A – B' means 'A is son of B'.

34. Which of the following means 'T is father of P'?
A. P + Q × R – T
B. P ، R – T × Q
C. P + Q ، R × T
D. P – Q + T ، R
E. None of these

35. How is Y related to Z if 'Y × V + W ، Z'?
A. Daughter
B. Father-in-law
C. Wife
D. Daughter-in-law
E. Cannot be determined

Direction (Qs. 36–40): *Each of the questions below consists of a question and two statements numbered I and II are given below it. You have to decide whether the data provided in the statements are sufficient to answer the question. Read both the statements and–*
Give answer
A. if the data in Statement I alone are sufficient to answer the question, while the data in Statement II alone are not sufficient to answer the question.
B. if the data in Statement II alone are sufficient to answer the question, while the data in Statement I alone are not sufficient to answer the question.
C. if the data in Statement I alone or in Statement II alone are sufficient to answer the question.
D. if the data in both the Statements I and II are not sufficient to answer the question.
E. if the data in both the Statements I and II together are necessary to answer the question.

36. How is Sanjay related to Anil?
I. Sanjay's son is the brother of only sister of Anil.
II. Radhika, the only daughter of Sanjay has only two brothers.

37. How many children does Seema have?
I. Seema, the mother of Varsha's sister has only one son.
II. Varsha has only three siblings.

38. What is the code for 'your' in the code language?
I. In the code language 'Buy your own book' is written as 'ta na pi la' and 'do try your best, is written as 'sa jo ta be'.
II. In the code language 'please submit your reports' is, written as 'ke si do ta' and 'your house is grand' is written as 'fi ta go hi'.

39. Who amongst P, R, S, T and V, each having a different height, is the tallest?
I. T is taller than R and V.
II. P is shorter than R.

40. How many children are there in the class?
I. Radhika's rank is 10th from the top and she is 3 ranks above Shraddha.

II. Namita's rank is 6th from the top and is 5 ranks above Karan who is 20th from the bottom.

Directions (Qs. 41-45): *In each question below are three statements followed by three conclusions numbered I, II and III. You have to take the three given statements to be true even if they seem to be at variance from commonly known facts and then decide which of the given conlusions logically follows from the three given statements disregarding commonly known facts. Then decide which of the answers (A), (B), (C), (D) and (E) is the correct answer and indicate it on the answersheet.*

41. **Statements** : Some desks are chairs.
    All chairs are tables.
    Some tables are mats.
    Conclusions : I. Some mats are desks.
    II. Some tables are desks
    II. Some mats are chairs.
    A. Only I follows
    B. Only II follows
    C. Only III follows
    D. Only II and III follow
    E. None of these

42. **Statements** : All sweets are fruits.
    No fruit is pencil.
    Some pencils are glasses.
    Conclusions : I. Some glasses are sweets.
    II. Some pencils are sweets.
    II. No glass is sweet.
    A. Only I follows
    B. Only II follows
    C. Only III follows
    D. Only either I or III follows
    E. None of these

43. **Statements** : Some books are flowers.
    Some flowers are chains.
    Some chains are hammers.
    Conclusions : I. Some hammers are flowers.
    II. Some chains are books.
    II. Some hammers are books.
    A. None follows   B. Only I follows
    C. Only II follows   D. Only III follows
    E. Only II and III follow

44. **Statements** : All roofs are cameras.
    Some cameras are photographs.
    Some photographs are stores.
    Conclusions : I. Some stores are cameras.
    II. Some stores are roofs.
    II. Some cameras are roofs.
    A. Only I follows
    B. Only II follows
    C. Only III follows
    D. Only II and III follow
    E. None of these

45. **Statements** : Some nails are hourses.
    All horses are tablets.
    All tablets are crows.
    Conclusions : I. Some crows are nails.
    II. Some tablets are nails.
    II. Some crows are horses.
    A. Only I follows
    B. Only I and II follow
    C. Only I and III follow
    D. Only II and III follow
    E. All I, II and III follow

Directions (Qs. 46–50): *Study the following information carefully and answer the questions given below:*

P, Q, R, S, T, U, V and W are sitting around a circle facing at the center. T is to the immediate right of W and fourth to the left of P. S is third to the right of Q who is not an immediate neighbour of either P or W. R is third to the left of U who is not an immediate neighbour of S.

46. Who is to the immediate right of Q?
    A. V   B. P
    C. U   D. Data inadequate
    E. None of these

47. Who is second to the right of V?
    A. P   B. S
    C. U   D. R
    E. None of these

48. Who is second to the right of R?
    A. Q
    B. P
    C. U
    D. Data inadequate
    E. None of these

49. What is Q's position with respect to R?
A. Fifth to the right
B. Third to the left
C. Fifth to the left
D. Fourth to the left
E. Third to the right

50. The persons in which of the following pairs are immediate neighbours of U?
A. QV   B. QP
C. TQ   D. TW
E. None of these

Directions (Qs. 51-55): *Each of the questions given below is based on the given diagram. The diagram shows students studying either Physics, Chemistry, Biology or combinations of these subjects.*

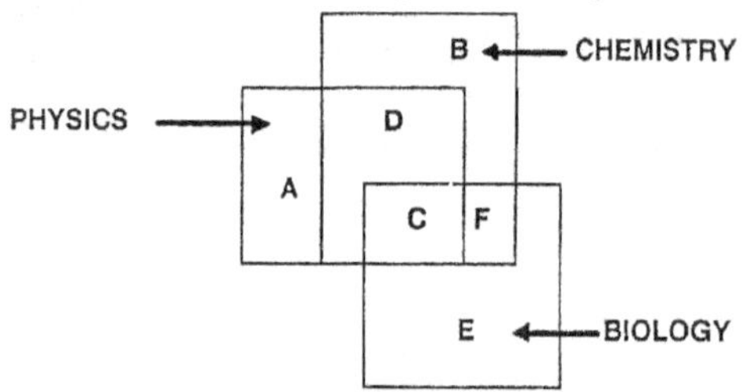

51. In which of the following groups are the students studying all the three subjects included?
A. A   B. B
C. C   D. D
E. None of these

52. Which of the following is **not** represented in the above diagram?
A. The students who study Biology, Chemistry as well as Physics.
B. The students who study Chemistry and Biology but not Physics
C. The students who do not study any of the three subjects.
D. The students who study Biology but not Physics and Chemistry.
E. The students who study Physics and Chemistry but not Biology

53. If a lecture is being attended by students from group B and group F together, on which of the following subjects could the lecture be?
A. Chemistry or Biology

B. Only Chemistry
C. Only Biology
D. Physics, Chemistry or Biology
E. Only Physics

54. Which of the following correctly represents the students studying both Physics and Chemistry but not biology?
A. Only C   B. C and D
C. C, D and F   D. Only D
E. Only F

55. Which of the following groups represents the students who do not study Chemistry?
A. E and F   B. Only A
C. A, C and E   D. D, C and F
E. A and E

56. In a certain code language 'Ne Pe Le' means 'what is this'. 'Bo Le Se' means 'is that okay' and 'Se Ni Di' means 'that was easy'. What is the code for 'okay' in that code language?
A. Le   B. Se
C. Ne   D. Ni
E. None of these

57. In a certain code 'GIVE' is written as 'VIEG' and 'OVER' is written as 'EVRO'. How will 'DISK' be written in that code?
A. SIDK   B. KISD
C. KDSI   D. SIKD
E. None of these

58. What should come next in the following letter series?
AABABCABCDABCDEABCDEF
A. G   B. C
C. B   D. A
E. None of these

59. Four of the following five are alike in a certain way and so form a group. Which is one that **does not** belong to that group?
A. Sesame   B. Mustard
C. Patato   D. Coconut
E. Groudnut

60. How many such pairs of digits are there in the number 5234816 each of which has as many digits between them in the number as when the digits are arranged in descending order within the number?

A. None   B. One
C. Two   D. Three
E. More than three

Directions (Qs. No. 61-65): *Study the information and answer the given question:*

In a certain code language:

'work never goes waste' is written as **'rb mk ni tj'**
'never waste your time' is written as **'ni ap sy rb'**
'focus on your work' is written as **'mk ap cn or'**
'Focus goes with time' is written as **'sy tj cn ke'**
(All the codes are two letter codes only)

61. In the given code language, what does the code 'tj' stand for?
A. never   B. goes
C. on   D. work
E. waste

62. What is the code for 'focus' in the given code language?
A. ap   B. ni

C. sy   D. cn
E. mk

63. What is the code for 'time' in the given code language?
A. tj   B. sy
C. ni   D. cn
E. rb

64. Which of the possibly means 'work on projects'?
A. sy cn tj   B. gt cn or
C. mk gt or   D. mk cn gt
E. mk or sy

65. In the given code language, what does the code 'rb' stand for'?
A. either 'never' or 'waste'
B. goes
C. your
D. work
E. time

Quantitative Aptitude

Directions (Qs. 66–80): *What will come in place of question mark (?) in the following questions?*

66. The value of $8\dfrac{1}{3}+5\dfrac{1}{4}\times13\dfrac{1}{5}\div6\dfrac{3}{5}=?$

A. $19\dfrac{1}{3}$ B. $18\dfrac{5}{6}$

C. $21\dfrac{1}{3}$ D. $22\dfrac{1}{2}$

E. None of these

67. What will be the value of

$11^2 - 6^2 \div 6\times\dfrac{5}{2}+2$ of 10?

A. 126   B. 108
C. 110   D. 125
E. None of these

68. $832.58 - 242.31 = 779.84 - ?$
A. 220.085   B. 189.57
C. 199.57   D. 205.05
E. None of these

69. $40.83 \times 1.02 \times 1.2 = ?$
A. 58.7952   B. 49.97592
C. 42.479532   D. 41.64660
E. None of these

70. What will be the value of $\sqrt[3]{\sqrt{144}+\sqrt{16}+\sqrt{4}}$?
A. 3   B. 2
C. 4   D. 5
E. 7

71. If $\sqrt{2+\dfrac{2}{49}}=\dfrac{x}{14}$, what will be the value of x?
A. 15   B. 18
C. 20   D. 30
E. None of these

72. The sum of present ages of two brothers is 36 years. After 4 years their age will be 5 : 6. What is the age of elder brother?
A. 20 years   B. 25 years
C. 35 years   D. 28 years
E. 22 years

73. The average of 13 numbers is 52. The average of first-seven of these numbers is 48 and the average of the last seven number is 58. What is the seventh number?
A. 60 B. 62
C. 64 D. 66
E. 68

74. The average of Mukesh's marks in 7 subjects is 75. His average in 6 subjects excluding science is 72. How many marks did he get in science?
A. 75 B. 85
C. 93 D. 88
E. 95

75. The sum of five consecutive numbers is 190. What is the product of second and 3rd numbers?
A. 1406 B. 1208
C. 1396 D. 1256
E. 1436

76. If 10% of a number is subtracted from it, the result is 1800. What is the number?
A. 1800 B. 2200
C. 2400 D. 2000
E. None of these

77. A car can complete a journey in 6 hrs if it travels at 45 km/hr. At what speed must it travel in order to complete the journey in 5 hours?
A. 60 km/hr B. 54 km/hr
C. 65 km/hr D. 72 km/hr
E. 58 km/hr

78. A and B working together complete a work in 35 days. If A takes 60 days to complete it, how long would B alone take to complete it?
A. 64 days B. 72 days
C. 81 days D. 84 days
E. None of these

79. In an examination 60% of the candidates passed in English, 55% in Mathematics and 25% failed in both subjects. What is the pass percentage?
A. 30% B. 35%
C. 25% D. 40%
E. 32%

80. A's income is 10% more than B's. How much per cent is B's income is less than A's?
A. 10% B. 7%
C. $9\dfrac{1}{11}\%$ D. $6\dfrac{1}{2}\%$
E. 8%

Directions (Qs. 81–85): *What will come in the place of the question mark (?) in the following number series?*

81. 1, 3, 5, 7, 9, ?
A. 11 B. 14
C. 17 D. 19
E. 15

82. 2, 7, 14, 23, 34, ?
A. 48 B. 45
C. 47 D. 52
E. 51

83. 1, 8, 27, 64, 125, ?
A. 225 B. 216
C. 420 D. 320
E. 215

84. 2, 5, 10, 17, 26, ?
A. 132 B. 140
C. 142 D. 37
E. 136

85. 10, 17, 26, ?, 50, 65
A. 42 B. 37
C. 38 D. 41
E. 29

86. A man travels a certain distance at the rate of 10 km/hr and returns the same point at the rate of 15 km/hr. His average rate for the whole journey is:

A. 12 km/hr B. $12\dfrac{1}{2}$ km/hr
C. 13 km/hr D. 14 km/hr
E. 11 km/hr

87. A train 150 m long passes an electric pole in 5 seconds. How long will it take to cross a bridge of 180 m long?
A. 10 sec B. 11 sec
C. 12 sec D. 9 sec
E. 8 sec

88. Mohan spent 20% of his income on food, 30% on house rent and 25% on clothes. If he saved ₹ 750, then find his income.
A. ₹ 2500   B. ₹ 2800
C. ₹ 3000   D. ₹ 3200
E. ₹ 2400

89. A dishonest shopkeeper claims to sell his goods at cost price but uses a weight of 800 gm in place of the standard 1 kg weight. His gain per cent is:
A. 25%   B. 20%
C. 16%   D. 8%
E. 12%

90. A man borrowed a sum at 15% simple interest. He paid ₹ 2250 as interest after 5 years. The sum borrowed by him is:
A. ₹ 3000   B. ₹ 4500
C. ₹ 4000   D. ₹ 2500
E. ₹ 3200

91. The difference between compound interest and simple interest on a certain sum of money in 2 years at 5% p.a. is ₹ 12.50. Find the sum:
A. ₹ 5000   B. ₹ 2500
C. ₹ 3000   D. ₹ 6000
E. ₹ 4000

92. The average of 15 numbers is 15 and the average of the first 8 numbers is 8. The average of the last 7 numbers is:
A. 15   B. 8
C. 7   D. 23
E. 18

93. Ravi and Rahim are two partners in a firm sharing the profit in the ratio 4 : 5. If the firm earns a profit of ₹ 14130, the profit to be received by Rahim is:
A. ₹ 1280   B. ₹ 7850
C. ₹ 6550   D. ₹ 6150
E. ₹ 3100

94. A, B and C share the profit in the ratio of 3 : 5 : 7. If the gain is ₹ 2040, then C's share is:
A. ₹ 360   B. ₹ 600
C. ₹ 700   D. ₹ 952
E. ₹ 380

95. A man gave $\frac{2}{5}$ th of his sum of money to his son and $\frac{1}{4}$ th to his daughter and half of the remaining money to a school. If he has ₹ 1750 now with him, find his sum of money.
A. ₹ 10000
B. ₹ 12000
C. ₹ 8000
D. ₹ 11000
E. ₹ 9000

Directions (Qs. 96–100): *Study the following graph carefully and answer the questions given below:*
Percentage of different types of employees in a company in two consecutive years

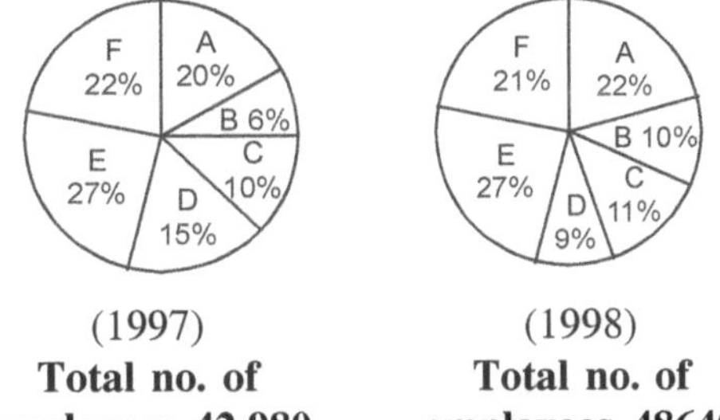

Total no. of employees 42,980   **Total no. of employees 48640**

96. In 1997 the total number of which of the following types of pairs of employees was approximately equal to A type of employees in 1998?
A. B and C   B. A and C
C. D and E   D. C and D
E. None of these

97. From 1997 to 1998 in the case of which of the following type of employees the change was maximum?
A. B   B. D
C. C   D. A
E. None of these

98. What was the approximate difference in the number of B type of employees during 1997 and 1998?
A. 2285   B. 2325
C. 2085   D. 2620
E. 1975

99. If the number of D type of employees in 1998 was 5000, what would have been its approximate percentage in the company?
A. 8 B. 12
C. 14 D. 10
E. 13

100. The number of A type of employees in 1998 was approximately what per cent of the number of A type of employees in 1997?
A. 11.5% B. 14.0%
C. 12.5% D. 13.0%
E. 12.0%

ANSWERS

1	2	3	4	5	6	7	8	9	10
E	C	A	A	E	B	D	C	B	E

11	12	13	14	15	16	17	18	19	20
C	B	A	C	D	C	A	D	A	E

21	22	23	24	25	26	27	28	29	30
B	B	A	A	A	D	A	B	D	B

31	32	33	34	35	36	37	38	39	40
D	D	C	C	D	E	D	C	D	B

41	42	43	44	45	46	47	48	49	50
B	C	A	C	E	A	B	E	D	C

51	52	53	54	55	56	57	58	59	60
C	C	B	D	E	E	D	D	C	B

61	62	63	64	65	66	67	68	69	70
B	D	B	C	A	B	A	B	B	A

71	72	73	74	75	76	77	78	79	80
C	A	D	C	A	D	B	D	D	C

81	82	83	84	85	86	87	88	89	90
A	C	B	D	B	A	B	C	A	A

91	92	93	94	95	96	97	98	99	100
A	D	B	D	A	D	A	A	D	C

Some Selected Explanatory Answers

34.
P Q R T
Brother Daughter Wife
Therefore T is father of P.

35.
Y V W Z
Wife Brother Daughter
Therefore Y is daughter's in law of Z.

41. 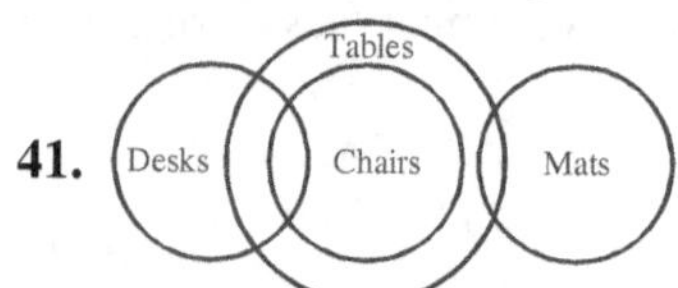

I. Some mats are desks. (False)
II. Some tables are desks. (True)
III. Some mats are chairs. (False)

45. 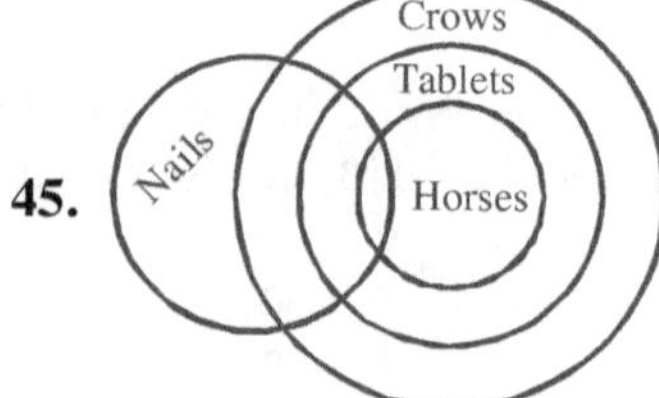

I. Some crows are nails. (True)

II. Some tablets are nails. (True)

III. Some crows are horses. (True)

For Qs. 46–50

Their sitting arrangement is shown below:

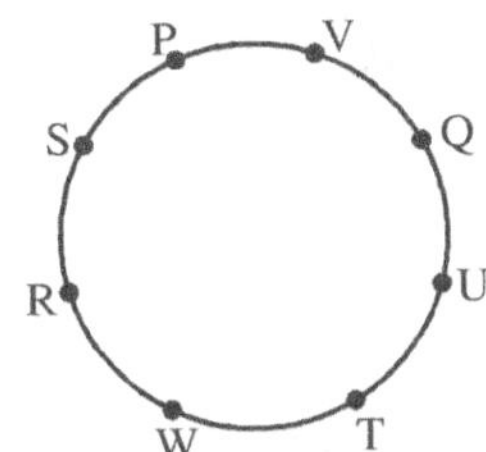

56. Ne Pe L̲e̲ → What i̲s̲ this

$\boxed{\text{Bo}}$ L̲e̲ S̲e̲ → i̲s̲ that $\boxed{\text{okay}}$

S̲e̲ Ne De → t̲h̲a̲t̲ way easy

Thus, Okay → Bo

57. As, $\overset{1\,2\,3\,4}{\text{GIVE}} \longrightarrow \overset{3\,2\,4\,1}{\text{VIEG}}$

$\overset{1\,2\,3\,4}{\text{OVER}} \longrightarrow \overset{3\,2\,4\,1}{\text{EVRO}}$

Similarly, $\overset{1\,2\,3\,4}{\text{DISK}} \longrightarrow \overset{3\,2\,4\,1}{\text{SIKD}}$

60.
5	2	3	4	8	1	6
8	6	5	4	3	2	1

, *i.e.*, one pair.

61-65.

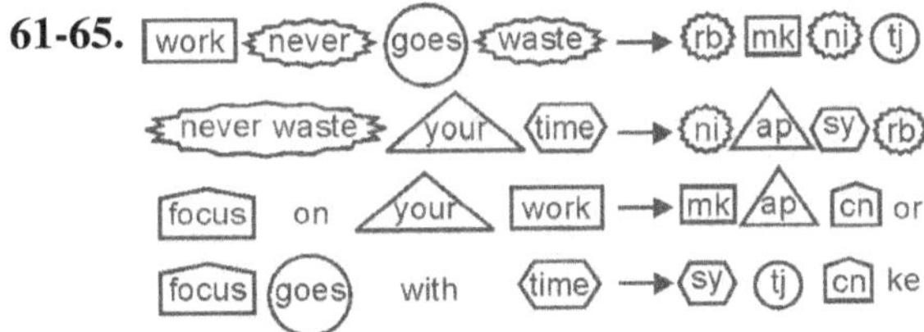

61. tj ⇒ goes

62. focus ⇒ cn

63. time ⇒ sy

64. work ⇒ mk; on ⇒ or

The code for 'projects' may be 'gt'.

65. rb ⇒ never or waste.

66. $8\dfrac{1}{3} + 5\dfrac{1}{4} \times 13\dfrac{1}{5} \div 6\dfrac{3}{5}$

$= \dfrac{25}{3} + \dfrac{21}{4} \times \dfrac{66}{5} \times \dfrac{5}{33}$

$= \dfrac{25}{3} + \dfrac{21}{2} = \dfrac{50+63}{6}$

$= \dfrac{113}{6} = 18\dfrac{5}{6}$

67. $11^2 - 6^2 \div 6 \times \dfrac{5}{2} + 2$ of 10

$= 11^2 - 36 \div 6 \times \dfrac{5}{2} + 2 \times 10$

$= 121 - 6 \times \dfrac{5}{2} + 20$

$= 121 - 15 + 20 = 126$

68. $x = (779.84 + 242.31) - 832.58$

$= 1022.15 - 832.58 = 189.57$

69. $x = 40.83 \times 1.02 \times 1.2$

$= 41.6466 \times 1.2$

$= 49.97592$

70. $\sqrt[3]{\sqrt{441} + \sqrt{16} + \sqrt{4}}$

$= \sqrt[3]{21 + 4 + 2} = \sqrt[3]{27} = 3$

71. $\because \sqrt{2 + \dfrac{2}{49}} = \dfrac{x}{14}$

$\sqrt{2 + \dfrac{2}{49}} = \sqrt{\dfrac{100}{49}} = \dfrac{10}{7}$

$\Rightarrow \quad \dfrac{10}{7} = \dfrac{x}{14}$

$\Rightarrow \quad 7x = 10 \times 14$

$\quad\quad x = \dfrac{10 \times 14}{7} = 20$

72. Let the age of the elder brother be x years.

∴ Age of the younger brother $= 36 - x$ years

According to the question,

$\dfrac{36 - x + 4}{x + 4} = \dfrac{5}{6}$

$\Rightarrow \dfrac{40 - x}{x + 4} = \dfrac{5}{6}$

$\Rightarrow 5x + 20 = 240 - 6x$

$\Rightarrow \qquad 11x = 220$

$\Rightarrow \qquad\quad x = 20$

Hence, age of elder brother = 20 years.

73. Seventh number $= (7 \times 58 + 7 \times 48) - 13 \times 52$

$$= 742 - 676 = 66$$

74. Marks in Science $= 7 \times 75 - 6 \times 72$

$$= 525 - 432 = 93$$

75. Let five consecutive numbers are

$x, x + 1, x + 2, x + 3$ and $x + 4$

According to the question,

$x + x + 1 + x + 2 + x + 3 + x + 4 = 190$

$\Rightarrow 5x + 10 = 190$

$\Rightarrow \qquad 5x = 180 \Rightarrow x = 36$

The product of 2nd and 3rd number

$$= (x + 2)\,(x + 1)$$
$$= (36 + 2)\,(36 + 1)$$
$$= 38 \times 37 = 1406$$

76. Let the number be x

According to the question,

$x - 10\%$ of $x = 1800$

$\Rightarrow \quad x - \dfrac{10}{100} \times x = 1800$

$\Rightarrow \qquad\qquad 90x = 100 \times 1800$

$\Rightarrow \qquad\qquad x = \dfrac{100 \times 1800}{90}$

$$= 100 \times 20 = 2000$$

Hence, required number = 2000

77. $\because \quad$ Speed $= \dfrac{\text{distance}}{\text{time}}$

$\Rightarrow$ distance = speed $\times$ time

$$= 45 \times 6 = 270 \text{ km}$$

Speed $= \dfrac{\text{distance}}{\text{time}}$

$$= \dfrac{270}{5} = 54 \text{ km/hr}$$

78. (A + B) can do a work in 35 days

(A + B)'s 1 day work $= \dfrac{1}{35}$

$\because$ A can do this work in 60 days

$\therefore$ A's 1 day work $= \dfrac{1}{60}$

B's 1 day work $= \dfrac{1}{35} - \dfrac{1}{60}$

$$= \dfrac{12 - 7}{420} = \dfrac{5}{420}$$

Hence, B alone can do this work in $\dfrac{420}{5}$

$$= 84 \text{ days.}$$

79. Those failing in Mathematics

$$= 100 - 55 = 45\%$$

Those failing in English

$$= 100 - 60 = 40\%$$

Failing in one or both the subjects

$$= (45 + 40 - 25) = 60\%$$

$\therefore \quad$ Pass $\% = 100 - 60 = 40\%$

80. Required $\% = \left[\dfrac{10}{(100 + 10)} \times 100 \right]\%$

$$= \dfrac{10}{110} \times 100 = \dfrac{100}{11} = 9\dfrac{1}{11}\%$$

81. 1, 3, 5, 7, 9, $\boxed{11}$

$\quad$ +2 $\quad$ +2 $\quad$ +2 $\quad$ +2 $\quad$ +2

82. 2, 7, 14, 23, 34, $\boxed{47}$

$\quad$ +5 $\quad$ +7 $\quad$ +9 $\quad$ +11 $\quad$ +13

83. 1, 8, 27, 64, 125, $\boxed{216}$

$\quad 1^3 \quad 2^3 \quad 3^3 \quad 4^3 \quad 5^3 \quad 6^3$

84. 2, 5, 10, 17, 26, $\boxed{37}$

$\quad 1^2+1 \quad 2^2+1 \quad 3^2+1 \quad 4^2+1 \quad 5^2+1 \quad 6^2+1$

85. 10, 17, 26, $\boxed{37}$, 50, 65

$\quad 3^2+1 \quad 4^2+1 \quad 5^2+1 \quad 6^2+1 \quad 7^2+1 \quad 8^2+1$

86. Average Speed $= \left(\dfrac{2xy}{x+y} \right)$

$$= \dfrac{2 \times 10 \times 15}{10 + 15}$$

$$= \dfrac{2 \times 10 \times 15}{25} = 12 \text{ km/hr}$$

87. Distance = 150 m, time = 5 sec

Speed of the train

$$= \dfrac{\text{distance}}{\text{time}}$$

$$= \dfrac{150}{5} = 30 \text{ m/s}$$

Now, Speed = 30 m/s

Distance = (150 + 180) m

$\qquad = 330$ m

$$\text{Time} = \dfrac{\text{distance}}{\text{speed}}$$

$$= \dfrac{330}{30} = 11 \text{ sec}$$

88. Let, Mohan's income = ₹ 100

Money spent = (20 + 30 + 25) = ₹ 75

Saving = 100 − 75 = ₹ 25

When saving is ₹ 25 then Income = ₹ 100

When saving is ₹ 750 then Income $= \dfrac{100}{25} \times 750$

$$= ₹ \; 100 \times 30 = ₹ \; 3000$$

89. Using formula,

$$\text{Gain \%} = \dfrac{\text{Error}}{\text{True Value} - \text{Error}} \times 100$$

$$= \dfrac{200}{1000 - 200} \times 100$$

$$= \dfrac{200}{800} \times 100 = 25\%$$

90. $P = \dfrac{\text{S.I.} \times 100}{r \times t} = \dfrac{2250 \times 100}{15 \times 5} = ₹ \; 3000$

91. Let, $\qquad$ P = ₹ 100

$$\text{S.I.} = \dfrac{100 \times 2 \times 5}{100} = ₹ \; 10$$

$$A = 100 \left(1 + \dfrac{5}{100} \right)^2$$

$$= 100 \times \dfrac{21}{20} \times \dfrac{21}{20}$$

$$= \dfrac{441}{4}$$

$$\text{C.I.} = A - P = \dfrac{441}{4} - 100$$

$$= \dfrac{441 - 400}{4} = \dfrac{41}{4}$$

$$\text{Difference} = \text{C.I.} - \text{S.I.} = \dfrac{41}{4} - 10$$

$$= \dfrac{41 - 40}{4} = \dfrac{1}{4}$$

When difference is ₹$\dfrac{1}{4}$ then P = ₹ 100

When difference is ₹$\dfrac{25}{2}$ then P

$$= 100 \times 4 \times \dfrac{25}{2} = ₹ \; 5000$$

92. Average of 15 numbers = 15

Total of 15 numbers = 15 × 15 = 225

Again, Average of first 8 numbers = 8

Total of first 8 numbers = 8 × 8 = 64

Hence, Total of last 7 numbers = 225 − 64 = 161

Average of the last 7 numbers $= \dfrac{161}{7} = 23$

93. Rahim's share $= \dfrac{5}{4+5} \times 14130$

$$= \dfrac{5}{9} \times 14130 = ₹ \; 7850$$

94. C's share $= \dfrac{7}{3+5+7} \times 2040$

$$= \dfrac{7}{15} \times 2040$$

$$= 7 \times 136 = ₹\ 952$$

95. Let, man's property be ₹ x

Son's share $= \dfrac{2 \times x}{5} = \dfrac{2x}{5}$

Daughter's share $= \dfrac{1 \times x}{4} = \dfrac{x}{4}$

$$\dfrac{2x}{5} + \dfrac{x}{4} = \dfrac{8x+5x}{20} = \dfrac{13x}{20}$$

Remaining amount $= x - \dfrac{13x}{20} = \dfrac{7x}{20}$

According to the question,

$$\dfrac{7x}{20 \times 2} = 1750$$

$$\Rightarrow \qquad x = \dfrac{40 \times 1750}{7}$$

$$= 40 \times 250 = ₹\ 10{,}000$$

$\therefore$ Man's property $= ₹\ 10{,}000$

96. Number of A type of employees in 1998

$$= 22\% \text{ of } 48640$$

$$= \dfrac{22}{100} \times 48640$$

$$= 10700$$

In 1997,

$$A = \dfrac{20}{100} \times 42980 = 8596$$

$$B = \dfrac{6}{100} \times 42980 = 2579$$

$$C = \dfrac{10}{100} \times 42980 = 4298$$

$$D = \dfrac{15}{100} \times 42980 = 6447$$

$$E = \dfrac{27}{100} \times 42980 = 11605$$

$$F = \dfrac{22}{100} \times 42980 = 9455$$

$\therefore$ C + D $= 4298 + 6447 = 10745$

98. $4864 - 2579 = 2285$

99. $\dfrac{5000}{48640} \times 100 = 10.3\% \approx 10\%$

100. $\dfrac{10700}{8596} \times 100 = 12.5\%$

SBI Junior Associates & Junior Agricultural Associates
(Clerical Cadre Exam)

General English

Directions (Qs. 1–15): *Read the following passage carefully and answer the questions given below it. Certain words/phrases have been printed in* **bold** *to help you locate them while answering some of the questions.*

Scientist Henry Mosely was born in a reputed family on November 23, 1887. His father—a Professor of anatomy at the University of Oxford—had an **untimely** death in 1891. However, his mother had sufficient income from family estates to **keep** her three children in school and to **allow** young Henry to build and equip a simple private laboratory. Thus, as a boy he was most familiar with a variety of neighbourhood birds and bird's nests. He also would search for prehistoric artefacts with his sister or his mother on his weekends and holiday vacations. On one occasion, Henry **found** a beautiful arrow-head on a visit to the Shetland Islands. His pride in this find was so **great** that he had to show it to two of his friends, Julian Huxley and Charles Darwin. All the three boys were of approximately the same age and were grandchildren of three famous scientists.

Henry **spent** five years at Eton, after which he entered Trinity College, Oxford with a scholarship in Natural Science. Before he graduated with honours in Natural Science, he was aleady dreaming of a career in pure science. He was greatly inspired **to do** research by Scientist Rutherford whom he met at Manchester.

1. Which of the following statements is not true in the context of the passage?
   A. Henry's mother and sister were interested in pre-historical articles
   B. The financial position of Henry's family was quite comfortable
   C. Henry had collected rare birds and bird's nests
   D. Henry got a scholarship ever before he graduated from his college
   E. Henry wanted to do research after he met Rutherford

2. Why did Henry set up his laboratory?
   A. His mother had sufficient money
   B. Not given in the passage
   C. To Spend his weekends and holidays
   D. To carry out research under Scientist Rutherford
   E. None of these

3. Why did Henry decide to make a career in Science?
   A. He was given a scholarship
   B. His father was a scientist
   C. Rutherford advised him accordingly
   D. To fulfil his father's dream
   E. Not given in the passage

4. Where did Henry finish his college education?
   A. Eton   B. Shetland
   C. Oxford   D. Manchester
   E. None of these

5. What helped Henry to develop, keen interest in natural beauty of surrounding area?
   A. Not given in the passage
   B. His inheritence of large family estate

C. His friendship with grandchildren from scientists's families
D. His knowledgeable mother and sister
E. None of these

6. Where Henry used to spend his weekends and holidays?
   A. His family estate at Shetland
   B. At Manchester with Rutherford
   C. At Oxford with his friends
   D. In his laboratory at Eton

7. Which of the following seems to be the probable reason for Henry's developing friendship with Julian and Charles?
   A. They were contemporaries and came from respectable families
   B. He wanted to become Scientist with their help
   C. They were interested in setting up a private laboratory
   D. They were impressed by Henry's immense knowledge
   E. None of the above

8. Why did Henry show the arrow-head to his friends?
   A. It was very beautiful and belonged to his family
   B. It was very ancient and had historical value
   C. He had received it from his father
   D. It was of a rare bird even at that time
   E. It was developed in his private laboratory

Directions (Qs. 9–12): *Which of the following is most nearly the SAME in meaning as the word/ group of words printed in bold as used in the passage?*

9. **KEEP**
   A. withhold
   B. preserve
   C. save
   D. continue
   E. pack

10. **UNTIMELY**
    A. prematurely
    B. quick
    C. timeless
    D. eternal
    E. unfortunate

11. **FOUND**
    A. established
    B. discovered
    C. organised
    D. laid
    E. concluded

12. **TO DO**
    A. to construct
    B. to build
    C. to develop
    D. to follow
    E. to carry on

Directions (Qs. 13–15): *Which of the following is most OPPOSITE in meaning of the word printed in bold as used in the passage?*

13. **ALLOW**
    A. permit
    B. forbid
    C. avoid
    D. recover
    E. cancel

14. **GREAT**
    A. infinite
    B. minor
    C. less
    D. short
    E. minute

15. **SPENT**
    A. installed
    B. established
    C. recouped
    D. saved
    E. avoided

Directions (Qs. 16–20) : *Each sentence below has a blank, each blank indicating that something has been omitted. Choose the word for each blank which best fits the meaning of the sentence as a whole.*

16. The passengers and crew members of the aeroplane had a ..... escape when it was taking off from the runway.
    A. little
    B. narrow
    C. brief
    D. large
    E. better

17. Eight scientists have ..... the national awards for outstanding contribution and dedication to the profession.
    A. picked
    B. conferred
    C. bagged
    D. discovered
    E. bestowed

18. There has been a ..... lack of efficiency in all the crucial areas of the working of Public Sector Undertakings.
    A. conspicuous
    B. stimulative
    C. insignificant
    D. surprising
    E. positive

19. Shailendra is too ..... as far as his food habits are concerned.
    A. curious
    B. enjoyable
    C. interesting
    D. involved
    E. fastidious

20. Some people ..... themselves into believing that they are indispensable to the organisation they work for.
   A. force   B. delude
   C. denigrate   D. fool
   E. keep

Directions (Qs. 21–25): *Read each sentence to find out whether there is any grammatical error or idiomatic error in it. The error, if any, will be in one part of the sentence. The number of that part is the answer. If there is "No Error" the answer is 'E'. (Ignore errors of punctuation if any.)*

21. (A) One of the most effective/(B) solutions is that/(C) she should work on Sunday/(D) and complete the assignment./(E) No error.

22. (A) He had to/(B) seek legal help in/(C) order for settling/(D) the dispute./(E) No error.

23. (A) Since I had been gone/(B) through the book/(C) long back, I could/(D) not remember the contents./(E) No error.

24. (A) We have to take/(B) him to the hospital yesterday/(C) because he was/(D) suffering from fever./(E) No error.

25. (A) The interviewer asked the actress/(B) how could she/(C) manage to attain fame/(D) in a short period./(E) No error.

Directions (Qs. 26–30): *Which of the phrases A, B, C and D given below should replace the phrase given in **bold** in the following sentence to make the sentence grammatically meaningful and correct? If the sentence is correct as it is and 'No correction is required', mark E as the answer.*

26. He is too impatient **for tolerating** any delay.
   A. to tolerate
   B. to tolerating
   C. at tolerating
   D. with tolerating
   E. No correction required

27. Why **should the candidates be** afraid of English Language is not clear.
   A. the candidates should be
   B. do the candidates be
   C. should be the candidates
   D. are the candidates
   E. No correction required

28. Ramesh is **as tall if not,** taller than Mahesh.
   A. not as tall but
   B. not so tall but as
   C. as tall as, if not
   D. as if not
   E. No correction required

29. The easiest **of the thing to do** is to ask the address to the postman.
   A. of the things to do
   B. among the things did
   C. of the thing to be done
   D. of all the things done
   E. No correction required

30. The player was asked **that why he had not** attended the prayer.
   A. why had he not
   B. that why had he not
   C. why he was not
   D. is hesitated to listen to
   E. No correction required

Reasoning Ability

Directions (Qs. 31–33): *Read the information/ statement given in each question carefully and answer the questions.*

31. Which of the following expressions will be true if the expression 'A > B ≥ C < D' is definitely true?
   A. A > D   B. C ≤ A
   C. D > B   D. D ≥ A
   E. None is true

32. Which of the following expressions will not be true if the expression 'F ≤ G = H < K' is definitely true?
   A. K ≥ F   B. H ≥ F
   C. G < K   D. F < K
   E. None of these

33. In which of the following expressions will the expression 'P < Q' be **definitely true?**
   A. P ≥ R > N = Q   B. Q < R ≥ N > P

C. $P < R \leq Q > R$ D. $P \geq N \geq M > Q$
E. None is true

Directions: (Qs. 34 & 35): *Read the following information carefully and answer the questions which follow:*
Point B is 4 m towards the North of point A.
Point E is 8 m towards the East of point B.
Point C is 5 m towards the East of point A.
Point D is 9 m towards the West of point C.

34. How far should one walk from point A in order to reach point D?
   A. 4 m   B. 9 m
   C. 5 m   D. 14 m
   E. 8 m

35. If a person walks 4 m towards the South from point E and then walks after taking a right turn, which of the following points would he reach first?
   A. A   B. B
   C. C   D. D
   E. Can not be determined

Directions (Qs. 36–40): *In each question below is given a group of number/symbol followed by four combinations of letters numbered A, B, C and D. You have to find out which of the combinations correctly represents the group of number/symbol based on the following coding system and the conditions and mark the number of that combination as your answer. If none of the four combinations correctly represents the group of number/symbol, give E i.e. 'None of these' as your answer.*

Number/ : % 6 # 5 @ 7 3 ★ β 8 $ 2 © 9 4
Symbol
Letter : F I H U T K A C W R M E Q B P
Code

Conditions :
   (i) If the first element is a symbol and the last an odd number, the codes for both these are to be interchanged.
   (ii) If both first and last elements are even digits, both these are to be coded as the code for the first even digit.
   (iii) If first element is a symbol and last element a perfect square, both these are to be coded as '£'.

36. #57★93
   A. HUKCBA   B. HUKCBH
   C. AUKBCH   D. AUKCBH
   E. None of these

37. 4@92%6
   A. ITBEFP   B. PTBEFP
   C. PTBFEP   D. £TBEF£
   E. None of these

38. @$9674
   A. £MKBI£   B. PMBIKT
   C. TMBIKT   D. £MBIK£
   E. None of these

39. ©%7263
   A. QFKEIA   B. AFKEIQ
   C. AKFEIQ   D. £FKEI£
   E. None of these

40. 5β86©9
   A. UWQRIB   B. £WQRIT
   C. BWRIQB   D. £WRIQ£
   E. None of these

Direction (Qs. 41–45): *In each question below are three statements followed by two conclusions numbered I and II. You have to take the three given statements to be true even if they seem to be at variance from commonly known facts and then decide which of the given conclusions logically follows from the three statements disregarding commonly known facts.*

Give answer (A) if only conclusion I follows.
Give answer (B) if only conclusion II follows.
Give answer (C) if either conclusion I or II follows.
Give answer (D) if neither conclusion I nor II follows.
Give answer (E) if both conclusion I and II follow.

41. Statements : All letters are words. Some pages are words. All pages are books.
   Conclusions : I. Some words are books.
   II. Some pages are letters.

42. Statements : Some trees are leaves. Some leaves are roots. Some roots are flowers.
   Conclusions : I. Some roots are trees.
   II. Some leaves are flowers.

43. Statements : All walls are floors. All floors are ceilings. All ceilings are roofs.

Conclusions : I. All walls are ceilings.
II. All floors are roofs.

44. Statements : Some squares are circles. All circles are rectangles. Some rectangles are cones.

Conclusions : I. Some cones are squares.
II. Some squares are rectangles.

45. Statements : Some computers are televisions. Some televisions are radios. All radios are mobiles.

Conclusions : I. No mobile is a computer.
II. Some computers are mobiles.

Directions (Qs. 46-50): *Study the following arrangement carefully and answer the questions given below:*

M, D, K, R, T, H, W and A are sitting around a circle facing at the centres. D is second to the right of M who is fifth to the left of T. K is third to the right of R who is second to the right of D. H is second to the right of W.

46. Who is third to the left of M?
A. A
B. T
C. H
D. D
E. Data inadequate

47. Who is fourth to the right of H?
A. A
B. T
C. R
D. K
E. None of these

48. In which of the following combinations is the first person sitting between the second and the third person?
A. KMW
B. MWD
C. RHT
D. TAK
E. None of these

49. If A and W interchange their positions who will be third to the left of R?
A. M
B. D
C. A
D. K
E. None of these

50. In which of the following pairs is the second person sitting to the immediate left of the first person?
A. MW
B. AK
C. TA
D. RH
E. WD

Directions (51-55): *Each of the questions given below is based on the given diagram. You have to take the given diagram to be true even if it seems to be at variance from commonly known facts and then decide which of the five alternatives following each question logically follows from the given diagram.*

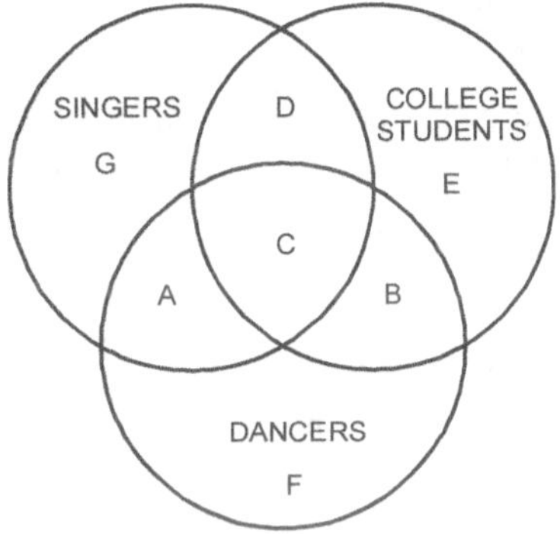

51. Which of the following represents such dancers who are also singers but not college students?
A. Only C
B. Only A
C. F and G
D. C and F
E. Only B

52. Which of the follwing represents the college students who are neither singers nor dancers?
A. E and B
B. Only C
C. B and C
D. Only E
E. Only B

53. Which of the following is **true** about C?
A. It represents all dancers from the college
B. It represents dancers who are not college students and also who are not singers
C. It represents such college students who are both singers as well as dancers
D. It represents all the dancers who are also singers
E. It represents singers who are not college students

54. Which of the following comprises of college students who are only singers and not dancers?
A. Only E
B. C and D
C. B, C and D
D. Only B
E. Only D

55. Which of the following represents all those singers who are **not** dancers?
A. E, D and G
B. Only E
C. B and C
D. Only D
E. D and G

56. In a certain code MODE is Written as #8%6 and DEAF is written as %67$. How is FOAM written in that code?
A. $87#
B. $#7%
C. #87%
D. $87%
E. None of these

57. What will come next in the series?
1 2 1 3 2 4 1 3 5 2 4 6 1 3 5
A. 2
B. 9
C. 6
D. 7
E. None of these

58. If '+' means '−', '−' means '×', '×' means '÷' and '÷' means '+' then what is the value of $9 - 7 + 85 \times 17 \div 15$?
A. 73
B. 83
C. 79
D. 68
E. None of these

Directions (Qs. 59 & 60): *In each of the following series determine the order of the letters. Then from the given options select the one which will complete the given series.*

59. KUZ, MOX, OIV, QET, ?
A. SAT
B. PAM
C. SAR
D. PBR
E. None of these

60. ABP, CDQ, EFR,?
A. GHS
B. GIS
C. GGS
D. GJS
E. None of these

Directions (Qs. 61–65) : *Study the following information carefully and answer the given question:*

Eight friends L, M, N O, P, Q, R and S are sitting around a square table in such a way that four of them sit at four corners of the square while four sit in the middle of each of the four sides. The ones who sit at the four corners face outside while those who sit in the middle of the sides face the centre.

- Only one person sits between L and Q. L sits at middle of one of the side.
- O sits third to the right of Q.
- Both R and S are immediate neighbours of L.
- M sits second to left of N.
- N is neither an immediate neighbour of Q nor S.

61. Four of the following five are alike in a certain way and so form a group. Which is the one that does not belong to that group?
A. L
B. R
C. S
D. O
E. P

62. Who sits third to the left of Q?
A. M
B. S
C. R
D. N
E. P

63. How many people sit between M and S when counted from the right hand side of S?
A. One
B. Three
C. None
D. Two
E. Four

64. Which of the following is true regarding P?
A. P sits exactly between M and N
B. O sits second to right of P.
C. None of the given options is true.
D. L sits immediate right of P.
E. Q is an immediate neighbour of P.

65. What is the position of P with respect to S?
A. Fourth to the left
B. second to the right
C. second to the left
D. Third to the right
E. Third to the left

Quantitative Aptitude

66. What is the sum of 3 + 0.3 + 0.03 + 0.003
- A. 3.320
- B. 3.333
- C. 3.350
- D. 3.303
- E. None of these

67. Find the value of $\dfrac{5+5\times19-15-7}{13\times13-156}$

A. 4	B. 8
C. 6	D. 9
E. 5	

68. Simplify: $0.00175 \div 0.025 \div 0.07$

A. 1	B. 0.1
C. 10	D. 100
E. 0.02	

69. If x is positive and $6 - x^2 = \dfrac{15}{16}$ then $\sqrt{x} = ?$

- A. $\dfrac{81}{16}$
- B. $\dfrac{9}{4}$
- C. $\dfrac{3}{2}$
- D. $\dfrac{\sqrt{3}}{2}$
- E. $\dfrac{27}{8}$

70. If $\dfrac{x^2-1}{x+1}=8,$ then find the value of x.

A. 5	B. 8
C. 6	D. 9
E. 4	

71. Simplify $\dfrac{\dfrac{3}{2}\div\dfrac{1}{2}\times\dfrac{3}{2}}{\dfrac{3}{2}\div\dfrac{1}{2}\text{ of }\dfrac{3}{2}}\div\dfrac{1}{8}$

A. 18	B. 21
C. 16	D. 24
E. 12	

72. Find the least number by which 336 be multiplied to make it a perfect square.

A. 21	B. 36
C. 48	D. 50
E. 40	

73. The average weight of 20 students in a class decreased by 500 g, when one boy whose weight is 45 kg is replaced by a new boy. What is the weight of the new boy?

A. 35 kg	B. 32 kg
C. 36 kg	D. 34 kg
E. 38 kg	

74. The value of $\dfrac{3.6\times0.48\times2.50}{0.12\times0.09\times0.5}$ is:

A. 80	B. 800
C. 8000	D. 80000
E. None of these	

75. $\dfrac{0.0203\times2.92}{0.0073\times14.5\times0.7}=?$

A. 0.8	B. 1.45
C. 2.40	D. 3.25
E. 4.45	

76. $108 \div 36 \text{ of } \dfrac{1}{4}+\dfrac{2}{5}\times3\dfrac{1}{4} = ?$

- A. $13\dfrac{3}{10}$
- B. $11\dfrac{3}{5}$
- C. $9\dfrac{3}{7}$
- D. $12\dfrac{5}{8}$
- E. $7\dfrac{7}{10}$

77. What value will replace the question mark in the given equation?

$$4\dfrac{1}{2}+3\dfrac{1}{6}+?+2\dfrac{1}{3}=13\dfrac{2}{5}$$

- A. $3\dfrac{1}{7}$
- B. $3\dfrac{2}{5}$

C. $3\dfrac{3}{5}$ D. $2\dfrac{3}{5}$

E. $3\dfrac{1}{5}$

78. The value of $\sqrt{10+\sqrt{25+\sqrt{108+\sqrt{154+\sqrt{225}}}}}$

is equal to:
A. 4 B. 6
C. 8 D. 10
E. 12

79. $\dfrac{\sqrt{625}}{11}\times\dfrac{14}{\sqrt{25}}\times\dfrac{11}{\sqrt{196}}$ is equal to:

A. 5 B. 6
C. 8 D. 11
E. 9

80. Find the average of all the numbers between 6 and 34 which are divisible by 5.
A. 18 B. 20
C. 24 D. 30
E. 26

Directions (Qs. 81–85): *What will come in place of the question mark (?) in the following number series?*

81. 14, 78, 252, ?
A. 420 B. 412
C. 512 D. 620
E. 612

82. 84, 260, 630, ?
A. 1302 B. 1032
C. 1230 D. 1941
E. 1532

83. 18, 45, 72, 99, ?
A. 125 B. 216
C. 140 D. 128
E. 126

84. 1, 12, 123, 1234, ?, 123456
A. 13245 B. 12345
C. 12432 D. 1231
E. 1347

85. 4, 20, 60, ?, 900
A. 250 B. 300
C. 330 D. 160
E. 310

86. The sum of four consecutive even integers is 1284. The greatest of them is:
A. 320 B. 322
C. 324 D. 326
E. 328

87. The sum of three consecutive odd numbers is 20 more than the first of these numbers. What is the middle number?
A. 7 B. 9
C. 11 D. Data inadequate
E. None of these

88. Sachin is younger than Rahul by 4 years. If their ages are in the respective ratio of 7 : 9, how old is Sachin?
A. 16 years
B. 18 years
C. 28 years
D. Can not be determined
E. None of these

89. If 120 is 20% of a number, then 120% of that number will be:
A. 20 B. 120
C. 360 D. 720
E. 80

90. If 35% of a number is 175, then what per cent of 175 is that number?
A. 35% B. 65%
C. 280% D. 45%
E. None of these

91. By selling 33 metres of cloth, one gains the selling price of 11 metres. Find the gain per cent.
A. 25% B. 20%
C. 50% D. 35%
E. 45%

92. If ₹ 782 be divided into three parts proportional to $\dfrac{1}{2}:\dfrac{2}{3}:\dfrac{3}{4}$, then the first part is:
A. ₹ 182 B. ₹ 190

C. ₹ 196   D. ₹ 204

E. ₹ 175

93. Simran started a software business by investing ₹ 50,000. After six months, Nanda joined her with a capital of ₹ 80000. After 3 years, they earned a profit of ₹ 24500. What was Simran's share in the profit?

A. ₹ 9423

B. ₹ 10250

C. ₹ 12500

D. ₹ 14000

E. None of these

94. 36 men can complete a piece of work in 18 days. In how many days will 27 men complete the same work?

A. 12

B. 18

C. 22

D. 24

E. None of these

95. A fort had provision of food for 150 men for 45 days. After 10 days, 25 men left the fort. The number of days for which the remaining food will last, is:

A. $29\dfrac{1}{5}$ B. $37\dfrac{1}{4}$

C. 42   D. 54

E. 48

Directions (Qs. 96–100): *Study the following graph carefully and answer the questions given below:*

Distribution of candidates who were enrolled for MBA Entrance Exam and the candidates (out of those enrolled) who passed the exam in different institutes.

Candidates Enrolled = 8550

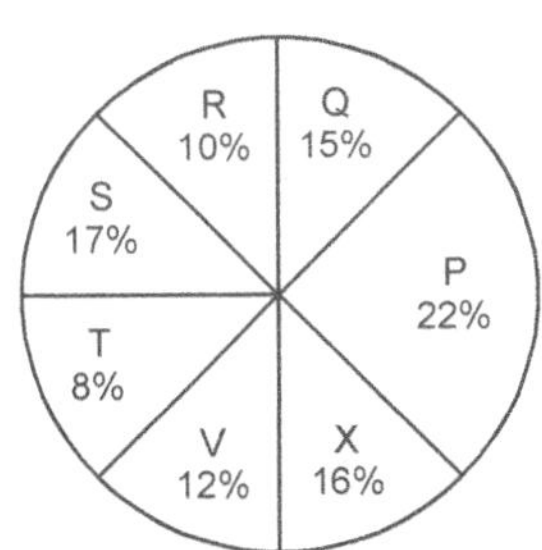

Candidates Who Passed The Exam = 5700

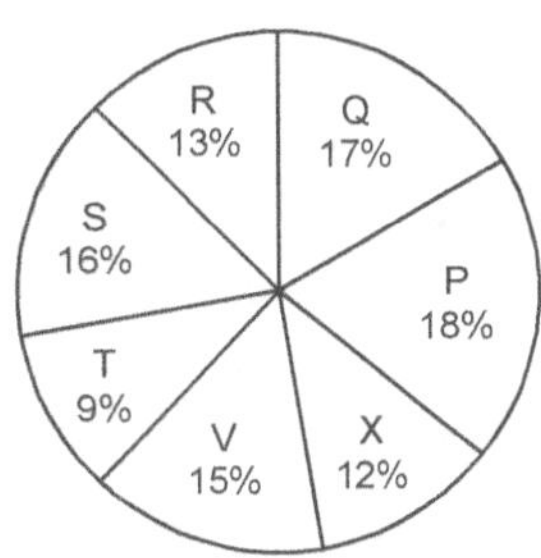

96. What percentage of candidates passed the exam from institute T out of the total number of candidates enrolled from the same institute?

A. 48%   B. 68%

C. 72%   D. 75%

E. 55%

97. What is the ratio of candidates passed to the candidates enrolled from institute P?

A. $\dfrac{7}{11}$ B. $\dfrac{6}{11}$

C. $\dfrac{12}{17}$ D. $\dfrac{8}{17}$

E. $\dfrac{5}{11}$

98. What is the percentage of candidates passed to the candidates enrolled for institute Q and R together?

A. 72%   B. 74%

C. 80%   D. 76%

E. 78%

99. Which institute has the highest percentage of candidates passed to the candidates enrolled?

A. Q   B. R

C. V   D. T

E. None of these

100. The number of candidates passed from institutes S and P together exceeds the number of candidates enrolled from institutes T and R together by:

A. 228   B. 279

C. 399   D. 407

E. 295

ANSWERS

1	2	3	4	5	6	7	8	9	10
C	B	C	C	A	E	A	B	D	A

11	12	13	14	15	16	17	18	19	20
B	E	B	E	D	B	C	A	E	B

21	22	23	24	25	26	27	28	29	30
E	C	A	A	B	A	A	C	A	D

31	32	33	34	35	36	37	38	39	40
E	A	C	A	C	D	B	D	B	E

41	42	43	44	45	46	47	48	49	50
A	D	E	B	C	B	D	C	C	D

51	52	53	54	55	56	57	58	59	60
B	D	C	E	E	A	D	A	C	A

61	62	63	64	65	66	67	68	69	70
A	C	E	E	C	B	C	A	C	D

71	72	73	74	75	76	77	78	79	80
A	A	A	B	A	A	B	A	A	B

81	82	83	84	85	86	87	88	89	90
D	A	E	B	B	C	B	E	D	E

91	92	93	94	95	96	97	98	99	100
C	D	E	D	C	D	B	C	B	C

Some Selected Explanatory Answers

33. $P < R \leq Q$

∴ $P < Q$

For (Q. 34-35):

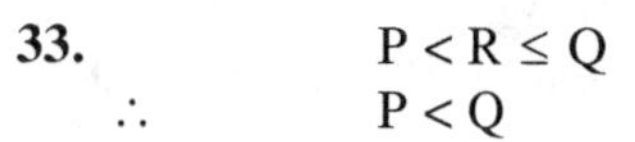
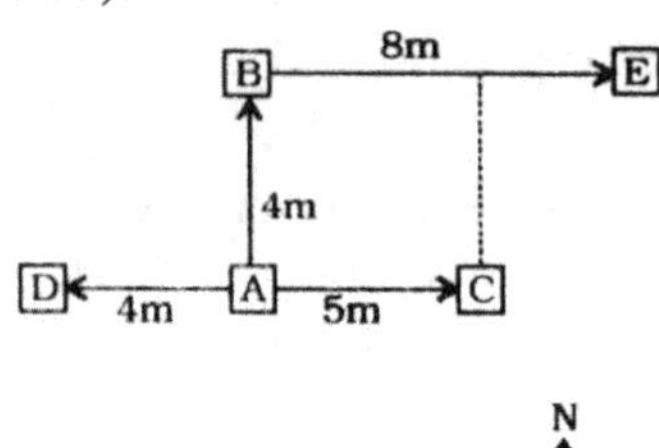
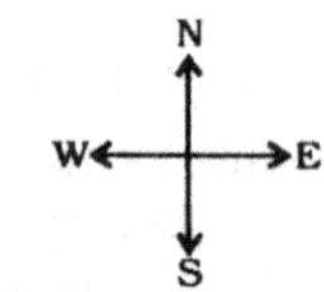

36. # 5 7 ★ 9 3
 ↓ ↓ ↓ ↓ ↓ ↓
 A U K C B H

Condition (i) is applied.

37. 4 @ 9 2 % 6
 ↓ ↓ ↓ ↓ ↓ ↓
 P T B E F P

Condition (ii) is applied.

38. @ S 9 6 7 4
 ↓ ↓ ↓ ↓ ↓ ↓
 £ M B I K £

Condition (iii) is applied.

39. © % 7 2 6 3
 ↓ ↓ ↓ ↓ ↓ ↓
 A F K E I Q

Condition (i) is applied.

40. 5 β 8 6 © 9
 ↓ ↓ ↓ ↓ ↓ ↓
 U W R I Q B

No condition is applied.

41.

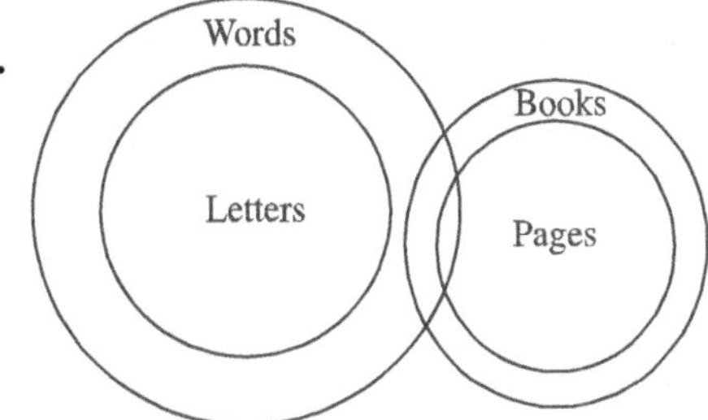

42.

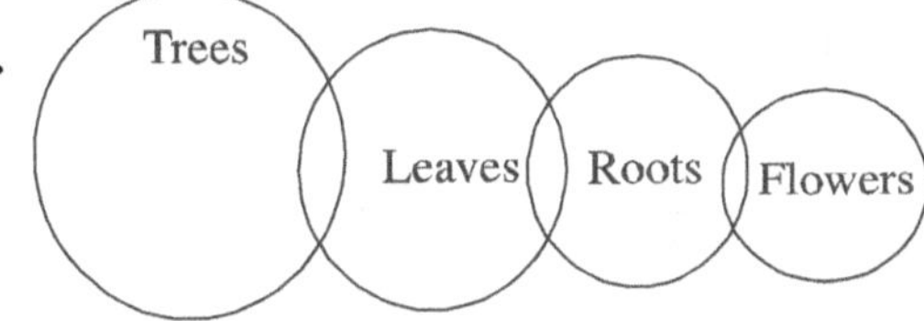

43.

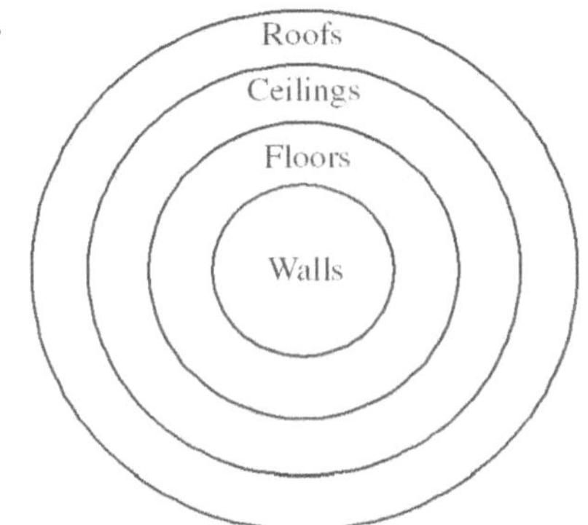

44.

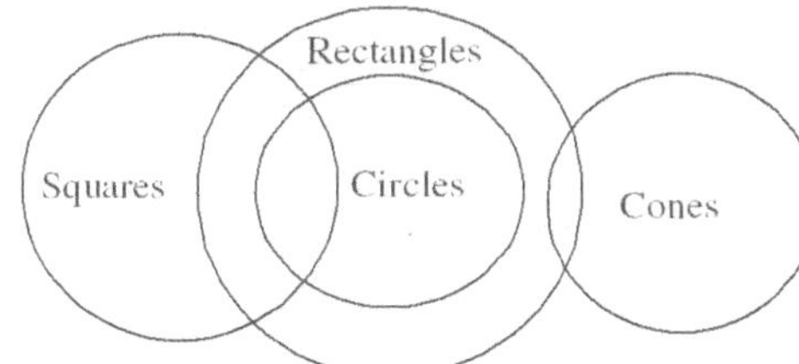

45.

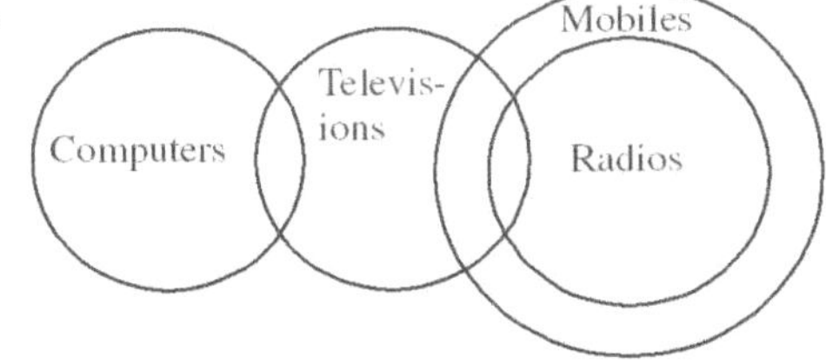

For Q. Nos. 46 to 50

Their sitting arrangement is shown below:

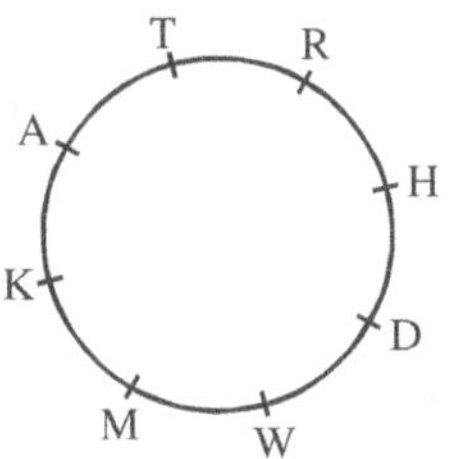

58. $? = 9 - 7 + 85 \times 17 \div 15$

$ = 9 \times 7 - 85 \div 17 + 15$

 (Putting original symbols)

$ = 9 \times 7 - 5 + 15$

$ = 63 - 5 + 15 = 73$

59. The letters in one group correspond to the letters in the next group in the manner +2, –6, –2 respectively till the third group and then +2, –4, –2 respectively, *i.e.,*

KUZ	MOX	OIV	QET	SAR
+2	+2	+2	+2	
–6	–6	–4	–4	
–2	–2	–2	–2	

60. The letters in one group correspond to the letters in the next group in the manner +2, +2, +1 respectively, *i.e.,*

ABP	CDQ	EFR	GHS
+2	+2	+2	
+2	+2	+2	
+1	+1	+1	

61-65.

61. Except L, all others sit at the corners of the square.

62. R sits third to the left of Q.

63. Four persons–L, R, N and O–sit between M and S when counted from the right hand side of S.

64. P sits exactly between M and Q. O sits second to the left of P. L sits third to the right of P.

65. P is second to the left of S.

66. $3 + 0.3 + 0.03 + 0.003 = 3.333$

67. $\dfrac{5+95-22}{169-156} = \dfrac{100-22}{13} = \dfrac{78}{13} = 6$

68. $\dfrac{175}{100000} \times \dfrac{1000}{25} \times \dfrac{100}{7} = \dfrac{175}{175} = 1$

69. $\because \quad 6 - x^2 = \dfrac{15}{16}$

$\Rightarrow \quad 6 - \dfrac{15}{16} = x^2 \Rightarrow \dfrac{96-15}{16} = x^2$

$\Rightarrow \quad \dfrac{81}{16} = x^2 \Rightarrow x = \dfrac{9}{4}$

$\therefore \quad \sqrt{x} = \dfrac{3}{2}$

70. $\because \quad \dfrac{x^2-1}{x+1} = 8$

$\Rightarrow \quad \dfrac{(x+1)(x-1)}{(x+1)} = 8$

$\Rightarrow \quad x - 1 = 8 \Rightarrow x = 9$

71. $\dfrac{\frac{3}{2} \times \frac{2}{1} \times \frac{3}{2}}{\frac{3}{2} \times \frac{4}{3}} \times \dfrac{8}{1} = \dfrac{36}{2} = 18$

72.

```
2 | 336
2 | 168
2 |  84
2 |  42
3 |  21
  |   7
```

$\therefore 336 = \underline{2 \times 2} \times \underline{2 \times 2} \times 3 \times 7$

If we multiply 336 by 21 then it becomes a perfect square.

$\therefore$ required number = 21

73. Total decrease $= \left(20 \times \dfrac{1}{2}\right)$ kg = 10 kg

Weight of new man $= (45 - 10)$ kg $= 35$ kg

74. $\dfrac{36 \times 48 \times 250}{12 \times 9 \times 5} = 800$

75. $\dfrac{203 \times 292}{73 \times 145 \times 7} = \dfrac{29 \times 4}{145} = \dfrac{4}{5} = 0.8$

76. $108 \div 9 + \dfrac{2}{5} \times \dfrac{13}{4}$

$= 12 + \dfrac{13}{10} = \dfrac{120+13}{10} = \dfrac{133}{10} = 13\dfrac{3}{10}$

77. $\dfrac{9}{2} + \dfrac{19}{6} + x + \dfrac{7}{3} = \dfrac{67}{5}$

$\Rightarrow \quad x = \dfrac{67}{5} - \dfrac{9}{2} - \dfrac{19}{6} - \dfrac{7}{3}$

$= \dfrac{402 - 135 - 95 - 70}{30}$

$= \dfrac{402 - 300}{30} = \dfrac{102}{30} = \dfrac{34}{10}$

$= \dfrac{17}{5} = 3\dfrac{2}{5}$

78. $\sqrt{10 + \sqrt{25 + \sqrt{108 + \sqrt{154 + 15}}}}$

$= \sqrt{10 + \sqrt{25 + \sqrt{108 + 13}}}$

$= \sqrt{10 + \sqrt{25 + 11}} = \sqrt{10 + 6} = 4$

79. $\dfrac{25}{11} \times \dfrac{14}{5} \times \dfrac{11}{14} = 5$

80. Numbers between 6 and 34 which are divisible by 5 are 10, 15 20, 25, 30

$\text{Average} = \dfrac{10+15+20+25+30}{5}$

$= \dfrac{100}{5} = 20$

81.

$$14 \qquad 78 \qquad 252 \qquad \boxed{620}$$
$$\downarrow \qquad \downarrow \qquad \downarrow \qquad \downarrow$$
$$2^4 - 2 \quad 3^4 - 3 \quad 4^4 - 4 \quad 5^4 - 5$$

82.

$$84 \qquad 260 \qquad 630 \qquad \boxed{1302}$$
$$\downarrow \qquad \downarrow \qquad \downarrow \qquad \downarrow$$
$$3^4 + 3 \quad 4^4 + 4 \quad 5^4 + 5 \quad 6^4 + 6$$

83.

$$18 \quad 45 \quad 72 \quad 99 \quad \boxed{126}$$
$$+27 \quad +27 \quad +27 \quad +27$$

84. $1 \quad 12 \quad 123 \quad 1234 \quad \boxed{12345} \quad 123456$

In the given series elements of the series have been arranged in the following manner:

First term = 1

2nd term = $1 \times 2 = 12$

3rd term = $1 \times 2 \times 3 = 123$

4th term = $1 \times 2 \times 3 \times 4 = 1234$

∴ fifth term in place of the question mark

$$= 1 \times 2 \times 3 \times 4 \times 5 = 12345$$

85.

$$4 \quad 20 \quad 60 \quad \boxed{300} \quad 900$$
$$\times 5 \quad \times 3 \quad \times 5 \quad \times 3$$

Terms of the series are alternately multiplied by 5 and 3 to obtain the next term. Therefore correct answer is (B).

86. Let, $x, x + 2, x + 4, x + 6$ are four consecutive even integers

According to the question,

$$x + x + 2 + x + 4 + x + 6 = 1284$$
$$\Rightarrow \qquad 4x + 12 = 1284$$
$$\Rightarrow \qquad 4x = 1284 - 12 = 1272$$
$$\Rightarrow \qquad x = \frac{1272}{4} = 318$$

∴ Greatest number = $x + 6 = 318 + 6 = 324$

87. Let the numbers be $x, x + 2$ and $x + 4$

then, $x + (x + 2) + (x + 4) = x + 20$
$$\Rightarrow \qquad 3x + 6 = x + 20$$
$$\Rightarrow \qquad 3x - x = 20 - 6$$
$$\Rightarrow \qquad 2x = 14 \Rightarrow x = 7$$

∴ Middle number = $x + 2 = 7 + 2 = 9$

88. Let, Rahul's age = x years

∴ Sachin's age = $(x - 4)$ years

According to the question,

$$\frac{x-4}{x} = \frac{7}{9}$$
$$\Rightarrow \qquad 9x - 36 = 7x$$
$$\Rightarrow \qquad 9x - 7x = 36$$
$$\Rightarrow \qquad 2x = 36 \Rightarrow x = 18$$

Hence, Sachin's age = $x - 4 = 18 - 4 = 14$ years.

89. Let, number = x

$$120 = 20\% \text{ of } x$$
$$\Rightarrow \qquad 120 = \frac{20}{100} \times x = \frac{x}{5}$$
$$\Rightarrow \qquad x = 120 \times 5 = 600$$

Now, 120% of $x = \dfrac{120}{100} \times 600 = 720$

90. Let, number = x

$$35\% \text{ of } x = 175$$
$$\Rightarrow \qquad \frac{35}{100} \times x = 175$$
$$\Rightarrow \qquad x = \frac{175 \times 100}{35}$$
$$= 5 \times 100 = 500$$

Now, $y\%$ of $175 = 500$
$$\Rightarrow \qquad \frac{y}{100} \times 175 = 500$$
$$\Rightarrow \qquad y = \frac{500 \times 100}{175} = \frac{500 \times 4}{7}$$
$$= \frac{2000}{7} = 285\frac{5}{7}\%$$

91. (SP of 33 m) – (CP of 33 m)

$$= \text{Gain} = \text{SP of 11 m}$$

SP of 33 m – SP of 11 m = CP of 33 m

SP of 22 m = CP of 33 m

Let CP of each metre be ₹ 1. Then CP of 22 m = ₹ 22, SP of 22 m = ₹ 33

∴ Gain% = $\left(\dfrac{11}{22} \times 100\right)\% = 50\%$

92. $A : B : C \quad\quad \dfrac{1}{2} : \dfrac{2}{3} : \dfrac{3}{4}$

LCM of 2, 3 and 4 = 12

$\therefore \quad A : B : C \quad\quad 6 : 8 : 9$

A's share $= \dfrac{6}{23} \times 782 = 6 \times 34 = ₹\ 204$

93. Simran : Nanda $= 50000 \times 36 : 80000 \times 30$

$\qquad\qquad = 1800000 : 2400000$

$\qquad\qquad = 18 : 24 = 3 : 4$

$\therefore$ Simran's share $= \dfrac{3}{7} \times 24500$

$\qquad\qquad = ₹\ 3 \times 3500 = ₹\ 10500$

94. $\because$ 36 men can complete a work in 18 days

$\therefore$ 1 man can complete the same work in 18×36 days

$\therefore$ 27 men can complete the same work in

$\dfrac{18 \times 36}{27} = 6 \times 4 = 24$ days.

95. 150 men – 25 men = 125 men

45 days – 10 days = 35 days

Food last for 150 men in 35 days

Food last for 125 men in $\dfrac{150 \times 35}{125}$ days

$\qquad\qquad = 6 \times 7 = 42$ days

96. Required percentage

$= \dfrac{9\% \text{ of } 5700}{8\% \text{ of } 8550} \times 100 = \dfrac{9 \times 5700}{8 \times 8550} \times 100 = 75\%$

97. Required ratio

$= \left(\dfrac{18\% \text{ of } 5700}{22\% \text{ of } 8550} \right) = \dfrac{18 \times 5700}{22 \times 8550} = \dfrac{6}{11}$

98. Candidates passed from institutes Q and R together $= [(13\% + 17\%) \text{ of } 5700] = 30\%$ of 5700

Candidate enrolled from institutes Q and R

together $= \left(\dfrac{30\% \text{ of } 5700}{25\% \text{ of } 8550} \times 100 \right)$

$= [(15\% \text{ of } 10\%) \text{ of } 8550] = 25\%$ of 8550

$\therefore$ Required percentage

$= \left(\dfrac{30\% \text{ of } 5700}{25\% \text{ of } 8550} \times 100 \right)$

$= \dfrac{30 \times 5700}{25 \times 8550} \times 100 = 80\%$

99. The percentage of candidates passed to candidates enrolled can be determined for each institute as under:

(i) $P = \left[\left(\dfrac{18\% \text{ of } 5700}{22\% \text{ of } 8550} \right) \times 100 \right]$

$\qquad = \left(\dfrac{18 \times 5700}{22 \times 8550} \times 100 \right) = \left(\dfrac{18 \times 2}{22 \times 3} \times 100 \right)$

$\qquad = 54.55\%$

(ii) $Q = \left[\left(\dfrac{17\% \text{ of } 5700}{15\% \text{ of } 8550} \right) \times 100 \right] = 75.56\%$

(iii) $R = \left[\left(\dfrac{13\% \text{ of } 5700}{10\% \text{ of } 8550} \right) \times 100 \right] = 86.67\%$

(iv) $S = \left[\left(\dfrac{16\% \text{ of } 5700}{17\% \text{ of } 8550} \right) \times 100 \right] = 62.75\%$

(v) $T = \left[\left(\dfrac{9\% \text{ of } 5700}{8\% \text{ of } 8550} \right) \times 100 \right] = 75\%$

(vi) $V = \left[\left(\dfrac{15\% \text{ of } 5700}{12\% \text{ of } 8550} \right) \times 100 \right] = 83.33\%$

(vii) $X = \left[\left(\dfrac{12\% \text{ of } 5700}{16\% \text{ of } 8550} \right) \times 100 \right] = 50\%$

Highest of these is 86.67% corresponding to institute R.

100. Required difference

$= [(16\% + 18\%) \text{ of } 5700] -$

$\qquad\qquad\qquad [(8\% + 10\%) \text{ of } 8550]$

$= 34\% \text{ of } 5700 - 18\% \text{ of } 8550$

$= 1938 - 1539 = 399.$

SBI Junior Associates & Junior Agricultural Associates
(Clerical Cadre Exam)

General English

Directions (Qs. 1–15): *Read the following passage carefully and answer the questions given below it. Certain words/phrases have been printed in **bold** to help you locate them while answering some of the questions.*

Believe it or not, once a wonderful plate made of gold fell from heaven into the court of a temple at Banares. On the plate these words were inscribed: "A gift from Heaven to him who loves best." The priest at once made a proclamation that everyday, all those who would like to claim the plate should **assemble** at the temple to have their kind deeds **judged.**

Everyday for a whole year all kinds of holy men, hermits, scholars and nobles came and related to the priests their deeds of charity. The priests heard their claims. At last they decided that the one who seemed to be the greatest lover of mankind was a rich man who had every year given all his wealth to the-poor. So they gave him the plate of gold. But when he took it in his hand, it **turned** to worthless lead. When he dropped it in his amazement on to the floor, it became gold again.

For another year claimants came and the priests presented the heavenly gift three times. But the same thjng happened, showing that Heaven did not consider these men **worthy** of the gift.

Meanwhile a large number of beggars came and lay about the temple gate, hoping that the claimants who came would give them alms to prove they were worthy of the golden plate. It was a good thing for the beggars because the pilgrims gave them money but showed no sympathy, nor even a look of pity.

At last a peasant who had heard nothing about the plate of gold came near the temple. He was so **touched** by the sight of the miserable beggars that he wept. When he saw a poor blind and maimed wretch at the temple gate, he knelt at his side and **comforted** him with kind words. When this peasant went inside the temple, he was shocked to find it full of men boasting of their kind deeds and quarrelling with the priests. The priest who held the golen plate in his hand saw the peasant standing there and beckoned to him to know what he wanted. The peasant went near the priest and knowing nothing about the plate, accidentally touched it. At once it shone out with three times its former splendour and the priest said: "Son, the gift is yours, "for you are the one who loves best."

1. The gift from Heaven was meant for those who
   A. were scholars
   B. were highly religious and loved God best
   C. gave money to the poor
   D. loved others in the best way
   E. were poor peasants

2. What did the peasant see inside the temple?
   A. Miserable beggars and blind men
   B. Priests quarrelling among themselves
   C. People speaking high of their kind deeds and fighting with the priests
   D. The golden plate being converted to worthless lead
   E. None of these

3. For which of the following was the proclamation made by the priest?
   A. To find the richest person in the town
   B. To find the rightful owner of the plate
   C. To judge the worth of the golden plate
   D. To judge his own deeds with the help of the people

4. What happened to the plate when it was touched by the peasant?
   A. It started glowing with greater splendour
   B. It changed from gold to lead
   C. It became heavier and fell on the ground
   D. It turned into gold
   E. Not mentioned in the passage

5. The rich man dropped the golden plate to the floor as he was
   A. not intersted in possessing it
   B. afraid of holding it
   C. curious to know about its purity
   D. surprised to see it turning to lead
   E. the rightful owner of the plate

6. Why did the beggars stay near the temple gate? They
   A. wanted to prove their claim on the golden plate
   B. had come to pray in the temple
   C. knew that the visitors would given them alms
   D. wanted to seek the sympathy of the peasant
   E. wanted to have a glimpse of the golden plate

7. The priests could decide on the rightful owner of the plate when the peasant
   A. met with an accident
   B. entered the temple and stood there
   C. put forward his claim on the heavenly gift
   D. touched the plate unknowingly
   E. comforted the poor blind man with kind words

8. Which of the following statements is *true* in the context of the passage?
   A. The rich man did not turn out to be the greatest lover of humanity
   B. The peasant touched the plate to know whether he was its rightful owner

C. The priest told the peasant to narrate his kind deeds
D. The plate shone out in splendour when the peasant dropped it on the floor
E. The peasant went near the priest to ask for the golden plate

9. What made the peasant weep?
   A. The quarrel between the priests and some people
   B. The greediness of the rich people
   C. The boastful crowd inide the temple
   D. The pitiable condition of the beggars
   E. None of the above

Directions (Qs. 10–12): *Choose the word which is most nearly the SAME in meaning as the word given in* **bold** *as used in the passage.*

10. **TURNED**
    A. bent   B. moved
    C. changed   D. revolved
    E. fell

11. **WORTHY**
    A. useful   B. promising
    C. successful   D. necessary
    E. deserving

12. **JUDGED**
    A. ordered   B. justified
    C. announced   D. explained
    E. assessed

Directions (Qs. 13–15): *Choose the word which is most OPPOSITE in meaning of the word given in* bold *as used in the passage.*

13. **COMFORTED**
    A. consoled   B. ignored
    C. advised   D. scolded
    E. controlled

14. **ASSEMBLE**
    A. distribute   B. gather
    C. partition   D. disperse
    E. dismantle

15. **TOUCHED**
    A. moved   B. indifferent
    C. disconnected   D. excited
    E. arrogant

Directions (Qs. 16–20): *Read each sentence to find out whether there is any grammatical error or idiomatic error in it. The error, if any, will be in one part of the sentence. The number of that part is the answer. If there is "No Error" the answer is 'E'. (Ignore errors of punctuation if any.)*

16. (A) The Head of the Department/(B) advised all the staff/(C) to not to/(D) indulge in gossip./(E) No error.

17. (A) I shall be able/(B) to complete the work in/(C) stipulated time provide/(D) you do not disturb me./(E) No error.

18. (A) Having learn my lessons/(B) I was very careful/(C) in dealing with him/(D) in front of his room-mate./(E) No error.

19. (A) In spite of his/(B) being a Quiz Master/(C) show was/(D) a big flop./(E) No error.

20. (A) No sooner the/(B) clock strike six than/(C) all the employees/(D) rushed out of office./(E) No error.

Directions (Qs. 21–30) : *In the following passage there are blanks, each of which has been numbered. These numbers are printed below the passage, against each, five words are suggested, one of which fits the blank appropriately. Find out the appropriate word in each case.*

..... **(21)** ..... can be injected ..... **(22)** ..... human blood for ..... **(23)** ..... diptheria, pneumonia and severe wounds. ..... **(24)** ..... surgical operations, penicillin is given to ..... **(25)** ..... to ..... **(26)** ..... the bacterial infections from spreading. After this ..... **(27)** ..... several other antibiotics ..... **(28)** ..... discovered.

Today, these antibiotics are ..... **(29)** ..... the lives of lakhs of ..... **(30)** ..... all over the world.

21. A. Antibiotics   B. Penicillin
    C. Streptomycin   D. Teramycin
    E. Medicine

22. A. within   B. through
    C. on   D. into
    E. over

23. A. treating   B. operating
    C. discovering   D. spreading
    E. monitoring

24. A. In   B. Over
    C. While   D. After
    E. During

25. A. children   B. injured
    C. patients   D. doctors
    E. nurses

26. A. study   B. prevent
    C. dismiss   D. spread
    E. remove

27. A. treatment   B. patient
    C. cause   D. discovery
    E. operation

28. A. were   B. may be
    C. have   D. are
    E. would be

29. A. multiplying   B. providing
    C. saving   D. infecting
    E. growing

30. A. children   B. species
    C. women   D. medicos
    E. people

Reasoning Ability

Directions (Qs. 31–35): *Following questions are based on five words given below:*

    RAG   FIN   PUT   LOW   SUE

(The new words formed after performing the mentioned operations may or may not necessarily be meaningful English words.)

31. If in each of the given words, each of the consonants is changed to previous letter and each vowel is changed to next letter in the English alphabetical series, in how many words thus formed will no vowels appear?
    A. None   B. One
    C. Two   D. Three
    E. More than three

32. If third alphabet in each of the word is changed to next alphabet in the English alphabetical order, how many words having two vowels (same or different vowels) will be formed?

A. None   B. One
C. Two   D. Three
E. Four

33. How many letters are there in the English alphabetical series between the second letter of the word which is second from the right and the second letter of the word which is second from the left of the given words?
A. Two   B. Five
C. Six   D. Nine
E. Three

34. If the positions of the first and the second alphabets of each of the words are interchanged, which of the following will form a meaningful English word?
A. Both SUE and PUT
B. FIN
C. Both Put and LOW
D. LOW
E. SUE

35. If the given words are arranged in the order as they would appear in a dictionery from left to right, which of the following will be second from the right?
A. RAG   B. FIN
C. PUT   D. LOW
E. SUE

36. Rahul started from point A and travelled 8 kms towards the North to point B, he then turned right and travelled 7 kms to point C, from point C he took the first right and drove 5 kms to point D, he took another right and travelled 7 kms to point E and finally turned right and travelled for another 3 kms to point F. What is the distance between point F and B?
A. 1 km   B. 2 km
C. 3 km   D. 4 km
E. None of these

37. Among R, L, T and J each having different weights, T is heavier than only L. R is not as heavy as J. Who is the heaviest?
A. R
B. J
C. T
D. Cannot be determined
E. None of these

38. How many meaningful English words can be formed with the letters STIF starting with F, using each letter only once in each word ?
A. None   B. One
C. Two   D. Three
E. More than three

Direction (Qs. 39 to 43): *The questions are based on following set of numbers.*

319   869   742   593   268

39. If one is subtracted from the first and third digits of each of the numbers, what will be the difference between the first digit of the highest number and the first digit of the lowest number?
A. 2   B. 3
C. 4   D. 5
E. None of these

40. If in each number the first and the third digits are interchanged then which number will be the highest?
A. 319   B. 869
C. 742   D. 593
E. 268

41. If in each number first digit is replaced by the third digit, second digit is replaced by the first digit and third digit is replaced by the second digit, then which number will be the second highest?
A. 319   B. 869
C. 742   D. 593
E. 268

42. If all the numbers are arranged in descending order, what will be the difference between the second digit of third number and third digit of second number?
A. 5   B. 9
C. 6   D. 7
E. None of these

43. If in each number all the digits are arranged in ascending order, which number will be second lowest?
A. 319   B. 869
C. 742   D. 593
E. 268

Directions (Qs. 44-48): *In each of the questions below are given three statements followed by two conclusions numbered I & II. You have to take the given statements to be true even if they seem to be at variance from commonly known facts. Read all the conclusions and then decide which of the given conclusions logically follows from the given statements disregarding commonly known facts.*

Give answer (A) if only conclusion I follows.
Give answer (B) if only conclusion II follows.
Give answer (C) if either I or II follows.
Give answer (D) if neither I nor II follows.
Give answer (E) if both I and II follow.

44. Statements : Some leaves are roots. Some roots are stems. All flowers are stems.

   Conclusions : I. No flower is a leaf.
   II. Some leaves are stems.

45. Statements : All numbers are digits. All alphabets are numbers. All words are alphabets.

   Conclusions : I. All words are digits.
   II. Some numbers are not words.

46. Statements : All plastics are wood. No wood is a metal. Some metals are gases.

   Conclusions : I. No plastic is a metal.
   II. Some gases are plastic.

47. Statements : All stars are moons. All moons are dust. All asteroids are dust.

   Conclusions : I. Some moons are asteroids.
   II. All stars are dust.

48. Statements : All umbrellas are rains. Some rains are clouds. All clouds are storms.

   Conclusions : I. Some storms are umbrellas.
   II. Some storms are not rains.

Directions (Qs. 49-53): *Study the following information carefully and answer the questions given below:*

   A, M, P, D, Q, R, W and B are sitting around a circle facing at the center. D is fourth to the left of A who is third to the right of M. P is third to the left of Q who is third to the left of M. R is third to the right of W who is second to the right of B.

49. Who is second to the left of D?
   A. W   B. B
   C. Q   D. Data inadequate
   E. None of these

50. Who is third to the left of P?
   A. M   B. D
   C. R   D. Data inadequate
   E. None of these

51. Who is the immediate right of Q?
   A. W   B. D
   C. B   D. Data inadequate
   E. None of these

52. Which of the following pairs represents the first and second respectively to the right of W?
   A. DM   B. QB
   C. MR   D. Data inadequate
   E. None of these

53. In which of the following pairs is the second person sitting to the immediate right of the first person?
   A. MD   B. RM
   C. AB   D. QB
   E. None of these

Directions (Qs. 54-56) : *From the five logical Diagrams, select one which best illustrates the relationship among three given classes in the questions.*

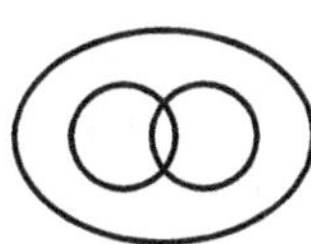

A.   B.

C.   D.

E.

54. Birds, fruits, mangoes

55. Criminals, lawyers, bandits

56. Swimmers, bachelors, men

57. In a certain code GROWN is written as 7@%36 and NAME is written as 64★$. How is GEAR writeen in that code?
   A. 74$@
   B. 7$4@
   C. 7%4@
   D. 7@$4
   E. None of these

58. In a certain code DISPLAY is written as RHCQZBM. How is GROUPED written in that code?
   A. PSHTEFQ
   B. NQFVCDO
   C. NQFVEFQ
   D. PSHTCDO
   E. None of these

59. How may meaningful English words can be formed with the letters OWH using each letter only once in each word?
   A. None
   B. One
   C. Two
   D. Three
   E. More than three

60. Which of the following will come in the place of question mark?

AC   EG   JL   ?   WY
   A. NP   B. MO
   C. PR   D. OP

Directions (Qs. 61–65) : *In these questions the symbols @, %, ©, $ and # are used with the following meaning as illustrated below:*

'P @ Q' means 'P is neither smaller than nor equal to Q'.

'P % Q' means 'P is neither greater than nor equal to Q'.

'P © Q' means 'P is not greater than Q'.

'P $ Q' means 'P is not smaller than Q'.

'P # Q' means 'P is neither smaller than nor greater than Q'.

Each of these questions has three statements followed by two conclusions numbered I and II. Assuming the given statements to be true, find which conclusion is definitely true:

61. *Statements   : H @ K, K % M, M © D*
Conclusion I : H @ D
Conclusion II : K % D
   A. Either conclusion I or II is true
   B. Only conclusion I is true
   C. Neither conclusion I nor II is true
   D. Only conclusion II is true
   E. Both conclusions I and II are true

62. *Statements   : R % H, H © T, T @ K*
Conclusion I : T © R
Conclusion II : K % H
   A. Either conclusion I or II is true
   B. Only conclusion I is true
   C. Neither conclusion I nor II is true
   D. Only conclusion II is true
   E. Both conclusions I and II are true

63. *Statements   : R © D, D $ M, M # J*
Conclusion I : J # D
Conclusion II : J % D
   A. Either conclusion I or II is true
   B. Only conclusion I is true
   C. Neither conclusion I nor II is true
   D. Only conclusion II is true
   E. Both conclusions I and II are true

64. *Statements   : W # D, D © B, B $ H*
Conclusion I : H # D
Conclusion II : B % W
   A. Either conclusion I or II is true
   B. Only conclusion I is true
   C. Neither conclusion I nor II is true
   D. Only conclusion II is true
   E. Both conclusions I and II are true

65. *Statements   : F $ N, N @ D, D % B*
Conclusion I : F @ D
Conclusion II : B @ N
   A. Either conclusion I or II is true
   B. Only conclusion I is true
   C. Neither conclusion I nor II is true
   D. Only conclusion II is true
   E. Both conclusions I and II are true

Quantitative Aptitude

66. 337.62 + 8.591 + 34.4 = ?
  A. 365.311   B. 375.411
  C. 380.611   D. 362.211
  E. None of these

67. 3889 + 12.952 − ? = 3854.002
  A. 47.95   B. 47.035
  C. 47.095   D. 47.85
  E. 47.125

68. A man spends $\dfrac{2}{5}$ of his salary on house rent, $\dfrac{3}{10}$ of his salary on food and $\dfrac{1}{8}$ of his salary on conveyance. If he has ₹ 1400 left with him, find his monthly salary.
  A. ₹ 5000   B. ₹ 8000
  C. ₹ 6000   D. ₹ 9000
  E. ₹ 10000

69. If $a^2 + b^2 = 117$ and $ab = 54$, then find the value of $\dfrac{a+b}{a-b}$.
  A. 2   B. 3
  C. 4   D. 5
  E. 1

70. 2 − [2 − {2 − 2 (2 + 2)}] = ?
  A. − 4   B. − 6
  C. 3   D. 5
  E. 6

71. $\dfrac{3}{5}$ of $\dfrac{4}{7}$ of $\dfrac{5}{9}$ of $\dfrac{21}{24}$ of 504 = ?
  A. 63   B. 69
  C. 96   D. 109
  E. None of these

72. $6\dfrac{5}{6} \times 5\dfrac{1}{3} + 17\dfrac{2}{3} \times 4\dfrac{1}{2} = ?$
  A. $112\dfrac{1}{3}$ B. $116\dfrac{2}{3}$
  C. 240   D. 663
  E. None of these

73. $\dfrac{3}{8}$ of 168 × 15 ÷ 5 + ? = 549 ÷ 9 + 235
  A. 107   B. 127
  C. 117   D. 1
  E. 137

74. How many $\dfrac{1}{8}$ s are there in $37\dfrac{1}{2}$?
  A. 300   B. 400
  C. 500   D. 350
  E. 430

75. A 70 cm long wire is to be cut into two pieces such that one piece will be $\dfrac{2}{5}$ as long as the other. How many centimetres will the shorter piece be?
  A. 10   B. 14
  C. 20   D. 28
  E. 24

76. The perimeter of a right angled triangle is 60 cm. Its hypotenuse is 26 cm. The area of the triangle is:
  A. 120 cm^2 B. 240 cm^2
  C. 390 cm^2 D. 780 cm^2
  E. None of these

77. A tank is 25 m long, 12 m wide and 6 m deep. The cost of plastering its wall and bottom at 75 paise per square metre is:
  A. ₹ 456   B. ₹ 458
  C. ₹ 558   D. ₹ 568
  E. ₹ 356

78. What will be the compound interest on a sum of ₹ 25000 after 3 years at the rate of 12% per annum?
  A. ₹ 9000.30   B. ₹ 9720
  C. ₹ 10123.20   D. ₹ 10483.20
  E. None of these

79. A train is moving at a speed of 132 km/hr. If the length of the train is 110 metres, how long will it take to cross a railway platform 165 metres long?

A. $7\dfrac{1}{2}$ sec   B. $8\dfrac{1}{2}$ sec

C. $9\dfrac{1}{2}$ sec   D. $6\dfrac{1}{2}$ sec

E. None of these

80. How many minutes does Aditya take to cover a distance of 400 m, if he runs at a speed of 20 km/hr?

A. 2 min   B. $2\dfrac{1}{5}$ min

C. 3 min   D. $1\dfrac{1}{5}$ min

E. $3\dfrac{1}{2}$ min

Directions (Qs. 81–85): *What will come in place of the question mark (?) in the following number series?*

81. 51, 68, 85, ?, 119
A. 101   B. 102
C. 103   D. 104
E. 105

82. 2, 7, 14, ?, 34
A. 23   B. 21
C. 18   D. 25
E. 28

83. ?, 15, 24, 35, 48
A. 6   B. 7
C. 8   D. 3
E. 5

84. 9, 14, 21, 30, ?
A. 45   B. 44
C. 49   D. 41
E. 50

85. 13, 31, 15, ?, 17
A. 18   B. 27
C. 25   D. 46
E. 35

86. If P% of P is 36, then P is equal to:
A. 15   B. 60
C. 600   D. 3600
E. None of these

87. The product of the ages of Ankit and Nikita is 240. If twice the age of Nikita is more than Ankita's age by 4 years. What is Nikita's age?
A. 12 years   B. 15 years
C. 14 years   D. 16 years
E. 13 years

88. The difference between a number and its three-fifth is 50. What is the number?
A. 75   B. 100
C. 125   D. 150
E. None of these

89. The average weight of a class of 24 students is 35 kg. If the weight of the teacher be included, the average rises by 400 g. The weight of the teacher is:
A. 45 kg   B. 50 kg
C. 53 kg   D. 55 kg
E. 48 kg

90. Peter purchased a machine for ₹ 80,000 and spent ₹ 5000 on repair and ₹ 1000 on transport and sold it with 25% profit. At what price did he sell the machine?
A. ₹ 105100   B. ₹ 106250
C. ₹ 107500   D. ₹ 117500
E. None of these

91. The ratio of the cost price and the selling price is 4 : 5. The profit per cent is:
A. 10%   B. 20%
C. 25%   D. 30%
E. 35%

92. The cost of 16 packets of salt, each weighing 900 grams is ₹ 28. What will be the cost of 27 packets, if each packet weighs 1 kg?
A. ₹ 52.50   B. ₹ 56
C. ₹ 58.50   D. ₹ 64.75
E. None of these

93. If 8 men can reap 80 hectares in 24 days, then how many hectares can 36 men reap in 30 days?
A. 350   B. 400
C. 425   D. 450
E. 375

94. A and B together can complete a piece of work in 4 days. If A alone can complete the

same work in 12 days, in how many days can B alone complete the work?
A. 10 days
B. 8 days
C. 6 days
D. 9 days
E. 7 days

95. A train when moves at an average speed of 40 km/hr, reaches its destination on time. When its average speed becomes 35 km/hr, then it reaches its destination 15 minutes late. Find the length of Journey.
A. 30 km
B. 40 km
C. 70 km
D. 80 km
E. 50 km

Directions (Qs. 96–100): *Study the following pie-diagrams carefully and answer the questions given below it.*

Percentage Composition of Human Body

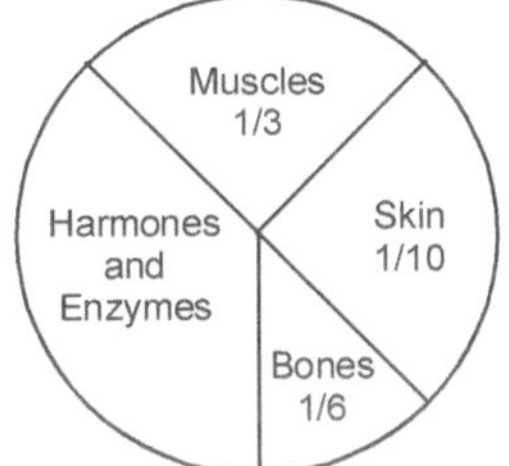

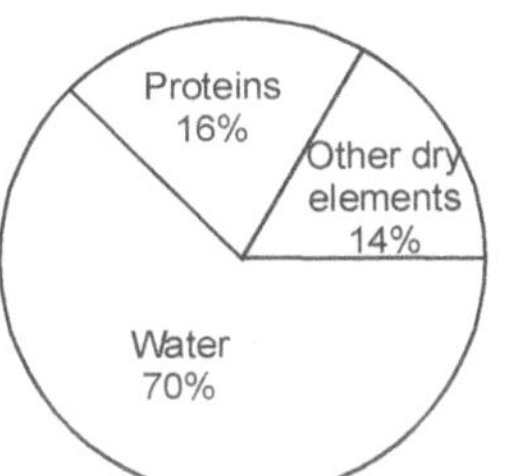

96. In the human body, what part is made of neither bones nor skin?

A. $\dfrac{1}{40}$

B. $\dfrac{3}{80}$

C. $\dfrac{2}{5}$

D. $\dfrac{11}{15}$

E. None of these

97. What is the ratio of the distribution of proteins in the muscles to that of the distribution of proteins in the bones?
A. 1 : 18
B. 1 : 2
C. 2 : 1
D. 18 : 1
E. None of these

98. What will be the quantity of water in the body of a person weighing 50 kg?
A. 20 kg
B. 35 kg
C. 41 kg
D. 42.5 kg
E. 43 kg

99. What per cent of the total weight of human body is equivalent to the weight of the proteins in skin in human body?
A. 0.016
B. 1.6
C. 0.16
D. 0.61
E. 0.106

100. To show the distribution of proteins and other dry elements in the human body, the arc of the circle should subtend at the centre an angle of:
A. 54°
B. 126°
C. 108°
D. 252°
E. None of these

ANSWERS

1	2	3	4	5	6	7	8	9	10
D	C	B	A	D	C	D	A	D	C

11	12	13	14	15	16	17	18	19	20
E	E	D	D	B	C	C	A	C	A

21	22	23	24	25	26	27	28	29	30
B	D	A	D	C	B	D	A	C	E

31	32	33	34	35	36	37	38	39	40
D	C	B	E	A	B	B	C	E	B

41	42	43	44	45	46	47	48	49	50
A	D	A	D	A	A	B	D	C	B

51	52	53	54	55	56	57	58	59	60
A	A	C	A	A	B	B	C	C	C

61	62	63	64	65	66	67	68	69	70
D	C	A	C	B	C	A	B	D	B
71	72	73	74	75	76	77	78	79	80
E	E	A	A	C	A	C	C	A	D
81	82	83	84	85	86	87	88	89	90
B	A	C	D	E	B	A	C	A	C
91	92	93	94	95	96	97	98	99	100
C	A	D	C	C	D	C	B	B	C

Some Selected Explanatory Answers

31. R A G   F I N   P U T   L O W   S U E
   ↓↓↓ ↓↓↓ ↓↓↓ ↓↓↓ ↓↓↓
Q B F   E J M   O V S   K P V   R V F

32. RAG FIN PUT LOW SUE
RAH **FIO** **PUU** LOX SUF

34. RAG FIN PUT LOW SUE
ARG IFN UPT OLW USE

35. FIN, LOW, PUT, RAG and SUE
Second word from right will be RAG.

36.

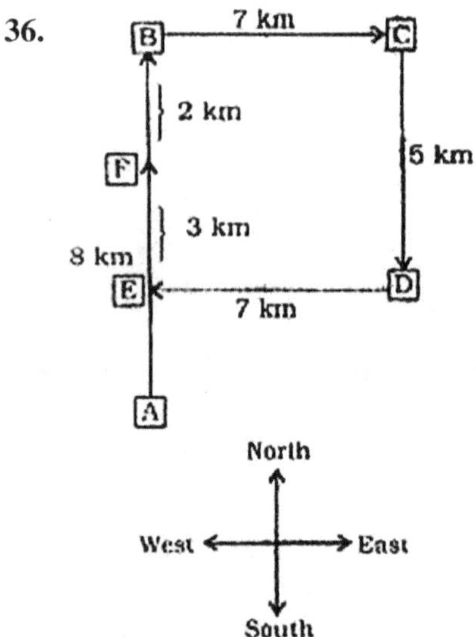

Distance between F and B = 2 km.

37. J > R > T > L

38. Meaningful words
= FIST : FITS

For Qs. 49–53

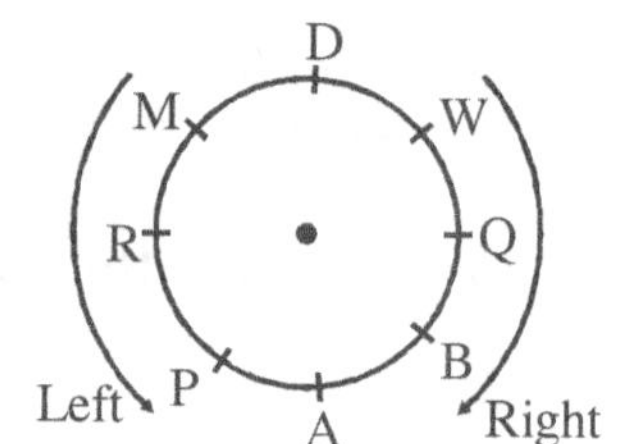

54.

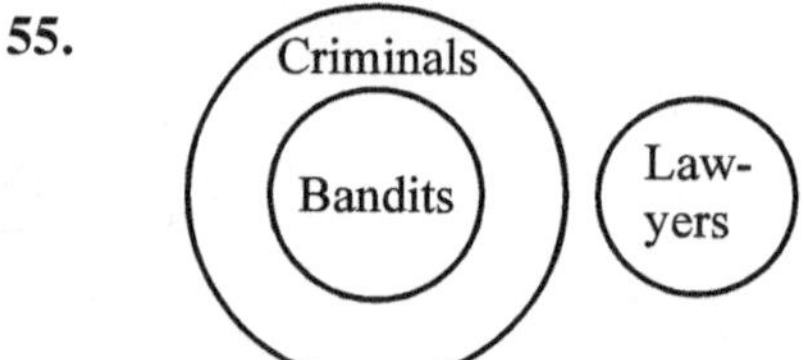

All mangoes are fruits, but neither fruits, nor mangoes can be birds.

55.

All bandits are criminal, but neither criminals nor bandits can be lawyers.

56.

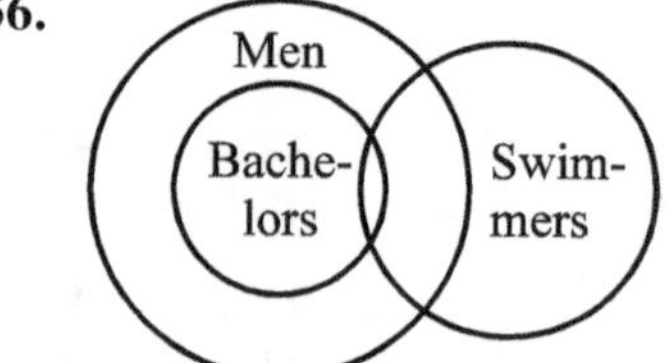

All bachelors are men and some men and bachelors can be swimmers.

57. As, G R O W N   N A M E
↓ ↓ ↓ ↓ ↓   ↓ ↓ ↓ ↓
7 @ % 3 6   6 4 ★ $

Similarly, G E A R
↓ ↓ ↓ ↓
7 $ 4 @

58. As,

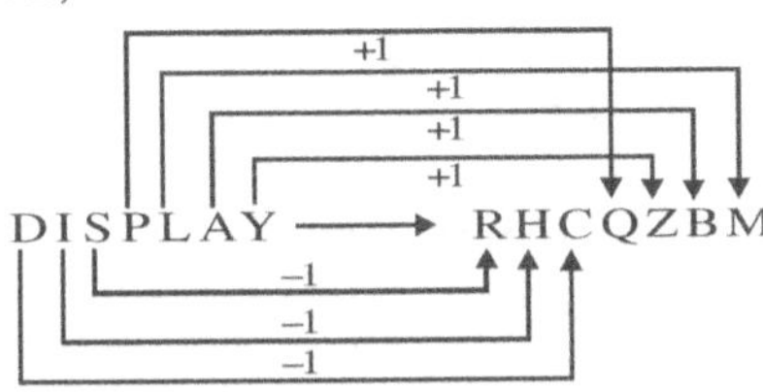

Similarly,

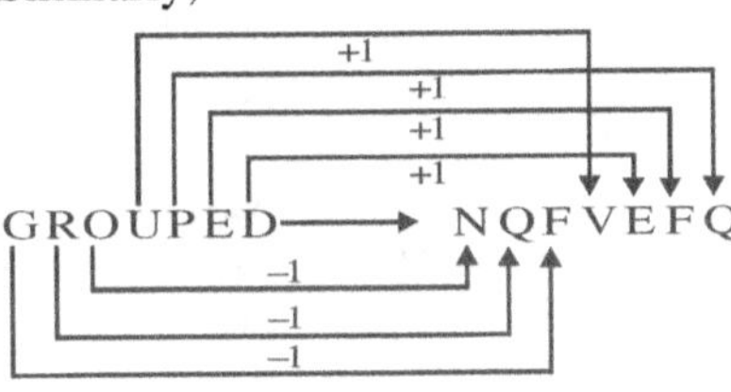

60.

$$\text{A} \;\; \text{C} \;\; \text{E} \;\; \text{G} \;\; \text{J} \;\; \text{L} \;\; \boxed{\text{P} \;\; \text{R}} \;\; \text{W} \;\; \text{Y}$$

(top: +4, +5, +6, +7 ; bottom: +4, +5, +6, +7)

61-65.
  (i) $P @ Q \Rightarrow P \nleq Q : P > Q$
  (ii) $P \% Q \Rightarrow P \ngeq Q : P < Q$
  (iii) $P © Q \Rightarrow P \ngtr Q : P \leq Q$
  (iv) $P \$ Q \Rightarrow P \nless Q : P \geq Q$
  (v) $P \# Q \Rightarrow P \ngtr Q : P \nless Q : P = Q$

$@ \Rightarrow >$	$\% \Rightarrow <$	$© \Rightarrow \leq$
$\$ \Rightarrow \geq$	$\# \Rightarrow =$	

61. $H @ K \Rightarrow H > K$ $K \% M \Rightarrow K < M$
$M © D \Rightarrow M \leq D$
Therefore, $H > K < M \leq D$
Conclusions
I. $H @ D \Rightarrow H > D$: Not True
II. $K \% D \Rightarrow K < D$: True

62. $R \% H \Rightarrow R < H$ $H © T \Rightarrow H \leq T$
$T @ K \Rightarrow T > K$
Therefore, $R < H \leq T > K$
Conclusions
I. $T © R \Rightarrow T \leq R$: Not True
II. $K \% H \Rightarrow K < H$: Not True

63. $R © D \Rightarrow R \leq D$ $D \$ M \Rightarrow D \geq M$
$M \# J \Rightarrow M = J$
Therefore, $R \leq D \geq M = J$
Conclusions
I. $J \# D \Rightarrow J = D$: may be
II. $J \% D \Rightarrow J < D$: may be
J is either smaller than or equal to D. Therefore, either conclusion I or conclusion II is true.

64. $W \# D \Rightarrow W = D$ $D © B \Rightarrow D \leq B$
$B \$ H \Rightarrow B \geq H$
Therefore, $W = D \leq B \geq H$
Conclusions
I. $H \# D \Rightarrow H = D$: Not True
II. $B \% W \Rightarrow B < W$: Not True

65. $F \$ N \Rightarrow F \geq N$
$N @ D \Rightarrow N > D$
$D \% B \Rightarrow D < B$
Therefore, $F \geq N > D < B$
Conclusions
I. $F @ D \Rightarrow F > D$: True
II. $B @ N \Rightarrow B > N$: Not True

66.
$$\begin{array}{r} 337.62 \\ 8.591 \\ + \; 34.4 \\ \hline 380.611 \end{array}$$

67.
$$3889 + 12.952 - x = 3854.002$$
$$\Rightarrow \quad 3901.952 - 3854.002 = x$$
$$\Rightarrow \quad 47.950 = x$$
$$\Rightarrow \quad x = 47.95$$

68. Let, man's monthly salary = ₹ x
Total money spent
$$= \frac{2x}{5} + \frac{2x}{10} + \frac{x}{8}$$
$$= \frac{16x + 12x + 5x}{40} = \frac{33x}{40}$$

Money saved $= x - \dfrac{33x}{40} = \dfrac{40x - 33x}{40} = \dfrac{7x}{40}$

According to the question,
$$\frac{7x}{40} = 1400$$
$$\Rightarrow \quad x = \frac{40 \times 1400}{7} = 8000$$
∴ Man's monthly salary = ₹ 8000

69.
$$(a + b)^2 = a^2 + b^2 + 2ab$$
$$= 117 + 2(54)$$
$$= 117 + 108 = 225$$
$$\therefore \quad a + b = 15$$

Now $(a - b)^2 = (a + b)^2 - 4ab$
$$= 225 - 4 \times 54 = 225 - 216 = 9$$
$$\therefore \quad a - b = 3$$
$$\therefore \quad \frac{a+b}{a-b} = \frac{15}{3} = 5$$

70. $2 - [2 - (2 - 8)] = 2 - [2 + 6]$
$$= 2 - 8 = -6$$

71. $\dfrac{3}{5} \times \dfrac{4}{7} \times \dfrac{5}{9} \times \dfrac{21}{24} \times 504 = \dfrac{504}{6} = 84$

72. $\dfrac{41}{6} \times \dfrac{16}{3} + \dfrac{53}{3} \times \dfrac{9}{2} = \dfrac{41 \times 8}{9} + \dfrac{159}{2}$

$$= \frac{656 + 1431}{18} = \frac{2087}{18} = 115\frac{17}{18}$$

73. $\dfrac{3}{8} \times 168 \times 15 \div 5 + x = 61 + 235$

$$3 \times 21 \times 3 + x = 296$$
$$x = 296 - 189 = 107$$

74. $\dfrac{75}{2} \div \dfrac{1}{8} = \dfrac{75}{2} \times \dfrac{8}{1} = 75 \times 4 = 300$

75. Let, length of one piece = x cm
length of 2nd piece = $70 - x$
According to the question,
$$\frac{2x}{5} = 70 - x$$
$$\Rightarrow \quad 2x = 350 - 5x$$
$$\Rightarrow \quad 7x = 350 \Rightarrow x = 50$$
length of first piece = 50 cm
length of 2nd piece = $70 - 50 = 20$ cm
$\therefore$ length of the shorter piece = 20 cm.

76.

$$\because x + y + 26 = 60$$
$$\therefore \quad x + y = 60 - 26 = 34$$

Now, $x^2 + y^2 = (26)^2$
$$(x + y)^2 = x^2 + y^2 + 2xy$$
$$(34)^2 = (26)^2 + 2xy$$
$$\Rightarrow \quad 2xy = (34)^2 - (26)^2$$
$$= (34 + 26)(34 - 26)$$
$$= 60 \times 8$$
$$\therefore \quad xy = \frac{60 \times 8}{2} = 240$$

Area of the right triangle,
$$= \frac{1}{2} \times xy = \frac{1}{2} \times 240 = 120 \text{ cm}^2$$

77. Area of the four walls = $2(l + b) \times h$
$$= 2(25 + 12) \times 16$$
$$= 2 \times 37 \times 6 \text{ m}^2$$
$$= 444 \text{ m}^2$$
Area of bottom = $25 \times 12 = 300$ m²
Total Area = $444 + 300 = 744$ m²

Cost of plastering of 1 m² = ₹ $\dfrac{3}{4}$

Cost of plastering of 744 m² = $744 \times \dfrac{3}{4}$
$$= ₹ 558$$

Hence, cost of plastering of walls and bottom
$$= ₹ 558$$

78. $A = P\left(1 + \dfrac{r}{100}\right)^t = 25000\left(1 + \dfrac{12}{100}\right)^3$

$$= 25000 \times \frac{28}{25} \times \frac{28}{25} \times \frac{28}{25}$$

$$= ₹ 35123.20$$

$\therefore$ CI = A – P
$$= 35123.20 - 25000$$
$$= ₹ 10123.20$$

79. Speed of the train = 132 km/hr

$$= 132 \times \frac{5}{18} \text{ m/s}$$

$$= \frac{22 \times 5}{3} \text{ m/s} = \frac{110}{3} \text{ m/s}$$

Total length = 110 + 165 = 275 m

$$\text{Time taken} = \frac{\text{distance}}{\text{speed}} = \frac{275}{\frac{110}{3}} = \frac{275 \times 3}{110}$$

$$= \frac{55 \times 3}{22} = \frac{15}{2} = 7\frac{1}{2} \text{ sec.}$$

80. Aditya's speed = 20 km/hr

$$= 20 \times \frac{5}{18} \text{ m/s} = \frac{50}{9} \text{ m/s}$$

$$\text{Time taken} = \frac{400 \times 9}{50} = 72 \text{ seconds}$$

$$= 1 \text{ min } 12 \text{ sec}$$

$$= 1\frac{12}{60} \text{ min} = 1\frac{1}{5} \text{ min}$$

81. 51 68 85 102 119
      +17 +17 +17 +17

82. 2 7 14 23 34
      2 + 5   7 + 7   14 + 9   23 + 11

83. 8 15 24 35 48
      + 7   + 9   + 11   + 13

84. 9 14 21 30 41
      + 5   + 7   + 9   + 11

85. 13 31 15 35 17
      13 + 2   15 + 2

Here, there are two types of series.

(*i*)   13, 15, 17, 19

(*ii*)   31, 35, ...

86. $\because$ P% of P = 36

$\Rightarrow$ $\dfrac{P}{100} \times P = 36$

$\Rightarrow$ $P^2 = 3600$

$\Rightarrow$ $P = \sqrt{3600} = 60$

87. Let, Nikita's age = x years

And, Ankit's age = y years

$$x \times y = 240$$

$\Rightarrow$ $x = \dfrac{240}{y}$

According to the question,

$$2x = y + 4$$

$\Rightarrow$ $2\left(\dfrac{240}{y}\right) = y + 4$

$\Rightarrow$ $y^2 + 4y - 180 = 0$

$\Rightarrow$ $y^2 + 24y - 20y - 480 = 0$

$\Rightarrow$ $y (y + 24) - 20 (y + 24) = 0$

$\Rightarrow$ $(y - 20) (y + 24) = 0$

$$y = 20, \ y = -24$$

$\therefore$ $x = \dfrac{240}{20} = 12$

Hence, Nikita's age = 12 years.

88. Let, the number be x

According to the question,

$$x - \frac{3x}{5} = 50$$

$\Rightarrow$ $5x - 3x = 250$

$\Rightarrow$ $2x = 250$

$\Rightarrow$ $x = 125$

Hence, number = 125

89. Total weight of 24 students

$$= 24 \times 35 = 840 \text{ kg}$$

Total weight of 24 students with teacher

$$= 25 \times 35.4 \text{ kg} = 885 \text{ kg}$$

$\therefore$ Weight of the teacher

$$= 885 - 840 = 45 \text{ kg}$$

90. CP of Machine = 80000 + 5000 + 1000

$$= ₹ \ 86000$$

$$\text{Profit} = \frac{25}{100} \times 86000$$

$$= ₹ \ 21500$$

Selling price = CP + Profit

$$= 86000 + 21500$$
$$= ₹\ 107500$$

91. Let, CP = $4x$

And, SP = $5x$

Profit = SP – CP

$$= 5x - 4x = x$$

$$\text{Profit\%} = \frac{\text{Profit}}{\text{CP}} \times 100 = \frac{x}{4x} \times 100 = 25\%$$

92. Total weight of 16 packets

$$= 16 \times 900 = 14400 \text{ g}$$

Total weight of 27 packets

$$= 27 \times 1000 = 27000 \text{ g}$$

Cost of 14400 g = ₹ 28

Cost of 27000 g = $\dfrac{28}{14400} \times 27000 = ₹\ 52.50$

93. In 24 days 8 men can reap 80 hectare

In 1 day 1 man can reap $\dfrac{80}{24 \times 8}$

In 30 day 36 men can reap

$$\frac{80 \times 30 \times 36}{24 \times 8} = 480 \text{ hectare.}$$

94. (A + B) can do a work in 4 days

(A + B)'s 1 day work = $\dfrac{1}{4}$

A alone can do this work in 12 days

A's 1 day work = $\dfrac{1}{12}$

B's 1 day work = $\dfrac{1}{4} - \dfrac{1}{12}$

$$= \frac{3-1}{12} = \frac{2}{12} = \frac{1}{6}$$

Hence, B alone can do this work in 6 days.

95. Let, length of the Journey = x km

$$\frac{x}{35} - \frac{x}{40} = \frac{15}{60} = \frac{1}{4}$$

$$\Rightarrow \quad \frac{8x - 7x}{280} = \frac{1}{4}$$

$$\Rightarrow \quad \frac{x}{280} = \frac{1}{4}$$

$$\Rightarrow \quad 4x = 280$$

$$\Rightarrow \quad x = \frac{280}{4} = 70$$

∴ length of the Journey = 70 km.

96. Part of the body made of neither bones nor

$$\text{skin} = 1 - \left(\frac{1}{6} + \frac{1}{10}\right) = \frac{11}{15}$$

97. Required ratio = $\dfrac{16\% \text{ of } \dfrac{1}{3}}{16\% \text{ of } \dfrac{1}{6}} = \dfrac{6}{3} = \dfrac{2}{1}$

98. Quantity of water in the body of a person weighing 50 kg = (70% of 50) kg = 35 kg.

99. Let, the body weight be x kg

Then, weight of skin protein in the body

$$= \left[16\% \text{ of } \left(\frac{1}{10} \text{ of } x\right)\right] \text{kg} = \left(\frac{16x}{1000}\right) \text{kg}$$

∴ Required percentage

$$= \left[\frac{\left(\dfrac{16x}{1000}\right)}{x} \times 100\right] = 1.6\%$$

100. Percentage of proteins and other dry elements in the body = (16% + 14%) = 30%

∴ Central angle corresponding to proteins and other dry elements together

$$= 30\% \text{ of } 360° = 108°$$

SBI Junior Associates & Junior Agricultural Associates
(Clerical Cadre Exam)

General English

Directions (Qs. 1–15): *Read the following passage carefully and answer the questions given below it. Certain words/phrases have been printed in **bold** to help you locate them while answering some of the questions.*

The balance wheel whirled and the rusty foot pedal clattered up and down. The needle hopped over the smooth-stitching pleats, folds and moving **smoothly** around the neckline. The reel of cotton thread jumped and shook on its needle stand. "Stop, you are making me dizzy," said the reel. "Stop, **grumbling,** you foolish thing," said the pedal. "If anyone should grumble, it is me," said the small reeel inside the bobbin. When the needle moved, it took the thread from the bobbin and made stitches under the cloth "I do all the **important** work and here I am stuck up day and night in this stuffy box. You all have a fine time sitting there staring at the world," he continued.

"Now children," said the kindly old balance wheel, "You all know what important work the lady is doing today. She is stitching a school dress for her daughter who will be admitted in school tomorrow. We must all work hard and stitch it beautifully." "I have had enough food today. It is too hot here and I am tired of the needle poking his nose in all the time," said the small reel. "Listen my children," continued the old wheel. "I have been with this machine for about hundred years. At first we belonged to a dress maker. He made us work hard. One day this lady's grandfather come to the shop. He liked the machine and bought it. The old gentleman wanted his daughters to learn sewing but they did not use us much. Still, we were fed **regularly** with oil and cleaned by the servants for years. We have stood in this corner and seen many things. We saw the old gentleman die. His children then started quarrelling. Slowly they became poor. The servants were **dismissed**. Then one by one, the children went away and the house was closed. After many years this lady came with her husband. She had a daughter after a few years. The lady started using us after pouring oil into these old joints. She did not listen to her husband's suggestion to sell us off to a scrapdealer."

As the wheel finished everyone was quiet for sometime. Then the reef said, "We are very sorry and we would rather break into pieces than let down the lady." They all continued to work till the scissors **snipped** the thread and the beautiful dress was ready.

1. What was the lady doing on the sewing machine?
   A. She was stitching a dress for herself
   B. She was winding cotton thread on the reel
   C. She was stitching a dress to sell
   D. She was stitching a school dress for her daughter
   E. None of these

2. Why was the reel of thread feeling dizzy?
   A. It was moving on the needle stand
   B. It was being shaken by the needle
   C. It was being wound with thread
   D. It was made to rotate at a very fast rate
   E. None of these

3. Who brought the sewing machine to the house?
   A. The child's grandfather
   B. The lady's father
   C. The grandfather of the child's mother
   D. The lady's husband's father
   E. None of these

4. What did the reel say after listening to the old balance wheel's story?
   A. That they would work and perish rather than disappoint the lady
   B. That they should break themselves into pieces after helping the lady
   C. That they should not create any problem for the lady by destroying themselves
   D. That there is no need to work so hard and break themselves into pieces
   E. None of these

5. Which of the following did not happen after the old gentleman's death?
   A. The infighting among his children
   B. The cleaning of the machine by the servants
   C. The gradual abandoning of the house by the children
   D. The old man's children becoming economically weak
   E. The dismissal of the servants

6. What was the suggestion of the lady's husband?
   A. To get the sewing machine repaired
   B. To consider the sewing machine as a scrap
   C. To give the sewing machine to the dress maker
   D. To dispose of the sewing machine as a scrap item
   E. To retain and use the sewing machine occasionally

7. Who, among the following, complained that it was stuck-up day and night in the stuffy box?
   A. The bobbin
   B. The needle
   C. The old balance wheel
   D. The pedal
   E. None of these

8. The house is presently inhabited by
   A. the lady, her husband and her grandfather
   B. the lady, her daughter and the lady's grandfather
   C. the lady, her husband and their daughter
   D. the lady, her husband and her father-in-law
   E. The lady, her daughter and the lady's father-in-law

9. Who is the narrator of the story of the lady's ancestors?
   A. The sewing machine
   B. The big reel of cotton thread
   C. The pedal
   D. The small reel inside the bobbin
   E. None of these

Directions (Qs. 10–12): *Choose the word or group of words which is most nearly the SAME in meaning. as the word given in bold capitals as used in the passage.*

10. **GRUMBLING**
    A. quarrelling
    B. roaring
    C. complaining
    D. disturbing
    E. interfering

11. **DISMISSED**
    A. let out
    B. laid off
    C. given away
    D. got over
    E. put down

12. **SNIPPED**
    A. attached
    B. removed
    C. opened
    D. cut
    E. loosened

Directions (Qs. 13–15): *Choose the word or group of words which is most nearly the OPPOSITE in meaning as the word given in bold capitals as used in the passage.*

13. **SMOOTHLY**
    A. clearly
    B. nicely
    C. noisily
    D. roughly
    E. strongly

14. **IMPORTANT**
    A. major
    B. trivial
    C. dirty
    D. tough
    E. bad

15. REGULARLY
   A. daily
   B. occasionally
   C. slightly
   D. frequently
   E. timely

Directions (Qs. 16–20) : *Each sentence below has a blank, each blank indicating that something has been omitted. Choose the word for each blank which best fits the meaning of the sentence as a whole.*

16. Mahesh had to drop his plan of going to picnic as he had certain ..... to take of during that period.
   A. transactions   B. preparations
   C. commitments   D. urgencies
   E. observations

17. No country can ..... to practise a constant, rigid foreign policy in view of the world power dynamics.
   A. envisage   B. anticipate
   C. afford   D. visualise
   E. obliviate

18. After a recent mild paralytic attack his movements are ..... restricted; otherwise he is still very active.
   A. not   B. entirely
   C. slightly   D. nowhere
   E. frequently

19. ..... he woke up, he saw that his bag was stolen.
   A. If   B. When
   C. Where   D. So
   E. Neither

20. I am going to Bhopal today and plan to ..... by tomorrow evening.
   A. returning
   B. returned
   C. have returned
   D. be returning
   E. return

Directions (Qs. 21–25): *Read each sentence to find out whether there is any grammatical error or idiomatic error in it. The error, if any, will be in one part of the sentence. The number of that part is the answer. If there is "No Error" the answer is 'E'. (Ignore errors of punctuation if any.)*

21. (A) Naren could not/(B) decide as to which/(C) course he should do/(D) after obtaining his Degree./(E) No error.

22. (A) One of the objective/(B) of the meeting which/(C) was held today was to/(D) elect new office-bearers./(E) No error.

23. (A) Ketaki would have/(B) surely got the job/(C) if she would have/(D) attended the interview./(E) No error.

24. (A) When the national/(B) anthem was being/(C) sung, everyone were/(D) standing in silence./(E) No error.

25. (A) Rosy herself wash/(B) all the clothes and/(C) never gives them/(D) to the laundry./(E) No error.

Directions (Qs. 26–30): *Which of the phrases A, B, C and D given below should replace the phrase given in* **bold** *in the following sentence to make the sentence grammatically meaningful and correct? If the sentence is correct as it is and 'No correction is required', mark 'E' as the answer.*

26. He **hesitated to listen to** what his brother was saying.
   A. listened to hesitate
   B. hesitated listen to
   C. hesitates to listening
   D. is hesitated to listen to
   E. No correction required

27. Hardly **does the sun rise** when the stars disappeared.
   A. have the sun rose
   B. had the sun risen
   C. did the sun rose
   D. the sun rose
   E. No correction required

28. The police has **so far succeeded in recovering** only a part of the stolen property.
   A. thus far succeeded for recovery
   B. so far succeed in the recovery of
   C. as far as succeeded in recovery of
   D. so far succeed to recover
   E. No correction required

29. What happens to all those travellers on the ship was not known?
 A. What happened of
 B. That is what happens to
 C. What is that happens to
 D. What happened to
 E. No correction required

30. Because of his ill health, the doctor has advised him **not to refrain** from smoking.
 A. to not refrain from
 B. to resort to
 C. to refrain from
 D. to be refrained from
 E. No correction required

Reasoning Ability

Directions (Qs. 31-35) : *Study the following information carefully and answer the questions given below :*

Seven persons—A, B, C, D, E, F and G—are standing in a straight line facing north at equal distances but not necessarily in the same order. Each of them is a different professional viz. Actor, Reporter, Doctor, Engineer, Lawyer, Teacher and Painter but not necessarily in the same order.

G is standing at the fifth position to the left of C. Reporter is standing at the third position to the right of G. F is standing at the fifth position to the right of A. E is standing second to the left of B. Engineer is standing at the second position to the left of D. Three persons are sitting between Engineer and Painter. Doctor is to the immediate left of Engineer. Lawyer is to the immediate right of teacher.

31. How many persons are there to the left of Reporter?
 A. None   B. One
 C. Two   D. Three
 E. More than three

32. Which of the following pairs of persons are sitting at the extreme ends?
 A. A and Actor
 B. Engineer and C
 C. Doctor and E
 D. F and Lawyer
 E. Teacher and Doctor

33. Who among the following is sitting exactly in the middle of the row?
 A. Doctor   B. F
 C. Lawyer   D. B
 E. Teacher

34. Who among the following is sitting second to the right of Teacher?
 A. Painter   B. B
 C. A   D. Actor
 E. Lawyer

35. Who among the following are the immediate neighbours of Painter?
 A. Actor and Teacher   B. B and Lawyer
 C. B and Engineer   D. Reporter and C
 E. Doctor and Lawyer

Directions (Qs. 36 & 37) : *Study the following information carefully and answer the questions given below:*

Point A is 11 metre to the north of point B. Point C is 11 metre to the east of point B. Point D is 5 metre to the north of point C. Point E is 7 metre to the west of the point D. Point F is 9 metre to the north of point E. Point G is 4 metre to the west of point F.

36. Point D is in which direction with respect to point F?
 A. North-East   B. South-East
 C. South   D. North-West
 E. East

37. Which of the following three points lie in a straight line?
 A. A, E and D   B. F, E and C
 C. G, F and B   D. G, A and B
 E. None of these

Directions (Qs. 38-40) : *Study the following information carefully and answer the questions given below :*

Among six persons—K, L, M, N, O and P— each lives on a different floor of a building having six floors numbered one to six (the ground floor is numbered 1, the floor above it is numbered 2 and so on and the top most floor is numbered 6).

L lives on an even numbered floor. L lives on a floor immediately below K's floor and immediately above M's floor. P lives on a floor immediately above N's floor. P lives on an even numbered floor. O does not live on floor number 4.

38. Who amongst the following live on the floors exactly between K and P?
A. O and L
B. L and N
C. L and M
D. M and N
E. M and O

39. On which floor does O live?
A. 6th
B. 2nd
C. 3rd
D. 5th
E. Cannot be determined

40. Who amongst the following does live on floor 5?
A. O
B. M
C. N
D. K
E. Cannot be determined

Directions (Qs. 41-45) : *Each of the questions below consists of a question and two statements numbered I and II given below it. You have to decide whether the data provided in the statements are sufficient to answer the question. Read both the statements and—*

Give answer (A) if the data in statement **I alone** are sufficient to answer the question, while the data in statement II alone are not sufficient to answer the question.

Give answer (B) if the data in statement **II alone** are sufficient to answer the question, while the data in statement I alone are not sufficient to answer the question.

Give answer (C) if the data **either** in statement I alone or in statement II alone are sufficient to answer the question.

Give answer (D) if the data given in both the statements I and II together are **not** sufficient to answer the question, and

Give answer (E) if the data in both the statements I and II together are necessary to answer the question.

41. Is D the mother of S?
I. L is the husband of D. L has only three children.
II. N is the brother of S and P. P is the daughter of L.

42. How many students are there in the class?
I. There are more than 20 but less than 27 students in the class.
II. There are more than 24 but less than 31 students in the class. When the students are divided into groups, each group contains five students.

43. Among J, K, L, M and N, each has different height. Who amongst them is the second tallest?
I. N is taller than M and K. K is shorter than M.
II. L is taller than N. J is not the tallest.

44. Five persons—A, B, C, D and E—are sitting in a circle facing the centre. Who is sitting to the immediate left of D?
I. C is sitting second to the left of A. B and D are immediate neighbours of each other.
II. D is sitting to the immediate left of B. E is not an immediate neighbour of D and B.

45. How is 'cost' written in a code language?
I. 'tell me the cost' is written as '@ 0 # 9' and 'cost was very high' is written as '& 6 # 1' in that code language.
II. 'some cost was discount' is written as '1 8 7 #' and 'some people like discount' is wrttten as '8 7 5 %' in that code language.

Directions (Qs. 46-50) : In these questions, relationship between different elements is shown in the statements. These statements are followed by two conclusions.

Mark answer   **If**
A.   Only conclusion I follows.
B.   Only conclusion II follows.
C.   Either conclusion I or II follows.
D.   Neither conclusion I nor II follows.
E.   Both conclusions I and II follow.

46. Statements : $K > I \geq T \geq E$;
                 $O < R < K$

Conclusions : I. R < E

II. O < T

47. Statements : B > A > S < I > C > L < Y

Conclusions : I. B > L

II. A > Y

48. Statements : C < L < O = U = D ≥ S > Y

Conclusions : I. O > Y

II. C < D

49. Statements : B > R > E > A > K;

H > A > S

Conclusions : I. H > K

II. S < B

50. Statements : J = A; C ≥ K ≥ S ≥ A

Conclusions : I. C > J

II. C = J

Directions (Qs. 51-55) : *In each of the questions/ set of questions below are given two statements followed by two conclusions numbered I and II. You have to assume everything in the statements to be true even if they seem to be at variance from commonly known facts and then decide which of the two given conclusions logically follows from the information given in the statement.*

Give answer A. if only conclusion I follows.

Give answer B. if only conclusion II follows.

Give answer C. if either conclusion I or conclusion II follows.

Give answer D. if neither conclusion I nor conclusion II follows.

Give answer E. if both conclusions I and II follow.

51. Statements : All alphabets are numbers.

Some alphabets are digits.

Conclusions : I. At least some digits are numbers.

II. No digit is a number.

52. Statements : Some squares are circles.

Some circles are rectangles.

Conclusions : I. At least some rectangles are squares.

II. No rectangle is a square.

53. Statements : No office is a palace.

All colleges are places.

Conclusions : I. All palaces are colleges.

II. No college is an office.

54. Statements : All mountains are rivers.

All rivers are lakes.

Conclusions : I. All mountains are lakes.

II. At least some lakes are rivers.

55. Statements : Some wins are losses.

All trophies are losses.

Conclusions : I. All trophies are wins.

II. All losses are trophies.

Directions (Qs. 56-60) : *Study the following information carefully answer the questions given below:*

C E B A C D B C D A C E D E D C A B A D A
C E D U B A N B D

56. How many such Ds are there in the above arrangement each of which is immediately preceded by a consonant and also immediately followed by a vowel?

A. None   B. One

C. Two   D. Three

E. More than three

57. How many Ds are there in the above arrangement?

A. Four   B. Three

C. Five   D. Seven

E. Six

58. If all the Bs are deleted from the above arrangement, which of the following will be eleventh from the left end?

A. D   B. C

C. E   D. A

E. None of these

59. How many such As are there in the above arrangement each of which is immediately preceded by B and also immediately followed by a consonant?

A. None   B. One

C. Two   D. Three

E. More than three

60. Which of the following is ninth to the right of the 22nd from the right end of the above arrangement?

A. A   B. C

C. B   D. D

E. E

Directions (Qs. 61-65) : *Study the following information carefully and answer the questions given below :*

Eight people—S, T, U, V, W, X, Y and Z—are sitting around a circle but not necessarily in the same order. Two of them S and T are facing towards the centre while other people are facing towards the outside. Y sits second to the left of W. S sits second to the left of Y. Only one person sits between S and Z. T sits to the immediate right of S. T is not an immediate neighbour of Y. V is not an immediate neighbour of Y. Both the immediate neighbours of X face towards the outside.

61. What is the position of X with respect to S?
   A. Third to the right
   B. Fourth to the left
   C. Third to the left
   D. Fourth to the right
   E. Second to the right

62. Who sits to the immediate left of Z?
   A. T   B. W
   C. S   D. X
   E. V

63. Which of the following pairs represents the immediate neighbours of W?
   A. V and X   B. V and Z
   C. X and Y   D. Z and T
   E. S and U

64. What is the position of U with respect to W?
   A. Second to the left   B. Fifth to the right
   C. Sixth to the left   D. Third to the right
   E. Fifth to the left

65. How many people sit between U and V?
   A. Two   B. Four
   C. One   D. Three
   E. Five

Quantitative Aptitude

66. Simplify : $\dfrac{5.32\times56+5.32\times44}{(7.66)^2-(2.34)^2}$
   A. 7.2   B. 8.5
   C. 10   D. 12
   E. 9.5

67. $(7.5 \times 7.5 + 37.5 + 2.5 \times 2.5)$ is equal to:
   A. 30   B. 60
   C. 80   D. 100
   E. 90

68. A tin of oil was $\dfrac{4}{5}$ full. When 6 bottles of oil were taken out and four bottles of oil were poured into it, it was $\dfrac{3}{4}$ full. How many bottles of oil can the tin contain?
   A. 40   B. 35
   C. 30   D. 45
   E. 50

69. Kiran had 85 currency notes in all, some of which were of ₹ 100 denomination and remaining of ₹ 50 denomination. The total amount of all these currency notes was ₹ 5000. How much amount did she have in the denomination of ₹ 50?
   A. ₹ 2500   B. ₹ 2800
   C. ₹ 3500   D. ₹ 4200
   E. ₹ 3800

70. What should come in place of both the question marks in the equation $\dfrac{?}{\sqrt{128}} = \dfrac{\sqrt{162}}{?}$.
   A. 12   B. 14
   C. 144   D. 196
   E. 28

71. The average of 25 results is 18. The average of first 12 of them is 14 and that of last twelve is 17. Find the thirteen result.
   A. 65   B. 78
   C. 68   D. 71
   E. 88

72. Out of 9 persons 8 persons spent ₹ 30 each for their meals. The ninth one spent ₹ 20 more than the average expenditure of all the nine. The total money spent by all of them was:

A. ₹ 260 B. ₹ 290
C. ₹ 292.50 D. ₹ 400
E. ₹ 325

73. The average age of 35 students in a class is 16 years. The average age of 21 students is 14. What is the average age of remaining 14 students?
A. 15 years B. 17 years
C. 18 years D. 19 years
E. 21 years

74. In a pair of fractions, fraction A is twice the fraction B and the product of two fractions is $\dfrac{2}{25}$, what is the value of fraction A?

A. $\dfrac{1}{5}$ B. $\dfrac{1}{25}$

C. $\dfrac{2}{5}$ D. $\dfrac{3}{5}$

E. $\dfrac{2}{25}$

75. 45% of 1500 + 35% of 1700 = ?% of 3175
A. 30 B. 35
C. 45 D. 40
E. None of these

76. A shopkeeper expects a gain of $22\dfrac{1}{2}\%$ on his cost price. If in a week, his sale was of ₹ 392, what was his profit?
A. ₹ 18.20 B. ₹ 70
C. ₹ 72 D. ₹ 88.25
E. None of these

77. 60 kg of an alloy A is mixed with 100 kg of alloy B. If alloy A has lead and tin in the ratio 3 : 2 and alloy B has tin and copper in the ratio 1 : 4, then the amount of tin in the new alloy is:
A. 36 kg B. 44 kg
C. 53 kg D. 80 kg
E. None of these

78. In a camp, 95 men had provisions for 200 days. After five days, 30 men left the camp. For how many days will the remaining food last now?
A. 180 B. 285

C. $139\dfrac{16}{19}$ D. 240
E. None of these

79. A can finish a work in 24 days, B in 9 days and C in 12 days. B and C start the work but are forced to leave after 3 days. The remaining work will be done by A in:
A. 5 days B. 6 days
C. 10 days D. $10\dfrac{1}{2}$ days
E. 8 days

80. A room is 15 feet long and 12 feet broad. A mat has to be placed on the floor of this room leaving $1\dfrac{1}{2}$ feet space from the walls. What will be the cost of the mat at the rate of ₹ 3.50 per square feet?
A. ₹ 378 B. ₹ 472.50
C. ₹ 496 D. ₹ 630
E. None of these

Directions (Qs 81–85): *What will come in place of the question mark (?) in the following number series?*

81. 1, 3, 6, 10, ?
A. 12 B. 15
C. 16 D. 20
E. 18

82. 2, 6, 12, 20, 30, 42, 56, ?
A. 60 B. 64
C. 70 D. 72
E. 80

83. 13, 25, 51, 101, 203, ?
A. 405 B. 406
C. 407 D. 411
E. None of these

84. 6, 11, 21, 36, 56, ?
A. 42 B. 72
C. 81 D. 91
E. 51

85. 5, 8, 12, 17, 23, ?, 38
A. 26 B. 28
C. 29 D. 30
E. 32

86. The diameter of a wheel is 1.26 m. How far will it travel in 500 revolution?
  A. 1492 m   B. 1980 m
  C. 2530 m   D. 2880 m
  E. None of these

87. The number of revolutions a wheel of diameter 40 cm makes in travelling a distance of 176 m is:
  A. 140   B. 150
  C. 160   D. 166
  E. 177

88. The difference between the compound interest and simple interest on a certain sum at 10% per annum for 2 years is ₹ 631. Find the sum.
  A. ₹ 63100   B. ₹ 62200
  C. ₹ 58100   D. ₹ 66200
  E. None of these

89. The simple interest on a sum of money will be ₹ 600 after 10 years. If the principal is trebled after 5 years, what will be the total interest at the end of the tenth year?
  A. ₹ 600   B. ₹ 900
  C. ₹ 1200   D. ₹ 1500
  E. ₹ 1000

90. If a boat goes 7 km up stream in 42 minutes and the speed of the stream is 3 km/hr, then the speed of the boat in still water is:
  A. 4.2 km/hr   B. 9 km/hr
  C. 13 km/hr   D. 21 km/hr
  E. 15 km/hr

91. Two trains of equal lengths take 10 seconds and 15 seconds respectively to cross a telegraph post. If the length of each train be 120 metres, in what time (in seconds) will they cross each other travelling in opposite direction?
  A. 10   B. 12
  C. 15   D. 20
  E. 18

92. A car covers a distance of 715 km at a constant speed. If the speed of the car would have been 10 km/hr more, then it would have taken 2 hours less to cover the same distance. What is the original speed of the car?
  A. 45 km/hr   B. 50 km/hr
  C. 55 km/hr   D. 65 km/hr
  E. 60 km/hr

93. Two pipes can fill a tank in 20 and 24 minutes respectively and a waste pipe can empty 3 gallons per minute. All the three pipes working together can fill the tank in 15 minutes, the capacity of the tank is:
  A. 60 gallons   B. 100 gallons
  C. 120 gallons   D. 180 gallons
  E. 140 gallons

94. If 18 binders bind 900 books in 10 days, how many binders will be required to bind 660 books in 12 days?
  A. 22   B. 14
  C. 13   D. 11
  E. 20

95. Arun, Kamal and Vinay invested ₹ 8000, ₹ 4000 and ₹ 8000 respectively in a business. Arun left after six months. If after eight months, there was a gain of ₹ 4005, then what will be the share of Kamal?
  A. ₹ 890   B. ₹ 1335
  C. ₹ 1602   D. ₹ 1780
  E. ₹ 1050

Directions (Qs. 96–100): *The circle-graph given here shows the spendings of a country on various sports during a particular year. Study the graph carefully and answer the questions given below it.*

96. What per cent of the total spendings is spent on Tennis?
  A. $12\frac{1}{2}\%$ B. $22\frac{1}{2}\%$
  C. 25%   D. 45%
  E. 18%

97. How much per cent more is spent on Hockey than that of Golf?

A. 27%   B. 35%
C. 37.5%   D. 75%
E. 32%

98. How much per cent less is spent on Football than that on Cricket?

A. $22\frac{2}{9}\%$ B. 27%

C. $33\frac{1}{3}\%$ D. $37\frac{1}{2}\%$

E. 25%

99. If the total amount spent on sports during the year was ₹ 2 crores, the amount spent on Cricket and Hockey together was:
A. ₹ 8,00,000   B. ₹ 80,00,000
C. ₹ 1,20,00,000   D. ₹ 1,60,00,000
E. ₹ 4,10,000

100. If the total amount spent on sports during the year be ₹ 1,80,00,000. The amount spent on Basketball exceeds that on Tennis by:
A. ₹ 2,50,000   B. ₹ 3,60,000
C. ₹ 3,75,000   D. ₹ 4,10,000
E. None of these

ANSWERS

1	2	3	4	5	6	7	8	9	10
D	D	C	A	B	D	E	C	D	C
11	**12**	**13**	**14**	**15**	**16**	**17**	**18**	**19**	**20**
B	D	D	B	B	C	C	C	B	E
21	**22**	**23**	**24**	**25**	**26**	**27**	**28**	**29**	**30**
E	A	C	C	A	E	B	E	D	C
31	**32**	**33**	**34**	**35**	**36**	**37**	**38**	**39**	**40**
E	A	C	B	D	B	D	C	A	D
41	**42**	**43**	**44**	**45**	**46**	**47**	**48**	**49**	**50**
E	E	D	E	A	D	D	E	E	C
51	**52**	**53**	**54**	**55**	**56**	**57**	**58**	**59**	**60**
A	C	B	E	D	B	D	A	D	B
61	**62**	**63**	**64**	**65**	**66**	**67**	**68**	**69**	**70**
C	E	A	B	D	C	D	A	C	A
71	**72**	**73**	**74**	**75**	**76**	**77**	**78**	**79**	**80**
B	C	D	C	D	C	B	B	C	A
81	**82**	**83**	**84**	**85**	**86**	**87**	**88**	**89**	**90**
B	D	A	C	D	B	A	A	C	C
91	**92**	**93**	**94**	**95**	**96**	**97**	**98**	**99**	**100**
B	C	C	D	A	A	D	C	B	A

Some Selected Explanatory Answers

31-35. Based on the given data, the arrangement will be like this:

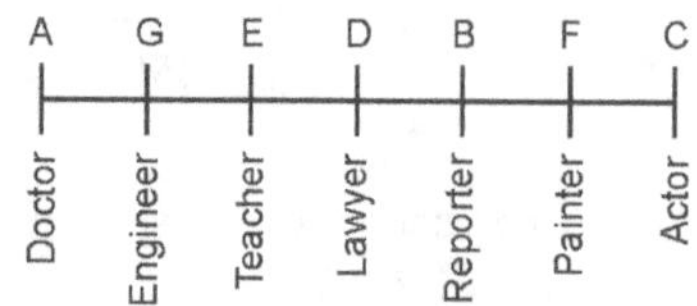

36–37.

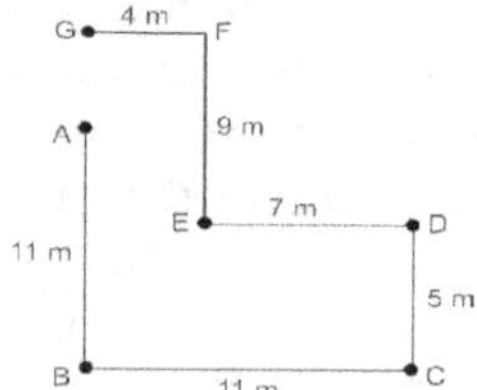

36. Point D is in South-East w.r.t. point F.

37. Point A, B, G are collinear points.

38-40. Floor

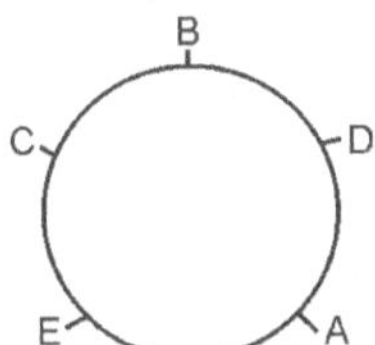

43. There is no clear point about height of J and N. So, both statements are not enough to give the answer.

44. Based on both statements together, the arrangement is like:

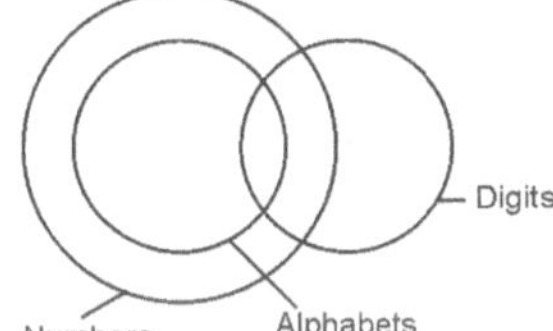

Hence, A is immediate left of D.

45. Code for 'Cost' is #.

51.

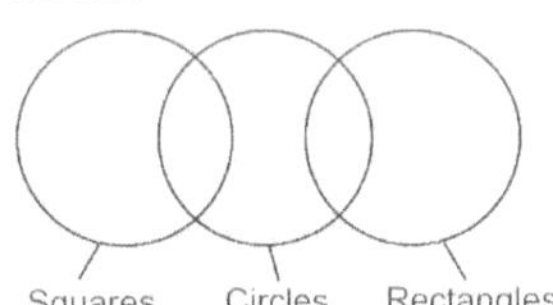

52.

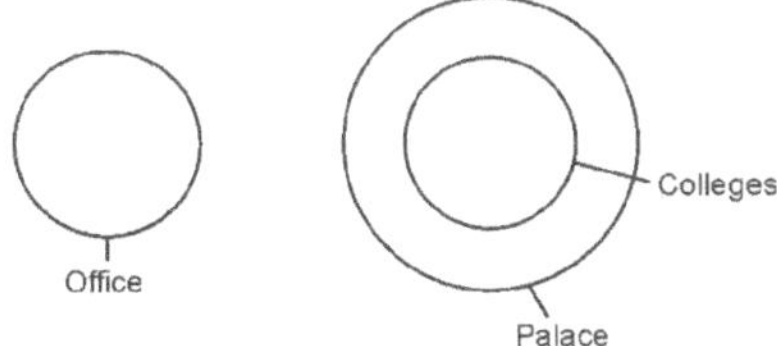

No rectangle is a square.

or

At least some rectangles are squares.

53.

No college is an office.

54.

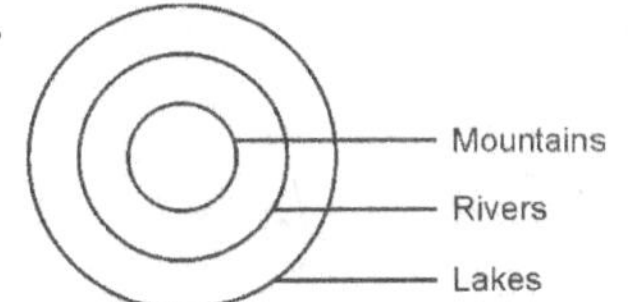

Both conclusions are correct.

55.

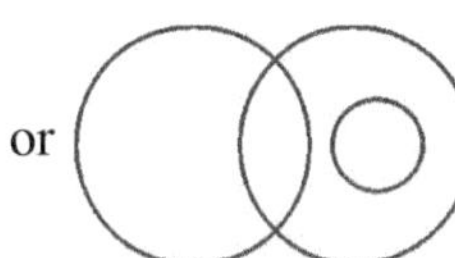

Neither of the conclusion follows.

61-65.

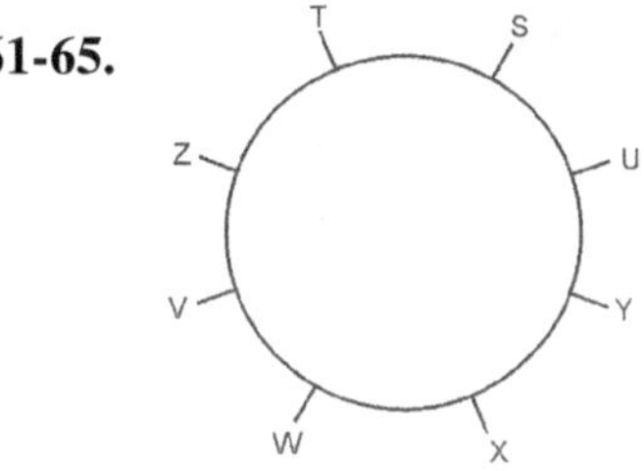

66. $\dfrac{5.32(56+44)}{(7.66+2.34)(7.66-2.34)}$

$= \dfrac{5.32 \times 100}{10 \times 5.32} = \dfrac{100}{10} = 10$

67. $(7.5)^2 + 2(7.5)(2.5) + (2.5)^2$

$= (7.5 + 2.5)^2 = (10)^2 = 100$

68. Suppose x bottles can fill the tin completely.

Then, $\dfrac{4}{5}x - \dfrac{3}{4}x = (6-4)$

$\Rightarrow \dfrac{16x - 15x}{20} = 2$

$\Rightarrow \dfrac{x}{20} = 2$

$\Rightarrow x = 2 \times 20 = 40$

$\therefore$ Required no. of bottles = 40

69. Let, the number of 50 rupee notes be x then, the number of 100 rupees notes $= (85 - x)$

$\therefore 50x + 100(85 - x) = 5000$

$\Rightarrow x + 2(85 - x) = 100$

$\Rightarrow x = 70$

So, required amount $= (50 \times 70)$

$= ₹\ 3500$

70. $\dfrac{x}{\sqrt{128}} = \dfrac{\sqrt{162}}{x}$

$\Rightarrow \quad x^2 = \sqrt{128 \times 162} = 8\sqrt{2} \times 9\sqrt{2}$

$\Rightarrow \quad x^2 = 72 \times 2 = 144$

$\Rightarrow \quad x = \sqrt{144} = 12$

71. Total of 25 results $= 25 \times 18 = 450$

Total of first 12 $= 12 \times 14 = 168$

Total of last 12 $= 12 \times 17 = 204$

$\therefore$ Required result $= 450 - (168 + 204)$

$= 450 - 372 = 78$

72. Let, the average expenditure be ₹ x

then, $\quad 9x = 8 \times 30 + (x + 20)$

$\Rightarrow \quad 9x - x = 240 + 20 = 260$

$\Rightarrow \quad 8x = 260 \Rightarrow x = \dfrac{260}{8} = 32.50$

$\therefore$ Total money spent

$= 9x = 9 \times 32.50$

$= ₹\ 292.50$

73. Sum of the ages of 14 students

$= (16 \times 35) - (14 \times 21)$

$= 560 - 294 = 266$

$\therefore$ Required average $= \dfrac{266}{14} = 19$ years

74. $\qquad A = 2B \Rightarrow B = \dfrac{1}{2}A$

So, $\quad AB = \dfrac{2}{25} \Rightarrow \dfrac{1}{2}A^2 = \dfrac{2}{25} \Rightarrow A^2 = \dfrac{4}{25}$

$\Rightarrow \quad A = \dfrac{2}{5}$

75. $\dfrac{45}{100} \times 1500 + \dfrac{35}{100} \times 1700 = \dfrac{x}{100} \times 3175$

$\Rightarrow \quad 45 \times 15 + 35 \times 17 = \dfrac{3175x}{100}$

$\Rightarrow \qquad 675 + 595 = \dfrac{3175x}{100}$

$\Rightarrow \qquad 1270 \times 100 = 3175x$

$\Rightarrow \qquad x = \dfrac{1270 \times 100}{3175}$

$= 10 \times 4 = 40$

76. $\qquad CP = ₹\left(\dfrac{100}{122.50} \times 392\right)$

$= ₹\dfrac{1000}{1225} \times 392 = ₹\ 320$

$\therefore$ Profit $= ₹\ (392 - 320) = ₹\ 72$

77. Quantity of tin in 60 kg of A

$= \left(60 \times \dfrac{2}{5}\right) kg = 24$ kg

Quantity of tin in 100 kg of B

$= \left(100 \times \dfrac{1}{5}\right) kg = 20$ kg

Quantity of tin in the new alloy

$= (24 + 20)$ kg $= 44$ kg

78. Let, the remaining food will last for x days

95 men had provisions for 195 days

65 men had provisions for x days

Less men, more days $\qquad$ Indirect properties

$\therefore \ 65 : 95 : : 195 : x$

$\Rightarrow \qquad 65 \times x = 95 \times 195$

$\Rightarrow \qquad x = \dfrac{95 \times 195}{65} = 285$

79. $(B + C)$'s 1 day work $= \left(\dfrac{1}{9} + \dfrac{1}{12}\right) = \dfrac{7}{36}$

Work done by B and C in 3 days

$= \dfrac{7}{36} \times 3 = \dfrac{7}{12}$

Remaining work $= 1 - \dfrac{7}{12} = \dfrac{5}{12}$

Now, $\dfrac{1}{24}$ work is done by A in 1 day

$\therefore \ \dfrac{5}{12}$ work is done by A in $24 \times \dfrac{5}{12} = 10$ days

80. Area of the mat $= [(15 - 3) \times (12 - 3)]$

$= 108$ square feet

Cost of the mat $= 108 \times 3.5 = ₹\ 378$

81. $\quad 1 \qquad 3 \qquad 6 \qquad 10 \qquad \boxed{15}$

$\qquad +2 \qquad +3 \qquad +4 \qquad +5$

82. 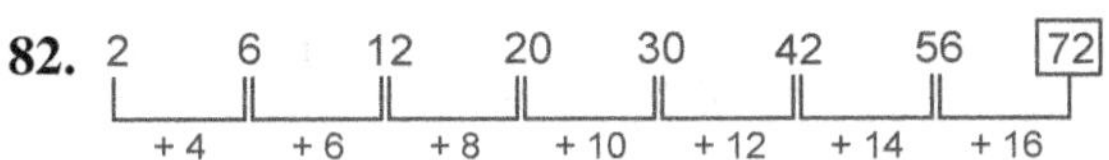

$$2 \quad 6 \quad 12 \quad 20 \quad 30 \quad 42 \quad 56 \quad \boxed{72}$$
$$+4 \quad +6 \quad +8 \quad +10 \quad +12 \quad +14 \quad +16$$

83.
$$13 \quad 25 \quad 51 \quad 101 \quad 203 \quad \boxed{405}$$
$$13 \times 2 - 1 \quad 25 \times 2 + 1 \quad 51 \times 2 - 1 \quad 101 \times 2 + 1 \quad 203 \times 2 - 1$$

84.
$$6 \quad 11 \quad 21 \quad 36 \quad 56 \quad \boxed{81}$$
$$+5 \quad +10 \quad +15 \quad +20 \quad +25$$

85.
$$5 \quad 8 \quad 12 \quad 17 \quad 23 \quad \boxed{30} \quad 38$$
$$+3 \quad +4 \quad +5 \quad +6 \quad +7 \quad +8$$

86. Distance covered in 1 revolution $= 2\pi r$

$$= 2 \times \frac{22}{7} \times 0.63 = \frac{99}{25} \text{ m}$$

Distance covered in 500 revolutions

$$= \frac{99}{25} \times 500 = 1980 \text{ m}$$

87. Distance covered in 1 revolution

$$= 2\pi r = 2 \times \frac{22}{7} \times 20 = \frac{880}{7} \text{ cm}$$

Required number of revolutions

$$= 17600 \times \frac{7}{880} = 140$$

88. Let, $P = ₹\ 100$

$$A = P\left(1 + \frac{r}{100}\right)^t = 100\left(1 + \frac{10}{100}\right)^2$$

$$= 100 \times \frac{11}{10} \times \frac{11}{10} = ₹\ 121$$

$$C.I = A - P$$
$$= 121 - 100 = ₹\ 21$$

$$S.I = \frac{P \times r \times t}{100}$$

$$= \frac{100 \times 10 \times 2}{100} = ₹\ 20$$

Difference $= 21 - 20 = ₹\ 1$

When difference is $₹\ 1$ then $P = ₹\ 100$

When difference is $₹\ 631$ then $P = ₹\ 631 \times 100$

$$= ₹\ 63100$$

89. Let the sum be $₹\ x$, S.I $= ₹\ 600$, $t = 10$ years

$$\text{Rate} = \frac{100 \times 600}{x \times 10} = \frac{6000}{x}\%$$

$$\text{S.I for 5 years} = ₹\left(\frac{x \times 5 \times 6000}{x \times 100}\right)$$

$$= ₹\ 300$$

$$\text{Again, S.I for 5 years} = ₹\left(3x \times 5 \times \frac{6000}{x \times 100}\right)$$

$$= ₹\ 900$$

$$\therefore \quad \text{Total interest} = ₹\ 300 + ₹\ 900$$
$$= ₹\ 1200$$

90. Let, speed of the boat $= x$ km/hr

According to the question,

$$\frac{7}{x-3} = \frac{42}{60}$$

$$\Rightarrow \quad \frac{7}{x-3} = \frac{7}{10} \quad \Rightarrow \quad x - 3 = 10$$

$$\Rightarrow \quad x = 13$$

$\therefore$ Speed of the boat $= 13$ km/hr

91. Speed of the first train $= \dfrac{120}{10} = 12$ m/s

Speed of the 2nd train $= \dfrac{120}{15} = 8$ m/s

Relative speed $= (12 + 8)$ m/s $= 20$ m/s

$\therefore$ Required time $= \dfrac{120 + 120}{20}$

$$= \frac{240}{20} = 12 \text{ seconds}$$

92. Let, speed of the car $= x$ km/hr

$$\frac{715}{x} - \frac{715}{x+10} = 2$$

$$\Rightarrow \quad 715\left(\frac{1}{x} - \frac{1}{x+10}\right) = 2$$

$$\Rightarrow \quad 715\left[\frac{x+10-x}{x(x+10)}\right] = 2$$

$$\Rightarrow \quad \frac{7150}{x^2 + 10x} = 2$$

$\Rightarrow \qquad x^2 + 10x - 3575 = 0$

$\Rightarrow \quad x^2 + 65x - 55x - 3575 = 0$

$\Rightarrow \qquad x(x + 65) - 55(x + 65) = 0$

$\Rightarrow \qquad (x - 55)(x + 65) = 0$

$\Rightarrow \quad x = 55, x = -65$ but $x \neq -65$

$\therefore$ Speed of the car = 55 km/hr

93. Work done by the waste pipe in 1 minute

$$= \frac{1}{15} - \left(\frac{1}{20} + \frac{1}{24}\right) = \left(\frac{1}{15} - \frac{11}{120}\right) = -\frac{1}{40}$$

[–ve sign means emptying]

Volume of $\dfrac{1}{40}$ part = 3 gallons

Volume of whole = 3 × 40 gallons

$\qquad\qquad\qquad = 120$ gallons

94. Let, the required number of binders be x

Less books, Less binders

(Direct proportion)

More days, Less binders

(Indirect proportion)

Books $\quad 900 : 600$
Days $\qquad 12 : 10$ $\Big\}$ $:: 18 : x$

$\therefore \ 900 \times 12 \times x = 600 \times 10 \times 18$

$$\Rightarrow \quad x = \frac{600 \times 10 \times 18}{900 \times 12} = 11$$

95. Arun : Kamal : Vinay

$= (8000 \times 6) : 4000 \times 8 : 8000 \times 8$

$= 48 : 32 : 64 = 3 : 2 : 4$

$\therefore$ Kamal's share $= \dfrac{2}{9} \times 4005 = ₹\ 890$

96. Percentage of money spent on Tennis

$$= \frac{45}{360} \times 100 = \frac{25}{2} = 12\frac{1}{2}\%$$

97. Let, the total spendings on sports be ₹ x

Then,

Amount spent on Golf $= \dfrac{36}{360} \times x = ₹\ \dfrac{x}{10}$

Amount spent on Hockey $= \dfrac{63}{360} \times x = ₹\ \dfrac{7x}{40}$

Difference $= \dfrac{7x}{40} - \dfrac{x}{10} = ₹\ \dfrac{3x}{40}$

$\therefore$ Required percentaqge $= \dfrac{3x/40}{x/10} \times 100$

$$= \frac{3x}{40} \times \frac{10}{x} \times 100$$

$$= 75\%$$

98. Let, the total spendings on sports be x

Then,

Amount spent on Cricket $= \dfrac{81}{360} \times x = ₹\ \dfrac{9}{40}x$

Amount spent on Football $= \dfrac{54}{360} \times x = ₹\ \dfrac{3}{20}x$

Difference $= \dfrac{9x}{40} - \dfrac{3x}{20} = ₹\ \dfrac{3x}{40}$

$\therefore$ Required percentage $= \dfrac{3x/40}{9x/40} \times 100$

$$= \frac{3x}{40} \times \frac{40}{9x} \times 100$$

$$= \frac{100}{3} = 33\frac{1}{3}\%$$

99. Amount spent on Cricket and Hockey together

$$= ₹\left(\frac{81 + 63}{360}\right) \times 2 \text{ crores}$$

$$= ₹\ 0.8 \text{ crores}$$

$$= ₹\ 8000000$$

100. Amount spent on Basketball exceeds that on Tennis by

$$\frac{50 - 45}{360} \times 18000000 = ₹\ 250000$$

SBI Junior Associates & Junior Agricultural Associates
(Clerical Cadre Exam)

General English

Directions (Qs. 1–15): *Read the following passage carefully and answer the questions given below it. Certain words/phrases have been printed in **bold** to help you locate them while answering some of the questions.*

There was an old weaver in a village, who had been praying to Lord Shiva for the last twenty-five years to give them enough money to live in comfort. Each morning and evening, he would walk round the Shiva temple one hundred and one times, prostrate himself before the image and then come back home. In spite of having prayed for such a long period, there was no sign of wealth coming to him. He, however, never lost faith in God and waited for the time to come.

As time passed, the poor weaver grew old. It was difficult for him to go round and round the temple and he was to help himself through a stick to walk. Lord Shiva did hear the weaver's prayer but did nothing to help him. However, Parvati, Shiva's wife, felt sorry at this and spoke to her husband "Why are you so hard on that old weaver who has been worshipping you for such a long time? He is grown so old now that he cannot even walk properly. Why don't you make life easier for him?" Shiva smiled and replied to Parvati, "Do you think 1 would have refused to give him wealth if he could make use of it? What can I do for someone who is not destined to be rich?" Parvati, however, was not convinced with the view that a man cannot make use of wealth if it is given to him.

One day both Shiva and Parvati came down to earth and went to that temple. Shiva put a pot of gold on the way of the weaver when he was taking a round of the temple so that he can pick it up. The weaver walked on. "Oh, my Lord", he prayed, "How long have I to coninue this **wretched** life? You have not been kind enough to me. But I can still play my trade. My eyes are still good. How fortunate I am that even in my old age I can still weave well." Then a terrible thought struck the weaver. "Suppose I were to lose my eyesight. But still I would be able to walk round the temple. Let me try. I could walk like this." He **firmly** closed his eyes and walked on. He passed by the pot of gold with his eyes closed. He smiled when he opened his eyes. "Yes," he said, "I need not worry. Even if I become blind, I can still walk round the temple." The weaver then went home. Shiva looked at Parvati and said, "But there is something I can do for him." He will not lose all interest in wealth. He will be very happy."

1. According to this passage, what made Parvati feel sorry?
   A. The old age of the weaver
   B. The attitude of the weaver
   C. Shiva not helping the weaver
   D. Shiva not listening to her appeal
   E. None of the above

2. Why did the weaver think himelf fortunate?
   A. That he could carry out his profession in old age
   B. That he could walk around the temple even without eyesight
   C. That Parvati was kind enough to convince Shiva for him
   D. Not given in the passage
   E. None of these

3. When the weaver opened his eyes
   A. he found the pot of gold
   B. he was cheerful
   C. he was worried
   D. he saw Shiva and Parvati
   E. None of these

4. The weaver took how many rounds of the temple everyday?
   A. 101   B. 102
   C. 111   D. 202
   E. None of these

5. Which of the following statements is not true regarding the weaver?
   A. He lost faith in God
   B. He worshipped for more than 25 years
   C. He continued taking rounds of temple even in old age
   D. He spent a miserable life
   E. All are true

6. On which of the following views did Shiva and Parvati have differences of opinion?
   A. Every devotee can be blessed with the fulfilment of his wish
   B. Without eyesight one can locate the pot of gold
   C. Taking a positive attitude towards the weaver
   D. One cannot make use of the wealth if it is given to him
   E. None of these

7. Had the weaver got enough money from the God, he would
   A. have a peaceful life
   B. have an easy life with no financial constraints
   C. not have further prayed to the God
   D. not have to stick to the weaver's job any more
   E. not have to work in his old age

8. After keeping the pot of gold on the passage around the temple, Shiva and Parvati
   A. returned to heaven
   B. hid themselves near the temple
   C. closely watched the weaver as invisible entities

   D. Not given in the passage
   E. None of these

9. How did Shiva favour the old weaver?
   A. By availing him the pot of gold
   B. By giving him strength to work
   C. By asking Parvati to help him
   D. Not given in the passage
   E. None of these

Directions (Qs. 10–12): *Choose the word which is most nearly SAME in meaning as the word printed in bold capitals as used in the passage.*

10. FELT
   A. realised   B. thought
   C. expressed   D. told
   E. beg

11. WRETCHED
   A. unsatisfactory   B. dirty
   C. poor   D. difficult
   E. unfortunate

12. HARD
   A. rigorous   B. cruel
   C. indifferent   D. strict
   E. rigid

Directions (Qs. 13–15): *Choose the word which is most OPPOSITE in meaning of the word printed in bold as used in the passage.*

13. STRUCK
   A. prevented   B. occurred
   C. avoided   D. slipped
   E. facilitated

14. FIRMLY
   A. liberally   B. openly
   C. lightly   D. closely
   E. freely

15. LOSE
   A. collect   B. gain
   C. obtain   D. restore
   E. retain

Directions (Qs. 16–20) : *Each sentence below has a blank, each blank indicating that something has been omitted. Choose the word for each blank which best fits the meaning of the sentence as a whole.*

16. Since the priest did not arrive in time, the ceremony was ..... late.
   A. begins
   B. begun
   C. began
   D. beginning
   E. begin

17. He succeeded in getting possession ..... his land after a long court case.
   A. to
   B. against
   C. of
   D. with
   E. for

18. The villagers have not ..... over the shock of losing everything in the earthquake.
   A. got
   B. made
   C. forgotten
   D. freed
   E. felt

19. Vinayak is the ..... head of the family and commands a lot of respect from the family members.
   A. solely
   B. strongest
   C. undisputed
   D. full
   E. controversial

20. The blood donation camp was organised ..... the Naval Youth Club.
   A. to
   B. by
   C. from
   D. with
   E. along

Directions (Qs. 21–25): *Read each sentence to find out whether there is any grammatical error or idiomatic error in it. The error, if any, will be in one part of the sentence. The number of that part is the answer. If there is "No Error" the answer is 'E'. (Ignore errors of punctuation if any.)*

21. (A) But for your/(B) kind help this/(C) task could not/(D) have been completed./(E) No error.

22. (A) Since it was a memory test/(B) the students were instructed/(C) to learn the/(D) passage with heart./(E) No error.

23. (A) So longer as/(B) you are honest/(C) and forthright I will/(D) support you in this task./(E) No error.

24. (A) The customer scarcely had/(B) enough money to pay/(C) to the cashier/(D) at the cash counter./(E) No error.

25. (A) Neither the earthquake/(B) nor the subsequent fire/(C) was able to dampen/(D) the spirit of the residents./(E) No error.

Directions (Qs. 26–30): *Which of the phrases A, B, C and D given below should replace the phrase given in* **bold** *in the following sentence to make the sentence grammatically meaningful and correct? If the sentence is correct as it is and 'No correction is required', mark E as the answer.*

26. The courts **are actively to safeguard** the interests and the rights of the poor.
   A. are actively to safeguarding
   B. have been actively safeguarding
   C. have to active in safeguarding
   D. are actively in safeguarding
   E. No correction required

27. He is a singer of repute, but his **yesterday's performance was** quite disappointing.
   A. performances for yesterday were
   B. yesterday performance was
   C. yesterday performances were
   D. performances about yesterday were
   E. No correction required

28. **Despite of their** differences on matters of principles, they all agree on the demand of hike in salary?
   A. Despite their
   B. Despite of the
   C. Despite for their
   D. Despite off their
   E. No correction required

29. The orator **had been left** the auditorium before the audience stood up.
   A. had been leaving
   B. was left
   C. left
   D. would leave
   E. No correction required

30. This is one of the most important **inventions of this century**.
   A. invention of this century
   B. invention of these centuries
   C. inventions of centuries
   D. inventions of the centuries
   E. No correction required

Reasoning Ability

Directions (Q. 31-33) : *Following questions are based on the five three digit numbers given below:*

473   169   825   692   538

31. If two is subtracted from the middle digit of each of the numbers, how many numbers thus formed will be divisible by three?
   A. None
   B. One
   C. Two
   D. Three
   E. Four

32. If all the digits in each of the numbers is arranged in descending order within the number, which of the following will form the lowest number in the new arrangement of numbers?
   A. 473
   B. 169
   C. 825
   D. 692
   E. 538

33. If all the numbers are arranged in ascending order from left to right, which of the following will be the product of the second and the third digits of the number which is second from the left end of the new arrangement?
   A. 18
   B. 54
   C. 24
   D. 21
   E. 10

34. D walked 30 metres towards South, took a left turn and walked 20 metres. He then took a right turn and walked 30 metres and turned towards his right and stopped. Towards which direction was he facing when he stopped?
   A. East
   B. West
   C. North
   D. Data inadequate
   E. None of these

35. 'R is brother of T'. 'M is sister of R'. 'K is brother of M'. 'W is father of T'. How many sons does W have?
   A. Two
   B. Three
   C. One
   D. Data inadequate
   E. None of these

36. Pointing to a girl, Samir said "She is the daughter of my grandfather's only son". How is the girl related to Samir?
   A. Sister
   B. Cousin
   C. Daughter
   D. Cannot be determined
   E. None of these

Directions (Qs. 37-41): *In the following questions, the symbols #, %, @, © and δ are used with the following meanings illustrated.*

'P % Q' means 'P is not greater than Q'.

'P δ Q' means 'P is not smaller than Q'.

'P # Q' means 'P is neither equal to nor smaller than Q'.

'P © Q' means 'P is neither equal to nor greater than Q'.

'P @ Q' means 'P is neither smaller than nor greather than Q.

In each questions, three statements showing relationships have been given, which are followed by three conslusions I, II & III. Assuming that the given statements are true, find out which conclusion(s) is/are **definitely true.**

37. Statements: M © K, K δ T, T © J
   Conclusions: I. J # K
            II. T # M
            II. M # J
   A. None is true
   B. Only I is true
   C. Only II is true
   D. Only III is true
   E. Only II and III are true

38. Statements: F @ T, T % M, M # R
   Conclusions: I. R © T
            II. F @ M
            II. F © M
   A. Only I is true
   B. Only II is true
   C. Only III is true
   D. Only either II or III is true
   E. Only II and III are true

39. Statements: J δ H, H @ B, B % N
   Conclusions: I. N δ H
            II. N @ J
            II. J δ B

A. Only I and II are true
B. Only II and III are true
C. Only I and III are true
D. All I, II and III are true
E. None of these

40. Statements: B # T, T © K, K % M
Conclusions: I. K # B
           II. M # T
           II. B # M

A. Only I is true
B. Only II is true
C. Only III is true
D. Only II and III are true
E. None of these

41. Statements: D % F, F δ K, K @ R
Conclusions: I. R % F
           II. R % D
           II. R @ D

A. Only I is true
B. Only II is true
C. Only III is true
D. Only I and II are true
E. None of these

Directions (Qs. 42–46): *Each of the questions below consists of a question and two statements numbered I and II given below it. You have to decide whether the data provided in the statements are sufficient to answer the question. Read both the statements and—*

Give answer (A) if the data in statement I alone are sufficient to answer the question, while the data in statement II alone are not sufficient to answer the question.

Give answer (B) if the data in statement II alone are sufficient to answer the question, while the data in statement I alone are not sufficient to answer the question.

Give answer (C) if the data either in statement I alone or in statement II alone are sufficient to answer the question.

Give answer (D) if the data given in both the statements I & II together are not sufficient to answer the question, and

Give answer (E) if the data in both the statements I & II together are necessary to answer the question.

42. What is M's rank from top in the group of twenty successful students?
  I. There are six students between M and R.
  II. R's position is twelfth from the bottom.

43. How is 'now' written in a code language?
  I. 'now or never' is written as 'ha na pa' in that code language.
  II. 'you may come now' is written as 'ja ta ha da' in that code language.

44. How is M related to R?
  I. M has only one brother and two sisters of which one is N.
  II. R is mother of N.

45. How many daughters does D have?
  I. B and F are brothers of H.
  II. D is father of H.

46. On which date in March is Ravi's mother's birthday?
  I. Ravi correctly remembers that his mother's birthday is after sixteenth but before twentieth March.
  II. Ravi's sister correctly remembers that their mother's birthday is before twenty-third but after eighteenth March.

Directions (Qs. 47-51): *Study the following information carefully and answer the questions given below:*

A, B, C, D, E, F, G and H are sitting around a circular table facing the centre.
  (*a*) B sits third to right of F.
  (*b*) A sits second to the right of D. D is not an immediate neighbour of B and F.
  (*c*) C and E are immediate neighbours of each other.
  (*d*) H is not an immediate neighbour of A.
  (*e*) No one sits between C and F.

47. Four of the following five are similar in a certain way based on their position in the seating arrangement and so form a group. Which of the following **does not** belong to that group?
A. DA   B. BC

C. HG   D. AC
E. BD

48. Who sits to the immediate left of B?
A. H   B. G
C. A   D. E
E. None of these

49. What is the position of D with respect to E in the above arrangement?
A. Third to the right
B. Fourth to the left
C. Second to the right
D. Fourth to the right
E. Immediately to the right

50. In which of the following pairs, second person is sitting to the immediate right of the first person?
A. FA   B. BE
C. AD   D. HB
E. None of these

51. Who amongst the following sits between G and F?
A. A   B. C
C. E   D. H
E. None of these

Directions (Qs. 52–54): *From the five logical diagrams select one which best illustrates the relationship among three given classes in the questions.*

A.   B.

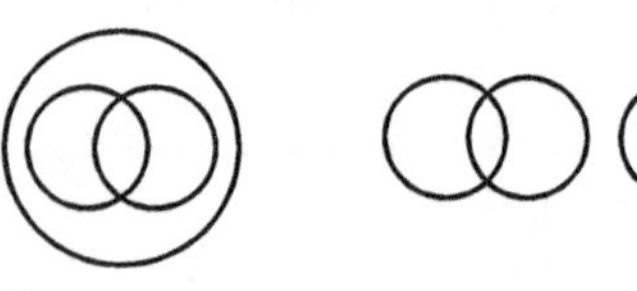

C.   D.

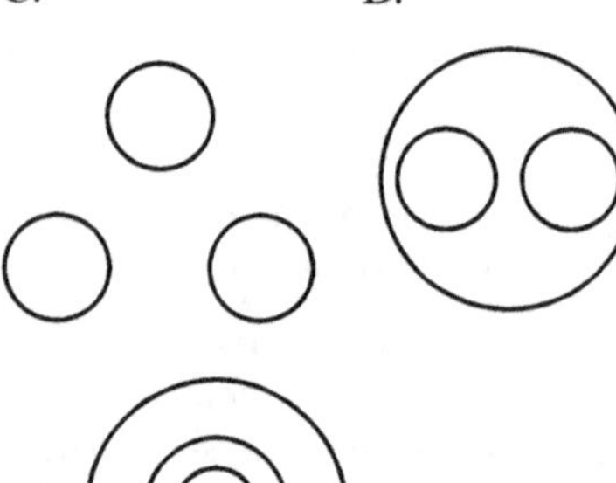

E.

52. Lizards, Reptiles, Crocodiles

53. Whales, Tortoise, Fishes

54. Birds, Crows, Parrots

55. In a certain code language 'tree is very beautiful' is written as 'ka na da ta' and 'this is strong tree' is written as 'na pa sa ka'. How is 'beautiful' written in that code language?
A. da   B. ta
C. sa   D. Data inadequate
E. None of these

56. In a certain code GIVE is written as '51@©' and FAIL is written as '%219'. How is LEAF written in that code?
A. 5©2%   B. 9©2%
C. 9@2%   D. 9©1%
E. None of these

Directions (Qs. 57 & 58): *In each of the following series determine the order of the letters. Then from the given options select the one which will complete the given series.*

57. QYK, ?, ISG, EPE
A. NWJ   B. MVI
C. NVI   D. MVJ
E. None of these

58. JMC, CLT, KND, ?, LOE, GPX
A. ENV   B. DMX
C. EOU   D. DRX
E. None of these

Directions (Qs. 59 & 60) : *Read the following statements and answer the questions given below :*

Raju has two sons 'X' and 'Y' and a daughter 'Z'. Biju has two sons 'A' and 'B' and daughter 'C'. 'A' and 'Z' are married and have two sons 'J' and 'K'. Laloo has a son 'P' and a daughter 'Q'. 'Q' is married to 'Y' and they have two daughters 'F' and 'G' and a son 'H'.

59. How is Raju related to 'Q'?
A. Uncle   B. Father-in-law
C. Brother   D. Son
E. None of these

60. How is 'Z' related to Biju?
A. Daughter   B. Sister
C. Sister-in-law   D. Daughter-in-law
E. None of these

Directions (Qs. 61–65): *Study the following information carefully and answer the questions given below :*

A, B, C, D, E, F, G and H are eight friends travelling in three different cars, viz. X, Y and Z with at least two in one car to three different places, viz. Delhi, Chandigarh and Agra.

There is at least one female member in each car. D is travelling with G to Delhi but not in car Y. A is travelling with only H in car Z but not to Chandigarh. C is not travelling with either D or E, F and D are studying in the same only girls' college. H, B and G are studying in the same only boys' college.

61. Which of the following represents the group of females among them?
A. F, C, A
B. F, G, A
C. D, C, A
D. Data inadequate
E. None of these

62. Which of the following combinations is **correct?**
A. Delhi – X – C
B. Chandigarh – X –F
C. Agra – Z – E
D. Delhi – Y – E
E. None of these

63. In which car are four of them travelling?
A. X or Z
B. Y
C. X or Y
D. Z
E. None of these

64. In which of the following cars is C travelling?
A. X
B. Y
C. Z
D. Either X or Y
E. Data inadequate

65. Passengers in which car are travelling to Chandigarh?
A. Y
B. X
C. Either X or Y
D. Data inadequate
E. None of these

Quantitative Aptitude

Directions (Qs. 66–80): *What will come in place of question mark (?) in the following questions?*

66. $18^2 + \sqrt{?} = 350$
A. 576
B. 676
C. 26
D. 28
E. None of these

67. $1530 \div 34 \times 360 \div 24 = ?$
A. 625
B. 765
C. 575
D. 645
E. None of these

68. $4966 + 285 - 1236 + ? = 4860$
A. 854
B. 848
C. 825
D. 875
E. None of these

69. $\dfrac{17 \times 4 + 18 \times 3}{\sqrt{441} \times 5 + 139} = ?$
A. $\dfrac{1}{4}$
B. $\dfrac{1}{2}$
C. $\dfrac{2}{3}$
D. $\dfrac{1}{3}$
E. None of these

70. $2820 \div 12 \times 8 = ?$
A. 1680
B. 1880
C. 1860
D. 1660
E. None of these

71. $1950 \div 26 \div 25 = ?$
A. 12
B. 8
C. 5
D. 3
E. None of these

72. 18% of $450 - 75\%$ of $96 = ?$
A. 15
B. 22
C. 12
D. 16
E. None of these

73. $75.75 - 48.32 + 146.92 = ?$
A. 174.35
B. 175.34
C. 173.45
D. 173.35
E. None of these

74. $8\dfrac{1}{3} \times 4\dfrac{2}{5} + ? = 44\dfrac{2}{5}$
A. $7\dfrac{11}{15}$
B. $7\dfrac{4}{15}$

C. $7\dfrac{8}{15}$ D. $8\dfrac{7}{15}$

E. None of these

75. $27.28 \div 2.2 + 4.7 \times 1.5 = ?$

A. 18.85   B. 19.25

C. 18.75   D. 19.45

E. None of these

76. $\dfrac{5}{9}$ of 315 + $\dfrac{3}{7}$ of 455 = ?

A. 370   B. 380

C. 360   D. 340

E. None of these

77. 145% of 780 + ?% of 250 = 1231

A. 25   B. 30

C. 40   D. 45

E. None of these

78. $\dfrac{5}{8}$ of $\dfrac{2}{3}$ of $\dfrac{3}{5}$ of 2104 = ?

A. 532   B. 536

C. 526   D. 528

E. None of these

79. $16.45 \times 5.2 \times 2.5 = ?$

A. 213.45   B. 218.45

C. 213.85   D. 218.25

E. None of these

80. 2.25% of 640 − 1.5% of 480 = ?

A. 6.4   B. 5.6

C. 4.8   D. 7.2

E. None of these

Directions (Qs. 81–85): *What will come in place of the question mark (?) in the following number series?*

81. 11   12   26   81   ?

A. 324   B. 328

C. 320   D. 280

E. None of these

82. 5120   1280   320   80   ?

A. 16   B. 24

C. 30   D. 40

E. None of these

83. 7   11   27   63   ?

A. 96   B. 118

C. 99   D. 127

E. None of these

84. 6   10   18   34   ?

A. 62   B. 64

C. 66   D. 50

E. None of these

85. 5   11   23   47   ?

A. 95   B. 93

C. 96   D. 97

E. None of these

86. A, B, C, D & E are five consecutive even numbers. Average of A and E is 46. What the largest number?

A. 52   B. 42

C. 50   D. 48

E. None of these

87. A train running at the speed of 66 kmph crosses a signal pole in 18 seconds. What is the length of the train?

A. 330 meters   B. 300 meters

C. 360 meters   D. 320 meters

E. None of these

88. Find the average of the following set of numbers

155, 128, 137, 140, 160, 132

A. 148   B. 140

C. 146   D. 144

E. None of these

89. Number obtained by interchanging the digits of a two digit number is less than the original number by 18, and the sum of the digits is 6. What is the original two digit number?

A. 46   B. 24

C. 42   D. 64

E. None of these

90. An amount of ₹ 45,000/- becomes ₹ 77,400/- on simple interest in eight years. What is the rate of interest p.c.p.a.?

A. 9   B. 11

C. 8   D. 10.5

E. None of these

91. Three-fifth of a number is more than its 40% by 85. What is 60% of that number?
  A. 245   B. 255
  C. 260   D. 250
  E. None of these

92. Rajesh spends 12% of his monthly income on entertainment, 18% of his monthly income on children's education, 50% of his monthly income on other household items and the remaining amount of ₹ 5,200/- he saves. What is his monthly income?
  A. ₹ 25,400/-
  B. ₹ 26,200/-
  C. ₹ 24,800/-
  D. ₹ 25,600/-
  E. None of these

93. 24 Men can complete a piece of work in 15 days. In how many days will 18 men complete that work?
  A. 16 days
  B. 20 days
  C. 22 days
  D. 25 days
  E. None of these

94. Rasika and Nikita invested amounts of ₹ 40,000/- and ₹ 75,000/- respectively. At the end of five years they got a total dividend of ₹ 46,000/-. What is Rasika's share in the dividend?
  A. ₹ 16,500/-
  B. ₹ 15,500/-
  C. ₹ 15,000/-
  D. ₹ 16,000/-
  E. None of these

95. Present ages of Rama and Shyama are in the ratio of 4 : 5 respectively. Five years hence the ratio of their ages become 5 : 6 respectively. What is Rama's present age?
  A. 25 years
  B. 22 years
  C. 20 years
  D. 30 years
  E. None of these

Directions (Qs. 96–100): *Study the following table carefully to answer these questions.*

Number of employees in different departments of five organizations

Organisaton \\ Department	A	B	C	D	E
HR	145	80	120	180	160
Finance	120	75	100	220	140
Marketing	150	90	115	200	190
IT	225	110	160	280	220
Administration	180	120	130	110	130

96. What is the average number of employees working in Marketing department of all the organizations?
  A. 149   B. 145
  C. 146   D. 148
  E. None of these

97. What is the total number of employees working in all the departments of organization B together?
  A. 350   B. 375
  C. 425   D. 475
  E. None of these

98. What is the ratio between number of employees from Finance and Marketing departments together of organization B and these two departments together of organization D respectively?
  A. 14 : 9   B. 9 : 14
  C. 11 : 28   D. 28 : 11
  E. None of these

99. What is the ratio between the total number of employees from all organizations together in HR and Administration departments respectively?
  A. 132 : 137   B. 137 : 132
  C. 122 : 137   D. 137 : 122
  E. None of these

100. Number of employees in IT department of organization C is what per cent of the total number of employees in organization C in all the departments together?
  A. 26.5   B. 25.6
  C. 25.4   D. 26.4
  E. None of these

ANSWERS

1	2	3	4	5	6	7	8	9	10
B	D	A	A	B	A	A	C	C	A

11	12	13	14	15	16	17	18	19	20
B	B	B	B	A	B	C	A	C	B

21	22	23	24	25	26	27	28	29	30
E	D	A	A	C	B	E	A	C	E

31	32	33	34	35	36	37	38	39	40
C	A	D	B	D	A	A	D	C	B

41	42	43	44	45	46	47	48	49	50
A	E	E	D	D	E	B	D	A	E

51	52	53	54	55	56	57	58	59	60
A	D	C	D	D	B	B	A	B	D

61	62	63	64	65	66	67	68	69	70
D	E	E	B	A	B	E	E	B	B

71	72	73	74	75	76	77	78	79	80
D	E	A	A	E	A	C	C	C	D

81	82	83	84	85	86	87	88	89	90
B	E	D	C	A	C	A	E	C	A

91	92	93	94	95	96	97	98	99	100
B	E	B	D	C	A	D	C	E	B

Some Selected Explanatory Answers

32. 743, 961, 852, 962, 853.
Obviously 743, which is derived from 473, is the lowest.

33. In ascending order : 169, 473, 538, 692, 825.
Now, 473 is second from left and $7 \times 3 = 21$.

37. $M © K \rightarrow M < K, K \delta T \rightarrow K \geq T,$
$T © J \rightarrow T < J \Rightarrow M < K \geq T < J$
I. $J \# K \rightarrow J > K$ (False)
II. $T \# M \rightarrow T > M$ (False)
III. $M \# J \rightarrow M > J$ (False)

38. $F @ T \rightarrow F = T, T \% M \rightarrow T \leq M,$
$M \# R \rightarrow M > R$
$\Rightarrow F = T \leq M > R$
I. $R © T \rightarrow R < T$ (False)
II. $F @ M \rightarrow F = M$
III. $F © M \rightarrow F < M$

39. $J \delta H \rightarrow J \geq H, H @ B \rightarrow H = B,$
$B \% N \rightarrow B \leq N$
$\Rightarrow J \geq H = B \leq N$
I. $N \delta H \rightarrow N \geq H$ (True)
II. $N @ J \rightarrow N = J$ (False)
III. $J \delta B \rightarrow J \geq B$ (True)

40. $B \# T \rightarrow B > T, T © K \rightarrow T < K,$
$K \% M \rightarrow K \leq M$
$\Rightarrow B > T < K \leq M$
I. $K \# B \rightarrow K > B$ (False)
II. $M \# T \rightarrow M > T$ (True)
III. $B \# M \rightarrow B > M$ (False)

41. $D \% F \rightarrow D \leq F, F \delta K \rightarrow F \geq K,$
$K @ R \rightarrow K = R$
$\Rightarrow D \leq F \geq K = R$
I. $R \% F \rightarrow R \leq F$ (True)

II. R % D → R ≤ D (False)

III. R @ D → R = D (False)

For Qs. (47-51):

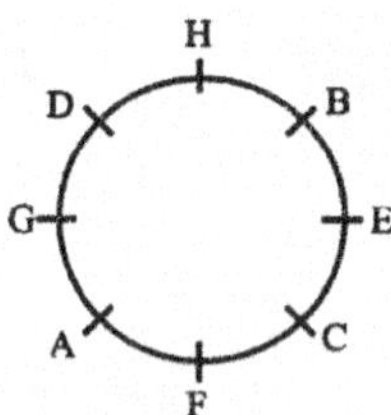

52.

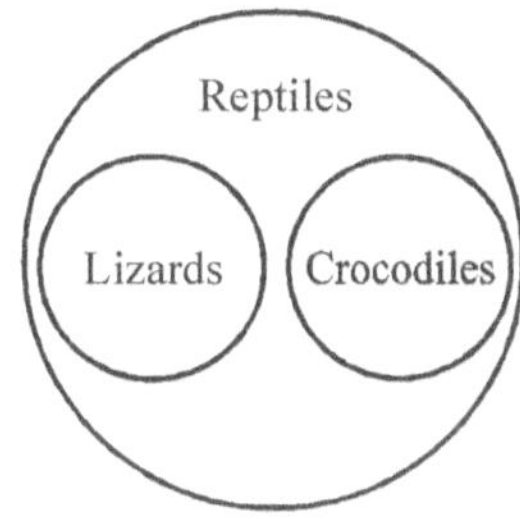

All lizards and crocodiles are reptiles, but neither is contained in the other. Some reptiles are lizards and some crocodiles.

53.

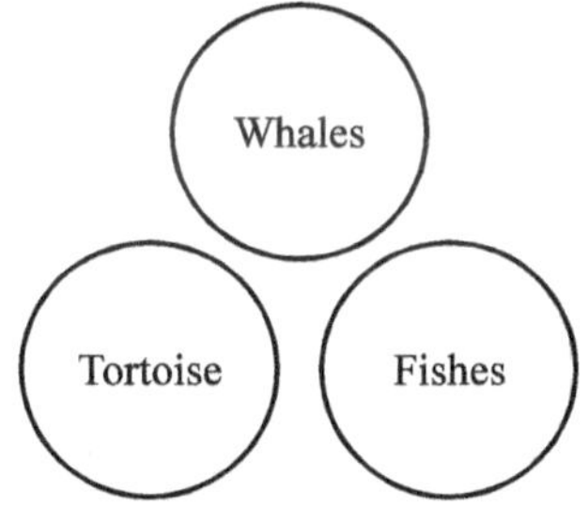

All three are different classes.

54.

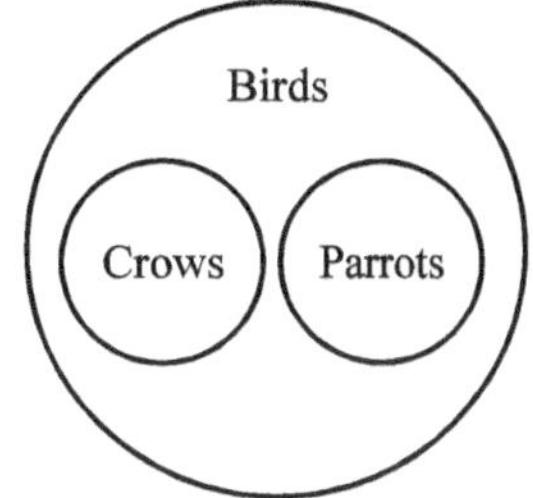

All crows and parrots are birds but neither is contained in the other. Some birds are crows and some parrots.

55. tree is very beautiful

→ ka na da ta   ...(*i*)

This is strong tree

→ na pa sa ka   ...(*ii*)

∴   is tree → na ka

Thus, data is inadequate to find the code of beautiful.

56.   GIVE → 51@©

And   FAIL → %219

∴   LEAF → 9©2%

57. The three letters in each group are moved 4, 3 and 2 steps backward respectively, *i.e.,*

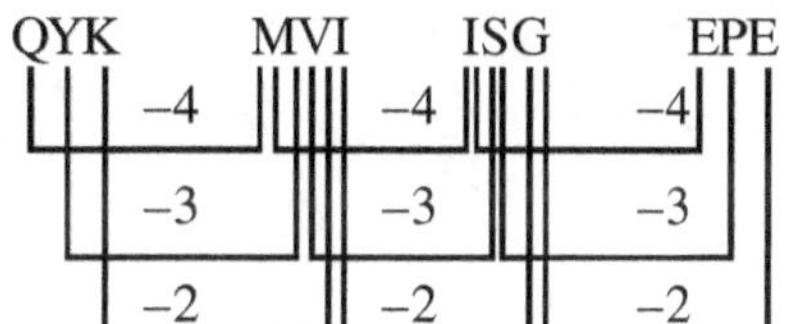

58. There are two alternate series :

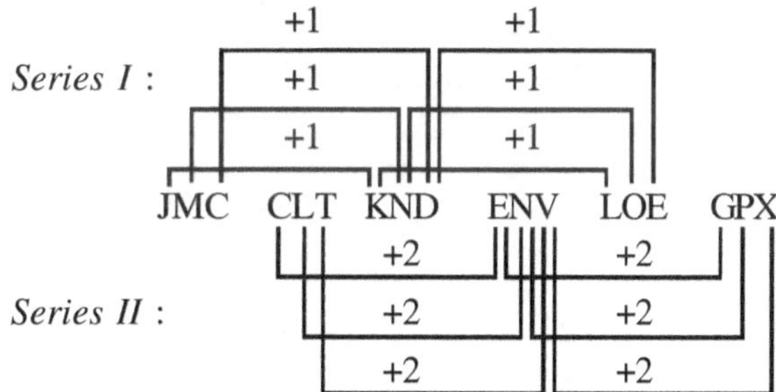

59. As seen in the chart 'Y' is the son of Raju and the husband of 'Q'. So Raju is the father-in-law of his son's 'Y' wife 'Q'.

60. 'A' is the son of Biju and husband of 'Z'. So, 'Z' is the daughter-in-law of her husband's (A) father Biju.

For Qs. (61–65)

From the following data, the arrangement is likely to be :

Person		Car	Distinction
Male	**Female**		
H	A	Z	Agra
G	D	X	Delhi
B, C	F	Y	Chandigarh

66. $\sqrt{?} = 350 - 18^2 = 350 - 324 = 26$

$\Rightarrow ? = (26)^2 = 676$

67. $? = 1530 \div 34 \times 360 \div 24$

$= 1530 \times \dfrac{1}{34} \times 360 \times \dfrac{1}{24} = 675$

68. $? = 4860 + 1236 - 4966 - 285$

$= 6096 - 5251 = 845$

69. $? = \dfrac{17 \times 4 + 18 \times 3}{\sqrt{441} \times 5 + 139} = \dfrac{68 + 54}{21 \times 5 + 139}$

$= \dfrac{122}{244} = \dfrac{1}{2}$

70. $? = 2820 \div 12 \times 8$

$= 2820 \times \dfrac{1}{12} \times 8 = 1880$

71. $? = 1950 \div 26 \div 25 = 1950 \times \dfrac{1}{26} \times \dfrac{1}{25} = 3$

72. $? = \dfrac{18}{100} \times 450 - \dfrac{75}{100} \times 96 = 81 - 72 = 9$

73. $? = 75.75 - 48.32 + 146.92$

$= 222.67 - 48.32 = 174.35$

74. $? = 44\dfrac{2}{5} - \left(8\dfrac{1}{3} \times 4\dfrac{2}{5}\right) = \dfrac{222}{5} - \left(\dfrac{25}{3} \times \dfrac{22}{5}\right)$

$= \dfrac{222}{5} - \dfrac{110}{3} = \dfrac{666 - 550}{15} = \dfrac{116}{15} = 7\dfrac{11}{15}$

75. $? = 27.28 \div 2.2 + 4.4 \times 1.5$

$= 27.28 \times \dfrac{1}{2.2} + 4.4 \times 1.5$

$= 12.4 - 6.6 = 5.8$

76. $? = \dfrac{5}{9} \times 315 + \dfrac{3}{7} \times 455 = 175 + 195 = 370$

77. $\dfrac{?}{100} \times 250 = 1231 - \dfrac{145}{100} \times 780$

$\Rightarrow ? \times \dfrac{5}{2} = 1231 - 1131$

$\Rightarrow ? = \dfrac{100 \times 2}{5} = 40$

78. $? = \dfrac{5}{8} \times \dfrac{2}{3} \times \dfrac{3}{5} \times 2104 = 526$

79. $? = 16.45 \times 5.2 \times 2.5$

$= 213.85$

80. $? = \dfrac{2.25}{100} \times 640 - \dfrac{1.5}{100} \times 480$

$= 14.4 - 7.2 = 7.2$

81.
$$11 \xrightarrow{\times 1+1} 12 \xrightarrow{\times 2+2} 26 \xrightarrow{\times 3+3} 81 \xrightarrow{\times 4+4} ?$$

Thus, $? = 81 \times 4 + 4 = 324 + 4 = 328$

82.
$$5120 \xrightarrow{\times \frac{1}{4}} 1280 \xrightarrow{\times \frac{1}{4}} 320 \xrightarrow{\times \frac{1}{4}} 80 \xrightarrow{\times \frac{1}{4}} ?$$

Thus, $? = 80 \times \dfrac{1}{4} = 20$

83.
$$7 \xrightarrow{+2^2} 11 \xrightarrow{+4^2} 27 \xrightarrow{+6^2} 63 \xrightarrow{+8^2} ?$$

Thus, $? = 63 + 8^2 = 63 + 64 = 127$

84.
$$6 \xrightarrow{+2^2} 10 \xrightarrow{+2^3} 18 \xrightarrow{+2^4} 34 \xrightarrow{+2^5} ?$$

Thus, $? = 34 + 2^5 = 34 + 32 = 66$

85.
$$5 \xrightarrow{\times 2+1} 11 \xrightarrow{\times 2+1} 23 \xrightarrow{\times 2+1} 47 \xrightarrow{\times 2+1} ?$$

Thus, $? = 47 \times 2 + 1 = 95$

86. Let, five consecutive even numbers A, B, C, D & E be x, $x + 2$, $x + 4$, $x + 6$ and $x + 8$ respectively, then

A + E = $x + x + 8 = 2 \times 46$

$\Rightarrow \qquad 2x = 92 - 8$

$\Rightarrow \qquad x = \dfrac{84}{2} = 42$

Thus, largest number, E $= x + 8$

$= 42 + 8 = 50$

87. 66 kmph $= 66 \times \dfrac{5}{18} = \dfrac{55}{3}$ m/s

Length of the train $= \dfrac{55}{3} \times 18 = 330$ m

88. Required average

$$= \frac{155 + 128 + 137 + 140 + 160 + 132}{6}$$

$$= \frac{852}{6} = 142$$

89. Let, the two digit number be $10x + y$,

Then $10x + y - 10y - x = 18$

$\Rightarrow \qquad 9\,(x - y) = 18$

$\Rightarrow \qquad x - y = 2 \qquad\qquad ...(i)$

And also, $\qquad x + y = 6 \qquad\qquad ...(ii)$

From equations (i) and (ii),

$$x = \frac{1}{2}(2 + 6) = 4;\ \ y = \frac{1}{2}(6 - 2) = 2$$

Thus, number $= 10x + y = 10 \times 4 + 2 = 42$

90. Simple Interest $= 77{,}400 - 45000 = ₹\ 32{,}400$

Rate of interest $= \dfrac{32400 \times 100}{45000 \times 8} = 9\%$ p.a.

91. Let, number be x,

Then $\quad \dfrac{3}{5} \times x - \dfrac{40}{100} \times x = 85$

$\Rightarrow \qquad \dfrac{3x}{5} - \dfrac{2x}{5} = 85$

$\Rightarrow \qquad\qquad \dfrac{x}{5} = 85$

$\Rightarrow \qquad\qquad x = 85 \times 5 = 425$

Thus, $\qquad \dfrac{60}{100} \times 425 = 225$

92. Let, this monthly income be $₹\ x$,

Then, $\ x - \left(\dfrac{12}{100} + \dfrac{18}{100} + \dfrac{50}{100} \right) \times x = 5200$

$\Rightarrow \quad x - \dfrac{80}{100} \times x = 5200$

$\Rightarrow \qquad\qquad \dfrac{x}{5} = 5200$

$\Rightarrow \qquad\qquad x = 5200 \times 5 = ₹\ 26000$

93.

Men	Days
24	15
18	x

Thus, $\ \dfrac{x}{15} = \dfrac{24}{18}$

$\Rightarrow \quad x = \dfrac{24}{18} \times 15 = 20\ \text{days.}$

94. Ratio of their dividend

$\qquad = (40{,}000) : (75{,}000) = 8 : 15$

Rasika's share in the dividend

$\qquad = \dfrac{8}{23} \times 46{,}000 = ₹\,16{,}000$

95. Let, present ages of Rama and Shyama be $4x$ and $5x$ years respectively

Then, $\ \dfrac{4x + 5}{5x + 5} = \dfrac{5}{6}$

$\Rightarrow \quad 24x + 30 = 25x + 5$

$\Rightarrow \qquad\qquad x = 5$

Thus, Rama's present age

$\qquad\qquad = 4x = 4 \times 5 = 20\ \text{years.}$

96. Required average

$$= \frac{150 + 90 + 115 + 200 + 190}{5} = \frac{745}{5} = 149$$

97. Required number of employees

$\qquad = 80 + 75 + 90 + 110 + 120 = 475$

98. Required ratio $= (75 + 90) : (220 + 200)$

$\qquad = 165 : 420 = 11 : 28$

99. Required ratio

$\qquad = \ (145 + 80 + 120 + 180 + 160) :$

$\qquad\qquad (180 + 120 + 130 + 110 + 130)$

$\qquad = \ 685 : 670 = 137 : 134$

100. Required percentage

$$= \frac{160}{(120 + 100 + 115 + 160 + 130)} \times 100$$

$$= \frac{160}{625} \times 100 = \frac{128}{5} = 25.6\%$$

SBI Junior Associates & Junior Agricultural Associates
(Clerical Cadre Exam)

General English

Directions (Qs. 1–15): *Read the following passage carefully and answer the questions given below it. Certain words/phrases have been printed in **bold** to help you locate them while answering some of the questions.*

It is **heartening** to know that if one had not had any heart attack earlier and he stops smoking, his chances of having a heart attack **drop** to that of a non-smoker in about six months' time. Stopping of smoking is also the single most effective means of secondary prevention (recurrence of a heart attack) in heart patients.

Smoking leads to pain and stiffness in the legs while walking. No amount of drugs can help. The only remedy is to give up smoking. If women smoke during pregnancy, there is an increased risk of death of the baby in the womb or soon after birth. Even where the baby survives, there is likelihood of delayed physical and intellectual development of the baby till it reaches 11 years of age.

Still worse the fact about smoking is that passive smoking is equally dangerous. Passive smokers are those who do not smoke but being in the company of smokers have to inhale smoke exhaled by the smokers They are equally prone to heart diseases, lung cancer and bronchitis, for no fault of theirs. It is seen that the incidence of these diseases is greater among women whose husbands are **heavy** smokers As such, every non-smoker has a fundamental right to safeguard himself against the danger of passive smoking. "Your smoking is injurious to my health and I have a right to stop you from smoking" could be the slogan against passive smoking. It is a great threat to the health of the individual, the family and the society. In fact one has to choose between health and smoking including passive smoking. **One cannot have both.**

Another matter of **grave concern** about smoking is the long time interval between the start of smoking habit and the manifestation of deadly diseases like cancer, chronic bronchitis and heart attack. People are generally not aware of the link between smoking and the misery they have to undergo years later and younger people often fall victim to this menacing habit under the wrong impression that they are **immune** to its disastrous effects, not realising that they are **heading** towards catastrophe. The prolonged incubation period of many tobacco-related diseases has prevented recognition of the size of the threat and the **grim** picture of chronic and life-threatening diseases.

1. What is "passive smoking"?
   A. Giving up the habit of smoking abruptly
   B. Exhaling smoke by a non-smoker
   C. Unintended intake of smoke exhaled by smokers
   D. Smoking cigarettes which are harmless in nature
   E. None of these

2. The effects of passive smoking are more and more prominently observed among
   A. the children
   B. the smokers
   C. the wives of smokers

D. the non-smokers

E. None of these

3. Which of the following is a heartening thing, according to the author?

A. People who have had a heart attack stop smoking

B. It takes only six months for any person to quit smoking

C. The smoker carries the risk of heart attack for six months

D. hazards of smoking can be seen after a six-month period

E. None of these

4. Which of the following statements is/are false in the context of the passage?

1. Passive smokers are not free from risk of heart diseases

2. Intake of certain medicines helps recover pain and stiffness in legs caused by smoking

3. Younger people are immune to the disastrous effects if their regular smoking is under control

A. 1 and 2 only   B. 2 and 3 only

C. 2 only   D. 3 only

E. All the three

5. Which of the following is not mentioned in the passage as a likely result of smoking by women during pregnancy?

A. Death of baby before birth

B. Death of baby after birth

C. Survival of baby with some abnormality

D. Abnormal delay in the childbirth

E. Slower mental development of the baby

6. Which of the following is considered by the author as a matter of "grave concern"?

A. Inordinate delay in appearance of symptoms of hazards of smoking

B. Long time required for giving up the habit of smoking

C. Manifestation of deadly diseases like cancer, brochitis, etc.

D. Lack of awareness of people regarding the hazards of smoking

E. None of these

7. The youth feel that they are immune to the hazardous effects of smoking because

A. these effects of smoking are not visible within a short time span

B. they do not realise that they are heading towards disaster

C. they feel a great thrill in acquiring the habit of smoking

D. the link between smoking and its disastrous effects cannot be established

E. they believe that their resistance power can counteract this effect

8. Which factor prevents people from realising the extent of threat of smoking hazards?

A. Their lack of awareness of civic responsibilities

B. Their firm belief that they are not immune to these hazards

C. The less disastrous effects of tobacco-related diseases

D. The long span of time required for giving up smoking

E. None of these

9. The last sentence of the third para "One cannot have both" means

A. active smoking and passive smoking

B. smoking and risk of heart diseases

C. threat to the individual and also to the family

D. freedom from health hazards and active smoking

E. None of these

Directions (Qs. 10–12): *Choose the word which is most nearly the SAME in meaning as the word given in bold capitals as used in the passage.*

10. HEADING

A. crowning   B. marching

C. adorning   D. title

E. mastering

11. HEAVY

A. excessive   B. bulky

C. large   D. thick

E. dense

12. DROP
A. roll
B. escape
C. remove
D. reduce
E. liquid

Directions (Qs. 13–15): *Choose the word which is most nearly the OPPOSITE in meaning of the word given in bold capitals as used in the passage.*

13. GRIM
A. dim
B. dark
C. presentable
D. ghostly
E. pleasant

14. IMMUNE
A. free
B. vulnerable
C. powerful
D. weak
E. ineffective

15. HEARTENING
A. cheerful
B. miserable
C. frightening
D. dangerous
E. harmful

Directions (Qs. 16–20): *Read each sentence to find out whether there is any grammatical error or idiomatic error in it. The error, if any, will be in one part of the sentence. The number of that part is the answer. If there is "No Error" the answer is 'E'. (Ignore errors of punctuation if any.)*

16. (A) Not one of the children/(B) has ever sang/(C) on any occasion/(D) in public before./(E) No error.

17. (A) If the by-stander had not been/(B) familiar with first-aid techniques,/(C) the driver which had met/(D) with the accident would have died./(E) No error.

18. (A) Even after requesting/(B) him, he did not/(C) tell us that how/(D) he solved the problem/(E) No error.

19. (A) We never thought/(B) that Mahesh is/(C) oldest than the other/(D) players in the team./(E) No error.

20. (A) No sooner did he/(B) got up from bed/(C) than he was sent/(D) to the dairy./(E) No error.

Directions (Qs. 21–30) : *In the following passage there are blanks, each of which has been numbered. These numbers are printed below the passage, against each, five words are suggested, one of which fits the blank appropriately. Find out the appropriate word in each case.*

Without science there is no future for any society. Even with science, ... **(21)** ..... it is controlled by some spiritual impulses, there is also no future. One great thing about science is that it does not accept anything on mere ..... **(22)** ..... . Everything has to be ..... **(23)** ..... beyond any doubt. All acceptance comes after experiment which has no room for any ..... **(24)** ..... . This is the reason ..... **(25)** ..... development of science and technology has revolutionised human life all over the world. There are very few spheres of human activity which have not experienced the ..... **(26)** ..... of such development. However, despite its manifold ..... **(27)** ..... science has not been ..... **(28)** ..... to solve any of man's moral or spiritual problems. Society is still ..... **(29)** ..... in the dark to find out what its future will be. The need, therefore, is to make science ..... **(30)** ..... for the ultimate truth.

21. A. unless
B. without
C. if
D. before
E. because

22. A. principles
B. conjecture
C. experiment
D. research
E. experience

23. A. accepted
B. demonstrated
C. proved
D. performed
E. understood

24. A. precision
B. exactness
C. confirmation
D. speculation
E. apprehension

25. A. for
B. how
C. that
D. about
E. why

26. A. impact
B. futility
C. causes
D. problems
E. nature

27. A. limitations
B. benefits
C. shortcomings
D. researches
E. inventions

28. A. employed
B. developed
C. able
D. entrusted
E. taught

29. A. engulfed   B. lost
C. enlightening   D. investigating
E. groping

30. A. useful   B. worthy
C. ready   D. search
E. fit

Reasoning Ability

Directions (Qs. 31–35): *In each question below are three statements followed by two conclusions numbered I and II. You have to take the three given statements to be true even if they seem to be at variance from commonly known facts and then decide which of the given conclusions logically follows from the three statements disregarding commonly known facts.*

Give answer A if only conclusion I follows.

Give answer B if only conclusion II follows.

Give answer C if either conclusion I or conclusion II follows.

Give answer D if neither conclusion I nor conclusion II follows.

Give answer E if both conclusion I and conclusion II follow.

31. Statements : All paints are colours.
All inks are paints.
No colour is a varnish.

Conclusions : I. No varnish is paint.
II. All inks are colours.

32. Statements : Some kites are planes.
All planes are birds.
All birds are balloons.

Conclusions : I. All birds are kites.
II. All planes are balloons.

33. Statements : All actors are producers.
Some producers are directors.
Some singers are producers.

Conclusions : I. Some actors are singers.
II. Some singers are directors.

34. Statements : All movies are dramas.
All plays are dramas.
All dramas are films.

Conclusions : I. All movies are films.
II. Some plays are not films.

35. Statements : Some grains are cereals.
Some cereals are rice.
Some rice are wheat.

Conclusions : I. Some grains are wheat.
II. Some wheat are cereals.

Directions (Qs. 36–40): *Study the following information carefully and answer the given questions.*

L, P, Q, R, S and T are sitting in a straight line facing North.

A. Q sits fourth to the left of T and Q does not sit at an extreme end of the line.

B. R is not an immediate neighbor of Q.

C. Only one person sits between R and T.

D. Neither S nor L sits at the extreme end of the line.

E. L is not an immediate neighbour of Q.

36. How many persons sit between Q and L?
A. None   B. One
C. Two   D. Three
E. Four

37. If all the persons are made to sit in alphabetical order from left to right, the positions of how many will remain unchanged as compared to the original seating positions?
A. None   B. One
C. Two   D. Three
E. Four

38. What is the position of Q with respect to L?
A. Second to the left
B. Immediately to the right
C. Second to the right
D. Third to the left
E. Third to the right

39. Who sits at the extreme left hand corner of the line?
A. P
B. R
C. T
D. Either T or R
E. None of these

40. Four of the following five are alike in a certain way based on their seating positions in the above arrangement and so form a group. Which is the one that **does not** belong to that group?

A. TR   B. SP

C. RQ   D. LS

E. QL

Directions (Qs. 41–45): *Following questions are based on the five three digit numbers given below:*

428   391   745   682   534

41. If '1' is added to the last digit of every odd number and '1' is subtracted from the last digit of every even number, what will be difference between the lowest odd number and the lower even number thus formed?

A. 211   B. 91

C. 38   D. 46

E. 35

42. If the positions of the first and the second digits of each of the numbers are interchanged, which of the following will be the difference between the highest and the second highest numbers thus formed?

A. 69   B. 106

C. 79   D. 121

E. 46

43. If '1' is subtracted from the middle digit of every number, how many numbers thus formed will be divisible by three?

A. None   B. One

C. Two   D. Three

E. Four

44. If all the numbers are arranged in descending order from left to right, which of the following will be sum of all the three digits of the number which is fourth from the left?

A. 16   B. 19

C. 14   D. 12

E. 13

45. What will be the resultant if second digit of the lowest number is divided by its first digit?

A. 2   B. 3

C. 1.33   D. 6

E. 1.2

Directions (Qs. 46 & 47) : *In the following diagram, rectangle represents Hindi Announcers, circle represents English Announcers, square represents French Announcers, and triangle represents German Announcers.*

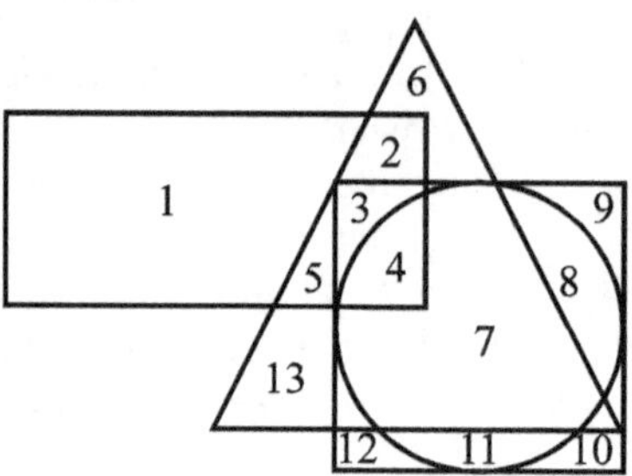

46. Which area represents those announcers who can present programmes in Hindi, French and German only?

A. 1   B. 2

C. 3   D. 4

E. 5

47. Which area represents those announcers who can present programmes in French and English only?

A. 7   B. 9

C. 11   D. 13

E. 6

48. In a certain code 'FAITH' is coded as 'HCKVJ' and 'NIGHT' is coded as 'PKIJV'. In the same code '............' will be coded as 'MTQOR'?

A. KRONP

B. OVSQT

C. TQSVO

D. PMORK

E. KROMP

49. In a certain code language 'it is dark outside' is written as 'ha no ti ju', 'is it still raining' is written as 'pa ha da no' and 'go and play outside' is written as 'su ju ye la'. How is 'dark' written in that code language?

A. ha

B. ti

C. su

D. ye

E. no

50. Peter walks 5 m towards West, takes a right turn and walks 5 m again. He then takes another right turn and walks 20 m. He then takes a final right turn and walks 5 m before stopping. How far is he from the starting point?
A. 20 m B. 5 m
C. 25 m D. 15 m
E. None of these

51. Pointing to a girl, Kiran said, "She is the only daughter of my grandfather's son". How is the girl related to Kiran?
A. Daughter B. Cousin
C. Sister D. Data inadequate
E. None of these

52. Suresh correctly remembers that his mother's birthday is before twentieth June but after seventeenth June whereas his brother correctly remembers that their mother's birthday is after eighteenth but before twenty-fourth June. On which date in June was definitely their mother's birthday?
A. Eighteenth B. Twentieth
C. Nineteenth D. Data inadequate
E. None of these

53. Sneha correctly remembers that last time when she travelled in the bus, she paid less than Rs. 10 but more than Rs. 4 for the ticket. Meenal correctly remembers that she paid more than Rs. 6 but less than Rs. 14 for the same distance. The conductor of the bus correctly mentions that the fare for that distance is not an odd number. Which of the following is definitely the fare for that particular distance?
A. Rs. 8 B. Rs. 6
C. Rs. 2 D. Rs. 12
E. Rs. 9

54. How many meaningful English words can be formed with the letters SWA using each letter only once in each word?
A. None B. One
C. Two D. Three
E. More than three

55. In an exam, A, B, C and D each scored different marks. B scored more than C and D. No one scored less than A. Who amongst them scored the maximum marks?
A. B
B. Either C or D
C. D
D. Cannot be determined
E. None of these

Directions (Qs. 56-60): *Following questions are based on five words given below*

AND FOR THE BIG SUM

(The new words formed after performing the mentioned operations may or may not necessarily be meaningful English words.)

56. If the third alphabet of each of the words is changed to the next alphabet in the English alphabetical series, which of the following will form a meaningful English word?
A. SUM
B. BIG
C. Both BIG and THE
D. FOR
E. Both FOR and BIG

57. If the given words are arranged in the order as they would appear in a dictionary from left to right, which of the following will be second from the right?
A. AND B. FOR
C. THE D. BIG
E. SUM

58. If second alphabet in each of the words is changed to next alphabet in the English alphabetical order, how many words having two vowels (same or different vowels) will be formed?
A. None B. One
C. Two D. Three
E. Four

59. How many letters are there in the English alphabetical series between the second letter of the word which is second from the right and the second letter of the word which is second from the left of the given words?
A. Two B. Five
C. Six D. Nine
E. Three

60. If in each of the given words, each of the consonants is changed to previous letter and each vowel is changed to next letter in the English alphabetical series, in how many words thus formed will no vowels appear?

A. None   B. One
C. Two   D. Three
E. More than three

Directions (Qs. 61-65): *In the following questions, a relationship is shown between the letters in the given statements followed by two conclusions.*
Give answer (A) if only conclusion I is true.
Give answer (B) if only conclusion II is true.
Give answer (C) if either I or II is true.
Give answer (D) if neither I nor II is true.
Give answer (E) if both I and II are true.

61. Statements   : $A \leq F \geq T = E \leq R$
    Conclusions I : $A < F$
               II : $R \geq F$

62. Statements   : $R \geq I < G \leq H > T$
    Conclusions I : $T < I$
               II : $H > I$

63. Statements   : $T = A \leq K > E = S$
    Conclusions I : $K \geq T$
               II : $S < K$

64. Statements   : $P < O = I \leq N > T$
    Conclusions I : $P < N$
               II : $O > T$

65. Statements   : $D > E \geq L > A \geq Y$
    Conclusions I : $Y \leq D$
               II : $A \geq E$

Quantitative Aptitude

Directions (Qs. 66–80): *What will come in place of question mark (?) in the following questions?*

66. $\dfrac{5}{11}$ of $\dfrac{4}{5}$ of $\dfrac{11}{16}$ of $848 = ?$

A. 216   B. 222
C. 208   D. 212
E. None of these

67. 1.4% of 750 + 2.2% of 480 = ?

A. 21.06   B. 21.16
C. 20.88   D. 21.18
E. None of these

68. $\dfrac{3}{4}$ of $116 - \dfrac{2}{3}$ of $87 = ?$

A. 31   B. 27
C. 29   D. 26
E. None of these

69. $6.96 \div 1.2 - 18.24 \div 7.6 = ?$

A. 3.4   B. 3.14
C. 3.04   D. 3.24
E. None of these

70. $32.25 \times 2.4 \times 1.6 = ?$

A. 128.84   B. 123.84
C. 112.88   D. 112.84
E. None of these

71. 136% of 250 + ?% of 550 = 670

A. 64   B. 55
C. 56   D. 65
E. None of these

72. $448 \div 16 \times 35 = ?$

A. 850   B. 890
C. 950   D. 980
E. None of these

73. $\dfrac{14 \times 25 - 5^3}{24 \times 5 + 8 \times 9} = ?$

A. $1\dfrac{9}{64}$ B. $\dfrac{64}{75}$

C. $1\dfrac{11}{64}$ D. $1\dfrac{11}{75}$

E. None of these

74. $78.45 + 128.85 + 1122.25 = ?$

A. 1329.55   B. 1239.55
C. 1329.45   D. 1239.45
E. None of these

75. $8729 - 4376 + 1245 = ? + 2785$

A. 2713   B. 2823
C. 2833   D. 2733
E. None of these

Directions (Qs. 76–80). *What will come in place of the question mark (?) in the following number series?*

76. 12 16 24 40 ?
   A. 76   B. 72
   C. 84   D. 88
   E. None of these

77. 9 19 39 79 ?
   A. 139   B. 129
   C. 159   D. 149
   E. None of these

78. 8 17 42 91 ?
   A. 170   B. 142
   C. 140   D. 172
   E. None of these

79. 7 8 18 57 ?
   A. 244   B. 174
   C. 186   D. 226
   E. None of these

80. 3840 960 240 60 ?
   A. 20   B. 18
   C. 12   D. 22
   E. None of these

81. 75% of a number is equal to three-seventh of another number. What is the ratio between the first number and the second number respectively?
   A. 4 : 7   B. 7 : 4
   C. 12 : 7   D. 7 : 12
   E. None of these

82. A 275 meter long train crosses a platform of equal length in 33 seconds. What is the speed of the train in kmph?
   A. 66
   B. 60
   C. 64
   D. 72
   E. None of these

83. What is compound interest accrued on an amount of ₹ 45,000/- in two years @ 9 percent per annum?
   A. ₹ 8,600/-
   B. ₹ 8,565.40/-
   C. ₹ 8,464.50/-
   D. ₹ 8,540/-
   E. None of these

84. Cost of 18 shirts and 45 trousers is ₹ 68,400/-. What is the cost of 10 shirts and 25 trousers?
   A. ₹ 38,000/-   B. ₹ 36,000/-
   C. ₹ 34,200/-   D. ₹ 36,200/-
   E. None of these

85. If the fractions $\dfrac{9}{11}, \dfrac{7}{9}, \dfrac{5}{6}, \dfrac{4}{5}$ and $\dfrac{11}{13}$ are arranged in ascending order, which one will be the fourth?
   A. $\dfrac{9}{11}$ B. $\dfrac{7}{9}$
   C. $\dfrac{5}{6}$ D. $\dfrac{4}{5}$
   E. $\dfrac{11}{13}$

86. Simple interest accrued on an amount in 8 years @ 12 per cent per annum is ₹ 5,520/-. What is the principal amount?
   A. ₹ 5,750/-   B. ₹ 8,500/-
   C. ₹ 5,650/-   D. ₹ 8,250/-
   E. None of these

87. Find the average of the following set of number:
148, 88, 184, 166, 96, 122
   A. 146   B. 142
   C. 136   D. 132
   E. None of these

88. Shrikant and Vividh started a business investing amounts of ₹ 1,85,000/- and ₹ 2,25,000/- respectively. If Vividh's share in the profit earned by them is Rs. 9,000/-, what is the total profit earned by them together?
   A. ₹ 17,400/-   B. ₹ 16,400/-
   C. ₹ 16,800/-   D. ₹ 17,800/-
   E. None of these

89. Present ages of father and the son are in the ratio of 6 : 1 respectively. Four years hence the ratio of their ages will become 4 : 1 respectively. What is the son's present age?
   A. 10 years   B. 6 years
   C. 4 years   D. 8 years
   E. None of these

90. A DVD player was purchased for ₹ 4,860/-. At what price should it be sold so that 25% profit is earned?
A. ₹ 6,225/-
B. ₹ 6,275/-
C. ₹ 6,075/-
D. ₹ 6,025/-
E. None of these

91. 65% of a number is more than its two-fifth by 140. What is 30% of that number?
A. 186   B. 168
C. 164   D. 182
E. None of these

92. Number obtained by interchanging the digits of a two digit number is more than the original number by 27 and the sum of the digits is 13. What is the original number?
A. 58   B. 67
C. 76   D. 85
E. None of these

93. 22 Men can complete a job in 16 days. In how many days will 32 men complete that job?
A. 14   B. 12
C. 16   D. 9
E. None of these

94. Mr. Davar spends 38% of his monthly income on food, 25% on children's education and 12% on transport and the remaining amount of ₹ 5,800/- he saves. What is Mr. Davar's monthly income?
A. ₹ 23,200/-
B. ₹ 24,200/-
C. ₹ 23,800/-
D. ₹ 24,400/-
E. None of these

95. A, B, C, D and E are five consecutive odd numbers. Average of A and C is 59. What is the smallest number?
A. 65
B. 63
C. 61
D. 57
E. None of these

Directions (Qs. 96 to 100): *Study the following table carefully to answer these questions*

Number of students appeared in SSC examination from five schools over the years

School \ Year	A	B	C	D	E
2009	650	760	820	800	780
2010	700	740	860	780	740
2011	800	820	940	750	730
2012	750	880	920	840	790
2013	850	840	900	860	770

96. Number of students appeared from school E in 2009 is **approximately** what percent of the total number of students appeared from all the schools together in that year?
A. 12   B. 28
C. 15   D. 30
E. 20

97. What is the average number of students appeared from school B for all the years?
A. 828   B. 808
C. 804   D. 812
E. None of these

98. Number of students appeared in 2011 from school A is what percent of the total number of students appeared from school A for all the years together?
A. $23\frac{2}{3}$ B. $22\frac{1}{3}$
C. $22\frac{2}{3}$ D. $21\frac{1}{3}$
E. None of these

99. What is the ratio between the total number of students appeared in 2009 and 2010 together from schools C and D respectively?
A. 84 : 79   B. 79 : 84
C. 48 : 79   D. 79 : 48
E. None of these

100. What is the average number of students appeared from all the schools in 2012?
A. 842   B. 856
C. 836   D. 830
E. None of these

ANSWERS

1	2	3	4	5	6	7	8	9	10
C	C	E	B	D	A	A	E	E	B

11	12	13	14	15	16	17	18	19	20
A	D	E	B	C	B	C	C	C	B

21	22	23	24	25	26	27	28	29	30
A	B	C	D	E	A	B	C	E	E

31	32	33	34	35	36	37	38	39	40
E	B	D	A	D	C	C	D	A	E

41	42	43	44	45	46	47	48	49	50
E	A	D	C	B	C	C	E	B	D

51	52	53	54	55	56	57	58	59	60
B	C	A	C	A	A	E	C	B	D

61	62	63	64	65	66	67	68	69	70
D	B	B	A	D	D	A	C	A	B

71	72	73	74	75	76	77	78	79	80
E	D	C	A	E	B	C	D	E	E

81	82	83	84	85	86	87	88	89	90
A	B	C	A	C	A	E	B	B	C

91	92	93	94	95	96	97	98	99	100
B	A	E	A	D	E	B	D	A	C

Some Selected Explanatory Answers

31. 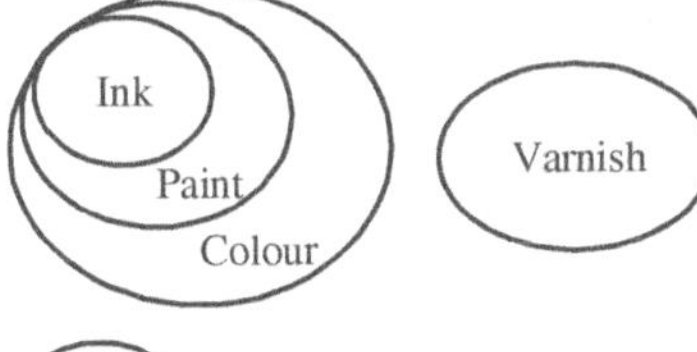

32. 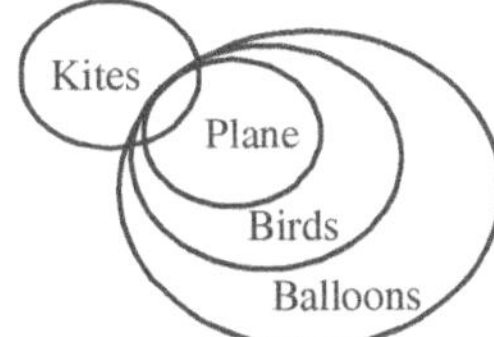

33. 

34. 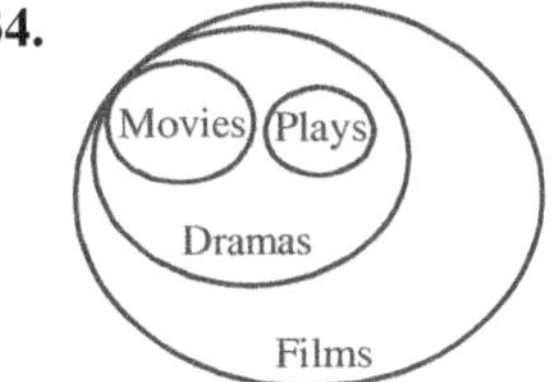

35. 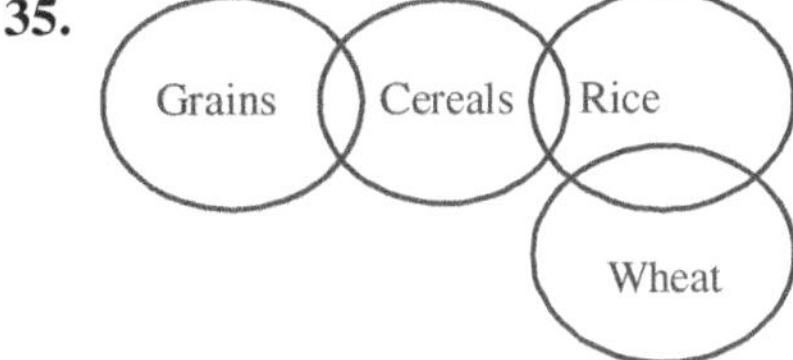

43. $428 \Rightarrow 418$;
$391 \Rightarrow 381$;
$745 \Rightarrow 735$;
$682 \Rightarrow 672$;
$534 \Rightarrow 524$

Numbers divided by 3.

$$\frac{381}{3} = 127; \frac{735}{3} = 245; \frac{672}{3} = 224$$

44. $745 > 682 > 534 > 428 > 391$
Required sum $= 4 + 2 + 8 = 14$

45. smallest number $\Rightarrow 391$

$$\frac{9}{3} = 3$$

For Qs. 46 & 47

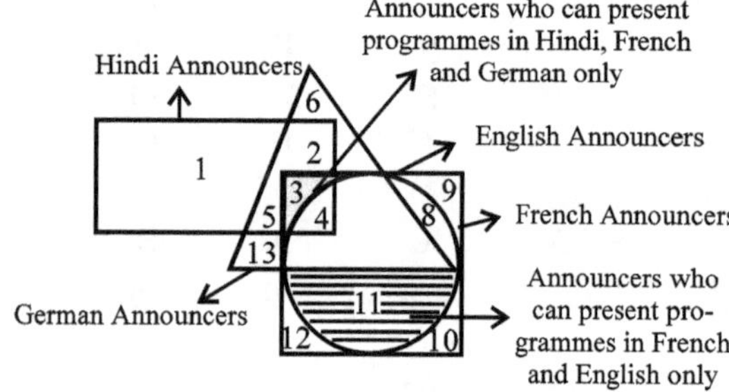

48. Each corresponding letter moves two positions forward in the alphabet.

49. it is dark outside = ha no ti ju ...(i)
is it still raining = pa ha da no ...(ii)
go and play outside = su ju ye la ...(iii)
From (i) and (ii), it is = ha no ...(iv)
From (i) and (iii), outside = ju ...(v)
Using (iv) and (v) in (i),
we get : dark = ti

50.
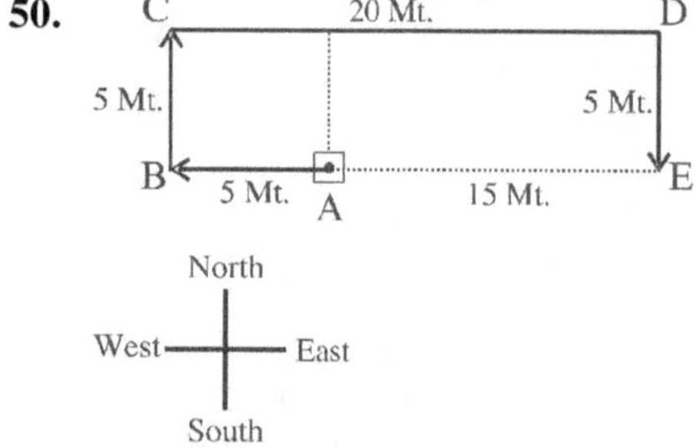

Requried distance = AE = 15 Mt.

51.

52. According to Suresh his mother's birthday = 18th/19th June.

According to Suresh's brother his mother's birthday = 19th/20th/21st/22nd/23rd June.

Common date = 19th June.

54. SAW and WAS

55. B > {C, D} > A

66. $? = \dfrac{5}{11} \times \dfrac{4}{5} \times \dfrac{11}{16} \times 848 = 212$

67. $? = \dfrac{1.4}{100} \times 750 + \dfrac{2.2}{100} \times 480$

$= 10.50 + 10.56 = 21.06$

68. $? = \dfrac{3}{4} \times 116 - \dfrac{2}{3} \times 87 = 87 - 58 = 29$

69. $? = 6.96 \div 1.2 - 18.24 \div 7.6$

$= 5.8 - 2.4 = 3.4$

70. $? = 32.25 \times 2.4 \times 1.6 = 123.84$

71. $\dfrac{136}{100} \times 250 + \dfrac{?}{100} \times 550 = 670$

$\Rightarrow \dfrac{?}{100} \times 550 = 670 - 340$

$\Rightarrow ? = \dfrac{330 \times 2}{11} = 60$

72. $? = 448 \div 16 \times 35$

$= 448 \times \dfrac{1}{16} \times 35 = 28 \times 35$

$= 980$

73. $? = \dfrac{14 \times 25 - 5^3}{24 \times 5 + 8 \times 9} = \dfrac{350 - 125}{120 + 72}$

$= \dfrac{225}{192} = \dfrac{75}{64} = 1\dfrac{11}{64}$

74. $? = 78.45 + 128.85 + 1122.25$

$= 1329.55$

75. $? = 8729 + 1245 - 4376 - 2785$

$= 9974 - 7161 = 2813$

76. $12 \xrightarrow{+4} 16 \xrightarrow{+8} 24 \xrightarrow{+16} 40 \xrightarrow{+32} ?$

Thus, ? = 40 + 32 = 72

77. $9 \xrightarrow{+10} 19 \xrightarrow{+20} 39 \xrightarrow{+40} 79 \xrightarrow{+80} ?$

Thus, ? = 79 + 80 = 159

78. $8 \xrightarrow{+3^2} 17 \xrightarrow{+5^2} 42 \xrightarrow{+7^2} 91 \xrightarrow{+9^2} ?$

Thus, ? = 91 + 9^2 = 91 + 81 = 172

79. $7 \xrightarrow{\times 1 + 1} 8 \xrightarrow{\times 2 + 2} 18 \xrightarrow{\times 3 + 3} 57 \xrightarrow{\times 4 + 4} ?$

Thus, ? = 57 × 4 + 4 = 228 + 4 = 232

80. $3840 \xrightarrow{\div 4} 960 \xrightarrow{\div 4} 240 \xrightarrow{\div 4} 60 \xrightarrow{\div 4} ?$

Thus, ? = 60 ÷ 4 = 15

81. $\dfrac{75}{100} \times x = \dfrac{3}{7} \times y \Rightarrow \dfrac{x}{y} = \dfrac{4}{3} \times \dfrac{3}{7} = \dfrac{4}{7}$

$\Rightarrow x : y = 4 : 7$

82. Speed of the train

$$= \frac{275 + 275}{33} = \frac{550}{33} = \frac{50}{3} \text{ m/s}$$

$$= \frac{50}{3} \times \frac{18}{5} \text{ km/hr} = 60 \text{ km/hr.}$$

83. C.I. = $45000 \left[\left(1 + \dfrac{9}{100} \right)^2 - 1 \right]$

$= 45000 \left[1.1881 - 1 \right]$

$= 45000 \times 0.1881$

= ₹ 8464.50

84. Cost of 10 shirts and 25 trousers

$$= \frac{68,400}{1.8} = ₹ 3800$$

85. $\dfrac{9}{11} = 0.\overline{81}, \dfrac{7}{9} = 0.\overline{7}, \dfrac{5}{6} = 0.8\overline{3}, \dfrac{4}{3} = 0.8, \dfrac{11}{13} = 0.846$

Thus, $\dfrac{7}{9} < \dfrac{4}{5} < \dfrac{9}{11} < \dfrac{5}{6} < \dfrac{11}{13}$

Thus, required fraction = $\dfrac{5}{6}$

86. Principal amount = $\dfrac{100 \times 5520}{8 \times 12}$ = ₹ 5750

87. Required average

$$= \frac{148 + 88 + 184 + 166 + 96 + 122}{6}$$

$$= \frac{804}{6} = 134$$

88. Ratio of their investments = 185000 : 225000

$$= 37 : 45$$

Thus, total profit = $\dfrac{900}{45} \times (37 + 45)$

$= 200 \times 82$

= ₹ 16,400

89. Let, present ages of father and son be $6x$ and x years respectively then,

$$\frac{6x + 4}{x + 4} = \frac{4}{1}$$

$\Rightarrow \quad 6x + 4 = 4x + 16$

$\Rightarrow \quad x = \dfrac{12}{2} = 6$ years

Thus, present age of son = 6 years.

90. Required S.P. = $\dfrac{125}{100} \times 4860$ = ₹ 6,075

91. $\dfrac{65}{100} \times x - \dfrac{2}{5} x = 140$

$\Rightarrow \quad \dfrac{25}{100} \times x = 140$

$\Rightarrow \quad \dfrac{30}{100} \times x = \dfrac{140}{25} \times 30 = 168$

Thus, 30% of that number = 168

92. Let, two digit-number = $10x + y$, then

$$y + x = 13 \qquad \qquad ...(i)$$

And Also,

$$10y + x - (10x + y) = 27$$

$$\Rightarrow \qquad 9(y - x) = 27$$
$$\Rightarrow \qquad y - x = 3 \qquad \qquad ...(ii)$$

Solving equations (*i*) and (*ii*), we get

$$x = 5, \quad y = 8$$

Thus, original number $= 10 \times 5 + 8 = 58$

93. Men   Days

$$22 \downarrow \qquad 16 \uparrow$$
$$32 \downarrow \qquad x \uparrow$$

Then, $\dfrac{x}{16} = \dfrac{22}{32} \Rightarrow x = \dfrac{16 \times 22}{32}$

$$= 11 \text{ days}$$

94. Let his monthly income be ₹ x, then

$$x - \left(38 + 25 + 12\right) \times \dfrac{1}{100} \times x \;=\; 5800$$

$$\Rightarrow \qquad x - \dfrac{75}{100} \times x \;=\; 5800$$

$$\Rightarrow \qquad \dfrac{x}{4} \;=\; 5800$$

$$\Rightarrow \qquad x = 4 \times 5800$$
$$= ₹\; 23{,}200$$

Thus, his monthly income $= ₹\; 23{,}200$

95. Average of A and C is 59

Thus, B will be 59

Thus, smallest number, A $= 59 - 2 = 57$

96. Required percentage

$$= \dfrac{780}{650 + 760 + 820 + 800 + 780} \times 100$$

$$= \dfrac{780}{3810} \times 100 \approx 20\%$$

97. Required average

$$= \dfrac{760 + 740 + 820 + 880 + 840}{5}$$

$$= \dfrac{4040}{5} = 808$$

98. Required percentage

$$= \dfrac{800}{650 + 700 + 800 + 750 + 850} \times 100$$

$$= \dfrac{800}{3750} \times 100 = \dfrac{64}{3}$$

$$= 21\dfrac{1}{3}\%$$

99. Required ratio

$$= (820 + 860) : (800 + 780)$$
$$= 1680 : 1580 = 84 : 79$$

100. Required average

$$= \dfrac{(750 + 880 + 920 + 840 + 790)}{5}$$

$$= \dfrac{4180}{5} = 836$$

SBI Junior Associates & Junior Agricultural Associates
(Clerical Cadre Exam)

General English

Directions (Qs. 1–15): *Read the following passage carefully and answer the questions given below it. Certain words/phrases have been printed in **bold** to help you locate them while answering some of the questions.*

The happy man is the man who lives objectively, who has free affections and wide interests, who secures his happiness through these interests and affections and through the fact that they, in turn, make him an object of interest and affection to many others. To be the recipient of affection is a potent cause of happiness, but the man who demands affection is not the man upon whom it is **bestowed**. The man who receives affection is, speaking broadly, the man who gives it. But it is useless to attempt to give it as a calculation, in the way in which one might lend money at interest, for a calculated affection is not genuine and is not felt to be so by the recipient.

What then can a man do who is unhappy because he is encased in self? So long as he continues to think about the causes of his unhappiness, he continues to be self-centred and therefore does not get outside the vicious circle, if he is to get outside it, it must be genuine interests, not by simulated interests adopted merely as a medicine. Although this difficulty is real, there is nevertheless much that he can do if he has rightly diagnosed his trouble. If, for example, his trouble is due to a sense of sin, conscious or unconscious, he can first persuade his conscious mind that he has no reason to feel sinful and then proceed, to plant his rational conviction in his unconscious mind, concerning himself meanwhile with some more or less neutral activity. If he succeeds in **dispelling** the sense of sin, it is possible that genuine objective interests will arise spontaneously. If his trouble is self pity, he can deal with it in the same manner after first persuading himself that there is nothing extraordinarily unfortunate in his circumstances.

If fear is his trouble, let him practise exercises designed to give courage. Courage has been recognised from time immemorial as an important virtue, and a great part of training of boys and young men has been devoted to producing a type of character capable of fearlessness in battle. But moral courage and intellectual courage have been much less studied, they also, however, have their technique. Admit to yourself everyday atleast one painful truth, you will find this quite useful. Teach yourself to feel that life still be worth living even if you were not, as of course you are, immeasurably superior to all your friends in virtue and in intelligence. Exercises of this sort prolonged through several years will at last enable you to admit facts **without flinching** and will, in so doing, free you from the empire of fear over a very large field.

1. Who according to the passage is the happy man?
   - A. who is encased in self
   - B. who has free affection and wide interests
   - C. who is free from wordly passions
   - D. who has externally centre passions
   - E. None of these

2. According to the passage, calculated affection
A. appears to be false and fabricated
B. makes other pen-on to love you
C. turns into permanent affection over a period of time
D. leads to self-pity
E. gives a feeling of courage

3. Which of the following virtues, according to the passage, has been recognised for long as an important virtue?
A. Patriotism
B. Sacrifice
C. Courage
D. Self-consciousness
E. None of these

4. Which of the following, according to the passage, has not been studied much?
A. Feeling of guilt and self-pity
B. The state of mind of an unhappy man
C. How to get absorbed in other interests
D. Moral and intellectual courage
E. None of these

5. If a man is suffering from a sense of sin
A. he should invite opinion of others
B. he should admit his sin at once
C. he should consciously realize that he has no reason to feel sinful
D. he should develop a fearless character
E. he should develop an internal locus of control

6. What happens to a man who demands affection?
A. His feelings are reciprocated by others
B. He tends to take a calculated risk
C. He becomes a victim of a viscious circle
D. He takes affection for granted from others
E. None of these

7. What should a man do who is suffering from the feeling of self-pity?
A. He should control his passions and emotions
B. He should persuade himself that everything is alright in his circumstances
C. He should seek affection from others
D. He should develop a feeling of fearlessness
E. He should consult an expert to diagnose his trouble

8. How to get out of the viscious circle mentioned in the passage?
A. By practicing skills of concentration
B. By inculcating the habits of self-absorption
C. Being true to others and one's internal circumstances
D. Admitting to oneself that others could be right
E. None of these

9. Which of the following statements is not *true* in the context of the passage?
A. Happy man has wide interests
B. Courage has been recognized as an important virtue
C. Unhappy man is encased in self
D. A man who suffers from the sense of sin must tell himself that he has no reason to be sinful
E. Issue of intellectual courage has been extensively studied

10. Which of the following words is SIMILAR in meaning of the word **'bestowed'** as used in the passage?
A. Conferred   B. Accommodated
C. Trusted   D. Withdrawn
E. Directed

11. Which of the following statements is *true* in the context of the passage?
A. All passions stem from unhappiness
B. The happy man lives in subjectively
C. Any virtue has a dark side also
D. One feels happy if one receives affection
E. Any affection is always genuine

12. Which of the following words is SIMILAR in meaning to the word **'flinching'** as used in the passage?
A. Wincing   B. Convincing
C. Explaining   D. Providing
E. Debating

13. What happens when you think about cause of your unhappiness?
A. You try to introspect and look critically at yourself
B. You realize that the life can be lived in different ways

C. You try to practice exercise designed to give courage
D. You remain a self-centred person
E. None of these

14. What according to the passage is the real cause of happiness?
A. Material rewards and incentives received
B. Critical analysis of the happy state of mind
C. Affection received from others
D. Calculated risks taken
E. None of these

15. Which of the following words is OPPOSITE in meaning of the word **'dispelling'** as used in the passage?
A. Giving
B. Accumulating
C. Projecting
D. Scattering
E. Receiving

Directions (Qs. 16–20) : *Each sentence below has a blank, each blank indicating that something has been omitted. Choose the word for each blank which best fits the meaning of the sentence as a whole.*

16. Last year the performance of this production unit was ..... .
A. tall
B. staggered
C. fantastic
D. below
E. upwards

17. We all must ..... that people are the most important assets of any organisation.
A. find
B. look
C. realise
D. involve
E. dispel

18. Since Vivek stays far away from our place, we do not meet each other .....
A. rarely
B. shortly
C. timely
D. frequently
E. momentarily

19. The lights ..... just as we sat down to watch the movie on television.
A. went off
B. shut out
C. put out
D. blew down
E. gave off

20. To ..... yourself from ..... wear warm clothes.
A. save, heat
B. suffer, cold
C. prevent, ice
D. protect, cold
E. prohibit, heat

Directions (Qs. 21–25): *Read each sentence to find out whether there is any grammatical error or idiomatic error in it. The error, if any, will be in one part of the sentence. The number of that part is the answer. If there is "No Error" the answer is 'E'. (Ignore errors of punctuation if any.)*

21. (A) By arresting the local criminals/(B) and encouraging good people/(C) we can end/(D) hostilities of that area./(E) No error.

22. (A) The apparently obvious solutions/(B) to most of his problems/(C) were overlook by/(D) many of his friends./(E) No error.

23. (A) In spite of the difficulties/(B) on the way,/(C) they enjoyed their/(D) trip to Gangotri./(E) No error.

24. (A) We decided not tell to/(B) the patient about/(C) the disease he was/(D) suffering from./(E) No error.

25. (A) The principals of equal justice/(B) for all is one of/(C) the cornerstones of our/(D) democratic way of life./(E) No error.

Directions (Qs. 26–30): *Which of the phrases A, B, C and D given below should replace the phrase given in **bold** in the following sentence to make the sentence grammatically meaningful and correct? If the sentence is correct as it is and 'No correction is required', mark E as the answer.*

26. Can you tell me **why did you not speak** the truth?
A. why did not you speak
B. that why did you not speak
C. why you did not speak
D. why did you not spoke
E. No correction required

27. The chemist **hadn't hardly any of those kind** of medicines.
A. had hardly any of those kinds
B. had hardly not any of those kind
C. had scarcely any of those kind
D. had hardly any of those kind
E. No correction required

28. She cooks, washes dishes, does her homework and **then relaxing.**

A. relaxing then   B. then is relaxing
C. relaxing is then   D. then relaxes
E. No correction required

29. Anyone interested in the use of computers can learn much if **you have access** to a personal computer.
A. they have access
B. access can be available

C. he or she has access
D. one of them have access
E. No correction required

30. By such time you finish that chapter, I will write a letter.
A. The time when   B. By the time
C. By that time   D. The time
E. No correction required

Reasoning Ability

Directions (Qs. 31–35): *In each question below are three statements followed by two conclusions numbered I and II. You have to take the three given statements to be true even if they seem to be at variance from commonly known facts and then decide which of the given conclusions logically follows from the three statements disregarding commonly known facts.*

Give answer (A) if only conclusion I follows.
Give answer (B) if only conclusion II follows.
Give answer (C) if either conclusion I or conclusion II follows.
Give answer (D) if neither Conclusion I nor Conclusion II follows.
Give answer (E) if both Conclusions I and II follow.

31. Statements: All stars are planets.
               All planets are moons.
               No moon is a sun.
    Conclusions: I. All stars are suns.
               II. No moon is a star.

32. Statements: Some computers are keyboards.
               Some keyboards are wires.
               Some wires are switches.
    Conclusions: I. Some computers are switches.
               II. Some wires are computers.

33. Statements: No cap is a hat.
               All hats are feather.
               All feathers are papers.
    Conclusions: I. All hats are papers.
               II. All feathers are caps.

34. Statements: All nylons are cottons.
               All cottons are wools.
               Some wools are polyesters.

    Conclusions: I. Some cottons are polyesters.
               II. Some wools are nylons.

35. Statements: All calculators are watches.
               All phones are watches.
               All watches are televisions.
    Conclusions: I. All phones are televisions.
               II. Some televisions are calculators.

Directions (Qs. 36–40): *Study the following information carefully and answer the questions given below:*

P, Q, R, S, T, V, W and Z are sitting around a circle facing the center. T is third to the left of Z who is third to the left of P. S is third to the right of P and fourth to the left of Q. R is second to the right of V.

36. What is R's position with respect to T?
A. Third to the left   B. Fifth to the right
C. Third to the right   D. Fifth to the left
E. Fourth to the left

37. In which of the following pairs is the first person sitting to the immediate right of the second person?
A. TS   B. PW
C. QP   D. VS
E. RQ

38. Who is fourth to the right of V?
A. Q   B. W
C. R   D. Data inadequate
E. None of these

39. Who is to the immediate right of P?
A. W   B. T

C. Q   D. Data inadequate
E. None of these

40. Who is second to the right of S?
A. V   B. Z
C. R   D. W
E. Data inadequate

Directions (Qs. 41 & 42) : *Following questions are based on the five three digit numbers given below:*

473 169 825 692 538

41. If the positions of the first and the third digits of each of the numbers are interchanged, in how many numbers thus formed will the third digit be a perfect square? ('1' is also a perfect square.)
A. None   B. One
C. Two   D. Three
E. Four

42. What will be the resultant if second digit of the lowest number is divided by the second digit of the highest number?
A. 4   B. 2.5
C. 1   D. 5
E. 3

Directions (Qs. 43 – 46) : *In the following diagram*

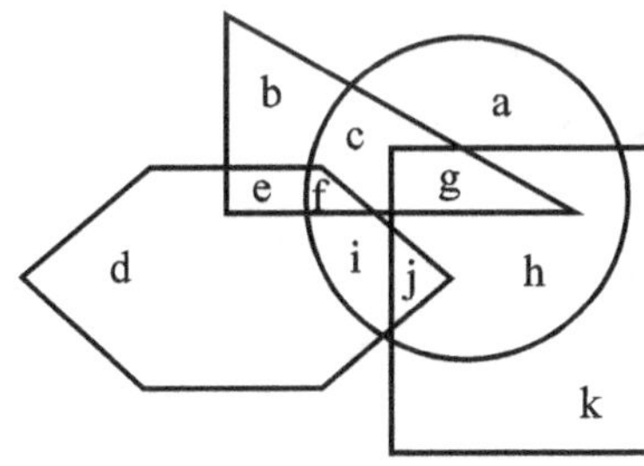

The Circle represents players
The Triangle represents outdoor games
The Hexagon represents indoor games and
The Square represents national level players
Study the diagram and answer the questions given below :

43. The letter in the section representing the players who play indoor games at national level is :
A. f   B. i
C. j   D. g
E. h

44. The letter representing the section of outdoor as well as indoor game players who do not play at the national level is :
A. c   B. f
C. e   D. i
E. k

45. The section representing national level players who do not play either outdoor or indoor games but still come under the category of players is :
A. k   B. g
C. c   D. h
E. a

46. Persons who play outdoor games but do not come under the category of players are represented in the section marked :
A. b   B. c
C. a   D. d
E. e

Directions (47-51): *In each question below is given a group of letters followed by five combinations of number/symbol codes numbered A, B, C, D and E. You have to find out which of the combinations correctly represents the group of letters based on the following coding system and the conditions and mark the number of that combination as your answer.*

Letters : F I H U T K A C W R M E Q B P
Number/ % 6 # 5 @ 7 3 ★ β 8 $ 2 © 9 4
Symbol Code :

Conditions :   (*i*) If both the third and the fourth elements are consonants, both these are to be coded as the code for the third element.

     (*ii*) If the third element is a vowel and the fourth a consonant, the codes for both these are to be interchanged.

     (*iii*) If both the second and the fifth elements are vowels, the second element is to be coded as' =

47. WKAECT
A. β723★@   B. β722★@
C. β7★32@   D. β=32★@
E. β732★@

48. TQAPHF
   A. @©34#%   B. @©#3#%
   C. @©43#%   D. @©43%#
   E. @43#©%

49. EUCMFK
   A. 25★★%7   B. 25★★7%
   C. 25$★%7   D. 25$$%7
   E. 2%5★★7

50. AQHRIM
   A. 3©##6$ B. 3©##$6
   C. 3©8#6$ D. 3= #86$
   E. 3##6©$

51. TIREUB
   A. @=8529   B. @=8259
   C. @68529   D. @=8859
   E. @=8952

52. Town R is towards East of town H and is towards South of town K. Town K is towards which direction of town H?
   A. South-East   B. South-West
   C. North-West   D. Data inadequate
   E. None of these

53. Suresh walked 30 metres towards North, took a left turn and walked 40 metres. He again took a left turn and walked 30 metres. How far is he from the starting point?
   A. 100 metres   B. 60 metres
   C. 70 metres   D. 40 metres
   E. Data inadequate

54. In a certain code SUBJECT is written as 'ATRIUDF'. How is ORDINAL written in that code?
   A. CQNHMBO   B. CQNHBMO
   C. NQCHMBO   D. ESPHMBO
   E. None of these

55. Complete the series

   1, 2, 2, 4, 16, ?, 65536
   A. 276   B. 64
   C. 256   D. 198
   E. None of these

56. Sushma is richer than Rashmi whereas Anand is richer than Priya. Arun is as rich as Rashmi. Shoba is richer than Sushma.
   Which of the following statements is correct according to the above propositions?

   A. Rashmi is poorer than Priya.
   B. Priya is richer than Arun
   C. Arun is poorer than Sushma.
   D. Anand is richer than Rashmi
   E. None of these

Directions (Qs. 57–60) : *Read the following directions and answer the questions given below :*

There are five books, out of which two books are on gardening, two on cookery and one on photography. Three of the books are in red cover and two in blue. There is a red cover on the photography book but not on the cookery book. There is no blue cover on the gardening books. B is a book on cookery, D on photography and E on gardening. C and D are not the books on gardening.

57. Which of the following books is in red cover and deals with gardening?
   A. E   B. C
   C. B   D. D
   E. None of the above

58. Which of the following books are in red cover and neither deals with cookery nor photography?
   A. B and C   B. A and E
   C. D and E   D. D and C
   E. None of the above

59. Which of the following are not the books on gardening?
   A. A and D   B. E and C
   C. B and D   D. E and D
   E. None of the above

60. Blue cover is not on the book dealing with the subject:
   A. Cookery   B. Gardening
   C. Photography   D. Both B and C
   E. None of the above

Directions (Qs. 61–65): *Each of the questions below consists of a question and two statements numbered I and II given below it. You have to decide whether the data provided in the statements are sufficient to answer the question. Read both the statements and*
_____

Give answer (A) if the data in statement **I alone** are sufficient to answer the question, while the data in statement **II alone** are not sufficient to answer the question.

Give answer (B) if the data in statement II alone are sufficient to answer the question, while the data in statement I alone are not sufficient to answer the question.

Give answer (C) if the data **either** in statement I alone or in statement II alone are sufficient to answer the question.

Give answer (D) if the data **given** in both the statements I & II together are **not** sufficient to answer the question, and

Give answer (E) if the data **given** in **both** the statements I & II together are necessary to answer the question.

61. Who among P, Q, R, S and T, each having a different age, is definitely the youngest?
  I. R is younger than only T and P.
  II. Q is younger than T but not the youngest.

62. Towards which direction was Q facing after he stopped walking?
  I. Q walked 30 metres towards West, took a left turn and walked 20 metres. He again took a left turn and stopped after walking 30 metres.
  II. Q walked 30 metres towards East, took a right turn and walked 20 metres and he took a left turn and stopped after walking 30 metres.

63. How is 'always' written in a code language?
  I. 'rain is always good' is written as '5 3 9 7' in that code language.
  II. 'he is always there' is written as '3 6 8 5' in that code language.

64. How is M related to D?
  I. M has only one son and two daughters.
  II. D's brother is son of M's wife.

65. On which date in April is definitely Pravin's mother's birthday?
  I. Pravin correctly remembers that his mother's birthday is after fourteenth but before nineteenth of April.
  II. Pravin's sister correctly remembers that their mother's birthday is after sixteenth but before twenty-first of April.

Quantitative Aptitude

Directions (Qs. 66–80): *What should come in place of the question mark (?) in the following questions?*

66. $630 \div 18 \div 5 = ?$
  A. 7 B. 14
  C. 10 D. 175
  E. None of these

67. $12\dfrac{3}{5} + 4\dfrac{1}{5} \times 3\dfrac{2}{3} = ?$
  A. $28\dfrac{1}{2}$ B. $27\dfrac{2}{15}$
  C. 28 D. $26\dfrac{7}{15}$
  E. None of these

68. $\dfrac{2}{5}$ of $\dfrac{3}{4}$ of $\dfrac{5}{8}$ of $480 = ?$
  A. 90 B. 120
  C. 240 D. 180
  E. None of these

69. $8934 - 3257 + 481 = ? + 2578$
  A. 6158 B. 3580
  C. 3040 D. 3400
  E. None of these

70. $8424 \div 135 \times 6 = ?$
  A. 124.8 B. 249.6
  C. 374.4 D. 274.4
  E. None of these

71. $12 \times 3.5 - 8.5 \times 3.2 = ?$
  A. 14.8 B. 18.4
  C. 69.2 D. 16.8
  E. None of these

72. $23.56 + 134.44 + 4142.25 = ?$
  A. 4302.25 B. 4300.75
  C. 4301.25 D. 4300.25
  E. None of these

73. 35% of 430 + ?% of 360 = 276.5
   A. 30   B. 25
   C. 45   D. 15
   E. None of these

74. $\dfrac{5}{9}$ of 567 + $\dfrac{3}{5}$ of 485 = ?

   A. 24   B. 606
   C. 480   D. 600
   E. None of these

75. 140% of 450 + 24% of 650 = ?
   A. 786   B. 474
   C. 800   D. 488
   E. None of these

76. $3\dfrac{3}{4} \times 4\dfrac{5}{6} + ? = 23\dfrac{3}{4}$

   A. $4\dfrac{5}{8}$ B. $5\dfrac{1}{2}$

   C. $5\dfrac{3}{8}$ D. $5\dfrac{5}{8}$

   E. None of these

77. $\sqrt{?} + 15^2 = 235$
   A. 10   B. 121
   C. 144   D. 100
   E. None of these

78. $\dfrac{34 \times 4 - 12 \times 8}{6^2 + \sqrt{196} + (11)^2} = ?$

   A. $\dfrac{40}{121}$ B. $\dfrac{36}{171}$

   C. $\dfrac{14}{171}$ D. $\dfrac{22}{171}$

   E. None of these

79. 2.03% of 1400 + 4.2% of 450 = ?
   A. 18.09   B. 10.33
   C. 24.42   D. 46.51
   E. None of these

80. 3960 ÷ 24 × 392 ÷ 14 = ?
   A. 4305   B. 193
   C. 4620   D. 2310
   E. None of these

Direction (Qs. 81–85): *What should come in place of the question mark (?) in the following number series?*

81. 8   39   155   464   ?
   A. 231   B. 463
   C. 1391   D. 927
   E. None of these

82. 4   5   14   51   ?
   A. 158   B. 156
   C. 260   D. 208
   E. None of these

83. 7   8   17   42   ?
   A. 67   B. 78
   C. 91   D. 106
   E. None of these

84. 5   6   15   50   ?
   A. 207   B. 157
   C. 155   D. 205
   E. None of these

85. 729   243   81   27   ?
   A. 18   B. 9
   C. 3   D. 15
   E. None of these

86. The ratio between the boys and girls in a class is 6 : 5 respectively. If 8 more boys join the class and two girls leave the class then the respective ratio becomes 11 : 7. What is the number of boys in the class now?
   A. 28   B. 38
   C. 44   D. 36
   E. None of these

87. Mohan purchased an article and sold it for ₹ 2817.50 and earned 15 per cent profit on the cost price. What was the cost price of the article?
   A. ₹ 2,500/-   B. ₹ 2,450/-
   C. ₹ 2,550/-   D. ₹ 3,315/-
   E. None of these

88. The difference between the average of three consecutive even numbers and the average of the next two consecutive even numbers is 5. What is first even number?
   A. 10
   B. 12
   C. 14

D. Cannot be determined
E. None of these

89. Cost of 24 bats and 32 sticks is ₹ 5,600/-.
What is the price of 3 bats and 4 sticks?
A. ₹ 1,400/-   B. ₹ 2,800/-
C. ₹ 700/-   D. Data inadequate
E. None of these

90. Which of the following has the fractions in descending order?

A. $\dfrac{5}{7}, \dfrac{9}{11}, \dfrac{7}{9}, \dfrac{3}{5}$ B. $\dfrac{3}{5}, \dfrac{5}{7}, \dfrac{7}{9}, \dfrac{9}{11}$

C. $\dfrac{9}{11}, \dfrac{7}{9}, \dfrac{5}{7}, \dfrac{3}{5}$ D. $\dfrac{9}{11}, \dfrac{5}{7}, \dfrac{3}{5}, \dfrac{7}{9}$

E. None of these

91. A 160 meter long train running at a speed of
90 km.ph crosses a platform in 18 seconds.
What is the length of the platform in meters?
A. 210   B. 240
C. 290   D. 310
E. None of these

92. 75% of a number is equal to four-fifth of
another number. What is the ratio between the
first number and the second number
respectively?
A. 16 : 15   B. 15 : 14
C. 5 : 6   D. 15 : 16
E. None of these

93. What will be the difference between the
compound interest and simple interest at the
rate of 5 per cent per annum on an amount of
₹ 4,000/- at the end of two years?
A. ₹ 10/-   B. ₹ 20/-
C. ₹ 25/-   D. Data inadequate
E. None of these

94. The difference between the digits of a two
digit number is 4 and the digit in the unit's
place is one-third of the digit in the tenth's
place. What is the two digit number?
A. 26   B. 31
C. 93   D. 62
E. Cannot be determined

95. The average of four consecutive even numbers
is 27. What is the highest number?
A. 32   B. 28
C. 30   D. 34
E. None of these

Directions (Qs. 96–100): *Study the following table carefully and answer the questions given below:*

NUMBER OF STUDENTS IN FIVE DISCIPLINES OF A COLLEGE OVER THE YEARS

Years \ Discipline	Arts	Science	Commerce	Management	Agriculture
2008	240	358	275	215	314
2009	260	390	286	234	365
2010	275	374	265	269	336
2011	284	368	290	255	348
2012	296	415	272	284	326
2013	312	432	364	276	383

96. In which year the percentage change in the
case of Agriculture discipline was highest from
the previous year?
A. 2009   B. 2010
C. 2011   D. 2012
E. 2013

97. What was approximate percentage increase in
the number of students in Commerce discipline
from 2010 to 2011?
A. 14   B. 18
C. 20   D. 9
E. 22

98. In which year was the difference in number of students in Arts and Science exactly 130?
   A. 2008   B. 2009
   C. 2011   D. 2013
   E. None of these

99. The total number of students in Agriculture in 2008 and 2012 together was **approximately** what per cent of number of students from the same discipline in 2009?

   A. 75   B. 165
   C. 65   D. 175
   E. 190

100. In which discipline was there a continuous increase of students over the given years?
   A. Science
   B. Agriculture
   C. Arts
   D. Commerce
   E. Management

ANSWERS

1	2	3	4	5	6	7	8	9	10
B	A	C	D	C	E	B	E	E	A
11	**12**	**13**	**14**	**15**	**16**	**17**	**18**	**19**	**20**
D	E	D	C	B	C	C	D	A	D
21	**22**	**23**	**24**	**25**	**26**	**27**	**28**	**29**	**30**
C	C	E	A	A	C	A	D	C	B
31	**32**	**33**	**34**	**35**	**36**	**37**	**38**	**39**	**40**
D	D	A	B	E	E	D	E	A	B
41	**42**	**43**	**44**	**45**	**46**	**47**	**48**	**49**	**50**
C	E	C	B	D	A	E	C	A	A
51	**52**	**53**	**54**	**55**	**56**	**57**	**58**	**59**	**60**
B	E	D	A	C	C	A	B	C	D
61	**62**	**63**	**64**	**65**	**66**	**67**	**68**	**69**	**70**
E	C	D	B	D	A	C	A	B	C
71	**72**	**73**	**74**	**75**	**76**	**77**	**78**	**79**	**80**
A	D	E	B	A	D	D	E	E	C
81	**82**	**83**	**84**	**85**	**86**	**87**	**88**	**89**	**90**
D	E	C	A	B	D	B	D	C	C
91	**92**	**93**	**94**	**95**	**96**	**97**	**98**	**99**	**100**
C	A	A	D	C	E	D	B	D	C

Some Selected Explanatory Answers

34. All nylongs are cotton.

All cottons are wool.

A + A

$\Rightarrow$ A type conclusion
"All nylons are wool."
Conclusion II is its converse.

35. All Phones are watches.

All watches are Television.

A + A

$\Rightarrow$ A type conclusion.
"All phones are television."
This is conclusion I.

All calculators are watches

All watches are Television.

A + A

$\Rightarrow$ A type conclusion.
"All calculators are television."
Conclusion II is its converse.

For Qs. (36-40) : Sitting arrangement

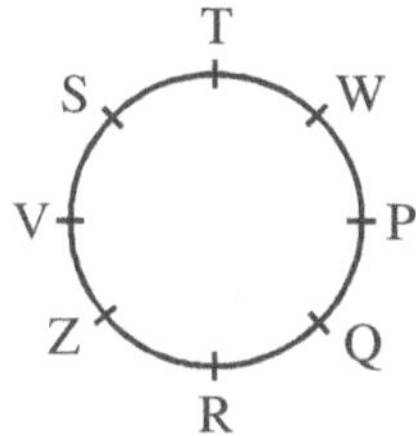

36. R is fourth the left of T.

37. V is just right of S.

38. P is fourth to the right of V.

39. W is the immidate right of P.

40. Z is second to the right of S.

41. In the given arrangement, look for first digits that are perfect squares.

42. 169 is the lowest and 825 the highest.
Now, 6 ÷ 2 = 3.

For Qs. (43-46)

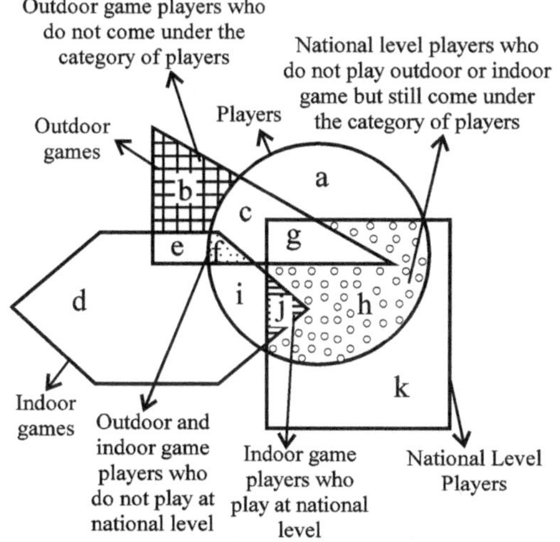

52.

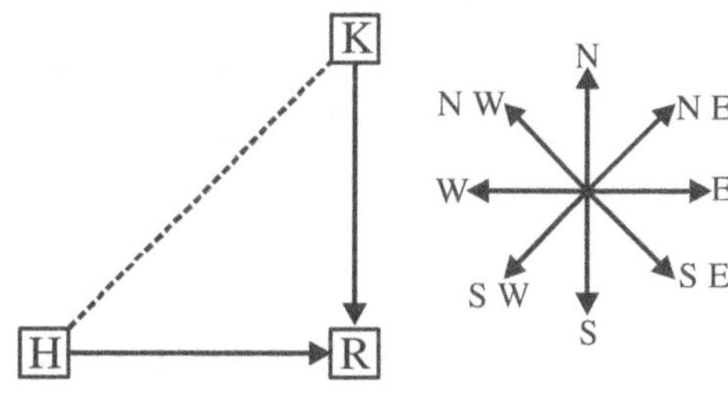

Town K, is in the NE of town H.

53.

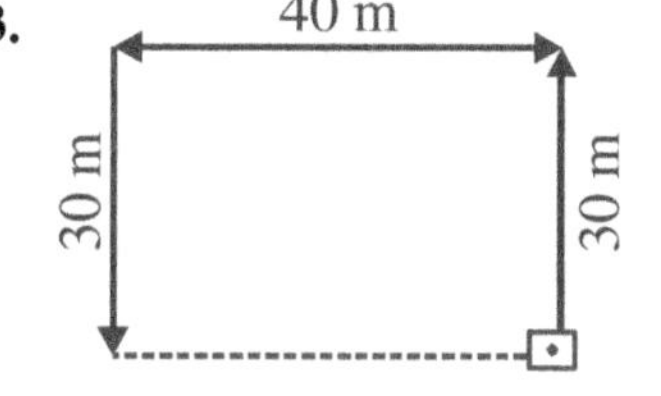

54.

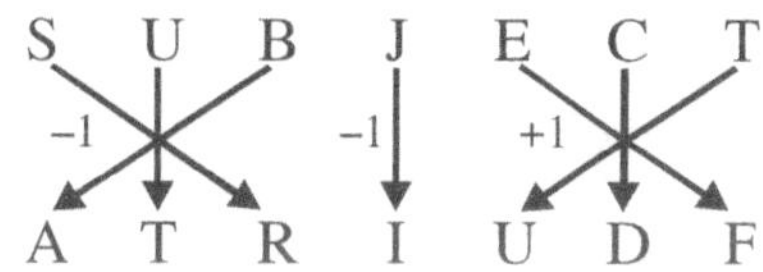

Similarly,

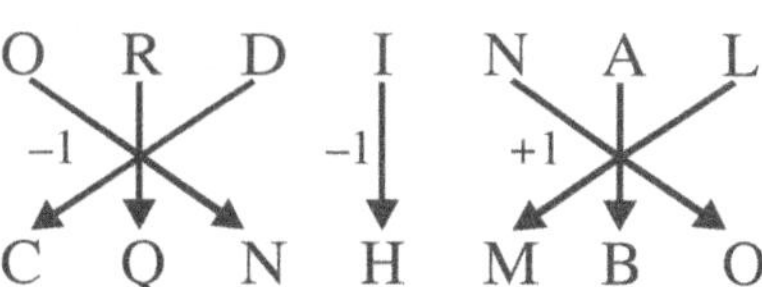

55. The number in the series is product of all the numbers preceding it.

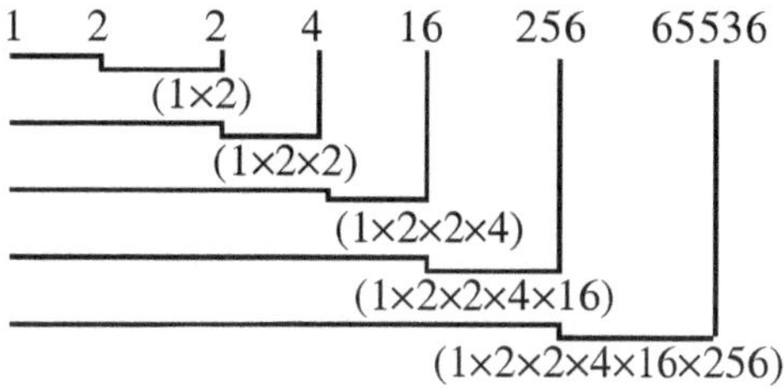

56. On the basis of wealth, the descending order will be :
1. Shobha, Sushma, Rashmi/Arun
2. Anand, *and* Priya
(The two statements are not inter-related.)

For Answers 57 to 60 the information chart will be:

Books	Cover colour	Subject
A	Red	Gardening
B	Blue	Cookery
C	Blue	Cookery
D	Red	Photography
E	Red	Gardening

61. From both the statements,

T P R Q S

62. From statement I,

Q was facing towards East.

From statement II,

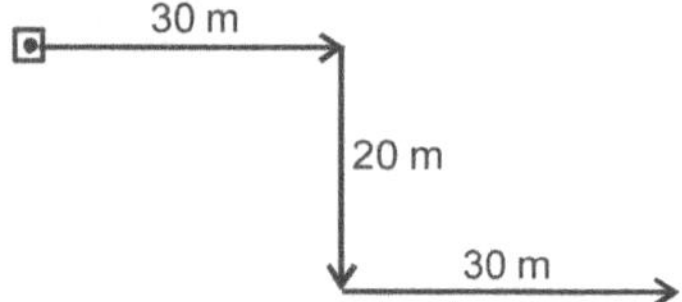

Q was facing towards East.

63. From both the statements

rain is always good → 5 3 9 7

he is always there → 3 6 8 5

64. From statement II,
M is father of D.

65. From both the statements,
According to Pravin, the birthday of his mother ⇒ 15th, 16th, 17th or 18th April
According to his sister, the birthday of Pravin's mother ⇒ 17th, 18th, 19th or 20th April.

66. $? = 630 \times \dfrac{1}{18} \times \dfrac{1}{5} = 7$

67. $? = \dfrac{63}{5} + \dfrac{21}{5} \times \dfrac{11}{3} = \dfrac{63}{5} + \dfrac{77}{5} = \dfrac{140}{5} = 28$

68. $? = \dfrac{2}{5} \times \dfrac{3}{4} \times \dfrac{5}{8} \times 480 = 90$

69. $? = 8934 - 3257 + 481 - 2578$
$= 9415 - 5835 = 3580$

70. $? = 8424 \times \dfrac{1}{135} \times 6 = \dfrac{1872}{5} = 374.5$

71. $? = 12 \times 3.5 - 8.5 \times 3.2$
$= 42 - 27.2$
$= 14.8$

72. $? = 23.56 + 134.44 + 4142.25$
$= 4300.25$

73. $\dfrac{?}{100} \times 360 = 276.5 - \dfrac{35}{100} \times 430$

$\Rightarrow ? \times \dfrac{18}{5} = 276.5 - 150.5$

$\Rightarrow ? = \dfrac{126 \times 5}{18} = 35$

74. $? = \dfrac{5}{9} \times 567 + \dfrac{3}{5} \times 485$
$= 315 + 291 = 606$

75. $? = \dfrac{140}{100} \times 450 + \dfrac{24}{100} \times 650$
$= 630 + 156 = 786$

76. $\dfrac{15}{4} \times \dfrac{29}{6} + ? = \dfrac{95}{4}$

$\Rightarrow ? = \dfrac{95}{4} - \dfrac{145}{8} = \dfrac{45}{8} = 5\dfrac{5}{8}$

77. $\sqrt{?} + 15^2 = 235$

$\Rightarrow \sqrt{?} = 235 - 225$
$\Rightarrow ? = (10)^2 = 100$

78. $? = \dfrac{34 \times 4 - 12 \times 8}{6^2 + \sqrt{196} + 11^2} = \dfrac{136 - 96}{36 + 14 + 121} = \dfrac{40}{171}$

79. $? = \dfrac{2.03}{100} \times 1400 + \dfrac{4.2}{100} \times 450$
$= 28.42 + 18.9 = 47.32$

80. $? = 3960 \times \dfrac{1}{24} \times 392 \times \dfrac{1}{14} = 165 \times 28 = 4620$

81.
$$\underset{8}{\Big|} \xrightarrow{\times 5-1} \underset{39}{\Big|} \xrightarrow{\times 4-1} \underset{155}{\Big|} \xrightarrow{\times 3-1} \underset{464}{\Big|} \xrightarrow{\times 2-1} \underset{?}{}$$

Thus, $? = 464 \times 2 - 1 = 928 - 1 = 927$

83.
$$\underset{7}{\Big|} \xrightarrow{+1^2} \underset{8}{\Big|} \xrightarrow{+3^2} \underset{17}{\Big|} \xrightarrow{+5^2} \underset{42}{\Big|} \xrightarrow{+7^2} \underset{?}{}$$

Thus, $? = 42 + 7^2 = 42 + 49 = 91$

85.
$$\underset{729}{\Big|} \xrightarrow{\div 3} \underset{243}{\Big|} \xrightarrow{\div 3} \underset{81}{\Big|} \xrightarrow{\div 3} \underset{27}{\Big|} \xrightarrow{\div 3} \underset{?}{}$$

Thus, $? = 27 \div 3 = 9$

86. Let, number of boys and girls be $6x$ and $5x$ respectively

Then, $\dfrac{6x+8}{5x-2} = \dfrac{11}{7}$

$\Rightarrow 42x + 56 = 55x - 22$

$\Rightarrow \qquad 13x = 78$

$\Rightarrow \qquad\quad x = 6$

Thus, number of boys in the class
$$= 6x = 6 \times 6 = 36$$

87. Cost price $= \dfrac{100}{115} \times 2817.50 = ₹\, 2450$

89. Cost of 3 bats and 4 sticks $= \dfrac{1}{8} \times ₹\, 5600$
$$= ₹\, 700$$

90. $\dfrac{5}{7} = 0.\overline{714285},\ \dfrac{9}{11} = 0.\overline{81},\ \dfrac{7}{9} = 0.\overline{7},\ \dfrac{3}{5} = 0.6$

Thus, their descending order will be
$$\dfrac{9}{11}, \dfrac{7}{9}, \dfrac{5}{7}, \dfrac{3}{5}$$

91. 90 km/hr $= 90 \times \dfrac{5}{18} = 25$ m/s

Length of the platform $= 25 \times 18 - 160$
$$= 450 - 160 = 290 \text{ m}$$

92. Let, two number be x and y,

Then, $\dfrac{75}{100} \times x = \dfrac{4}{5} \times y \Rightarrow \dfrac{x}{y} = \dfrac{4}{5} \times \dfrac{4}{3} = \dfrac{16}{15}$

Thus, $x : y = 16 : 15$

93. Required difference
$$= 4000\left[\left(1 + \dfrac{5}{100}\right)^2 - 1\right] - \dfrac{4000 \times 5 \times 2}{100}$$
$$= 4000 \times \dfrac{41}{100} - 400$$
$$= 410 - 400 = ₹\, 10$$

94. Let digit at the tenth's place and unit place be $3x$ and x respectively, then number will be
$10 \times 3x + x = 31x$
Now, $3x - x = 4 \quad \Rightarrow 2x = 4 \quad \Rightarrow x = 2$
Thus, two digit number $= 31 \times 2 = 62$

95. Let, the four consecutive even numbers be
$x, (x + 2), (x + 4)$ and $(x + 6)$ respectively, then
$x + x + 2 + x + 4 + x + 6 = 108$
$\Rightarrow 4x + 12 = 108$
$\Rightarrow 4x = 96$
$\Rightarrow x = 24$
Thus, highest number $= x + 6 = 24 + 6 = 30$

96. In 2013 percentage change
$$= \dfrac{383 - 326}{326} \times 100 = \dfrac{5700}{326} = 17.48\%,$$
which is highest.

97. Required percentage increase
$$= \dfrac{290 - 265}{265} = \dfrac{25}{265} \times 100 = \dfrac{500}{53} \approx 9\%$$

98. In 2009, required difference $= 390 - 260$
$$= 130$$

99. Required percentage
$$= \dfrac{(314 + 326)}{365} \times 100 = \dfrac{640}{365} \times 100 \approx 175\%$$

SBI Junior Associates & Junior Agricultural Associates
(Clerical Cadre Exam)

General English

Directions (Qs. 1–15): *Read the following passage carefully and answer the questions given below it. Certain words/phrases have been printed in **bold** to help you locate them while answering some of the questions.*

The Chinese have a **way** of giving a name to every new year, like the 'Year of the Dog.' In our country, each year according to the Tamil calendar gets a name. 1994 was called **Yuva Varsha** or the year of the youth. That brings us to our mind the Year of the Child. That description was given to 1979 by the United Nations (UN) which, too, baptises each year. Last year, it was the Year of the Family; 1995 was the Year of Tolerance.

In 1979, the UN urged every member-country to plan programmes for the welfare of children. In **subsequent** years, they formulated the Rights of the Child and held a World Conference of Children. By calling 1994 the Year of the Family, the United Nations stressed the importance of family ties which are safeguarded by **affection**, regard, and respect for each other among the several members of the family. Bhagavat Gita says: "Every person should be equally disposed towards friends and foes, towards the indifferent and the hateful, towards the righteous and unrighteous." This is **Tolerance**. The Gita calls such persons, who are tolerant of others, as "leaders whose perfect actions are worth **emulating**."

When differences of opinion occur, one is **often** advised to step into the other person's shoes and evaluate the problem from the other person's point of view. One need not even then agree to those views because of personal reasons, but tolerance will help him accept the right of the other to hold a different view.

Mahatma Gandhi would characterise religion as a way to attain 'Self-knowledge' or 'Self-realisation.' He once said: "I look at all religions with equanimity, because they speak the same truth." Among all acts of human behaviour, religious tolerance **assumes** the greatest importance.

1. Programmes of children welfare were planned as a result of the
   A. UN's celebration of the year of the family
   B. UN's appeal to the member countries
   C. Sacred teaching of the 'Bhagawat Gita'
   D. Lessons of tolerance
   E. None of these

2. How according to the passage should differences of opinion be resolved?
   A. By sticking firmly to one's own opinion
   B. By not agreeing to the view of others
   C. By requesting the other person to step in your shoes
   D. By judging the issues from the other person's view point
   E. None of these

3. For accepting the right of others to hold a different view point, one needs to have
   A. personal reason
   B. individual view point
   C. ability to evaluate
   D. an ability to achieve perfection
   E. tolerance

4. The Chinese and the United Nations have one-thing in common that both of them.....
   A. celebrated *Yuva Varsha*
   B. celebrated Gandhiji's birth anniversary
   C. have been working for world peace
   D. give some name to each year
   E. follow the Tamil calendar

5. The idea of celebrating the 'Year of the Child' was derived from the
   A. year of the youth
   B. Chinese way of giving names
   C. United Nations' scheme
   D. year of the family
   E. year of dog

6. What is the role of family ties in the society?
   A. They hinder the spirit of tolerance
   B. They teach us to be courteous to our enemies also
   C. They inculcate in us the spirit of Gita
   D. They teach us to attain perfection in action
   E. None of these

7. Which of the following statement(s) (1), (2) and/or (3) are True in the context of the passage?
   1. Speaking the same truth, according to Gandhiji, is the common factor among all religions
   2. United Nations gives names to years as per the Tamil calendar
   3. Evaluating problems from other person's view point is termed as tolerance
   A. Only (1)   B. Only (2)
   C. Only (1) and (2)   D. Only (2) and (3)
   E. None of these

8. Which of the following can be considered as 'Tolerance' as described in the passage?
   A. Affinity for friends and close associates
   B. Ability to differentiate between friends and foes
   C. Balanced and unbiased attitude towards everybody
   D. Ability to differentiate between right and wrong actions
   E. None of these

9. Which of the following statements (1), (2) and/or (3) is/are False in the context of the passage?
   1. According to Gita, persons whose actions are imitated by others are called tolerant persons
   2. The world conference of children was held with the initiative of China
   3. Religious tolerance is considered to be the most imprtant virtue
   A. All the three are false
   B. Only (1) and (2) are false
   C. Only (2) and (3) are false
   D. Only (3) is false
   E. Only (2) is false

Directions (Qs. 10–12): *Choose the word which is most OPPOSITE in meaning as the word given in **bold** capitals as used in the passage.*

10. OFTEN
   A. never   B. seldom
   C. always   D. frequent
   E. exceptional

11. SUBSEQUENT
   A. preceding   B. following
   C. current   D. future
   E. olden

12. AFFECTION
   A. love   B. jealous
   C. hatred   D. dissatisfaction
   E. expulsion

Directions (Qs. 13–15): *Choose the word which is most nearly the SAME in meaning as the word given in bold capitals as used in the passage.*

13. WAY
   A. road   B. manner
   C. hierarchy   D. mode
   E. system

14. ASSUMES
   A. imagines   B. loses
   C. expects   D. acquires
   E. insists

15. EMULATING
   A. criticising   B. codemning
   C. imitating   D. neglecting
   E. accepting

Directions (Qs. 16–20): *Read each sentence to find out whether there is any grammatical error or idiomatic error in it. The error, if any, will be in one part of the sentence. The number of that part* *is the answer. If there is "No Error" the answer is 'E'. (Ignore errors of punctuation if any.)*

16. (A) The Trust has succeeded/(B) admirably in raising/(C) money for/(D) its future programmes./(E) No error.

17. (A) Honesty, integrity and being intelligent/(B) are the qualities which/(C) we look for when/(D) we interview applicants./(E) No error.

18. (A) In order to save petrol,/(B) motorists must have to/(C) be very cautious/(D) while driving along the highways./(E) No error.

19. (A) The committee is thankful to Shri Desai/(B) for preparing not only the main report/(C) but also for preparing/(D) the agenda notes and minutes./(E) No error.

20. (A) All of you will agree with me/(B) that no problem faced by our society/(C) is as grave and intractable/(D) as this problem is./(E) No error.

Directions (Qs. 21–30) : *In the following passage there are blanks, each of which has been numbered. These numbers are printed below the passage, against each, five words are suggested, one of which fits the blank appropriately. Find out the appropriate word in each case.*

In the earlier days, some long distance trains were ..... **(21)** ..... more number of compartments, thus making the train ..... **(22)** ..... than even the length of the platforms. Therefore, the last compartment usually ..... **(23)** ..... outside the platform. Once a person travelling in the last compartment of such a train could not ..... **(24)** ..... tea, coffee, snacks or water as he failed to ..... **(25)** ..... on the platform. He remained hungry and thirsty throughout his ..... **(26)** ..... . On reaching his destination, he ..... **(27)** ..... a

written complaint in which he appealed, ... **(28)** ..... long distance train should ever have any last compartment. If at all, last compartment cannot be ..... **(29)** ..... it should be placed somewhere in the ..... **(30)** ....

21. A. attaching   B. shunting
C. travelling   D. manufacturing
E. having

22. A. bigger   B. longer
C. heavier   D. crowded
E. shorter

23. A. crowded   B. vacated
C. halted   D. derailed
E. collapsed

24. A. get   B. offer
C. eat   D. drink
E. sell

25. A. walk   B. run
C. wait   D. alight
E. stand

26. A. days   B. compartment
C. life   D. train
E. journey

27. A. wrote   B. submitted
C. alleged   D. withdrew
E. received

28. A. No   B. Each
C. Every   D. Any
E. Only

29. A. stopped   B. connected
C. attached   D. avoided
E. removed

30. A. wagon   B. station
C. middle   D. end
E. yard

Reasoning Ability

Directions (Q. 31–36): *In each of the questions below are given three statements followed by two conclusions numbered I & II. You have to take the given statements to be true even if they seem to be at variance from commonly known facts. Read all the conclusions and then decide which of the given conclusions logically follows from the given statements disregarding commonly known facts.*

Give answer (A) if only conclusion I follows.
Give answer (B) if only conclusion II follows.

Give answer (C) if either I or II follows.
Give answer (D) if neither I nor II follows.
Give answer (E) if both I and II follow.

31. Statements : All jugs are plates. All plates are cups. All cups are bottles.

Conclusions : I. Some bottles are jugs.
II. All plates are bottles.

32. Statements : Some jungles are mirrors. All mirrors are houses. All houses are roads.

Conclusions : I. All jungles are roads.
II. All jungles are houses.

33. Statements : All pigeons are trees. Some trees are channels. All channels are baskets.

Conclusions : I. Some baskets are trees.
II. Some channels are pigeons.

34. Statements : Some tents are ropes. All ropes are lanterns. Some lanterns are boxes.

Conclusions : I. Some boxes are tents.
II. Some lanterns are tents.

35. Statements : Some bags are clothes. Some clothes are papers. Some papers are glasses.

Conclusions : I. Some glasses are bags.
II. No glass is bag.

36. Statements : Some chains are trucks. No truck is car. All cars are trains.

Conclusions : I. Some trains are trucks.
II. Some cars are chains.

Directions (Qs. 37–41): *Read the following information to answer the questions given below :*

(*i*) Five friends A, B, C, D and E wore shirts of green, yellow, pink, red and blue colours and shorts of black, white, grey, blue and green colours.

(*ii*) Nobody wore shirt and short of same colour.

(*iii*) D wore blue shirt and C wore green short.

(*iv*) The one who wore green shirt, wore black short and the one who wore blue short, wore red shirt.

(*v*) A wore white short and pink shirt.

(*vi*) E did not wear red shirt.

37. What was the colour combination of D's shirt and short?
A. Green and black   B. Red and blue
C. Blue and grey   D. Blue and white
E. None of these

38. Who wore black short?
A. C   B. E
C. B   D. D
E. A

39. Who wore white short?
A. E   B. Data inadequate
C. B   D. A
E. None of these

40. Which colour shirt did C wear?
A. Yellow   B. Blue
C. Green   D. Pink
E. Data inadequate

41. Which colour short did B wear?
A. Grey   B. Blue
C. White   D. Black
E. Green

Directions (Qs. 42–46): *In the following questions, the symbols @, $, ★, © and # are used with the following meaning as illustrated below:*

'P ★ Q' means 'P is neither greater than nor smaller than Q'.

'P $ Q' means 'P is neither greater than nor equal to Q'.

'P @ Q' means 'P is not smaller than Q'.

'P © Q' means 'P is not greater than Q'.

'P # Q' means 'P is neither smaller than nor equal to Q'.

Now in each of the following questions assuming the given statements to be true, find which of the three conclusions I, II and III given below them is/ are **definitely true** and give your answer accordingly.

42. Statements: F ★ R, R © M, M $ D
Conclusions: I. D # R
II. D # F
III. M @ F
A. Only I and II are true
B. Only I and III are true
C. Only II and III are true
D. All I, II and III are true
E. None of these

43. Statements: V © M, M ★ B, B $ F
Conclusions: I. F # M
II. B @ V
III. F # V
A. Only I and II are true
B. Only II and III are true

C. Only I and III are true
D. All I, II and III are true
E. None of these

44. Statements: D # N, N @ B, B ★ F
Conclusions: I. F $ D
II. N # F
III. N ★ F
A. Only I is true
B. Only II is true
C. Only III is true
D. Only either II or III is true
E. Only I and either II or III are true

45. Statements: R $ T, T # K, K @ M
Conclusions: I. R $ M
II. T # M
III. R $ K
A. None is true   B. Only I is true
C. Only II is true   D. Only III is true
E. Only II and III are true

46. Statements: H # N, N $ T, T @ B
Conclusions: I. B $ N
II. H # T
III. B $ H
A. None is true   B. Only I is true
C. Only II is true   D. Only III is true
E. Only II and III are true

47. If Δ denotes =; + denotes >, − denotes <, □ denotes ≠, × denotes ≯ and ÷ denotes ≮ then a + b − c denotes
A. b Δ c □ a   B. b □ a ÷ c
C. a ÷ b × c   D. b − a + c
E. None of these

48. In the following question which one number can be placed at the sign of interrogation?

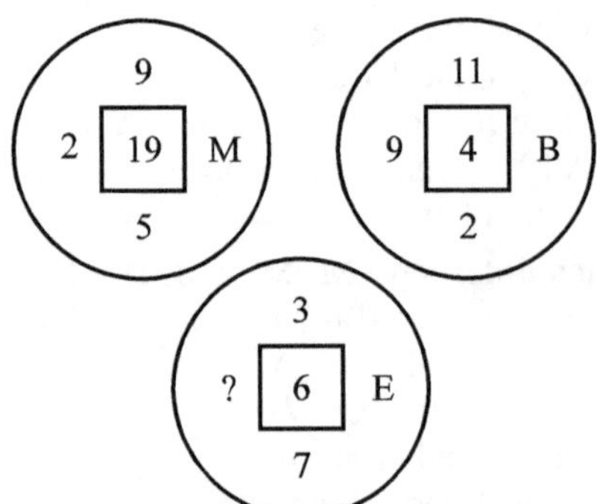

A. 1   B. 3
C. 9   D. 13
E. None of these

Directions (Qs. 49–53): *Study the following arrangement carefully and answer the questions given below:*

L 5 $ 9 N ★ S E # Q β U 6 % @ F ©
V & 8 A Z 7 K 4 W M 3 C 2

49. Four of the following five are alike in a certain way based on their positions in the above arrangement and so form a group. Which is the one that does not belong to that group?
A. %F@   B. 74K
C. 59$ D. #βQ
E. 87Z

50. How many such letters are there in the above arrangement, each of which is immediately preceded by a symbol and also followed by a symbol?
A. None
B. One
C. Two
D. Three
E. More than three

51. How many such numbers are there in the above arrangement, each of which is immediately preceded by a vowel and immediately followed by a number?
A. None   B. One
C. Two   D. Three
E. More than three

52. Which of the following is the fifth to the left of the sixteenth from the left end of the above arrangement?
A. A   B. 8
C. U   D. β
E. None of these

53. If all the numbers are dropped from the above arrangement, which of the following will be the seventh from the right end of the above arrangement?
A. A   B. &
C. V   D. #
E. Q

54. Which would be a meaningful order of the following?

1. Index   2. Contents
3. Title   4. Chapters
5. Introduction

A. 2 3 4 5 1   B. 3 2 5 4 1
C. 5 1 4 2 3   D. 3 2 5 1 4
E. 5 4 2 1 3

55. If S – T means 'S' is the wife of 'T', S + T means 'S' is the daughter of 'T' and S ÷ T means 'S' is the son of 'T'. What will M + J ÷ K mean?

A. 'K' is the father of 'M'
B. 'M' is the grand-daughter of K
C. 'J' is wife of 'K'
D. 'K' and 'M' are brothers
E. None of these

Directions (56–60): *Study the following arrangement carefully and answer the questions given below:*

1 8 5 9 4 71 2 5 8 3 6 5 9 2 7 6 4 5 2 9 2 6 4 1 2 3 5 1 4 2 8 3

56. Which of the following is fifth to the right of the twelfth digit from the right end of the above arranement?

A. 3   B. 1
C. 2   D. 7
E. None of these

57. How many 5s are there in the above arrangement, each of which is immediately followed by a digit which has a numerical value of less than five?

A. None
B. One
C. Two
D. Three
E. More than three

58. How many such 4s are there in the above arrangement each of which is immediately preceded by an even digit and also immediately followed by an odd digit?

A. None
B. One
C. Two
D. Three
E. More than three

59. If all the even digits are deleted from the above arrangement, which of the following will be seventh from the left end of the arrangement?

A. 9   B. 5
C. 1   D. 3
E. 7

60. How many such 1s are there in the above arrangement, each of which is immediately preceded by a perfect square?

A. None   B. One
C. Two   D. Three
E. More than three

Directions (Q.Nos. 61–65): *Study the following information carefully and answer the questions given below:*

P, Q, A, B, D, R and F are sitting around a circular table facing the centre. R is not second to the left of D and D is not an immediate neighbour of B. A is third to the right of F. B is second to the left of F. Q is not an immediate neighbour of B or F.

61. Who is second to the right of P?

A. R   B. Q
C. D   D. A
E. Data inadequate

62. Who is to the immediate left of F?

A. R   B. P
C. D   D. Data inadequate
E. None of these

63. Who is to the immediate right of D?

A. Q   B. A
C. F   D. P
E. None of these

64. What is D's position with respect to B?

A. Second to the right
B. Third to the left
C. Second to the left
D. Fourth to the right
E. Third to the right

65. Who is to the immediate right of Q?

A. D
B. R
C. A
D. B
E. None of these

Quantitative Aptitude

Directions (Qs. 66–70): *What will come in place of the question mark (?) in the following questions?*

66. 3.05% of 1200 + 6.4% of 800 = ?
   A. 36.6
   B. 51.2
   C. 87.8
   D. 14.6
   E. None of these

67. 14 × 4.5 – 7.4 × 3.5 = ?
   A. 44.5
   B. 35.1
   C. 88.9
   D. 37.1
   E. None of these

68. $4\dfrac{2}{5} \times 3\dfrac{1}{3} - ? = 5\dfrac{1}{3}$

   A. $8\dfrac{1}{3}$
   B. $9\dfrac{2}{3}$
   C. $6\dfrac{2}{3}$
   D. $7\dfrac{1}{3}$

   E. None of these

69. 7995 ÷ 123 ÷ 5 = ?
   A. 325
   B. 65
   C. 13
   D. 70
   E. None of these

70. 62.18 + 169.35 + 3046.81 = ?
   A. 3305.34
   B. 3277.44
   C. 3638.34
   D. 3278.44
   E. None of these

71. $\sqrt{?} + 19^2 = 21^2$
   A. 6400
   B. 4
   C. 64
   D. 16
   E. None of these

72. $6\dfrac{1}{2} + 5\dfrac{1}{4} \times 1\dfrac{3}{7} = ?$

   A. $14\dfrac{1}{5}$
   B. $13\dfrac{1}{3}$
   C. 14
   D. 15
   E. None of these

73. $\dfrac{3}{5}$ of $\dfrac{5}{7}$ of $\dfrac{2}{9}$ of 630 = ?
   A. 90
   B. 75
   C. 45
   D. 60
   E. None of these

74. 125% of 200 + 36% of 350 = ?
   A. 451
   B. 126
   C. 227
   D. 325
   E. None of these

75. $\dfrac{28 \times 5 - 14 \times 4}{8^2 + \sqrt{225} + (14)^2} = ?$

   A. $\dfrac{27}{83}$
   B. $\dfrac{84}{275}$
   C. $\dfrac{84}{285}$
   D. $\dfrac{42}{275}$
   E. None of these

76. $\dfrac{3}{7}$ of 413 + $\dfrac{2}{5}$ of 615 = ?
   A. 541
   B. 423
   C. 792
   D. 433
   E. None of these

77. 7865 – 4128 + 372 = ? + 2014
   A. 2095
   B. 2905
   C. 1915
   D. 2005
   E. None of these

78. 45% of 240 + ?% of 360 = 234
   A. 45
   B. 35
   C. 30
   D. 40
   E. None of these

79. 7986 ÷ 165 × 7 = ?
   A. 338.8
   B. 55.4
   C. 6.91
   D. 302.2
   E. None of these

80. 4495 ÷ 145 × 656 ÷ 16 = ?
   A. 1312
   B. 72
   C. 0.76
   D. 0.41
   E. None of these

Directions (Qs. 81–85): *What should come in place of the question mark (?) in the following number series?*

81. 4   6   16   54   ?
A. 280   B. 232
C. 228   D. 224
E. None of these

82. 5   39   272   1631   ?
A. 4892   B. 6523
C. 8154   D. 9785
E. None of these

83. 768   192   48   12   ?
A. 2   B. 3
C. 4   D. $\dfrac{1}{3}$
E. None of these

84. 12   16   32   68   ?
A. 84   B. 168
C. 104   D. 128
E. None of these

85. 7   15   32   67   ?
A. 138   B. 198
C. 137   D. 264
E. None of these

86. A sum of money fetches ₹ 408/- as compound interest at the rate of 4 p.c.p.a. at the end of two years. What is the sum?
A. ₹ 6,000/-
B. ₹ 5,000/-
C. ₹ 4,000/-
D. Cannot be determined
E. None of these

87. A train running at a speed of 60 kmph crosses a platform double its length in 32.4 seconds. What is the length of the platform?
A. 180 metres   B. 240 metres
C. 360 metres   D. 90 metres
E. Cannot be determined

88. Three-seventh of a number is equal to 45 per cent of another number. What is the respective ratio between the first and the second numbers?
A. 21 : 20   B. 20 : 21
C. 45 : 100   D. 45 : 300
E. None of these

89. Vishal sold an article for ₹ 1,840/- and made 15 per cent profit on the discounted price he bought. If the discount was 20 per cent, what was the original price?
A. ₹ 1,900/-
B. ₹ 1,600/-
C. ₹ 2,400/-
D. Cannot be determined
E. None of these

90. The sum of the average of three consecutive odd numbers and three consecutive even numbers is 21. If the highest even number is 16, what is the lowest odd number?
A. 5   B. 7
C. 9   D. 11
E. None of these

91. The ratio between the male and female existing employees in an organization in 7 : 3. THE RATIO between the male and female new recruits of 240 is 5 : 7. What will be new ratio between male and female employees after the recruits join the organization?
A. 6 : 5
B. 5 : 4
C. 3 : 2
D. Cannot be determined
E. None of these

92. The total cost of 45 pens and 24 pencils is ₹ 675/-. What is the total price of 8 pens and 15 pencils?
A. ₹ 225/-
B. ₹ 245/-
C. ₹ 337.5/-
D. Cannot be determined
E. None of these

93. Which of the following has the fractions in ascending order?
A. $\dfrac{2}{7}, \dfrac{3}{5}, \dfrac{5}{11}, \dfrac{6}{17}$ B. $\dfrac{2}{7}, \dfrac{6}{17}, \dfrac{5}{11}, \dfrac{3}{5}$

C. $\dfrac{6}{17}, \dfrac{2}{7}, \dfrac{5}{11}, \dfrac{3}{5}$ D. $\dfrac{2}{7}, \dfrac{6}{17}, \dfrac{3}{5}, \dfrac{5}{11}$

E. None of these

94. The average of five consecutive odd numbers is 84 per cent of the highest number. What is the sum of the first two of these numbers?
  A. 64   B. 32
  C. 36   D. 44
  E. None of these

95. Nikhil spent 45% of his monthly stipend on food and transport, 20% of the remaining on books and half of the remaining on other expenses. If he is left with ₹ 880/- now, how much is his monthly stipend?
  A. ₹ 6,000/-
  B. ₹ 4,500/-
  C. ₹ 3,000/-
  D. ₹ 3,600/-
  E. None of these

Directions (Qs. 96–100): *Study the following table carefully and answer the questions given below:*

No. of Marks obtained by Five Students in Five Subjects in an Examination
(Total marks in all the five subjects are 200)

Student \ Subject	English	Mathematics	History	Geography	Science
A	115	180	120	90	140
B	170	105	150	135	100
C	102	108	132	110	90
D	98	106	162	148	120
E	163	125	136	124	115

96. The total marks obtained by B in English and History together was **approximately** what percentage of marks obtained by E in English?
  A. 150   B. 100
  C. 200   D. 250
  E. 175

97. Marks obtained by C in History was **approximately** what percentage of marks obtained by A in Geography?
  A. 167   B. 67
  C. 133   D. 33
  E. 150

98. Who among them secured highest total marks in English, History and Geography?
  A. A   B. B
  C. C   D. D
  E. E

99. If the minimum pass percentage is 50 in each subject to be declared pass in the examination, how many of them failed in the examination?
  A. None   B. 2
  C. 1   C. 3
  E. 4

100. Who among them secured highest total percentage of marks?
  A. A   B. B
  C. C   D. D
  E. E

ANSWERS

1	2	3	4	5	6	7	8	9	10
B	D	E	D	B	C	A	C	B	A

11	12	13	14	15	16	17	18	19	20
A	C	E	D	C	E	A	B	C	B

21	22	23	24	25	26	27	28	29	30
E	B	C	A	D	E	B	A	D	C

31	32	33	34	35	36	37	38	39	40
E	D	A	B	C	D	C	B	D	A
41	42	43	44	45	46	47	48	49	50
B	D	D	E	C	A	D	B	E	D
51	52	53	54	55	56	57	58	59	60
A	D	B	B	B	A	C	C	D	B
61	62	63	64	65	66	67	68	69	70
C	B	A	E	C	C	D	E	C	E
71	72	73	74	75	76	77	78	79	80
A	C	D	E	B	B	A	B	A	E
81	82	83	84	85	86	87	88	89	90
D	C	B	E	A	B	C	E	E	A
91	92	93	94	95	96	97	98	99	100
D	D	B	C	E	C	E	B	D	E

Some Selected Explanatory Answers

Chart for Answers 37 to 41

Friend	*Shirt*	*Short*
A	Pink	White
B	Red	Blue
C	Yellow	Green
D	Blue	Grey
E	Green	Black

42.

$$F \star R - F = R$$
$$R © M - R \leq M$$

and $M \, \$ \, D - M < D$

∴ $F = R \leq M < D$

I. $D \# R \to D > R$ (True)

II. $D \# F \to D > F$ (True)

III. $M @ F \to M \geq F$ (True)

46.

$$H \# N - H > N$$
$$N \, \$ \, T - N < T$$

and $T @ B - T \geq B$

∴ $H > N < T \geq B$

I. $B \, \$ \, N \to B < N$ (False)

II. $H \# T \to H > T$ (False)

III. $B \, \$ \, H \to B < H$ (False)

47. What is given is $a > b < c$

The equations are :

A. $b = c \neq a$ which is wrong

B. $b \neq a < c$ which is wrong

C. $a \not< b \not> c$ which is wrong

D. $b < a > c$ which is correct

Therefore, 'D' is the answer.

48. Letter M is 13th in order of aphabetical series. So 13 (= M) × 2 (number on the opposite side) = 9 × 5 (product of numbers above and below the square) – 19 (number inside the square) *i.e.*

$$13 \times 2 = (9 \times 5) - 19$$
$$26 = (45 - 19)$$
$$26 = 26$$

Letter B is 2nd in order, so

$$2 \times 9 = (11 \times 2) - 4$$
$$18 = 22 - 4$$
$$18 = 18$$

Similarly, letter E is 5th in order

$$5 \times ? = (3 \times 7) - 6$$
$$5 \times ? = 21 - 6$$
$$5 \times ? = 15$$
$$? = 15 \div 5 = 3$$

49.

$$\% \xrightarrow{+2} F \xrightarrow{-1} @$$
$$7 \xrightarrow{+2} 4 \xrightarrow{-1} K$$
$$5 \xrightarrow{+2} 9 \xrightarrow{-1} S$$
$$\# \xrightarrow{+2} \beta \xrightarrow{-1} Q$$
$$8 \xrightarrow{-3} 7 \xrightarrow{-1} Z$$

54. A Title comprises Contents of Introduction for Chapter Index.

55. M + J means 'M' is the daughter of 'J'. J ÷ K means 'J' is the son of 'K'

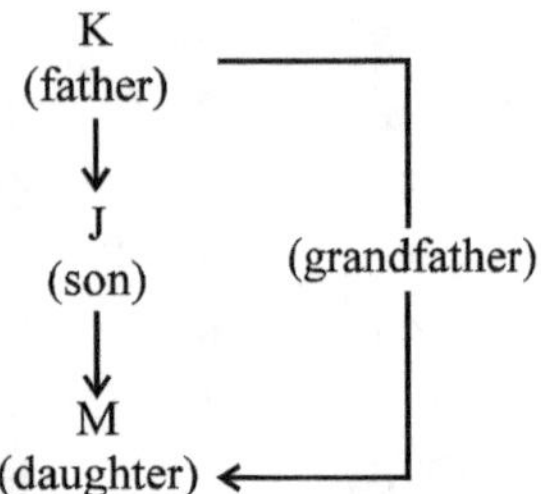

56. 12th digit from right will be 2 and 5th digit from 2 in right will be 3.

57. Combination $\boxed{4 \;|\; 5 \;|\; 2}$ and $\boxed{3 \;|\; 4 \;|\; 1}$

58. Required $\boxed{6 \;|\; 4 \;|\; 5}$ and $\boxed{6 \;|\; 4 \;|\; 1}$

59. New Combination is
1 5 9 7 1 5 3 5 9 7 5 9 1 3 5 1 3
Seventh digit from left is 3.

60. $\boxed{4 \;|\; 1 \;|\; 2}$

61-65.

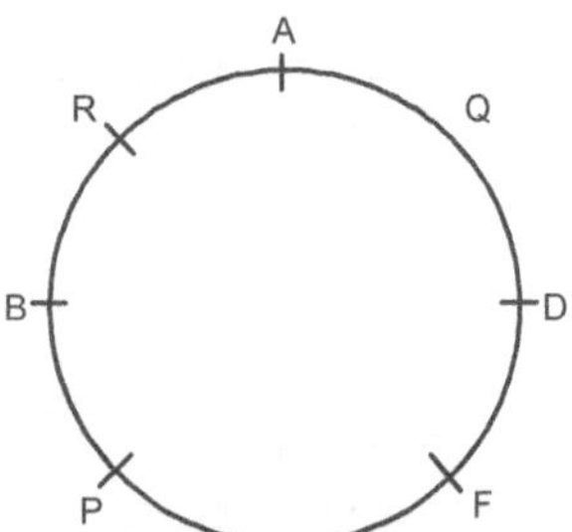

61. D is second to the right of P.
62. P is to the immediate left of F.
63. Q is to the immediate right of D.
64. D is third to the right of B. D is fourth to the left of B.
65. A is to the immediate right of Q.

66. $? = \dfrac{3.05}{100} \times 1200 + \dfrac{6.4}{100} \times 800$

$= 36.60 + 51.2 = 87.8$

67. $? = 14 \times 4.5 - 7.4 \times 3.5$

$= 63.0 - 25.9 = 37.1$

68. $? = \dfrac{22}{5} \times \dfrac{10}{3} - \dfrac{16}{3}$

$= \dfrac{44}{3} - \dfrac{16}{3} = \dfrac{28}{3} = 9\dfrac{1}{3}$

69. $? = 7995 \times \dfrac{1}{123} \times \dfrac{1}{5} = 13$

70. $? = 62.18 + 169.35 + 3046.81 = 3278.34$

71. $\sqrt{?} = 21^2 - 19^2 = 441 - 361 = 80$

$\Rightarrow ? = (80)^2 = 6400$

72. $? = \dfrac{13}{2} + \dfrac{21}{4} \times \dfrac{10}{7} = \dfrac{13}{2} + \dfrac{15}{2} = \dfrac{28}{2} = 14$

73. $? = \dfrac{3}{5} \times \dfrac{5}{7} \times \dfrac{2}{9} \times 630 = 60$

74. $? = \dfrac{125}{100} \times 200 + \dfrac{36}{100} \times 350 = 250 + 126$

$= 376$

75. $? = \dfrac{28 \times 5 - 14 \times 4}{8^2 + \sqrt{225} + (14)^2} = \dfrac{140 - 56}{64 + 15 + 196} = \dfrac{84}{275}$

76. $? = \dfrac{3}{7} \times 413 + \dfrac{2}{5} \times 615$

$= 177 + 246 = 423$

77. $? = 7865 + 372 - 4128 - 2014$

$= 8237 - 6142 = 2095$

78. $\dfrac{?}{100} \times 360 = 234 - \dfrac{45}{100} \times 240$

$\Rightarrow \dfrac{?}{5} \times 18 = 234 - 108$

$\Rightarrow ? = \dfrac{126 \times 5}{18} = 35$

79. $? = 7986 \times \dfrac{1}{165} \times 7 = \dfrac{1694}{5} = 338.8$

80. $? = 4495 \times \dfrac{1}{145} \times 656 \times \dfrac{1}{16}$

$= 31 \times 41 = 1271$

81.

	$\times 1+2$	$\times 2+4$	$\times 3+6$	$\times 4+8$
4	6	16	54	?

Thus, $? = 54 \times 4 + 8 = 216 + 8 = 224$

82.

	$\times 8-1$	$\times 7-1$	$\times 6-1$	$\times 5-1$
5	39	272	1631	?

Thus, $? = 1631 \times 5 - 1 = 8155 - 1 = 8154$

83. $768 \xrightarrow{\div 4} 192 \xrightarrow{\div 4} 48 \xrightarrow{\div 4} 12 \xrightarrow{\div 4} ?$

Thus, $? = 12 \div 4 = 3$

84. $12 \xrightarrow{+2^2} 16 \xrightarrow{+4^2} 32 \xrightarrow{+6^2} 68 \xrightarrow{+8^2} ?$

Thus, $? = 68 + 8^2 = 68 + 64 = 132$

85. $7 \xrightarrow{\times 2+1} 15 \xrightarrow{\times 2+2} 32 \xrightarrow{\times 2+3} 67 \xrightarrow{\times 2+4} ?$

Thus, $? = 67 \times 2 + 4 = 134 + 4 = 138$

86. $408 = x\left[\left(1+\dfrac{4}{100}\right)^2 - 1\right]$

$$\Rightarrow \quad x\left[\dfrac{676}{625} - 1\right] = 408 \Rightarrow x \times \dfrac{51}{625} = 408$$

$$\Rightarrow \quad x = \dfrac{408 \times 625}{51} = 5000$$

Thus, sum = ₹ 5000

87. Let, length of the train and platform be x m and $2x$ m respectively.

$$60 \text{ km/hr} = 60 \times \dfrac{5}{18} = \dfrac{50}{3} \text{ m/s}$$

Now, $2x + x = \dfrac{50}{3} \times 32.4 = 540$ m.

$$\Rightarrow \quad x = \dfrac{540}{3} = 180 \text{ m.}$$

Thus, length of the platform
$= 2x = 2 \times 180 = 360$ m.

88. Let, two numbers be x and y repectively, then,

$$\dfrac{3}{7}x = \dfrac{45}{100} \times y \qquad \Rightarrow \dfrac{x}{y} = \dfrac{21}{100}$$

$$\Rightarrow x : y = 21 : 100$$

89. Original price $= \dfrac{100}{115} \times \dfrac{100}{80} \times 1840$

$$= \text{Rs. } 2000$$

93. $\dfrac{2}{7} = 0.\overline{28571}$, $\dfrac{3}{5} = 0.6$, $\dfrac{5}{11} = 0.\overline{45}$,

$$\dfrac{6}{17} = 0.353$$

Thus, their ascending order will be

$$\dfrac{2}{7}, \dfrac{6}{17}, \dfrac{5}{11}, \dfrac{3}{5}$$

94. Let, five consecutive odd numbers be $(x + 1)$, $(x + 3)$, $(x + 5)$, $(x + 7)$ and $(x + 9)$ respectively

Then, $(x + 5) = \dfrac{84}{100}(x + 9)$

$\Rightarrow \quad 25x + 125 = 21x + 189$

$\Rightarrow \quad 4x = 64 \Rightarrow x = 16$

Thus, sum of first these two numbers
$= (x + 1) + (x + 3)$
$= (16 + 1) + (16 + 3) = 17 + 19 = 36$

95. Let, Nikhil's monthly stipend be ₹ x, then expenses on food and transport

$$= \dfrac{45}{100} \times x = ₹ \dfrac{9x}{20}$$

Remaining amount $= x - \dfrac{9x}{20} = ₹ \dfrac{11x}{20}$

Expense on books $= \dfrac{20}{100} \times \dfrac{11x}{20} = ₹ \dfrac{11x}{100}$

Remaining amount

$$= \dfrac{11x}{20} - \dfrac{11x}{100} = ₹ \dfrac{44x}{100} = ₹ \dfrac{11x}{25}$$

Then, other expenses $= \dfrac{11x}{25}$

Now, $\dfrac{11x}{50} = 880 \Rightarrow x = \dfrac{880 \times 50}{11} = ₹ 4000$

96. Required percentage

$$= \dfrac{170 + 150}{163} \times 100 = \dfrac{32000}{163} \approx 200\%$$

97. Required percentage $= \dfrac{132}{90} \times 100 \approx 150\%$

SBI Junior Associates & Junior Agricultural Associates
(Clerical Cadre Exam)

General English

Directions (Qs. 1–15): *Read the following passage carefully and answer the questions given below it. Certain words/phrases have been printed in **bold** to help you locate them while answering some of the questions.*

Yeshwant Patil — a poor farmer used to live in a village named Narasopur. He was hardworking and sincere. His father, Bhagirath, mother, Dhirubai and younger brother, Dadu, lived with hirp. They were gentle and affectionate. However, Yeshwant's wife— Sonabai was a loudmouthed woman. On each and every issue she would quarrel. Yeshwant was a peace loving man. He was not much ambitious. On the other hand, Sonabai was very cunning and would not get satisfied easily. She wanted to have all luxuries of life and all household articles. **Regular** quarrels was a **pan** of their family.

Sonabai in spare time used to visit neighbouring families. She would provoke other women. She would ask them to demand such things from their husbands. A lot of women started **following** her advice.

The farmer had a few animals including a mule. The mule would **draw** the small cart. The farmer used to love and take care of his animals as he knew their importance in farming. Sonabai, however, did not like this. Particularly, she did not like the mule. Whenever she was required to feed the animals, she would ignore the animal as far as possible. She also did not give adequate food to these animals. The animals also did not **like** her.

Once, Yeshwant was to go to visit his friend Kashinath. He left the house in the morning. He was to stay in that village for two-three days. Before leaving his house he patted all his animals. He instructed Sonabai to take proper care of the animals. Sonabai—as usual did not pay attention to the animals. The feeding time of the animals was over but they were not fed. The mule was standing on the ground and Sonabai with **great** force hit him with a burning stick. The mule turned its back and kicked her furiously. Alas! She collapsed and in a few minutes died. Messages were sent and Yeshwant returned to his village. The news of the death of Sonabai spread and people gathered in large numbers, A passing by traveller asked Devram, the elder brother of Yeshwant, "Oh, was she so popular! Why is there so much rush?" Someone said, "No, We are here to purchase the mule, high price is being quoted." People have not come to pay their respect for this lady. She was terrible! She had spoiled other ladies also.

1. Why did people offer high price for the mule?
   A. It was very strong
   B. The cost of feeding this mule was negligible
   C. It was capable of protecting the house
   D. It was considered to be very lucky
   E. None of these

2. Why did Yeshwant love his animals?
   A. He knew that animals were partners in his progress
   B. He knew that if animals are loved people will offer more value
   C. Bhagirath had asked him to love the animals

D. He had nothing else to offer to the animals
E. None of these

3. What activity Sonabai used to do in her free time?
   A. Look after the animals
   B. Visit Kashinajh's house
   C. Help the neighbours
   D. Not given in the passage
   E. None of these

4. People turned in large numbers to meet Yeshwant
   A. as this was a normal practice of the villagers
   B. as they were shocked and in grief
   C. to purchase the mule
   D. to console the parents of Kashinath
   E. to take care of the mule and other animals

5. Which of the following correctly describes the behaviour of Sonabai?
   (1) She would quarrel only occasionally
   (2) She was ambitious and strong willed
   A. Only (1)
   B. Only (2)
   C. Either (1) or (2)
   D. Neither (I) nor (2)
   E. Both (1) and (2)

6. Why did the mule attack Sonabai?
   A. She had beaten all the animals on that day
   B. Sonabai did not allow the mule to pull the cart
   C. Sonabai used to harass the family members
   D. It would not allow anyone to touch except Yeshwant
   E. None of these

7. Who among the following does not belong to Patil's family?
   A. Dadu   B. Bhagirath
   C. Dhirubai   D. Kashinath
   E. Devram

8. Why did Sonabai not give sufficient food to the animals?
   A. As per instructions of Yeshwant
   B. There was shortage of animal fodder
   C. The animals were lazy
   D. Not given in the passage
   E. Dhirubai did not like the animals

9. Sonabai had succeeded in
   A. creating a group of followers
   B. selling the mule
   C. taking care of the animals
   D. commanding love and respect of the villagers
   E. controlling her behaviour

Directions (Qs. 10–12): *Choose the word which is most OPPOSITE in meaning of the word given in bold capitals as used in the passage.*

10. FOLLOWING
   A. ignoring   B. leading
   C. beginning   D. closing
   E. observing

11. LIKE
   A. similar   B. hate
   C. differ   D. calm
   E. refuse

12. GREAT
   A. short   B. unknown
   C. weak   D. powerful
   E. ordinary

Directions (Qs. 13–15): *Choose the word which is most nearly the SAME in meaning as the word given in bold capitals as used in the passage.*

13. REGULAR
   A. big   B. large
   C. frequent   D. systematic
   E. disciplined

14. PART
   A. piece   B. feature
   C. sign   D. whole
   E. separate

15. DRAW
   A. ride   B. push
   C. run   D. pull
   E. sketch

Directions (Qs. 16–20) : *Each sentence below has a blank, each blank indicating that something has been omitted. Choose the word for each blank which best fits the meaning of the sentence as a whole.*

16. He is ..... to ..... any kind of work with due sincerity.
   A. determined, undertake

B. found, perform
C. eager, avoid
D. willing, ignore
E. reluctant, entrust

17. They wanted to ..... all these books, but they could not find ..... time to do so.
    A. buy, some   B. read, sufficient
    C. dispose, some   D. pursue, necessary
    E. cover, almost

18. They started their ..... branch in this city today; their other ..... branches are in the next by-lane.
    A. first, new   B. first, old
    C. second, old   D. third, two
    E. new, several

19. Due to ..... rainfall this year, there will be ..... cut in water supply
    A. meagre, least
    B. abundant, considerable
    C. enough, substantial
    D. surplus, abundant
    E. sufficient, no

20. The judge ..... him because he was found ..... on the basis of the evidence.
    A. acquitted, criminal
    B. punished, guilty
    C. sentenced, innocent
    D. suspended, involved
    E. pardoned, innocent

Directions (Qs. 21–25): *Read each sentence to find out whether there is any grammatical error or idiomatic error in it. The error, if any, will be in one part of the sentence. The number of that part is the answer. If there is "No Error" the answer is 'E'. (Ignore errors of punctuation if any.)*

21. (A) I would have lost/(B) my luggage and other belongings/(C) if I would have left the compartment/(D) and gone out to fetch drinking water./(E) No error.

22. (A) Ramesh did not like/(B) leaving his old parents alone in the house/(C) but he had no alternative/(D) as he has to go out to work./(E) No error.

23. (A) I was being astonished/(B) when I heard that/(C) he had left the country/(D) without informing anyone of us./(E) No error.

24. (A) According to one survey/(B) only those forests which were/(C) not under village management/(D) succumbed from fires recently./(E) No error.

25. (A) We can not handle/(B) this complicated case today/(C) unless full details are not given/(D) to us by now./(E) No error.

Directions (Qs. 26–30): *Which of the phrases A, B, C and D given below should replace the phrase given in **bold** in the following sentence to make the sentence grammatically meaningful and correct? If the sentence is correct as it is and 'No correction is required', mark E as the answer.*

26. **Had I realised** how close I was to the edge of the valley, I would not have carried the bags there.
    A. Had I been realised
    B. If I would have realised
    C. When I realised
    D. Had I had realised
    E. No correction required

27. Later he became unpopular because he tried **to lord it on** his followers.
    A. to lord it for   B. to lord over
    C. to lord it over   D. to lord it over on
    E. No correction required

28. **The long or short of it** is that I do not want to deal with that new firm.
    A. The long and short of it
    B. The long and short for it
    C. The long or short for it
    D. The short and long of it
    E. No correction required

29. The people generally try to **curry favour** with the corrupt but influential person.
    A. cook favour   B. seek favour
    C. extract favour   D. display favour
    E. No correction required

30. My hair **stood off ends** when I saw the horrible sight.
    A. stood at ends
    B. stood on ends
    C. stood to ends
    D. stands on ends
    E. No correction required

Reasoning Ability

Directions (Qs. 31–35): *In the following questions, the symbols @, ©, %, $ and ★ are used with the following meaning as illustrated below:*

'P © Q' means 'P is smaller than Q'.
'P % Q' means 'P is equal to Q'.
'P ★ Q' means 'P is greater than Q'.
'P @ Q' means 'P is either equal to or smaller than Q.'
'P $ Q' means 'P is either equal to or greater than Q.'

Now in each of the following questions assuming the given statements to be true, find which of the two conclusions I and II given below them is/are **definitely true**?

Give answer (A) if only Conclusion I is true.
Give answer (B) if only Conclusion II is true.
Give answer (C) if either Conclusion I or II is true.
Give answer (D) if neither Conclusion I nor II is true.
Give answer (E) if both Conclusion I and II are true.

31. Statements: J $ H, H © F, F ★ G
Conclusions: I. F ★ J
II. H © G

32. Statements: R % S, S @ T, T © U
Conclusions: I. U ★ S
II. T $ R

33. Statements: M @ N, N % L, L © K
Conclusions: I. L $ M
II. K ★ M

34. Statements: Z © Y, Y $ W, W ★ V
Conclusions: I. Z @ W
II. V © Y

35. Statements: A ★ B, B % C, C @ D
Conclusions: I. B @ D
II. A ★ D

Directions (Qs. 36–40) : *At an Electronic Data Processing Unit, five out of the eight program sets P, Q, R, S, T, U, V and W are to be operated daily. On any one day, except for the first day of a month, only three of the program sets must be the ones that were operated on the previous day. The program operating must also satisfy the following conditions :*

(*i*) If program 'P' is to be operated on a day, 'V' cannot be operated on that day.

(*ii*) If 'Q' is to be operated on a day, 'T' must be one of the programs to be operated after 'Q'.

(*iii*) If 'R' is to be operated on a day, 'V' must be one of the programs to be operated after 'R'.

(*iv*) The last program to be operated on any day must be either 'S' or 'U'.

36. If the program sets 'R' and 'W' are to be operated on the first day, which of the following could be the other programs on that day?
A. P, T, U   B. Q, S, V
C. Q, T, V   D. T, S, U
E. None of these

37. Which of the following is TRUE of any day's valid program set operation?
A. 'P' cannot be operated at third place
B. 'Q' cannot be operated at third place
C. 'T' cannot be operated at third place
D. 'R' cannot be operated at fourth place
E. 'U' cannot be operated at fourth place

38. If the program sets operated on a day, P, Q, W, T, U, each of the following could be the next day's program set EXCEPT
A. Q, R, V, T, U   B. Q, T, V, W, S
C. W, T, U, V, S   D. W, R, V, T, U
E. W, T, S, P, U

39. If 'R' is operated at third place in a sequence, which of the following CANNOT be the second program in that sequence?
A. Q   B. S
C. T   D. U
E. W

40. Which of the following could be the set of programs to be operated on the first day of a month?
A. P, R, V, S, U   B. Q, S, R, V, U
C. T, U, R, V, S   D. U, Q, S, T, W
E. V, Q, R, T, S

Directions (Qs. 41–45): *In the following questions, the symbols @, ©, %, $ and ★ are used with the following meaning as illustrated below :*
'P © Q' means 'P is neither equal to nor greater than Q'.

'P $ Q' means 'P is neither greater than nor smaller than Q'.

'P ★ Q' means 'P is neither smaller than nor equal to Q'.

'P % Q' means 'P is not smaller than Q'.

'P @ Q' means 'P is not greater than Q'.

Now in each of the following questions assuming the given statements to be true, find which of three conclusions I, II and III given below them is/are **definitely true** and give your answer accordingly.

41. Statements : H © N, N ★ B, B $ M, M @ K
   Conclusions: I. H © B
   II. K ★ B
   III. K $ B
   A. Only II is true
   B. Only III is true
   C. Only either II or III is true
   D. Only II and III are true
   E. None of these

42. Statements : W % F, F $ A, A © J, J ★ B
   Conclusions: I. A @ W
   II. J ★ W
   III. B ★ F
   A. Only I is true
   B. Only II is true
   C. Only III is true
   D. Only I and II are true
   E. None of these

43. Statements : K @ B, B © R, R $ H, H ★ V
   Conclusions: I. V © R
   II. R ★ K
   III. H ★ B
   A. Only I and II are true
   B. Only I and III are true
   C. Only II and III are true
   D. Only III is true
   E. All I, II and III are true

44. Statements : N $ T, T @ B, H $ B, K © H
   Conclusions: I. K © B
   II. B $ N
   III. B ★ N
   A. Only either II or III is true
   B. Only either II or III and I are true
   C. Only I is true

D. Only I and II are true
E. All I and III are true

45. Statements : R ★ K, K © M, M @ H, H % T
   Conclusions: I. T © M
   II. T $ M
   III. H ★ K
   A. None is true
   B. Only I is true
   C. Only II is true
   D. Only III is true
   E. Only either I or II and III are true

46. Which one would be a meaningful order of the following?
   1. Windows   2. Walls
   3. Floor   4. Foundation
   5. Roof   6. Room
   A. 4 2 1 5 3 6   B. 4 3 5 6 2 1
   C. 4 5 3 2 1 6   D. 4 1 5 6 2 3
   E. 4 1 5 3 6 2

47. If 'violet' is called 'yellow', 'yellow' is called 'blue', 'blue' is called 'red', 'red' is called 'fawn', 'fawn' is called 'green' what is the colour of brick?
   A. blue   B. green
   C. yellow   D. fawn
   E. red

Directions (Qs. 48–50) : *Read the following information to answer questions given below :*
   (A) A × B means 'A' is the brother of 'B'
   (B) A + B means 'A' is the mother of 'B'
   (C) A ÷ B means 'A' is the son of 'B'
   (D) A – B means 'A' is the husband of 'B'

48. Which of the following would mean 'M' is the father of 'N'?
   A. M ÷ N + O   B. M × O – N
   C. M + O ÷ N   D. M – O + N
   E. None of these

49. Which of the following is definitely true if 'N' is the son of 'M'?
   A. M + N × O
   B. M + N – O
   C. N ÷ M
   D. All the three are true
   E. None of the three are true

50. Which of the following would mean 'M' is the Aunt of 'N'?
A. M + N – O   B. M × O ÷ N
C. N + O × M   D. N ÷ M + O
E. None of these

Directions (Qs. 51–52): *In a certain code language :*

(A) 'pit na som' means 'bring me water'.
(B) 'na jo tod' means 'water is life'.
(C) 'tub od pit' means 'give me toy'.
(D) 'jo lin kot' means 'life and death'.

51. Which of the following represents 'is' in that language?
A. jo   B. na
C. tod   D. lin
E. None of these

52. To find out the answer to the above question, which of the following statements can be dispensed with?
A. A only   B. C only
C. D only   D. B or C only
E. None of these

53. What number in the dice, given below, will be on the side opposite to 6?

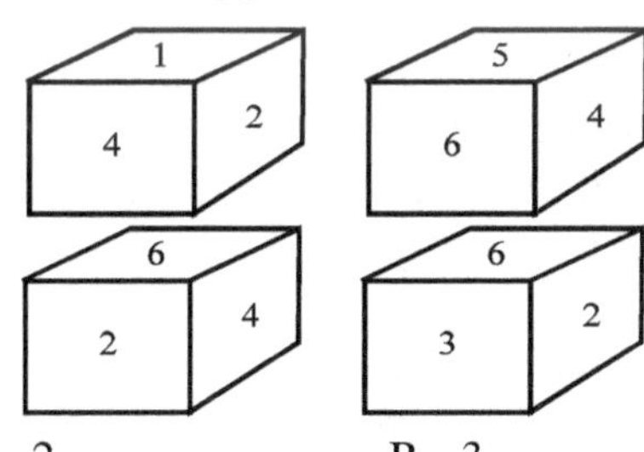

A. 2   B. 3
C. 1   D. 5
E. None of these

54. Twon D is 12 km. towards the North of town A. Town C is 15 km. towards the West of town D. Town B is 15 km. towards the West of town A. How far and in which direction is town B from town C?
A. 15 km. towards North
B. 12 km. towards North
C. 3 km. towards South
D. 12 km. towards South
E. Cannot be determined

Directions (Qs. 55–57) : *Following questions are based on the five three digit numbers given below:*

937   425   816   398   671

55. If the positions of the first and the third digits within each number are reversed, which of the following will be the third digit of the second lowest number?
A. 8   B. 9
C. 4   D. 6
E. None of these

56. Which of the following is the sum of the first and the second digits of the lowest number?
A. 12   B. 6
C. 9   D. 13
E. None of these

57. Which of the following is the second digit of the second highest number.
A. 3   B. 2
C. 1   D. 9
E. 7

Directions (Qs. 58–60) : *Read the following directions and answer the questions given below:*

There are four friends Ravi, Hari, Manu and Jatin. One of them lives at Kanpur and his hobbies are reading and writing. Hari and Jatin live at Lucknow. Hari's hobby is stamp collection. Common Hobby of two friends staying at Lucknow is coin collection. Ravi lives at Allahabad. One boy staying at Lucknow also loves to hear music. The boy staying at Allahabad loves to travel and read comics. If all the boys have two hobbies each answer the following questions :

58. Who lives at Kanpur?
A. Jatin   B. Manu
C. Ravi   D. Hari
E. None of the above

59. Coin collection and listening to music are the hobbies of :
A. Manu   B. Ravi
C. Hari   D. Jatin
E. None of the above

60. Which of the following is not the hobby of Ravi?
A. Reading comics
B. Reading

C. Travelling

D. Cannot be said

E. None of the above

Directions (Qs. 61–65): *Study the following information carefully and answer the given questions.*

A, B, C, D, E and F are sitting in a straight line (not necessarily in the same order) facing North.

    (a) D sits at the extreme left hand corner of the line.

    (b) Only three persons sit between D and B.

    (c) B sits second to right of F.

    (d) A is not an immediate neighbour of B.

    (e) E does not sit at the extreme end of the line.

61. Four of the following five are alike in a certain way based on their seating positions in the above arrangement and so form a group. Which is the one that **does not** belong to that group?

    A. FB   B. EC

    C. AE   D. AD

    E. DF

62. Who sits at the extreme right hand corner of the line?

    A. A   B. C

    C. D   D. F

    E. None of these

63. If all the persons are made to sit in alphabetical order from **right to left,** the positions of how many will remain unchanged as compared to the original seating positions?

    A. None   B. One

    C. Two   D. Three

    E. Four

64. What is the position of F with respect to D?

    A. Third to the left

    B. Second to the left

    C. Immediately to the right

    D. Third to the right

    E. Second to the right

65. How many persons sit between A and B?

    A. None   B. One

    C. Two   D. Three

    E. Four

Quantitative Aptitude

Directions (Qs. 66–80): *What will come in place of question mark (?) in the following questions?*

66. $\dfrac{5}{9}$ of $504 + \dfrac{3}{8}$ of $640 = ?$

    A. 520   B. 480

    C. 460   D. 540

    E. None of these

67. $\dfrac{4}{9}$ of $\dfrac{3}{8}$ of $\dfrac{2}{7}$ of $294 = ?$

    A. 24   B. 14

    C. 16   D. 22

    E. None of these

68. 16% of 250 + 115% of 480 = ?

    A. 522   B. 588

    C. 582   D. 498

    E. None of these

69. $16.45 \times 2.8 + 4.5 \times 1.6 = ?$

    A. 56.23   B. 56.32

    C. 53.26   D. 53.66

    E. None of these

70. 55% of 860 + ?% of 450 = 581

    A. 24   B. 28

    C. 32   D. 36

    E. None of these

71. $1740 \div 12 \times 4070 \div 110 = ?$

    A. 5635   B. 5365

    C. 5465   D. 5445

    E. None of these

72. $72.42 + 385.66 + 4976.38 = ?$

    A. 5234.46   B. 5434.46

    C. 5434.66   D. 5244.66

    E. None of these

73. $8\dfrac{5}{9} \times 4\dfrac{3}{5} - 6\dfrac{1}{3} = ?$

    A. $32\dfrac{11}{45}$ B. $33\dfrac{11}{45}$

C. $32\dfrac{1}{45}$ D. $33\dfrac{1}{45}$

E. None of these

74. $5760 \div 45 \times 15 = ?$

A. 1890   B. 1828

C. 1820   D. 1928

E. None of these

75. $9845 - 3896 + 486 = ? - 1128$

A. 7365   B. 7463

C. 7536   D. 7653

E. None of these

76. $22^2 + \sqrt{?} = 529$

A. 45   B. 2045

C. 2025   D. 48

E. None of these

77. $\dfrac{17 \times 4 + 4^2 \times 2}{90 \div 5 \times 12} = ?$

A. $\dfrac{25}{54}$ B. $\dfrac{22}{57}$

C. $\dfrac{11}{27}$ D. $\dfrac{13}{27}$

E. None of these

78. $2520 \div 14 \div 9 = ?$

A. 22   B. 18

C. 20   D. 16

E. None of these

79. $8\dfrac{2}{5} \times 5\dfrac{2}{3} + ? = 50\dfrac{1}{5}$

A. $3\dfrac{3}{5}$ B. $2\dfrac{2}{5}$

C. $3\dfrac{2}{5}$ D. $2\dfrac{3}{5}$

E. None of these

80. 3.2% of $250 + 1.8\%$ of $400 = ?$

A. 14.8   B. 15.75

C. 14.75   D. 15.2

E. None of these

Directions (Qs. 81–85): *What will come in place of question mark (?) in the following number series?*

81. 11   13   16   20   ?

A. 24   B. 26

C. 28   D. 27

E. None of these

82. 7   13   25   49   ?

A. 99   B. 97

C. 89   D. 87

E. None of these

83. 608   304   152   76   ?

A. 39   B. 36

C. 38   D. 37

E. None of these

84. 8   9   20   63   ?

A. 256   B. 252

C. 246   D. 242

E. None of these

85. 5   6   10   19   ?

A. 28   B. 37

C. 36   D. 35

E. None of these

86. Difference between the digits of a two digit number is 5 and the digit in the unit's place is six times the digit in the ten's place. What is the number?

A. 27   B. 72

C. 16   D. 61

E. None of these

87. Find the average of the following set of numbers.

132, 148, 164, 128, 120, 136

A. 142   B. 136

C. 138   D. 144

E. None of these

88. Which of the following has fractions in descending order?

A. $\dfrac{7}{8}, \dfrac{5}{7}, \dfrac{2}{3}, \dfrac{3}{5}$ B. $\dfrac{3}{5}, \dfrac{2}{3}, \dfrac{5}{7}, \dfrac{7}{8}$

C. $\dfrac{7}{8}, \dfrac{5}{7}, \dfrac{3}{5}, \dfrac{2}{3}$ D. $\dfrac{2}{3}, \dfrac{3}{5}, \dfrac{5}{7}, \dfrac{7}{8}$

E. None of these

89. Populations of two villages X and Y are in the ratio of 5 : 7 respectively. If the population of village Y increases by 25000 and the population of village X remains unchanged the respective ratio of their populations becomes 25 : 36. What is the population of village X?
A. 6,25,000
B. 6,75,000
C. 8,75,000
D. 9,00,000
E. None of these

90. 56% of a number is less than its 72% by 56. What is 70% of that number?
A. 300   B. 235
C. 240   D. 350
E. None of these

91. A 240 metre long train crosses a 300 metre long platform in 27 seconds. What is the speed of the train in kmph?
A. 66   B. 60
C. 76   D. 64
E. None of these

92. Vandana sells an article for ₹ 3,240/- and earns a profit of 20%. What is the cost price of the article?
A. ₹ 2,800/-   B. ₹ 2,820/-
C. ₹ 2,750/-   D. ₹ 2,700/-
E. None of these

93. 16 men can complete a piece of work in 7 days. In how many days will 28 men complete the same work?
A. 6 days   B. 8 days
C. 3 days   D 4 days
E. None of these

94. Sum of five consecutive even numbers is 380. What is the second number in ascending order?
A. 76   B. 78
C. 74   D. 72
E. None of these

95. Cost of 6 dozen apples and 8 dozen bananas is ₹ 1,400/-. What will be the cost of 15 dozen apples and 20 dozen bananas?
A. ₹ 3,200/-   B. ₹ 3,500/-
C. ₹ 3,600/-   D. ₹ 42,00/-
E. None of these

Directions (Qs. 96–100): *Study the following table carefully to answer these questions*

Number of Students studying five different disciplines from five Institutes

Institute \ Discipline	Arts	Commerce	Science	Management	Computer Science
A	350	260	450	140	300
B	240	320	400	180	320
C	460	300	360	160	380
D	440	480	420	120	340
E	280	360	340	200	330

96. Number of students studying Commerce from Institute D is what per cent of the total number of students studying all the disciplines together from this institute?

A. $28\dfrac{1}{3}$ B. $26\dfrac{2}{3}$

C. $24\dfrac{2}{3}$ D. $24\dfrac{1}{3}$

E. None of these

97. What is the average number of students studying all disciplines together from Institute E?
A. 312   B. 310
C. 302   D. 304
E. None of these

98. What is the ratio between total number of students studying Science from Institutes C and D together and the total number of students studying Computer Science from these two Institutes together respectively?

A. 13 : 12   B. 12 : 13
C. 13 : 15   D. 15 : 13
E. None of these

99. What is the average number of students studying Commerce from all the Institutes together?
A. 356   B. 360
C. 348   D. 340
E. None of these

100. Total number of students studying Arts from Institutes A and B together is **approximately** what per cent of the total number of students studying Computer Science from these two Institutes?
A. 84   B. 85
C. 88   D. 90
E. 95

ANSWERS

1	2	3	4	5	6	7	8	9	10
E	A	E	C	B	E	D	D	A	A
11	**12**	**13**	**14**	**15**	**16**	**17**	**18**	**19**	**20**
B	C	C	B	D	A	B	D	E	B
21	**22**	**23**	**24**	**25**	**26**	**27**	**28**	**29**	**30**
C	D	A	D	C	E	C	A	E	B
31	**32**	**33**	**34**	**35**	**36**	**37**	**38**	**39**	**40**
D	E	E	B	A	E	E	E	A	C
41	**42**	**43**	**44**	**45**	**46**	**47**	**48**	**49**	**50**
C	E	E	B	D	A	D	D	D	E
51	**52**	**53**	**54**	**55**	**56**	**57**	**58**	**59**	**60**
C	B	C	D	C	A	C	B	D	B
61	**62**	**63**	**64**	**65**	**66**	**67**	**68**	**69**	**70**
D	B	B	E	C	A	B	E	C	A
71	**72**	**73**	**74**	**75**	**76**	**77**	**78**	**79**	**80**
B	B	D	E	E	C	A	C	D	D
81	**82**	**83**	**84**	**85**	**86**	**87**	**88**	**89**	**90**
E	B	C	A	D	C	C	A	A	E
91	**92**	**93**	**94**	**95**	**96**	**97**	**98**	**99**	**100**
E	D	D	C	B	B	C	A	E	E

Some Selected Explanatory Answers

(Qs. 31–35):

© ⇒ <	% ⇒ =	★ ⇒ >
@ ⇒ ≤	$ ⇒ ≥	

31. $J \$ H \Rightarrow J \geq H$
$H © F \Rightarrow H < F$
$F ★ G \Rightarrow F > G$
Hence, $J \geq H < F > G$
Conclusion:
  I. $F ★ J \Rightarrow F > J$: False
  II. $H © J \Rightarrow H < G$: False

32. $R \% S \Rightarrow R = S$
$S @ T \Rightarrow S \leq T$
$T © U \Rightarrow T < U$

Hence, $R = S \leq T < U$

Conclusion:
  I. $U ★ S \Rightarrow U > S$: True
  II. $T \$ R \Rightarrow T \geq R$: True

33. M @ N ⇒ M ≤ N
N % L ⇒ N = L
L © K ⇒ L < K

Hence, M ≤ N = L < K

Conclusion:
  I. L $ M ⇒ L ≥ M   : True
  II. K ★ M ⇒ K > M : True

34. Z © Y ⇒ Z < Y
Y $ W ⇒ Y ≥ W
W ★ V ⇒ W > V

Hence, Z < Y ≥ W > V

Conclusion:
  I. Z @ W ⇒ Z ≤ W False
  II. V © Y ⇒ V < Y   True

36. Other programmes are : R, T, W, V, S

37. U can be the last programme on any day.

38. Four of the program sets cannot be operated the next day out of those operated on the first day.

41. H © N → H < N, N ★ B → N > B,
B $ M → B = M, M @ K → M ≤ K
From these four we get
H < N > B = M ≤ K
  (*i*) H © B → H < B (False)
  (*ii*) K ★ B → K > B
  (*iii*) K $ B → K = B

42. W % F → W ≥ F, F $ A → F = A,
A © J → A < J, J ★ B → J > B

From these four we get,
W ≥ F = A < J > B
  (*i*) A @ B → A ≥ B (False)
  (*ii*) J ★ W → J > W (False)
  (*iii*) B ★ F → B > F (False)

43. K @ B → K ≤ B, B © R → B < R,
R $ H → R = H, H ★ V → H > V
From these four, we get
K ≤ B < R = H > V
  (*i*) V © R → V < R (True)
  (*ii*) R ★ K → R > K (True)
  (*iii*) H ★ B → H > B (True)

44. N $ T → N = T, T @ B → T ≤ B,
H $ B → H = B, K © H → K < H

From these four, we get
N = T ≤ B = H > K
  (*i*) K © B → K < B (True)
  (*ii*) B $ N → B = N (True)
  (*iii*) B ★ N → B > N

45. R ★ K → R > K, K © M → K < M,
M @ H → M ≤ H, H % T → H ≥ T
From these four, we get
R > K < M ≤ H ≥ T
  (*i*) T © M → T < M (False)
  (*ii*) T $ M → T = M (False)
  (*iii*) H ★ K → H > K (False)

46. The order of words depict the right order of constructing a building/room.

47. Colour of brick is 'red' and 'red' is called 'fawn'.

48. M – O means 'M' is the husband of 'O' and O + N means 'O' is the mother of 'N'.

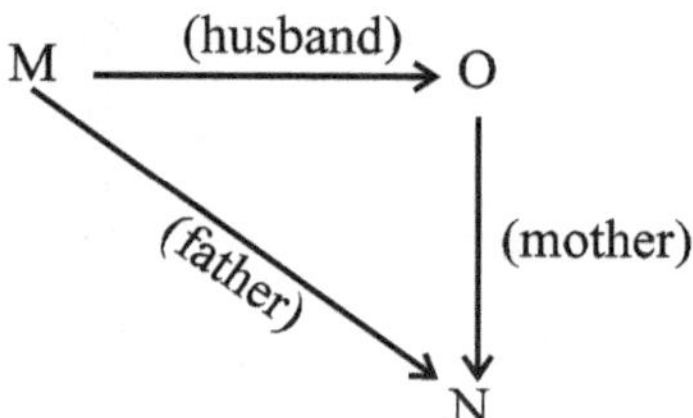

49. (A) M + N means 'M' is the mother of 'N' and N × O means 'N' is the brother of 'O'.

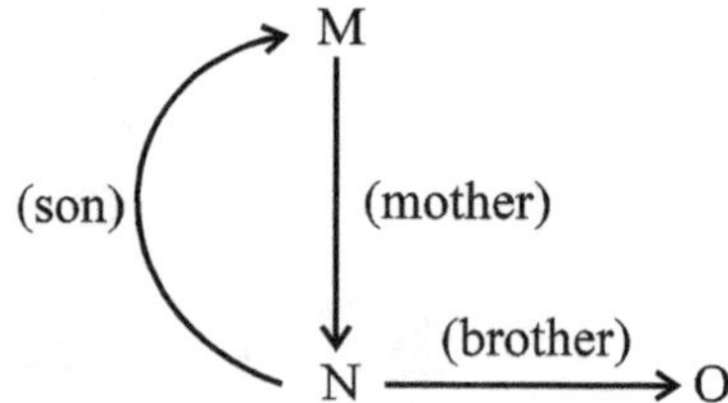

(B) M + N means 'M' is the mother of 'N' and N – O means 'N' is the husband of 'O'.

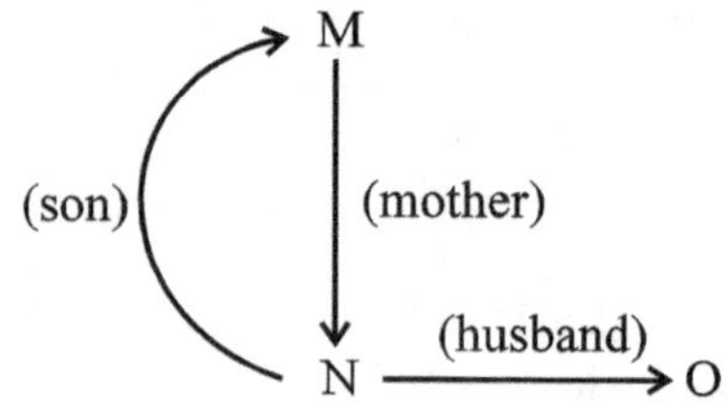

(C) N ÷ M means 'N' is the son of 'M'

50. The answer cannot be determined. Information about a sister's relationship is required to work out the relationship between 'M' and 'N'.

51.

Code	Sentence
A. pit *na* som	bring me *water*
B. *na jo* **tod**	*water* **is** *life*
C. tub od pit	give me toy
D. *jo* lin kot	*life* and death

The word 'is' is in Sentence 'B' only. The word 'water' is repeated in Sentence 'A' and so is the code 'na'. The word 'life' is repeated in sentence 'D' and so is the code 'jo'. The only code remaining is 'tod' which stands for 'is'.

52. The answer to the above question was arrived at by comparing codes and sentences A, B and D. Only sentence 'C' could be dispensed with.

53. According to the given figures of the same dice, the numbers adjacent to 6 are 5, 4, 2 and 3. So, the number opposite to the side 6 will be 1.

54.

Obviously, CB = AD = 12 km and B is south of C.

55. 937 $\Rightarrow$ 739; 425 $\Rightarrow$ 524; 816 $\Rightarrow$ 618; 398 $\Rightarrow$ 893; 671 $\Rightarrow$ 176;
Second least no. $\Rightarrow$ 524

56. Least no. $\Rightarrow$ 398
Required sum $\Rightarrow$ 3 + 9 = 12.

57. Second biggest no. $\Rightarrow$ 816.

Chart for Answers 58 to 60

Name	Staying at	Hobbies
Ravi	Allahabad	Travelling, Reading comics
Hari	Lucknow	Stamp & Coin collection
Manu	Kanpur	Reading, Writing
Jatin	Lucknow	Music, Coin collection

For Qs. 61–65:

D A F E B C

63.

D	A	F	E	B	C
F	E	D	C	B	A

66. $? = \dfrac{5}{9} \times 504 + \dfrac{3}{8} \times 640 = 280 + 240 = 520$

67. $? = \dfrac{4}{9} \times \dfrac{3}{8} \times \dfrac{2}{7} \times 294 = 14$

68. $? = \dfrac{16}{100} \times 250 + \dfrac{115}{100} \times 480$

$= 40 + 552 = 592$

69. $? = 16.45 \times 2.8 + 4.5 \times 1.6$

$= 46.06 + 7.20 = 53.26$

70. Here, ? % of 450 = 581 – 55% of 860

$\Rightarrow \dfrac{?}{100} \times 450 = 581 - \dfrac{55}{100} \times 860$

$\Rightarrow \dfrac{?}{2} \times 9 = 581 - 473$

$\Rightarrow ? = \dfrac{108 \times 2}{9} = 24$

71. $? = \dfrac{1740}{12} \times \dfrac{4070}{110} = 145 \times 37 = 5365$

72. $? = 72.42 + 385.66 + 4976.38$

$= 5434.46$

73. $? = \dfrac{77}{9} \times \dfrac{23}{5} - \dfrac{19}{3} = \dfrac{1771}{45} - \dfrac{19}{3}$

$= \dfrac{1486}{45} = 33\dfrac{1}{45}$

74. $? = 5760 \times \dfrac{1}{45} \times 15 = 1920$

75. $? = 9845 - 3896 + 486 + 1128$

$= 11459 - 3896$

$= 7563$

76. $\sqrt{?} = 529 - 22^2 = 529 - 484 = 45$

$\Rightarrow ? = (45)^2 = 2025$

77. $? = \dfrac{17 \times 4 + 4^2 \times 2}{90 \div 5 \times 12} = \dfrac{68 + 32}{18 \times 12}$

$= \dfrac{100}{18 \times 12} = \dfrac{25}{54}$

78. $? = 2520 \times \dfrac{1}{14} \times \dfrac{1}{9} = 20$

79. $? = \dfrac{251}{5} - \left(\dfrac{42}{5} \times \dfrac{17}{3}\right)$

$= \dfrac{251}{5} - \dfrac{238}{5}$

$= \dfrac{13}{5} = 2\dfrac{3}{5}$

80. $? = \dfrac{3.2}{100} \times 250 + \dfrac{1.8}{100} \times 400$

$= 8 + 7.2 = 15.2$

81.
$$\begin{array}{ccccc} \overset{+2}{} & \overset{+3}{} & \overset{+4}{} & \overset{+5}{} \\ 11 & 13 & 16 & 20 & ? \end{array}$$

Thus, $? = 20 + 5 = 25$

82.
$$\begin{array}{ccccc} \overset{+6}{} & \overset{+12}{} & \overset{+24}{} & \overset{+48}{} \\ 7 & 13 & 25 & 49 & ? \end{array}$$

Thus, $? = 49 + 48 = 97$

83.
$$\begin{array}{ccccc} \overset{\frac{1}{2}}{} & \overset{\frac{1}{2}}{} & \overset{\frac{1}{2}}{} & \overset{\frac{1}{2}}{} \\ 608 & 304 & 152 & 76 & ? \end{array}$$

Thus, $? = 76 \times \dfrac{1}{2} = 38.$

84. $\quad$ 8 $\quad$ 9 $\quad$ 20 $\quad$ 63 $\quad$?

The series is based on following way:

8 (8 × 1 + 1) (9 × 2 + 2) (20 × 3 + 3) ?

Thus, $? = 63 \times 4 + 4 = 252 + 4 = 256$

85.
$$\begin{array}{ccccc} \overset{+1^2}{} & \overset{+2^2}{} & \overset{+3^2}{} & \overset{+4^2}{} \\ 5 & 6 & 10 & 19 & ? \end{array}$$

Thus, $? = 19 + 4^2 = 19 + 16 = 35$

86. Let, digit in the ten's and unit's place be x and $6x$ respectively, then,

$6x - x = 5 \Rightarrow 5x = 5 \Rightarrow x = 1$

Thus, digits are 1 and 6

Thus, number = 10 × 1 + 6 = 16

87. Required average

$= \dfrac{132 + 148 + 164 + 128 + 120 + 136}{6}$

$= \dfrac{828}{6} = 138$

88. $\dfrac{7}{8} = 0.875$, $\dfrac{5}{7} = 0.\overline{714285}$,

$\dfrac{2}{3} = 0.\overline{6}$, $\dfrac{3}{5} = 0.6$

Thus, their descending order will be

$$\dfrac{7}{8}, \dfrac{5}{7}, \dfrac{2}{3}, \dfrac{3}{5}$$

89. Here, $\dfrac{5x}{7x + 25000} = \dfrac{25}{36}$

$\Rightarrow \qquad 180x = 175x + 625000$

$\Rightarrow \qquad 5x = 625000$

Thus, population of village X = 625000

90. Let number be x; then

$\Rightarrow \left(\dfrac{72 - 56}{100}\right) \times x = 56 \Rightarrow \dfrac{16}{100} \times x = 56$

$\Rightarrow \dfrac{70}{100} \times x = \dfrac{56}{16} \times 70 = 245$

Thus, 70% of that number = 245.

91. $\quad$ Speed $= \dfrac{240 + 300}{27} = \dfrac{540}{27} = 20$ m/s

$= 20 \times \dfrac{18}{5} = 72$ km/hr

92. $\quad$ CP $= \dfrac{100}{120} \times 3240 =$ Rs. 2700

93.

Men	Days
16 ↓	7 ↑
28 ↓	x ↑

Thus, $\dfrac{x}{7} = \dfrac{16}{28}$

$\Rightarrow \quad x = \dfrac{16}{28} \times 7$

$\qquad = 4$ days.

94. Here, $x + (x + 2) + (x + 4) + (x + 6) + (x + 8)$
$$= 380$$

$\Rightarrow \qquad 5x + 20 = 380$

$\Rightarrow \qquad 5x = 360$

$\Rightarrow \qquad x = \dfrac{360}{5} = 72$

Thus, required second number
$$= 72 + 2 = 74.$$

95. Cost of 6 dozen apples and 8 dozen bananas
$= ₹ 1400$.
Thus, cost of 15 dozen apples and 20 dozen

bananas $= \dfrac{5}{2} \times 1400 = ₹ 3500$.

96. Total number of students in Institute D
$= 440 + 480 + 420 + 120 + 340$
$= 1800$

Required percentage $= \dfrac{480}{1800} \times 100$

$$= \dfrac{80}{3} = 26\dfrac{2}{3}\%$$

97. Required average

$$= \dfrac{280 + 360 + 340 + 200 + 330}{5}$$

$$= \dfrac{1510}{5} = 302$$

98. Required ratio $= (360 + 420) : (380 + 340)$
$$= 780 : 720 = 13 : 12$$

99. Required average

$$= \dfrac{260 + 320 + 300 + 480 + 360}{5}$$

$$= \dfrac{1720}{5} = 344$$

100. Required percentage

$$= \dfrac{(350 + 240)}{(300 + 320)} \times 100$$

$$= \dfrac{590}{620} \times 100$$

$$= 95.16\% \approx 95\%$$

General English

Directions (Qs. 1–15): *Read the following passage carefully and answer the questions given below it. Certain words/phrases have been printed in **bold** to help you locate them while answering some of the questions.*

Ramarao was a merchant and moneylender. His village Kopapur was an important place of business. Ramarao was known for his honesty and **keen** sense of business. At the same time he was kind hearted. Any person approaching him with a request for charity would not go empty-handed. He had given donations to some institutes as well. Once, a youth from village Mangrule approached him. Ganesh, the youth, wanted money on loan basis for purchasing additional land. He had with him gold ornaments. He was a social worker as well. His wife Smita accompanied him.

Smita was from village Vadaon. Ramarao asked him, "Why have you come to such a distant village? You could have got money at some nearby place, say, Narayangao! Why have you come all the way to Kopapur?" Ganesh said, "Smita's mother comes from Kopapur. So Smita knows your reputation." Smita smiled **indicating** her concurrence.

"Well, then how much money do you need? What assurance do you give?" Ramarao asked. Ganesh took out the ornaments. Ramarao inspected it and said, "Well, I can give ₹ 10,000 on this." But, Sir, we need ₹ 500 more." Ramarao said, "Well, I cannot give more on these ornaments". Smita immediately took out her gold bangles and wedding ring and said "Will this **do**?" Ramarao saw the faith of the woman in her husband. He nodded his head and said to his personal assistant, "Subhash get ready! Start ..... !"

Turning to Smita he said, "I got the guarantee ...... please stay with us for lunch and **return** to your village in the afternoon. Now, I will go to the temple. Subhash will do the **needful**."

1. Needy persons approaching Ramarao for charity
   A. would prove their honesty
   B. would show him what a kind heart means
   C. would return with some loan
   D. would get some cash
   E. would provide certain guarantee

2. Initially, why was Ramarao not able to give the desired amount?
   A. He did not have the amount
   B. Smita was not ready to give bangles and ring
   C. He did no get sufficient gold as guarantee
   D. Ganesh approached him for the first time
   E. The couple did not approach nearby money lenders

3. Why did Smita smile?
   A. Ganesh had agreed to her suggestion
   B. Ramarao agreed to give the loan
   C. Ramarao belonged to her village
   D. They got the loan approved
   E. None of the above

4. Why did Ganesh meet Ramarao?
   A. To return the loan in terms of gold
   B. To seek money on loan basis

C. To sell his ornaments

D. To seek donation for his family

E. None of the above

5. It appears that Ganesh's wife

A. was having full faith in her husband

B. was against purchase of ornaments

C. was from a rich family

D. belonged to Narayangao

E. Did not bring the bangles and gold ring

6. Ramarao ultimately decided to lend the money to Ganesh because

A. Ganesh wanted the money for doing charitable work

B. he received additional gold ornaments

C. he decided not to take any guarantee from Ganesh

D. Subhash was ready to raise the necessary cash

E. None of the above

7. Which of the following is true in the context of the passage?

A. Smita comes from Kopapur

B. Subhash was a youth from Mangrule

C. Ganesh initially did not tell the required amount to Ramarao

D. Ramarao wanted Ganesh to come to the temple

E. Ganesh was impressed by Ramarao's honesty

8. The incident proves which of the following qualities of Ramarao?

A. Intelligence and money mindedness

B. Humanity and understanding

C. Religious and devotional

D. Charity and respect for elders

9. It appears that Smita succeeded in

A. making Ganesh approach Ramarao

B. purchasing land for herself

C. retaining all her old ornaments

D. getting money for social work

E. showing her keen sense of business

10. In the context of the passage, "Subhash, get ready, start....." means

A. forget about this transaction, we have other things to do

B. I am ready for going out to the temple, let us move

C. order lunch for this couple

D. prepare the documents and give them required money

E. return all the ornaments of this couple

Directions (Qs. 11–13): *Choose the word/group of words which is most nearly the SAME in meaning as the word given in **bold** capitals as used in the passage.*

11. NEEDFUL

A. likely   B. necessary

C. thoughtful   D. careful

E. must

12. DO

A. complete   B. prepare

C. make   D. perform

E. suffice

13. INDICATING

A. directing   B. suspecting

C. signifying   D. pointing

E. denying

Directions (Qs. 14 & 15): *Choose the word/group of words which is most nearly the OPPOSITE in the meaning of the word given in **bold** capitals as used in the passage.*

14. KEEN

A. blunt   B. stupid

C. slow   D. shallow

E. clever

15. RETURN

A. come back   B. go back

C. withhold   D. take away

E. retain

Directions (Qs. 16–20): *Read each sentence to find out whether there is any grammatical error or idiomatic error in it. The error, if any, will be in one part of the sentence. The number of that part is the answer. If there is "No Error" the answer is 'E'. (Ignore errors of punctuation if any.)*

16. (A) We will pack not only/(B) the material properly/(C) but will also deliver it/(D) to your valued customers./(E) No error.

17. (A) While Mahendra was away/(B) on a long official tour/(C) his office receive an important letter/(D) which was marked 'Urgent'./(E) No error.

18. (A) We now look forward for/(B) some great achievements/(C) which to some extent/(D) can restore the country's prestige once again./(E) No error.

19. (A) Mahatma Gandhi did not solve/(B) all the problems of the future/(C) but he did solve/(D) problems of his own age./(E) No error.

20. (A) No country can long endure/(B) if its foundations/(C) were not laid deep/(D) in the material prosperity./(E) No error.

Directions (Qs. 21–30): *In the following passage there are blanks, each of which has been numbered. These numbers are printed below the passage, against each, five words are suggested, one of which fits the blank appropriately. Find out the appropriate word in each case.*

Do women ..... **(21)** ..... leadership differently than men do? And if so, will feminine leadership ..... **(22)** ..... where ..... **(23)** ..... leadership does not? A recent study suggests somewhat paradoxically that female managers ..... **(24)** ..... their male ..... **(25)** ..... even when the personal characteristics of both are very ..... **(26)** .... Of the two schools of thought, the structualist theory argues that men and women do not receive the same treatment in the workplace and that stamping out ..... **(27)** ..... bias would stamp out the observed ..... **(28)** .... In contrast, the socialisation theory contends that men and women experience work differently because men see work as more ..... **(29)** ..... to their lives. These ..... **(30)** ..... explanations apart, today business appears to be undergoing a feminisation of leadership.

21. A. exercise   B. undertake
C. authorise   D. empower
E. tolerate

22. A. affect   B. succeed
C. compete   D. progress
E. dominate

23. A. traditional   B. charismatic
C. masculine   D. benevolent
E. authoritarian

24. A. out-live   B. out-cast
C. out-work   D. out-stand
E. out-do

25. A. employees   B. subordinates
C. managers   D. counterparts
E. superiors

26. A. minimal   B. distinct
C. unique   D. similar
E. constant

27. A. employment   B. culture
C. gender   D. class
E. category

28. A. variations   B. discriminations
C. resemblances   D. distortions
E. equalities

29. A. needy   B. desperate
C. preliminary   D. trivial
E. central

30. A. contradictory   B. corresponding
C. discriminating   D. analogical
E. identical

Reasoning Ability

31. How many meaningful English words can be formed with the letters ADIC using each letter only once in each word?
A. None   B. One
C. Two   D. Three
E. More than three

32. Four of the following five are alike in a certain way and so form a group, which is the one tat does not belong to that group?
A. Violin   B. Harp
C. Guitar   D. Flute
E. Sitar

33. If it is possible to make only one meaningful word with the first, fourth, fifth and tenth letters of the word Television, which of the following would be the second letter of that word from the right end? If no such word can be made, give 'X' as your answer and if more than one such word can be formed, give your answer as 'Y'.
A. X
B. L
C. N
D. E
E. Y

34. In a certain code TRUMP is written SUTQN. How is FIRED written in that code?
A. GJQEF
B. JGEQF
C. JQGEF
D. JGQFE
E. JGQEF

35. In a certain language 'give me more' is coded as '7 3 5', 'she has more' is coded as '9 7 1' and 'she asked me gently' is coded as '6 3 2 1'. Which of the following is the code for 'give' in that language?
A. 5
B. 7
C. 6
D. 9
E. 1

36. If each of the vowels in the word GOLIATHS is changed to the next letter in the English alphabetical series and each consonant is changed to the previous letter in the English alphabetical series, and then the alphabets so formed are arranged in alphabetical order from left to right, which of the following will be sixth from the left of the new arrangement thus formed?
A. S
B. P
C. G
D. J
E. F

37. In a certain language 'WEAK' is coded as '4$β7'. How will 'KEWRA' be coded in the same code?
A. 7 4 $ β #
B. β 7 $ 8 #
C. # β 9 7 4
D. $ β 7 9 4
E. 4 7 8 β $

38. How many such pairs of letters are there in the word FORMATION each of which has as many letters between them in the word (in both forward and backward directions) as they have between them in the English alphabetical order?
A. None
B. One
C. Two
D. Three
E. More than three

39. If the digits in the number 79246358 are arranged in descending order from left to right, what will be the difference between the difits which are third from the right and second from the left in the new arrangement?
A. 1
B. 2
C. 3
D. 4
E. 5

40. 'Music' is related to 'Notes' in the same way as 'Language' is related to ....
A. Sentences
B. Combination
C. Grammar
D. Alphabets
E. Syntax

Directions (Qs. 41–45): *Read the following information carefully and answer the questions which follow:*

If 'P * Q' means 'P is the mother of Q'.
If 'P × Q' means 'P is the father of Q'.
If 'P + Q' means 'P is the sister of Q'.
If 'P – Q' means 'P is the brother of Q'.
If 'P > Q' means 'P is the son of Q'.
If 'P < Q' means 'P is the daughter of Q'.

41. In the expression 'A × B + R > S' how is S related to A?
A. Daughter-in-law
B. Daugher
C. Wife
D. Sister
E. Cannot be determined

42. Which of the following means P is the father of S?
A. P × < R * S
B. R × P < Q – S
C. R + S > Q + P
D. S + Q – R * P
E. Cannot be determined

43. In the expression 'P + Q > A – B' how is P related to B?
A. Daughter
B. Son
C. Niece
D. Newphew
E. Cannot be determined

44. Which of the following means D is the aunt of C?

    A. D > B * A C

    B. D + B – C * A

    C. D – B – A × C

    D. D + B × A × C

    E. None of these

45. In the expression 'W > X < Y * Z' how is W related to Z?

    A. Nephew   B. Uncle

    C. Son   D. Brother-in-law

    E. None of these

Directions (Qs. 46–50): *In each question below are given three statements followed by two conclusions numbered I and II. You have to take the given statements to be true even if they seem to be at variance from commonly known facts and then decide which of the given conlusions logically follows from statements disregarding commonly known facts.*

    A. if only conclusion I follows.

    B. if only conclusion II follows.

    C. if either conclusion I or conclusion II follows.

    D. if neither conclusion I nor conclusion II follows.

    E. if both conclusions I and II follow.

46. Statements : All medicines are tablets. Some tablets are tonics. Some tonics are bitter.

    Conclusions : I. Some tablets are bitter.

                II. No medicines is a tonic,

47. Statements : All incomes are salaries. Some salaries are perks. Some perks are tangible.

    Conclusions : I. Some incomes are tangible.

                II. At least some perks are salaries.

48. Statements : All roses are red. Some red are colour. All colour are paints.

    Conclusions : I. Some red are paints.

                II. All red are roses.

49. Statements : Some casual are formal. All formal are expensive. All expensive are elegant.

    Conclusions : I. All formal are elegant.

                II. Some casual are expensive.

50. Statements : All towns are cities. All cities are urban. Some urban are rural.

    Conclusions : I. Some towns are rural.

                II. All rural are towns.

Directions (Qs. 51–55): *The following questions are based on five words given below:*

    RAT   ONE   BUT   AND   SAW

    (The new words formed after performing the mentioned operations may or may not necessarily be meaningful English words.)

51. If in each of the given words, each alphabet is changed to the next letter in the English alphabetical series, in how many words thus formed have the consonants changed to vowels?

    A. One   B. Two

    C. Three   D. Four

    E. Five

52. How many such pairs of letters are there in the word highlighted in **bold**, each of which has as many letters between them in the word (in both forward and backward directions) as they have between them in the English alphabetical order?

    A. None   B. One

    C. Two   D. Three

    E. Four

53. If in the given every words only consonants are changed with their successive letters and vowels are kept same then in how many words the vowel same or different will come twice or more than two times?

    A. None   B. One

    C. Two   D. Three

    E. Four

54. If the first letter of every words is changed with successive letter then how many meaningful word will be formed.

    A. One   B. two

    C. three   D. four

    E. five

55. If the given words are arranged alphabetically from left to right then which one of the following will be fourth from left.
   A. RAT   B. ONE
   C. BUT   D. AND
   E. SAW

Directions (Qs. 56–60): *Study the information carefully and answer the questions.*

Five friends P Q R S and T travel from Goa individually for the five cities *i.e.*, Chennai, Kolkata, Delhi, Hydrabad and Manglore by different means of transport *i.e.*, bus, train, aeroplane, car and boat.

One who traveled for Delhi did not use boat. R traveled for Manglore by car and S traveled by boat. Q traveled by aeroplane for Kolkata and T traveled by train. Delhi and Chennai in not connected with bus roate with Goa.

56. Which combination of place and transport of the following is true.
   A. Kolkata - bus   B. Delhi - aeroplane
   C. Manglore - train   D. Chennai - boat
   E. Hyderabad - car

57. Q : Kolkata Similarly, S : ?
   A. Hyderabad   B. Chennai
   C. Manglore   D. Delhi
   E. Can not be determined

58. Who of the following traveled for Delhi?
   A. T   B. R
   C. S   D. P
   E. Q

59. Which combination of the following is true for P.
   A. travelled by bus for Kolkata
   B. travelled by train for Delhi
   C. travelled by boat for Chennai
   D. travelled by bus for Hyderabad
   E. None of these

60. 5 travelled for .... by ....
   A. Hyderabad, train
   B. Chennai, boat
   C. Chennai, train
   D. Delhi, boat
   E. Delhi, train

Directions (Qs. 61–65) : *Study the following information carefully and answer the questions given below it :*

   (*i*) Eleven students A, B, C, D, E, F, G, H, I, J and K are sitting in the first row of the class facing the teacher.
   (*ii*) D who is to the immediate left of F is second to the right of C.
   (*iii*) A is second to the right of E, who is at one of the ends.
   (*iv*) J is the immediate neighbour of A and B and third to the left of G.
   (*v*) H is to the immediate left of D and third to the right of I.

61. In the above sitting arrangement which of the following statements is superfluous?
   A. (*i*)   B. (*ii*)
   C. (*iii*)   D. (*iv*)
   E. None is superfluous

62. Which of the following groups of friends is sitting to the right of G?
   A. IBJA   B. ICHDF
   C. CHDF   E. CHDE
   E. None of these

63. Who is sitting in the middle of the row?
   A. C   B. I
   C. B   D. G
   E. None of these

64. Which of the following statements is TRUE in the context of the above sitting arrangements?
   A. There are three students sitting between D and G
   B. G and C are neighbours sitting to the immediate right of H.
   C. B is sitting between J and I
   D. K is between A and J
   E. None of these

65. If E and D, C and B, A and H and K and F interchange their positions, which of the following pairs of students is sitting at the ends?
   A. D and E   B. E and F
   C. D and K   D. K and F
   E. None of these

Quantitative Aptitude

Directions (Qs. 66–75): *What should come in place of the question mark (?) in the following questions?*

66. $205 \times ? \times 13 = 33625 + 25005$
  A. 22 B. 27
  C. 33 D. 39
  E. None of these

67. $[(135)^2 \div 15 \times 32] \div ? = 45 \times 24$
  A. 18 B. 24
  C. 36 D. 44
  E. None of these

68. $(8.2\% \text{ of } 365) - (1.75\% \text{ of } 108) = ?$
  A. 16.02 B. 28.04
  C. 42.34 D. 53.76
  E. None of these

69. $(10)^{24} \times (10)^{-21} = ?$
  A. 3 B. 10
  C. 100 D. 1000
  E. None of these

70. $15.594 - 4.312 - 3.517 - 1.689 = ?$
  A. 6.706 B. 6.760
  C. 6.670 D. 6.607
  E. None of these

71. $69 \div 3 \times 0.85 + 14.5 - 3 = ?$
  A. 36.45 B. 23.85
  C. 42.95 D. 18.65
  E. None of these

72. $2172 \div ? = 1832 - 956 - 514$
  A. 6 B. 8
  C. 10 D. 12
  E. None of these

73. $4368 + 2158 - 596 - ? = 3421 + 1262$
  A. 1066 B. 1174
  C. 1247 D. 1387
  E. None of these

74. $666.06 + 66.60 + 0.66 + 6.06 + 6 + 60 = ?$
  A. 819.56 B. 805.38
  C. 826.44 D. 798.62
  E. None of these

75. $(96)^2 + (63)^2 = (?)^2 - (111)^2 - 8350$
  A. 33856
  B. 30276
  C. 174
  D. 184
  E. None of these

Directions (Qs. 76–80) : *Study the following table carefully to answer the questions that follow:–*

NUMBER OF BOYS AND GIRLS IN FIVE STREAMS OF A COLLEGE OVER THE YEARS

YEAR	STREAMS									
	Arts		Science		Commerce		Management		IT	
	Boys	Girls	Boys	Girls	Boys	Girls	Boys	Girls	Boys	Girls
2008	556	414	619	505	668	612	770	633	670	515
2009	763	608	793	612	781	616	667	439	866	722
2010	672	519	540	516	859	713	778	727	781	619
2011	809	602	928	908	870	811	849	729	977	817
2012	745	510	884	820	967	819	562	938	990	808
2013	698	413	765	616	571	515	1288	1016	1151	1010

76. What is the average number of Girls from Commerce Stream for the given years?
  A. 681 B. 675
  C. 618 D. 657
  E. None of these

77. What is the ratio of the total number of Boys to the total number of Girls, from all the Streams together, for the year 2013?
  A. 2 : 3 B. 14 : 13
  C. 52 : 49 D. 213 : 170
  E. None of these

78. What is the ratio of the total number of Boys to the total number of Girls in the Management Stream for all the years together?

   A. 9 : 8   B. 71 : 86

   C. 91 : 83   D. 27 : 23

   E. None of these

79. What is the total number of Boys, for all the Streams together, in the year 2010?

   A. 4148   B. 3630

   C. 4433   D. 3247

   E. None of these

80. The number of Boys in Arts Stream in the year 2010 is **approximately** what per cent of the total number of Boys for all the years together in Arts Stream?

   A. 27   B. 34

   C. 08   D. 39

   E. 16

Directions (Qs. 81–85) : *What should come in place of the question mark (?) in the following number series?*

81. 16 14 24 66 256 1270 ?

   A. 8564   B. 5672

   C. 4561   D. 7608

   E. 6340

82. 12 6.5 7.5 12.75 27.5 71.25 ?

   A. 225.75   B. 216.75

   C. 209.75   D. 236.75

   E. 249.75

83. 22 23 27 36 52 77 ?

   A. 111   B. 109

   C. 113   D. 117

   E. 115

84. 16 24 36 54 81 121.5 ?

   A. 182.25   B. 174.85

   C. 190.65   D. 166.55

   E. 158.95

85. 12 12 18 45 180 1170 ?

   A. 13485   B. 14675

   C. 15890   D. 16756

   E. 12285

Directions (Qs. 86–90) : *Study the information carefully to answer the following questions–*

In an organization consisting of 750 employees, the ratio of males to Females is 8 : 7 respectively. All the employees work in five different departments viz. HR, Management, PR, IT and Recruitment. 16 per cent of the Females work in Management Department. 32 per cent of males are in HR Department. One-fifth of the Females are in the Department of Recruitment. The ratio of males to Females in the Management Department is 3 : 2 respectively. 20 per cent of the total numbers of employees are in PR Department. Females working in Recruitment are 50 per cent of the Males working in the same Department. 8 per cent of the Males are in IT Department. The remaining Males are in PR Department. 22 per cent of the Females work in HR Department and the remaining Females are working in IT Department.

86. What is the total number of employees working in the Management Department?

   A. 128   B. 77

   C. 210   D. 140

   E. None of these

87. What is the total number of Females working in the IT and Recruitment Department together?

   A. 147   B. 83

   C. 126   D. 45

   E. None of these

88. What is the number of Females working in the HR Department?

   A. 77   B. 70

   C. 56   D. 134

   E. None of these

89. Number of Males working in HR Department forms **approximately** what per cent of total number of the employees in the Organization?

   A. 20   B. 28

   C. 32   D. 9

   E. 17

90. Number of Males working in PR Department forms what percent of the number of Females working in the same Department? (rounded off to two digits after decimal)

   A. 22.98   B. 15.68

   C. 11.94   D. 6.79

   E. 27.86

Directions (Qs. 91–95): *What approximate value should come in place of question mark (?) in the following questions? (You are not expected to calculate the exact value.)*

91. $628.306 + 6.1325 \times 44.0268 = ?$
   A. 820   B. 970
   C. 1050   D. 1175
   E. 900

92. $(935.82)^2 = ?$
   A. 870000   B. 867500
   C. 888800   D. 875800
   E. 899800

93. $814296 \times 36 = ? \times 96324$
   A. 326   B. 272
   C. 304   D. 358
   E. 260

94. $(739\% \text{ of } 383) \div 628 = ?$
   A. 10.00   B. 4.50
   C. 15.75   D. 19.25
   E. 24.15

95. $(9795 + 7621 + 938) \div (541 + 831 + 496) = ?$
   A. 9   B. 13
   C. 17   D. 23
   E. 29

Directions (Qs. 96–100): *Study the graph carefully to answer the questions that follow:*

NUMBER OF GIRLS ENROLLED IN DIFFERENT HOBBY CLASSES IN VARIOUS INSTITUTES IN A YEAR

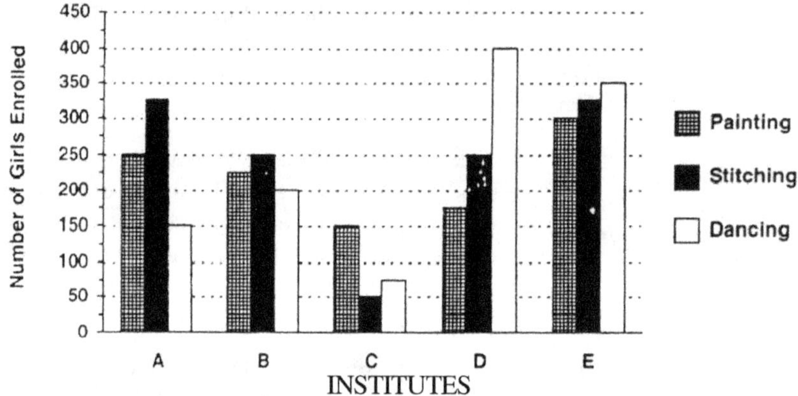

96. What is the total number of Girls Enrolled in Painting from all the Institutes together?
   A. 1150   B. 1200
   C. 1275   D. 1100
   E. None of these

97. What is the respective ratio of total number of Girls Enrolled in Painting, Stitching and Dancing from all the Institutes together?
   A. 44 : 48 : 47   B. 43 : 47 : 48
   C. 44 : 47 : 48   D. 47 : 48 : 44
   E. None of these

98. Number of Girls Enrolled in Dancing in Institute A forms what per cent of total number of Girls Enrolled in all the Hobby Classes together in that Institute? (rounded off to two digits after decimal)
   A. 23.87   B. 17.76
   C. 31.23   D. 33.97
   E. 20.69

99. Number of Girls Enrolled in Stitching in Institute B forms **approximately** what per cent of the total number of Girls Enrolled in Stitching in all the Institutes together?
   A. 29   B. 21
   C. 33   D. 37
   E. 45

100. What is the respective ratio of total number of Girls Enrolled in Painting in the Institutes A & C together to those Enrolled in Stitching in the Institutes D & E together?
   A. 5 : 4   B. 5 : 7
   C. 16 : 23   D. 9 : 8
   E. None of these

ANSWERS

1	2	3	4	5	6	7	8	9	10
D	C	C	B	A	C	C	B	C	D

11	12	13	14	15	16	17	18	19	20
B	E	C	A	A	A	C	A	B	C

21	22	23	24	25	26	27	28	29	30
B	B	C	E	D	D	C	B	E	A

31	32	33	34	35	36	37	38	39	40
B	D	C	E	A	B	E	D	D	A

41	42	43	44	45	46	47	48	49	50
C	A	D	E	B	D	B	D	E	D

51	52	53	54	55	56	57	58	59	60
E	D	E	B	A	D	B	A	D	B

61	62	63	64	65	66	67	68	69	70
E	C	B	C	C	A	C	B	D	D

71	72	73	74	75	76	77	78	79	80
E	A	C	B	D	A	D	C	B	E

81	82	83	84	85	86	87	88	89	90
D	B	C	A	E	D	B	A	E	C

91	92	93	94	95	96	97	98	99	100
E	D	C	B	A	D	A	E	B	C

Some Selected Explanatory Answers

31. Only one meaningful word ACID can be formed from the given letters.

32. Only flute is blowed with mouth out of the given murical instruments.

33. Only VENT a meaningful word can beformed with the first, the fourth, the fifth and the tenth letter of the given word TELEVISION, ie. T, E, V, N.

34.
```
T  R  U  M  P        F  I  R     E  D
 X  ↓  X  ↓           X  ↓        X
S  U  T  Q  N        J  G  Q     E  F
```

35. 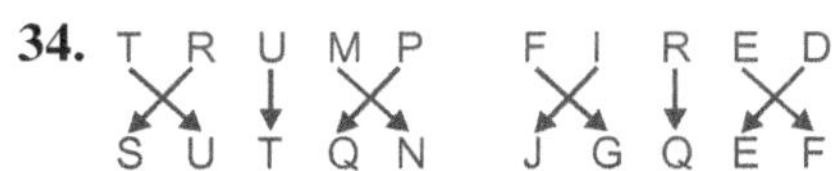

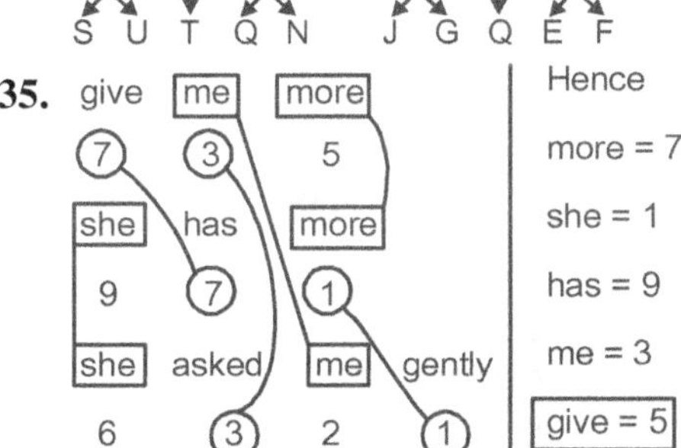

Hence

more = 7

she = 1

has = 9

me = 3

give = 5

36. F P K J B A G R $\Rightarrow$ B F G J K $\boxed{P}$ R S

37. The correct code of K E W R A is β$479

38.
```
F O R M A T I O N
```

39. 9 8 7 6 5 $\underline{4}$ 3 2 Required difference = 4 − 4 = 4.

41. $A \xrightarrow{Father} B \xrightarrow{Sister} R \xrightarrow{Son} S$

42. $P \xrightarrow{Father} Q \xrightarrow{Daughter} R \xrightarrow{Mother} S$

$R \xrightarrow{Father} P \xrightarrow{Daughter} Q \xrightarrow{Brother} S$

$R \xrightarrow{Sister} S \xrightarrow{Son} R \xrightarrow{Sister} P$

$S \xrightarrow{Sister} Q \xrightarrow{Brother} R \xrightarrow{Mother} P$

According of option A R is mother, 'Q' is sister and 'P' is father of 'S'

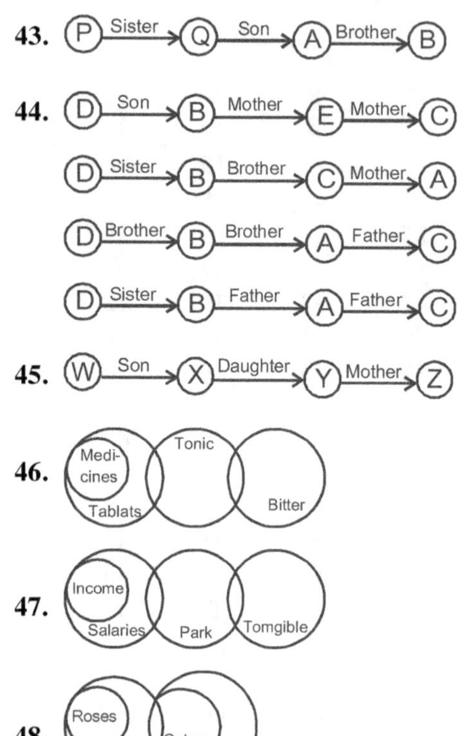

43. $P \xrightarrow{\text{Sister}} Q \xrightarrow{\text{Son}} A \xrightarrow{\text{Brother}} B$

44. $D \xrightarrow{\text{Son}} B \xrightarrow{\text{Mother}} E \xrightarrow{\text{Mother}} C$

$D \xrightarrow{\text{Sister}} B \xrightarrow{\text{Brother}} C \xrightarrow{\text{Mother}} A$

$D \xrightarrow{\text{Brother}} B \xrightarrow{\text{Brother}} A \xrightarrow{\text{Father}} C$

$D \xrightarrow{\text{Sister}} B \xrightarrow{\text{Father}} A \xrightarrow{\text{Father}} C$

45. $W \xrightarrow{\text{Son}} X \xrightarrow{\text{Daughter}} Y \xrightarrow{\text{Mother}} Z$

46. Medicines, Tonic, Tablats, Bitter

47. Income, Salaries, Park, Tomgible

48. Roses, Red, Colour, Paints

49. Casual, Formal, expensive, elegant

50. Town, Cities, urban, Rural

51. RAT, ONE BUT AND SAW
The required arrangement is %
SBU, POF, CVU, BOE, TBX

52. R A T   O N E   B U T

53. The required arrangement is:

S A U   O O E   C U U   A O E   T A X

54. The required arrangement is:
SAT   PNE   CUT   BND   TAW

55. The required arragement is:
AND   BUT   ONE   RAT   SAW

For Questions 56-60

Manglore	Hyderabad	Delhi	Kolkata	Chennai		Bus	Train	Aeroplane	Car	Boat
×	í	×	×	×	P	í	×	×	×	×
×	×	×	í	×	Q	×	×	í	×	×
í	×	×	×	×	R	×	×	×	í	×
×	×	×	×	í	S	×	×	×	×	í
×	×	í	×	×	T	×	í	×	×	×

For answers **61** to **64** the sitting arrangement of the students is :
E, K, A, J, B, I, G, C, H, D, F

65. The new sitting arrangement will be :
D, F, H, J, C, I, G, B, A, E, K

66. $205 \times ? \times 13 = 33625 + 25005$

$$\therefore \ ? = \frac{(33625 + 25005)}{205 \times 13} = \frac{58620}{205 \times 13} = 22$$

67. $\left[(135)^2 \div 15 \times 32\right] \div ? = 45 \times 24$

$\Rightarrow [135 \times 9 \times 32] \div ? = 45 \times 24$

$\Rightarrow [38880] \div ? = 45 \times 24$

$$\therefore \ ? = \frac{38880}{45 \times 24} = 36$$

70. $15.594 - 4.312 - 3.517 - 1.689$
$= 15.594 - 9.518 = 6.076$

71. $69 \div 3 \times 0.85 + 14.5 - 3$
$= 23 \times 0.85 + 14.5 - 3$
$= 19.55 + 14.5 - 3 = 34.05 - 3$
$= 31.05$

72. $2172 \div ? = 1832 - 956 - 514$
$\Rightarrow 2172 \div ? = 362$
$\therefore \ 2172 \div 362 = 6$

75. $(96)^2 + (63)^2 = (?)^2 - (111)^2 - 8350$

$\Rightarrow \ (?)^2 = (96)^2 + (63)^2 + (111)^2 + 8350$

$= 9216 + 3969 + 12321 + 8350$

$= 33{,}856$

$\therefore \ ? = \sqrt{33856} = 184$

76. The average number of Girls from Commerce stream for the given years

$$= \frac{(612 + 616 + 713 + 811 + 819 + 515)}{6}$$

$$= \frac{4086}{6} = 681$$

80. The required per cent

$$= \frac{674}{(556 + 763 + 672 + 809 + 745 + 698)} \times 100$$

$$= \frac{672 \times 100}{4243} = 15.83\% \simeq 16\%$$

81. Here,

$16 \times 1 - 2 = 16 - 2 = 14$

$14 \times 2 - 4 = 28 - 4 = 24$

$24 \times 3 - 6 = 72 - 6 = 66$

$66 \times 4 - 8 = 264 - 8 = 256$

$256 \times 5 - 10 = 1280 - 10 = 1270$

$1270 \times 6 - 12 = 7620 - 12 = 7608$

82. Here,

$12 \times 0.5 + 0.5 = 6 + 0.5 = 6.5$

$6.5 \times 1 + 1 = 6.5 + 1 = 7.5$

$7.5 \times 1.5 + 1 = 11.25 + 1.5 = 12.75$

$12.75 \times 2 + 2 = 25.5 + 2 = 27.5$

$27.5 \times 2.5 + 2.5 = 46.75 + 2.5 = 71.25$

$71.25 \times 3 + 3 = 213.75 + 3 = 216.75$

85. Here,

$12 \times 1 = 12$

$12 \times 1.5 = 18$

$18 \times (1 + 1.5) = 18 \times 2.5 = 45$

$45 \times (2.5 + 1.5) = 45 \times 4 = 180$

$180 \times (4 + 2.5) = 180 \times 6.5 = 1170$

$1170 \times (6.5 + 4) = 1170 \times 10.5 = 12285$

86–90:

Total number of employees = 750

Number of males = 400

Number of females = 350

Deptt.	Males	Females
HR	128	77
Mgmt.	84	56
PR	16	134
IT	32	13
Rect.	140	70

86. The required number of students = 84 + 56 = 140

87. The required number of students = 13 + 70 = 83

90. The required per cent $= \dfrac{16}{134} \times 100$

$$= \frac{800}{67} = 11.94\%$$

96. The required number of girls

$= 250 + 225 + 150 + 175 + 300 \ = 1100$

98. The required per cent

$$= \frac{150}{(250 + 325 + 150)} \times 100$$

$$= \frac{150}{725} \times 100 = \frac{600}{29}\% = 20.69\%$$

99. The required per cent

$$= \frac{250}{325 + 250 + 50 + 250 + 325}$$

$$= \frac{250}{1200} \times 100 = \frac{125}{6}$$

$= 20.83\% \simeq 21\%$

SBI Junior Associates & Junior Agricultural Associates
(Clerical Cadre Exam)

Directions (Qs. 1–15): *Read the following passage carefully and answer the questions given below it. Certain words/phrases have been printed in **bold** to help you locate them while answering some of the questions.*

Books are a great treasurehouse of knowledge. They are the living examples of man's **march** on the path to higher and higher civilisation. The great men who died long ago, live in their books. We feel their very personality and existence when we read their books. We feel as if they were conversing with us.

Books not only store civilization but also carry it forward. All coming generations get the light of knowledge from the books written by their ancestors and try to improve upon that knowledge. Civilization cannot make much **headway** in a country where there are not many **great** books. We get through books the latest knowledge in the fields of arts, science, commerce, etc. This knowledge is helpful to us and **enables** us to achieve success in the field of our choice.

Books are never failing friends. They never **desert** us, not even when all fair-weather friends have deserted us. They dispel the dark clouds of gloom from our minds and increase our happiness if we are already happy. Through the ages, the scriptures and other great books have provided immeasurable **solace** to the wounded and strife-torn humanity.

There may be books prescribed for some course or profession, but then there are books for general study. The books of literature—poetry, drama, novel, short stories, etc., are generally highly thrilling and inspiring if they are written by a good author. There may be tragic, comical or humorous books. The question is that of an individual's choice.

To be a lover of books, though not to be book-worm, is a sign of good luck. A voracious reader gets much **more pleasure** from reading books than a miser gets in hoarding money. The knowledge embedded in books is valueless; so is pleasure obtained from reading them. A good book absorbs the whole spirit of man; the reader's pleasure is indescribable.

1. Which of the following, according to the passage, is not true about books?
   A. They are source of inspiration
   B. They are source of knowledge
   C. They are source of happiness
   D. They are means of livelihood
   E. All are true

2. How do the books help in progress of civilization?
   A. Based on the earlier books new knowledge is obtained
   B. The books provide solution to many problems
   C. The books inspire the scientists
   D. Not mentioned in the passage
   E. None of these

3. How do the books make people more happy?
   A. They help the reader to overcome the shadows of uncertainty

B. They help bring in joy by amusing the reader through their content

C. They help the reader to understand the darker side of life

D. They give moral support to the reader in his loneliness

E. Not mentioned in the passage

4. Which of the following is the author's view about the knowledge and pleasure derived from books?

(1) We get more of knowledge and less of pleasure

(2) We get more of pleasure and less of knowledge

(3) We get knowledge and pleasure in equal measure

A. only (1)   B. only (2)
C. either (1) or (2)   D. only (3)
E. None of these

5. The high quality of books produced by a country indicates:

A. it has a high rate of literacy

B. it has a progressive civilization

C. it is no an industrialised nation

D. it has learned ancestors

E. None of these

6. Why are the books, according to the passage, called never-failing friends?

A. Books do not betray individuals

B. Books are inanimate

C. Books always give companionship to the reader

D. Books are available in the market anytime unlike others

E. None of these

7. How do the books help in bringing peace in the minds of people?

A. Books provide information about the past civilization

B. Books help people learn to take correct steps with the help of the recorded information

C. Books act as a window to the minds of the great men

D. Not mentioned in the passage

E. None of these

8. Which of the following has been described as a sign of good luck?

A. Being a miser

B. Having lot of money

C. Advancing the culture

D. A passion for books

E. None of these

Directions (Qs. 9–12): *Choose the word which is most nearly the SAME in meaning as the word given in bold capitals as used in the passage.*

9. SOLACE

A. peace   B. tranquillity
C. calmness   D. solidarity
E. console

10. ENABLES

A. helps   B. succeeds
C. promotes   D. stops
E. propels

11. HEADWAY

A. higher   B. forge
C. movement   D. prosper
E. improve

12. MARCH

A. move   B. progress
C. pass   D. register
E. parade

Directions (Qs. 13–15): *Choose the word which is most OPPOSITE in meaning of the word given in bold capitals as used in the passage.*

13. GREAT

A. small   B. thin
C. short   D. plain
E. ordinary

14. PLEASURE

A. displeasure   B. pain
C. happiness   D. hardship
E. sadness

15. DESERT

A. waterhole   B. bitter
C. accompany   D. propel
E. help

Directions (Qs. 16–20) : *Each sentence below has a blank, each blank indicating that something has been omitted. Choose the word for each blank which best fits the meaning of the sentence as a whole.*

16. The speaker's ..... over his subject was seen through his ..... discourse.
   A. mastery, fluent   B. efficiency, thorough
   C. lethargy, dull   D. grip, boring
   E. skill, pleasant

17. Workers in ealier days were ..... because of which the industries ..... a lot.
   A. honest, lost   B. rich, flourished
   C. autocrats, developed   D. inefficient, suffered
   E. idle, prospered

18. A close ..... of the bill shows that the provisions are ..... and there is a need to add certain crucial elements to them.
   A. examination, sufficient
   B. observation, helpful
   C. scrutiny, inadequate
   D. file, numerous
   E. account, excellent

19. His ..... speech has seriously ..... the young minds.
   A. audacious, delighted
   B. maiden, flattered
   C. humorous, damaged
   D. irresponsible, misled
   E. eccentric, questioned

20. On ..... of the enquiry, if it is found that the ..... are true, the enquiry officer will report the matter to the higher authority.
   A. demand, findings
   B. completion, allegations
   C. instituting, charges
   D. withdrawal, inferences
   E. establishment, results

Directions (Qs. 21–25): *Read each sentence to find out whether there is any grammatical error or idiomatic error in it. The error, if any, will be in one part of the sentence. The number of that part is the answer. If there is "No Error" the answer is 'E'. (Ignore errors of punctuation if any.)*

21. (A) Though he suffered of fever,/(B) he attended office/(C) and completed all the pending/(D) work by sitting late./(E) No error.

22. (A) As always have been said,/(B) parents should not/(C) impose their desires/(D) on their wards./(E) No error.

23. (A) Being a very fast worker,/(B) he is always liking/(C) by all his colleagues./(D) and superiors too./(E) No error.

24. (A) We fail to understand/(B) why do most educated people/(C) lose their temper even/(D) without any apparent reason./(E) No error.

25. (A) You may not always/(B) get whatever you deserve/(C) but that does not belittle/(D) the importance for your work./(E) No error.

Directions (Qs. 26–30): *Which of the phrases A, B, C and D given below should replace the phrase given in* **bold** *in the following sentence to make the sentence grammatically meaningful and correct? If the sentence is correct as it is and 'No correction is required', mark 'E' as the answer.*

26. "Friends and comrades, the light has gone **away from** our lives and there is darkness everywhere."
   A. off   B. out of
   C. out from   D. out off
   E. No correction required

27. We **can not always convey** ourselves in simple sentences.
   A. cannot always convey
   B. can not always express
   C. cannot always express
   D. can not always communicate
   E. No correction required

28. **Shapes** of gods and goddesses are worshipped by people.
   A. Images   B. Reflections
   C. Clay shapes   D. Clay toys
   E. No correction required

29. The crops are dying; **it must not had** rained.
   A. must had not   B. must not be
   C. must not have   D. must not have been
   E. No correction required

30. It is always better to make people realise the importance of discipline than to **impose them on it.**
   A. impose it with them
   B. impose them with it
   C. imposing them on it
   D. impose it on them
   E. No correction required

Reasoning Ability

Direction. (Qs. 31–35): *The letter group in each question below is to be codified in the following number codes:*

Letters : M T V B S A Z R P C
Number Codes : 7 4 1 9 6 8 2 5 0 3

You have to find out which of the answers A or B or C or D has the correct coded form of the given letters and indicate it on the answer sheet. If none of the coded form is correct mark E as the answer.

31. TACZMBP
A. 4832790	B. 4328790
C. 4823970	D. 4823790

E. None of these

32. SRMVPBA
A. 6751098	B. 6571089
C. 6571098	D. 6750198

E. None of these

33. VZBMPRC
A. 1927053	B. 1279503
C. 1297503	D. 1297053

E. None of these

34. ZTCAVSP
A. 2483160	B. 2438160
C. 2348160	D. 2431860

E. None of these

35. SMAVPTC
A. 6871043	B. 6780134
C. 6781034	D. 6870143

E. None of these

Directions (Qs. 36–40): *In each of the questions below are given three statements followed by two conclusions numbered I and II. You have to take the given statements to be true even if they seem to be at variance from commonly known facts. Read all the conclusions and then decide which of the given conclusions logically follows from the given statements disregarding commonly known facts.*

Give answer (A) if only conclusion I follows.
Give answer (B) if only conclusion II follows.
Give answer (C) if either conclusion I or II follows.
Give answer (D) if neither conclusion I nor II follows.
Give answer (E) if both conclusion I and II follow.

36. Statements: All rooms are tables.
Some tables are cards.
All cards are spoons.
Conclusions:
I. Some spoons are rooms.
II. Some spoons are tables.

37. Statements: Some chairs are windows.
Some windows are walls.
Some walls are houses.
Conclusions:
I. Some houses are chairs.
II. No house is chair.

38. Statements: Some pins are swords.
All swords are knives.
All knives are sticks.
Conclusions:
I. Some sticks are pins.
II. Some knives are pins.

39. Statements: All desks are plates.
All plates are mirrors.
All mirrors are boxes.
Conclusions:
I. Some boxes are plates.
II. All mirrors are desks.

40. Statements: All roads are buses.
No bus is train.
Some trains are platforms.
Conclusions:
I. Some platforms are roads.
II. Some trains are roads.

Directions (Qs. 41–45): *Study the following information carefully and answer the question given below:*

A, B, D, F, H, J, K, T and W are sitting around a circle facing at the center. D is third to the left of A who is fourth to the left of T. H is third to the right of F who is third to the right of T. B is third to the right of K who is not an immediate neighbour of F or D. J is not an immediate neighbour of A.

41. Who is to the immediate right of D?
A. F	B. B
C. W	D. Data inadequate

E. None of these

42. Who is second to the right of W?
A. A
B. K
C. H
D. Data inadequate
E. None of these

43. Who is fourth to the right of B?
A. W
B. A
C. H
D. Data inadequate
E. None of these

44. What is J's position with respect to B?
A. Third to the left
B. Third to the right
C. Second to the right
D. Fourth to the right
E. Second to the left

45. Which of the following pairs represents the immediate neighbours of H?
A. KW
B. AJ
C. JW
D. KA
E. Data inadequate

46. 'Teacher' is related to 'school' in the same way as 'cook' is related to '.......'
A. Food
B. Kitchen
C. Hostel
D. House
E. Market

47. Atul walks 20 metres towards South. Turning to the left he walks 30 metres, then turning right he walks 10 metres, then turning right he walks 40 metres, then turning right he walks 30 metres and stops. In what direction is he with respect to his starting point?
A. South-West
B. West
C. North-West
D. He is at starting point
E. None of these

48. What will come in place of question mark (?) in the following series?
TG   HU   VI   JW   ?
A. KY
B. KX
C. YK
D. XK
E. None of these

49. Satish is 15 ranks above Sushil who ranks 28th in a class of 50. What is Satish's rank from the bottom?
A. 39
B. 37
C. 38
D. 35
E. None of these

50. Four of the following five are alike in a certain way and hence form a group. Which one **does not** belong to the group?
A. Year
B. Month
C. Day
D. Week
E. Time

51. If Ramesh's mother's brother is Alok's father's brother, then Ramesh's mother is Alok's:
A. Grandmother
B. Aunt
C. Cousin
D. Sister-in-law
E. None of these

52. In a certain code language 'Ne Pe Le' means 'what is this'. 'Bo Le Se' means 'is that okay' and 'Se Ni Di' means 'that was easy'. What is the code for 'okay' in that code language?
A. Le
B. Se
C. Ne
D. Ni
E. None of these

53. Which of the following letters is as far away from M to the right as D is away from N ?
A B C D E F G H I J K L M N O P Q R S T U V W X Y Z
A. X
B. V
C. C
D. Y
E. None of these

54. Among P, Q, R, S and T, T is shorter than S and P. Q is shorter than only P. Who among them is the shortest?
A. Cannot be determined
B. R
C. T
D. Q
E. None of these

55. In a certain code 'GIVE' is written as 'VIEG' and 'OVER' is written as 'EVRO'. How will 'DISK' be written in that code?
A. SIDK
B. KISD
C. KDSI
D. SIKD
E. None of these

Directions (Qs. 56–58) : *Following questions are based on the five three digit numbers given below:*

937   425   816   398   671

56. If the positions of the first and the third digits within each number are reversed, which of the following will be the third digit of the second lowest number?

A. 8   B. 9
C. 4   D. 6
E. None of these

57. Which of the following is the sum of the first and the second digits of the lowest number?
A. 12   B. 6
C. 9   D. 13
E. None of these

58. Which of the following is the second digit of the second highest number?
A. 3   B. 2
C. 1   D. 9
E. 7

59. Town R is towards East of town H and is towards South of town K. Town K is towards which direction of town H?
A. South-East   B. South-West
C. North-West   D. Data inadequate
E. None of these

60. Suresh walked 30 metres towards North, took a left turn and walked 40 metres. He again took a left turn and walked 30 metres. How far is he from the starting point?
A. 100 metres   B. 60 metres
C. 70 metres   D. 40 metres
E. Data inadequate

Directions (Qs. 61–65) : *Study the following information carefully and answer the questions given below:*

P, Q, R, S, T, U, V and F are sitting around a circle facing the centre. U is third to the right of Q who is third to the right of F. P is third to the left of F. R is fourth to the left of P. T is third to the right of S. S is not a neighbour of P.

61. Four of the following five are similar in a certain way based on their positions in the seating arrangement and so form a group. Which of the following **does not** belong to that group?
A. RQT   B. QPV
C. SPU   D. FRT
E. RSF

62. Who is sitting third to the left of Q?
A. F   B. U
C. S   D. P
E. R

63. In which of the following pairs is the first person sitting to the immediate right of the second person?
A. TQ   B. VP
C. PU   D. FS
E. None of these

64. What is P's position with respect to F?
A. Third to the left   B. Third to the right
C. Second to the left   D. Immediate right
E. Fourth to the left

65. Who is sitting second to the left of U?
A. Q   B. P
C. V   D. F
E. T

Quantitative Aptitude

66. The difference between 42% of a number and 28% of the same number is 210. What is 59% of that number?
A. 630   B. 885
C. 420   D. 900
E. None of these

67. What **approximate** value should come in place of the question mark (?) in the following questions?
$4275 \div 496 \times (21)^2 = ?$
A. 3795   B. 3800
C. 3810   D. 3875
D. 3995

68. A canteen requires 112 kgs. of wheat for a week. How many kgs. of wheat will it require for 69 days?
A. 1,204 kgs.   B. 1,401 kgs.
C. 1,104 kgs.   D. 1,014 kgs.
E. None of these

69. If an amount of ₹ 41,910/- is distributed equally amongst 22 persons. How much amount would each person get?
A. ₹ 1,905/-   B. ₹ 2,000/-
C. ₹ 1,885/-   D. ₹ 2,105/-
E. None of these

70. The cost of 4 Cell-phones and 7 Digital cameras is ₹ 1,25,627/-. What is the cost of 8 Cell-phones and 14 Digital cameras?
A. ₹ 2,51,254/-
B. ₹ 2,52,627/-
C. ₹ 2,25,524/-
D. Cannot be determined
E. None of these

Directions (Qs. 71–75): *Each of the questions below consists of a questions and two statements numbered I and II are given below it. You have to decide whether the data provided in the statements are sufficient to answer the question. Read both the statements and —*

Give answer (A) if the data in Statement I alone are sufficient to answer the question, while the data in Statement II alone are not sufficient to answer the question.

Give answer (B) if the data in Statement II alone are sufficient to answer the question, while the data in Statement I alone are not sufficient to answer the question.

Give answer (C) if the data in Statement I alone or in Statement II alone are sufficient to answer the question.

Give answer (D) if the data in both the Statements I and II are not sufficient to answer the question.

Give answer (E) if the data in both Statements I and II together are necessary to answer the question.

71. What is the area of the circle?
I. Perimeter of the circle is 88 cms
II. Diameter of the circle is 28 cms

72. What is the rate of interest?
I. Simple interest accrued on an amount of ₹ 25,000/- in two years less than the compound interest for the same period by ₹ 250/-
II. Simple interest accrued in 10 years is equal to the principal

73. What is the number of trees planted in the field in rows and columns?
I. Number of columns is more than the number of rows by 4
II. Number of trees in each column is an even number

74. What is the area of the right-angled triangle?
I. Height of the triangle is three-fourth of the base
II. Diagonal of the triangle is 5 metres

75. What is the father's present age?
I. Father's present age is five times the son's present age
II. Five years ago the father's age was fifteen times the son's age that time

Directions (Qs. 76–80) : *Study the following graph carefully to answer these questions:*

Profit earned (in Crore Rs.) by Seven Companies during 2012-2013

76. What is the ratio between the profit earned by Company A in 2013 and the profit earned by Company B in 2012 respectively?
   A. 4 : 3   B. 3 : 2
   C. 3 : 4   D. 2 : 3
   E. None of these

77. What is the difference (in Crore ₹) between the total profit earned by Companies E, F and G together in 2012 and the total profit earned by these companies in 2013?
   A. 70   B. 75
   C. 78   D. 82
   E. None of these

78. What is the ratio between the total profit earned by Company C in 2012 & 2013 together and the total profit earned by Company E in these two years respectively?
   A. 11 : 9   B. 9 : 10
   C. 10 : 11   D. 11 : 10
   E. None of these

79. What was the average profit earned by all the companies in 2012? (In Crore ₹ Rounded-Off to two digits after decimal).
   A. 52.75   B. 53.86
   C. 52.86   D. 53.75
   E. None of these

80. Profit earned by Company B in 2013 is what per cent of the profit earned by the same company in 2012?
   A. 133.33   B. 75
   C. 67.66   D. 75.25
   E. None of these

Directions (Qs. 81–85): *Study the following table carefully to answer these questions.*

Table giving percentage of unemployed male and female youth and the total population for different states in 2012 and 2013

State	2012			2013		
	M	F	T	M	F	T
A	12	15	32	7	8	35
B	8	7	18	10	9	20
C	9	10	28	10	12	34
D	10	6	24	8	8	30
E	6	8	30	7	6	32
F	7	5	28	8	7	35

M = Percentage of unemployed Male youth over total population.
F = Percentage of unemployed female youth over total population.
T = Total population of the state in lakhs.

81. What was the total number of unemployed youth in State A in 2013?
   A. 2,20,000   B. 3,25,000
   C. 5,20,000   D. 5,25,000
   E. None of these

82. How many female youth were unemployed in State D in 2012?
   A. 14,400   B. 1,44,000
   C. 1,40,000   D. 14,000
   E. None of these

83. Number of unemployed male youth in State A in 2012 was what per cent of the number of unemployed female youth in State E in 2013?
   A. 66   B. 50
   C. 200   D. 133
   E. None of these

84. What was the difference between the number of unemployed male youth in State F in 2012 and the number of unemployed male youth in State A in 2013?
   A. 70,000   B. 45,000
   C. 68,000   D. 65,000
   E. None of these

85. What was the respective ratio between unemployed male youth in State D in 2012 and the unemployed male youth in State D in 2013?
   A. 1 : 1   B. 2 : 3
   C. 3 : 2   D. 4 : 5
   E. None of these

Directions (Qs. 86–90): *What should come in place of the question mark (?) in the following questions?*

86. 92.5% of 550 = ?
   A. 506.45   B. 521.65
   C. 518.55   D. 508.75
   E. None of these

87. $12^4 \times 12^{13}$ = ?
   A. 12^7 B. 12^{39}
   C. 12^{17} D. 12^{-7}
   E. None of these

88. 12.22 + 22.21 + 221.12 = ?
A. 250.55   B. 255.50
C. 250.05   D. 255.05
E. None of these

89. 464 ÷ (16 × 2.32) = ?
A. 12.5   B. 14.5
C. 10.5   D. 8.5
E. None of these

90. 78 ÷ 5 ÷ 0.5 = ?
A. 15.6   B. 31.2
C. 7.8   D. 20.4
E. None of these

91. A bus covers a distance of 2,924 kms. in 43 hours. What is the speed of the bus?
A. 72 kms./hr.
B. 60 kms./hr.
C. 68 kms./hr.
D. Cannot be determined
E. None of these

92. If $(9)^3$ is subtracted from the square of a number, the answer so obtained is 567. What is the number?
A. 36   B. 28
C. 42   D. 48
E. None of these

93. What would be the simple interest obtained on an amount of ₹ 5,760/- at the rate of 6 p.c.p.a. after 3 years?
A. ₹ 1,036.80   B. ₹ 1,666.80
C. ₹ 1,336.80   D. ₹ 1,063.80
E. None of these

94. What is 333 times 131?
A. 46,323   B. 43,623
C. 43,290   D. 42,957
E. None of these

95. The product of two successive numbers is 8556. What is the smaller number?
A. 89   B. 94
C. 90   D. 92
E. None of these

96. The owner of an electronics shop charges his customer 22% more than the cost price. If a customer paid ₹ 10,980/- for a DVD Player, then what was the cost price of the DVD Player?
A. ₹ 8,000/-   B. ₹ 8,800/-
C. ₹ 9,500/-   D. ₹ 9,200/-
E. None of these

97. What would be the compound interest obtained on an amount of ₹ 3,000/- at the rate of 8 p.c.p.a. after 2 years?
A. ₹ 501.50   B. ₹ 499.20
C. ₹ 495/-   D. ₹ 510/-
E. None of these

98. What is least number to be added to 4321 to make it a perfect square?
A. 32   B. 34
C. 36   D. 38
E. None of these

99. 45% of a number is 255.6. What is 25% of that number?
A. 162   B. 132
C. 152   D. 142
E. None of these

100. Find the average of the following Set of Scores?
221, 231, 441, 359, 665, 525
A. 399   B. 428
C. 407   D. 415
E. None of these

ANSWERS

1	2	3	4	5	6	7	8	9	10
D	A	E	D	B	A	D	D	E	A

11	12	13	14	15	16	17	18	19	20
E	B	E	B	C	A	D	C	D	B

21	22	23	24	25	26	27	28	29	30
A	A	B	B	D	B	C	A	C	D

31	32	33	34	35	36	37	38	39	40
A	C	D	B	E	B	C	E	A	D
41	42	43	44	45	46	47	48	49	50
A	C	B	E	D	B	B	D	E	E
51	52	53	54	55	56	57	58	59	60
B	E	E	A	D	C	A	C	E	D
61	62	63	64	65	66	67	68	69	70
D	A	D	A	C	B	B	C	A	A
71	72	73	74	75	76	77	78	79	80
C	C	D	E	E	E	E	A	C	B
81	82	83	84	85	86	87	88	89	90
D	B	C	E	A	D	C	E	A	B
91	92	93	94	95	96	97	98	99	100
C	A	A	B	D	E	B	E	D	C

Some Selected Explanatory Answers

36. 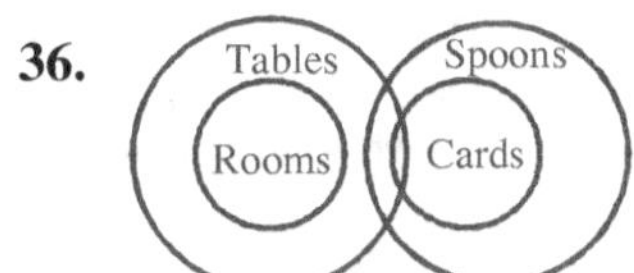

37. 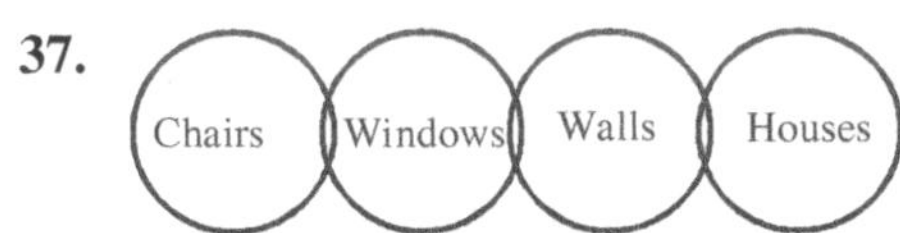

38. 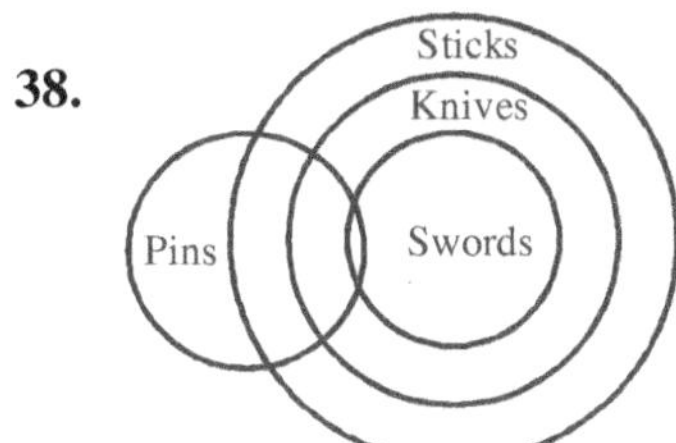

39. 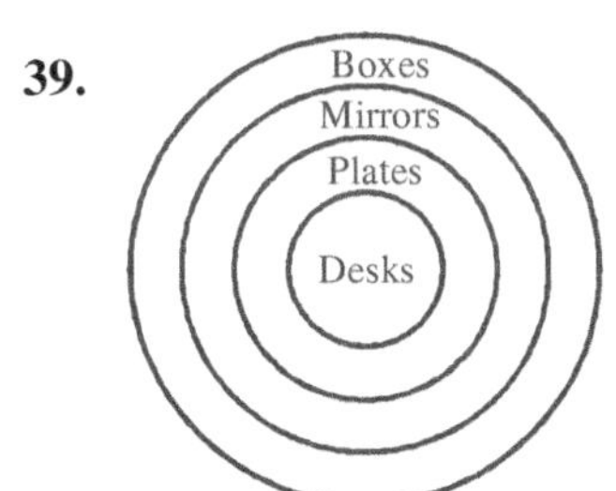

40. 

For Qs. (41–45)

Their sitting arrangement is shown below:

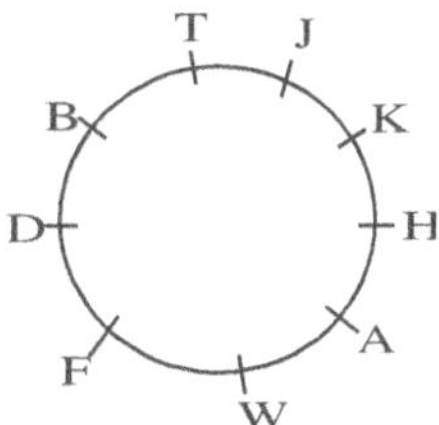

46. As teacher is related to school, similarly cook is related to kitchen.

47. 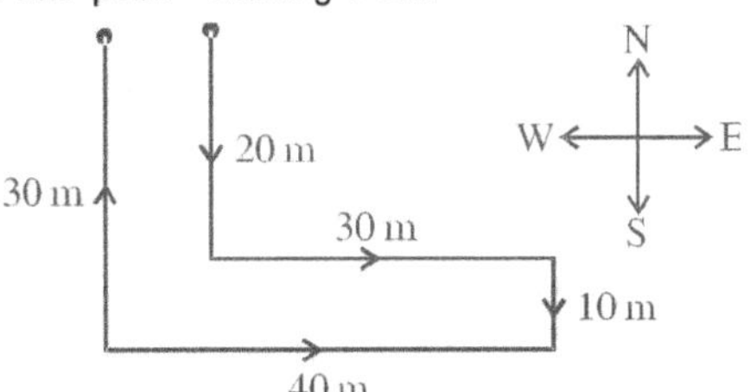

It is clear from the ray-diagram that Atul is in west direction with respect to his starting point.

48.

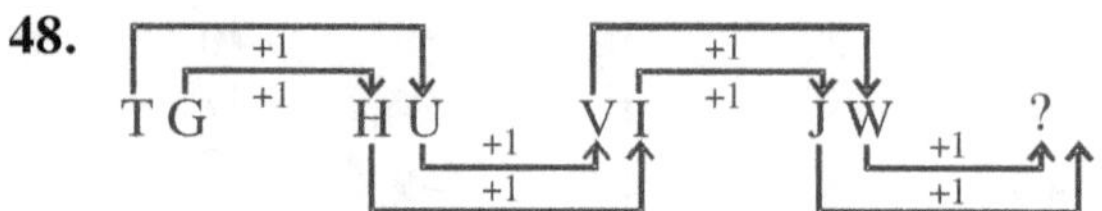

Thus, ? $\Rightarrow$ X K.

49. Sushil's rank from the bottom
$\quad$ = 50 − 28 + 1 = 23
Thus, Satish's rank from the bottom
$\quad$ = 23 + 15 = 38

52. Ne Pe Le $\rightarrow$ What is this

$\boxed{\text{Bo}}$ Le Se $\rightarrow$ is that $\boxed{\text{okay}}$

Se Ne De $\rightarrow$ that way easy

Thus, Okay $\rightarrow$ Bo

55. As, $\overset{1\,2\,3\,4}{\text{GIVE}} \longrightarrow \overset{3\,2\,4\,1}{\text{VIEG}}$

$\quad\overset{1\,2\,3\,4}{\text{OVER}} \longrightarrow \overset{3\,2\,4\,1}{\text{EVRO}}$

Similarly, $\overset{1\,2\,3\,4}{\text{DISK}} \longrightarrow \overset{3\,2\,4\,1}{\text{SIKD}}$

56. 937 $\Rightarrow$ 739; 425 $\Rightarrow$ 524; 816 $\Rightarrow$ 618;
$\quad$ 398 $\Rightarrow$ 893; 671 $\Rightarrow$ 176;

Second least no. = 524

57. Least no. = 398

Required sum = 3 + 9 = 12.

58. Second biggest no. = 816.

59.

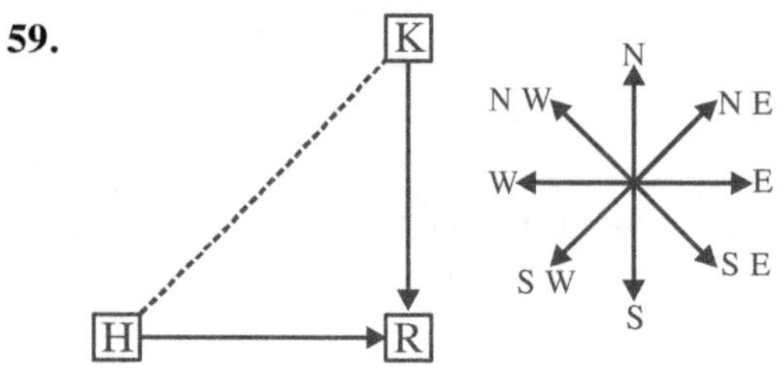

Town K, is in the NE of town H

60.

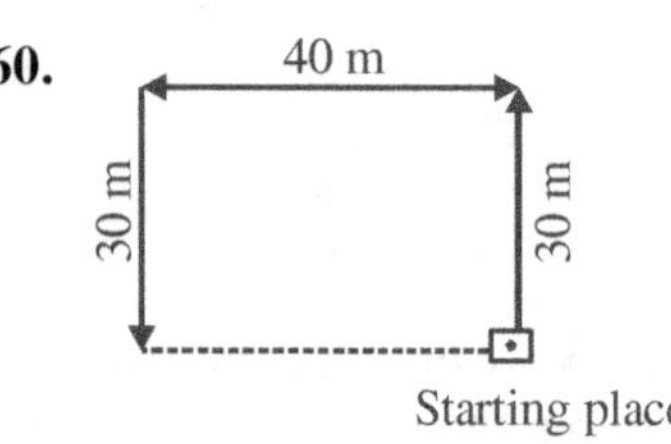

66. Let, the number be x

Then, $\dfrac{42}{100} \times x - \dfrac{28}{100} \times x = 210$

$\Rightarrow \qquad \dfrac{14}{100} \times x = 210$

$\therefore \qquad \dfrac{59}{100} \times x = \dfrac{210}{14} \times 59 = 885$

Hence, 59% of that number = 885

67. $4275 \div 496 \times (21)^2 = 4275 \times \dfrac{1}{496} \times 441$

$\qquad\qquad \simeq 4280 \times \dfrac{1}{500} \times 450$

$\qquad\qquad = 3809.2 \simeq 3800$

68. $\because$ In 7 days 112 kgs of wheat required

$\therefore$ In 69 days $\dfrac{112}{7} \times 69$ kgs of wheat required

$\qquad\qquad = 1104$ kgs.

69. The share of each person

$\qquad = \dfrac{41,910}{22}$

$\qquad = ₹ \ 1905$

70. The cost of 4 Cell-phones and 7 Digital cameras = ₹ 1,25,627
$\therefore$ The cost of 8 Cell-phones and 14 Digital cameras

$\qquad\qquad = 2 \times ₹ \ 1,25,627$
$\qquad\qquad = ₹ \ 2,51,254$

71. From (*i*),

Radius of the circle $= \dfrac{88}{2\pi} = \dfrac{88 \times 7}{2 \times 22} = 14$ cm

Area $= \pi r^2 = \dfrac{22}{7} \times 14 \times 14 = 616$ cm^2

From (*ii*),

Radius $= \dfrac{28}{2} = 14$ cm

Area $= \pi r^2 = \dfrac{22}{7} \times 14 \times 14 = 616$ cm^2

72. From (*i*)

Here, C.I. – P.I. = ₹ 250

$$\Rightarrow 25000\left[\left(1+\frac{r}{100}\right)^2 - 1\right] - \frac{25000 \times r \times 2}{100}$$

$$= ₹\ 250$$

$$\Rightarrow \left[1+\frac{2r}{100}+\frac{r^2}{10000}-1\right]-\frac{2r}{100} = \frac{250}{25000}$$

$$\Rightarrow \qquad \frac{r^2}{10000} = \frac{1}{100}$$

$$\Rightarrow \qquad r^2 = 100$$

$$\therefore \qquad r = \sqrt{100} = 10$$

∴ Rate of interest = 10% p.a.

From (*ii*) $\quad 25000 = \dfrac{25000 \times r \times 10}{100}$

$$\Rightarrow \qquad r = \frac{100}{10} = 10$$

∴ Rate of interest = 10% p.a.

73. Here, either number of rows or number of columns are not given in the both the statements. So, both the statements are not sufficient to answer the question.

74. From the statements I & II,

Let, base be x m then height will be $\dfrac{3}{4}x$ m

Now, $\qquad x^2 + \left(\dfrac{3}{4}x\right)^2 = 5^2$

$$\Rightarrow \qquad x^2 + \frac{9}{16}x^2 = 25$$

$$\Rightarrow \qquad \frac{25}{16}x^2 = 25$$

$$\Rightarrow \qquad x^2 = 16$$

$$\therefore \qquad x = 4$$

Now, $\qquad$ base = x m = 4 m

$$\text{Height} = \frac{3}{4}x$$

$$= \frac{3}{4} \times 4 = 3 \text{ m}$$

Area of the triangle $= \dfrac{1}{2} \times 4 \times 3 = 6 \text{ m}^2$

75. From the statements I & II,

Let the son's present age be x years, then the present age of father will be $5x$ years;

Now from the question,

$$\frac{5x-5}{x-5} = 15$$

$$\Rightarrow \qquad \frac{x-1}{x-5} = 3$$

$$\Rightarrow \qquad x-1 = 3x - 15$$

$$\Rightarrow \qquad 2x = 14$$

$$\therefore \qquad x = 7$$

Hence, present age of father

$$= 5x = 5 \times 7 = 35 \text{ years.}$$

76. Required ratio $= \dfrac{40}{40} = 1 : 1$

77. Profit earned by companies E, F & G in 2013

= 40 + 20 + 50 = ₹ 110 crores

Profit earned by companies E, F & G in 2012

= 50 + 80 + 60

= ₹. 190 crores.

Their difference =190 – 110 = ₹ 80 crores.

78. The profit earned by company C in 2012 & 2013

= 50 + 60 = ₹ 110 crores.

The profit earned by company E in 2012 & 2013

= 40 + 50 = ₹ 90 crores.

Hence, their required ratio $= \dfrac{110}{90} = 11 : 9$

79. The average profit earned by all companies in 2012

$$= \frac{20 + 40 + 50 + 70 + 50 + 80 + 60}{7}$$

$$= \frac{370}{7} = ₹\ 52.85 \text{ crores.}$$

80. Here, $40 \times \dfrac{x}{100} = 30$

$$\Rightarrow \quad x = \dfrac{30 \times 100}{40} = 75$$

Hence, required percentage = 75%

81. Total number of unemployed youth in state A in 2013

$$= \dfrac{15}{100} \times 35,00,000 = 5,25,000$$

82. The number of unemployed youth in state D in 2012

$$= \dfrac{6}{100} \times 24,00,000 = 1,44,000$$

83. The number of unemployed male youth in state A in 2012

$$= \dfrac{12}{100} \times 32,00,000$$

$$= 3,84,000$$

The number of unemployed female youth in state E in 2013

$$= \dfrac{6}{100} \times 32,00,000 = 1,92,000$$

Required percentage $= \dfrac{384000}{192000} \times 100$

$$= 200\%$$

84. The number of unemployed male youth in state F in 2012

$$= \dfrac{7}{100} \times 28,00,000$$

$$= 1,96,000$$

The number of unemployed male youth in state A in 2013

$$= \dfrac{7}{100} \times 35,00,000$$

$$= 2,45,000$$

Their difference

$$= 2,45,000 - 1,96,000 = 49,000$$

85. The number of unemployed male youth in state D in 2012

$$= \dfrac{10}{100} \times 24,00,000 = 2,40,000$$

The number of unemployed male youth in state D in 2013

$$= \dfrac{8}{100} \times 30,00,000 = 2,40,000$$

Hence, their required ratio

$$= \dfrac{2,40,000}{2,40,000} = 1 : 1$$

86. 92.5% of 550 $= \dfrac{92.5}{100} \times 550$

$$= \dfrac{92.5 \times 11}{2} = \dfrac{1017.5}{2} = 508.75$$

87. $12^4 \times 12^{13} = 12^{4 + 13} = 12^{17}$

88. $12.22 + 22.21 + 221.12 = 255.55$

89. $464 \div (16 \times 2.32)$

$$= 464 \times \dfrac{1}{37.12} = \dfrac{46400}{3712} = \dfrac{25}{2} = 12.5$$

90. $78 \div 5 \div 0.5 = 78 \times \dfrac{1}{5} \times \dfrac{1}{0.5} = \dfrac{780}{5 \times 5} = 31.2$

91. Speed $= \dfrac{2924}{43} = 68$ km/hr

92. Let, the required number be x,

Then, $\quad x^2 - 9^3 = 567$

$$\Rightarrow \quad x^2 = 567 + 729$$

$$\Rightarrow \quad x^2 = 1296$$

$$\therefore \quad x = \sqrt{1296} = 36$$

93. S.I. $= \dfrac{5760 \times 6 \times 3}{100} = \dfrac{5184}{5} = ₹\ 1036.80$

94. $131 \times 333 = 43,623$

95. Let, two successive numbers be x and $(x + 1)$

Then, $\quad x(x + 1) = 8556$

$$\Rightarrow \quad x^2 + x - 8556 = 0$$

$\Rightarrow x^2 + 93x - 92x - 8556 = 0$

$\Rightarrow x(x + 93) - 92(x + 93) = 0$

$\Rightarrow \qquad (x - 92)(x + 93) = 0$

Hence, either $x = 92$ or, $x = -93$ (Impossible)

So, smallest number = 92

96. Let, cost price be ₹ x

Then, $x + \dfrac{22}{100} \times x = 10{,}980$

$\Rightarrow \qquad \dfrac{122x}{100} = 10{,}980$

$\therefore \qquad x = \dfrac{10{,}980 \times 100}{122}$

$\qquad = 90 \times 100 = ₹ \; 9000$

Hence, $\qquad$ C.P. = ₹ 9000

97. $\qquad$ C.I. $= P\left[\left(1 + \dfrac{r}{100}\right)^n - 1\right]$

$\qquad = 3000\left[\left(1 + \dfrac{8}{100}\right)^2 - 1\right]$

$\qquad = 3000\left[\left(\dfrac{27}{25}\right)^2 - 1\right]$

$\qquad = 3000\left[\dfrac{729}{625} - 1\right]$

$\qquad = 3000 \times \dfrac{104}{625}$

$\qquad = \dfrac{2496}{5} = ₹ \; 499.20$

98.

$$
\begin{array}{r|l}
6 & \overline{43}\ \overline{21}\ (66 \\
 & \underline{36} \\
126 & \quad 721 \\
 & \quad \underline{756} \\
 & \quad -35
\end{array}
$$

Hence, required number = 35

99. Let, number be x

Then, $x \times \dfrac{45}{100} = 255.6$

$\therefore \; x \times \dfrac{25}{100} = \dfrac{255.6}{45} \times 25 = 28.4 \times 5 = 142.0$

Hence, 25% of that number = 142

100. Average scores

$\qquad = \dfrac{221 + 231 + 441 + 359 + 665 + 525}{6}$

$\qquad = \dfrac{2442}{6} = 407$

SBI Junior Associates & Junior Agricultural Associates
(Clerical Cadre Exam)

General English

Directions (Qs. 1–15): *Read the following passage carefully and answer the questions given below it. Certain words/phrases have been printed in **bold** to help you locate them while answering some of the questions.*

Education, particularly higher education is the obvious but crucially important instrument for nation building. As Confucious has said:

"If you are thinking of one year, plant rice. If you are thinking of a decade, plant trees. If you are thinking of a century, educate the people.

When we set about the task of higher education, we should be absolutely clear in our perception of the goals of education in the specific context of our nation's development. No **doubt**, one of the important aims of education would be to create the required range and nature of trained manpower assessed to be needed by different sectors of national growth. The entire educational apparatus must be geared progressively to fulfill the requirements of different phases of our growth in every sector— primary, secondary and **tertiary**. The aim must be to ensure that our country does not experience either **paucity**, or a **surfeit** of trained manpower in any specific segment of our economy. The requirements of our country, as a free, democratic, secular, socialist, nation, **aspiring** for rapid development, **entail** a specific recipe for our educational institutions, Today's educational institutions must therefore be developed accordingly and must regulate themselves to give the country the precise nature and quantum of trained manpower as projected by the requirements of our planned economy.

1. The author has quoted thoughts of Confucious to stress
   A. importance of planting trees for human beings
   B. the worthless efforts in planting rice
   C. the benefits of investing in education
   D. the need for assessing manpower requirement
   E. None of these

2. Which statement cannot be made on the basis of the passage?
   A. Higher education should keep in view the requirements of national economy
   B. Higher education has not been employed for nation building
   C. All levels of education have a role to play in nation's growth
   D. In our country we need to have a specially planned educational system
   E. The educational system should be modified to suit to our country's needs

3. The writer believes that
   A. there are no problems related to higher education
   B. investment in education is of long-range
   C. higher education should be used to assess manpower needs
   D. aims of higher education in India are absolutely clear
   E. None of these

4. The author's expectations from higher education, are essentially
   A. unrealistic   B. confusing
   C. critical   D. vague
   E. reasonable

5. The writer indicates that
   A. higher education did not play any role in national growth
   B. primary education did not play any role in national growth
   C. our nation experiences paucity of trained manpower in many sectors
   D. today's higher education has no precise goals to achieve
   E. None of these

6. Author has used the word 'apparatus' to indicate the
   A. scientific nature of education
   B. complicated organization demanded by education
   C. readily visible benefits of education
   D. entire equipment of education to perform particular function
   E. None of these

7. Which of the following has not been conveyed by the passage?
   A. Education at any level can contribute in nation building
   B. Manpower needs in many areas can be fulfilled through higher education
   C. Rapid development of our nation is possible through higher education
   D. Present higher education does not ensure surfeit of trained manpower

8. This passage is likely to be addressed to
   A. politicians only
   B. scientists only
   C. students only
   D. economists only
   E. cannot be said

9. Choose a suitable title to the passage
   A. Manpower Planning in India
   B. Importance of Higher Education
   C. Demands of Higher Education
   D. Role of Higher Education in India
   E. None of these

Directions (Qs. 10–12): *Choose the word which is most nearly the SAME in meaning as the word given in* **bold** *capitals as used in the passage.*

10. DOUBT
   A. suspicion   B. certain
   C. definite   D. sure
   E. evident

11. TERTIARY
   A. last   B. important
   C. third   D. terminal
   E. phenomenal

12. ASPIRING
   A. inquiring   B. awaiting
   C. involving   D. striving
   E. expecting

Directions (Qs. 13–15): *Choose the word which is most OPPOSITE in meaning as the word given in* **bold** *capitals as used in the passage.*

13. PAUCITY
   A. moderate   B. enormity
   C. mediocrity   D. littleness
   E. insignificance

14. SURFEIT
   A. abundance   B. redundancy
   C. repletion   D. congestion
   E. lack

15. ENTAIL
   A. entitled   B. ensure
   C. dismiss   D. retain
   E. originate

Directions (Qs. 16–20): *Read each sentence to find out whether there is any grammatical error or idiomatic error in it. The error, if any, will be in one part of the sentence. The number of that part is the answer. If there is "No Error" the answer is 'E'. (Ignore errors of punctuation if any.)*

16. (A) On resuming his duty,/(B) he asked his Superiors/(C) that whether he would be/(D) permitted to leave early./(E) No error.

17. (A) We don't deny/(B) your right to know/(C) whatever happened while/(D) you were not in the office./(E) No error.

18. (A) Jayesh loved his Guru immensely/(B) and gave him fullest loyalty,/(C) yet he had his own/(D) independent way of thinking./(E) No error.

19. (A) We have done everything/(B) that could be done/(C) to avert the storm/(D) which is now coming on./(E) No error.

20. (A) Our school is making/(B) every possible effort/(C) to provide best facilities/(D) and personal attention for each child./(E) No error.

Directions (Qs. 21–30) : *In the following passage there are blanks, each of which has been numbered. These numbers are printed below the passage, against each, five words are suggested, one of which fits the blank appropriately. Find out the appropriate word in each case.*

The last decade has been ..... **(21)** ..... for management education and development. When the economies of most western countries were ..... **(22)** ..... in the early 1980s there were ..... **(23)** ..... cuts both in corporate training and in higher education. During the boom years of the mid 1980s there was some ..... **(24)** ..... in both areas. In early 1990s industrialised countries were in the ..... **(25)** ..... of another severe recession and a ..... **(26)** ..... retrenchment was to be reasonably ..... **(27)** ..... throughout the training world. But this is not the case so far. Many leading companies are ..... **(28)** ..... their belief in training as the key to future competitiveness and governments have ..... **(29)** ..... an era of rapid ..... **(30)** ..... and came toward him with little steps just as the child had done when she came out of the river.

21. A. dogmatic   B. paradoxical
    C. outstanding   D. sluggish
    E. praiseworthy

22. A. galvanised   B. privatised
    C. dominant   D. faltering
    E. developing

23. A. severe   B. judicious
    C. marginal   D. proportionate
    E. dramatic

24. A. proactivity   B. curiosity
    C. downsizing   D. slashing
    E. reactivity

25. A. area   B. mood
    C. grip   D. light
    E. context

26. A. critical   B. light
    C. profound   D. possible
    E. tough

27. A. fabricated   B. projected
    C. lamented   D. expected
    E. advocated

28. A. managing   B. asserting
    C. criticising   D. rejecting
    E. developing

29. A. encouraged   B. established
    C. preached   D. circulated
    E. directed

30. A. degradation   B. communication
    C. expansion   D. projection
    E. exhibition

Reasoning Ability

Directions (Qs. 31–35): *In these questions, certain symbols have been used to indicate relationships between elements as follows:*

A % B means A is neither smaller than nor greater than B.

A $ B means A is greater than B.

A ★ B means A is either greater than or equal to B.

A @ B means A is smaller than B.

A # B means A is either smaller than or equal to B.

In each question, three statements showing relationships have been given, which are followed by two conclusions I & II. Assuming that the given statements are true, find out which conclusion(s) is/are **definitely true.**

Mark answer A   if only conclusion I is true.
Mark answer B   if only conclusion II is true.
Mark answer C   if either conclusion I or II is true.
Mark answer D   if neither conclusion I nor II is true.
Mark answer E   if both conclusions I and II are true.

31. Statements : P ★ Q, Q $ R, Q % S
    Conclusions : I. P @ S
               II. R @ P

32. Statements : T # V, V $ X, X ★ Y
    Conclusions : I. V $ Y
               II. X # T

33. Statements : C % E, E # W, W @ Z
    Conclusions : I. W ★ C
               II. C @ Z

34. Statements : L # M, M @ N, N $ P
    Conclusions : I. L # N
               II. M ★ P

35. Statements : F ★ G, G % H, H $ K
    Conclusions : I. H@F
               II. F % H

Directions (Qs. 36–40): *These questions are based on the following letter/number/symbol arrangement. Study it carefully and answer the questions.*

1 % B 7 @ 4 D G 2 I 9 A K 6 # E 3 © U C 8 Z $ 5

36. If all the symbols are dropped from the above arrangement, which element will be the eighth from the right end?
   A. E   B. K
   C. I   D. 6
   E. None of these

37. How many such symbols are there in the above arrangement each of which is immediately preceded by a number but not immediately followed by a letter?
   A. None   B. One
   C. Two   D. Three
   E. More than three

38. If the order of all the elements is reversed, which element will be fifth to the left of eighteenth from the left?
   A. K   B. 6
   C. 9   D. I
   E. None of these

39. Four of the following five are alike in a certain way based on their positions in the given arrangement and so form a group. Which is the one that does not belong to the group?
   A. 4G@   B. ©U3

   C. 9KI   D. 74B
   E. #36

40. Which element is fourth to the left of thirteenth from the left?
   A. 2   B. E
   C. G   D. 3
   E. None of these

Directions (Qs. 41–45): *Study the following information carefully to answer these questions.*

Eight friends A, B, C, D, E, F, G and H are sitting around a circle facing the centre. A sits third to the left of B, while second to the right of F. D does not sit next to A or B. C and G always sit next to each other. H never sits next to D and C does not sit next to B.

41. Which of the following pairs sits between H and E?
   A. F, D   B. H, B
   C. C, G   D. E, G
   E. None of these

42. Starting from A's position if all the eight were arranged in alphabetical order in clockwise direction the seating position of how many members (excluding A) would not change?
   A. None   B. One
   C. Two   D. Three
   E. Four

43. Which of the following pairs has only one person sitting between them, if the counting is done in clockwise direction?
   A. A, B   B. C, D
   C. F, E   D. G, H
   E. E, A

44. Who sits to the immediate right of E?
   A. A   B. D
   C. F   D. H
   E. None of these

45. What is the position of B with respect to C?
   A. Second to the left
   B. Third to the right
   C. Third to the left
   D. Can't be determined
   E. None of these

46. 'Smell' is to 'Flower' in the same way as 'taste' is to.
  - A. Tongue
  - B. Water
  - C. Sweet
  - D. Food
  - E. Good

47. Four of the following five are alike in a certain way and hence form a group. Which one **does not** belong to the group?
  - A. 36
  - B. 64
  - C. 49
  - D. 81
  - E. 16

48. Four of the following five are alike in a certain way and hence form a group. Which one **does not** belong to the group?
  - A. OP
  - B. IJ
  - C. TU
  - D. AB
  - E. EF

49. In the English alphabet 'BDG' is to 'CFJ' in the same way as 'EGJ' is to
  - A. FIL
  - B. FJM
  - C. FIM
  - D. FIN
  - E. None of these

50. In the case of how many digits in the number 7214658, their position in the number and the position when the digits of the numbers are arranged in the ascending order is identical?
  - A. Three
  - B. Four
  - C. One
  - D. Two
  - E. None of these

51. How many such pairs of letters are there in the word CONSUMER each of which has as many pairs of letters between them in the word as in the English alphabet?
  - A. None
  - B. One
  - C. Two
  - D. Three
  - E. More than three

52. How many meaningful English words can be made with the letters NNEO using each letter only once in each word?
  - A. None
  - B. One
  - C. Two
  - D. Three
  - E. More than three

53. How many such pairs of digits are there in the number 5134876, each of which has as many digits between them in the number as when the digits are rearranged in ascending order within the number?
  - A. None
  - B. One
  - C. Two
  - D. Three
  - E. More than three

54. If 'K' denotes '×'; 'B' denotes '÷' 'T' denotes '–' and 'M' denotes '+', then

40 B 8 T 6 M 3 K 4 = ?
  - A. 19
  - B. 11
  - C. –31
  - D. 23
  - E. None of these

55. What should come next in the following letter series?

A B C D P Q R S A B C D E P Q R S T A B C D E F P Q R S T
  - A. A
  - B. V
  - C. U
  - D. W
  - E. None of these

56. 'WT' is related to 'QN' in the same way as '———' is related to 'FC'.
  - A. KH
  - B. MJ
  - C. GJ
  - D. GK
  - E. LI

57. In a certain code language 'RISE' is written as '8419', and 'MEAL' is written as '5927'. How is 'RAIL' written in that code?
  - A. 8429
  - B. 8124
  - C. 8247
  - D. 8412
  - E. 2948

58. The positions of how many digits will remain the same if the digits in the number 94276153 are rearranged in the ascending order from left to right?
  - A. None
  - B. One
  - C. Two
  - D. Three
  - E. More than three

59. Pointing to a girl, Laxmi said, "She is the only daughter of my grandfather's son". How is the girl related to Laxmi?
  - A. Daughter
  - B. Cousin
  - C. Sister
  - D. Data inadequate
  - E. None of these

60. Among 1, 2, 3, 4 and 5 each having a different height, 3 is taller than only 1 and 2 is taller than 4 and 5. Who among them is the tallest?

A. 3   B. 2

C. 5   D. Data inadequate

E. None of these

Directions (Qs. 61-65): *In each question below is given a number/symbol followed by five combinations of letter codes numbered A, B, C, D and E. You have to find out which of the combinations correctly represents the number/symbol based on the following coding system and the conditions and mark the number of that combination as your answer. Two or more conditions may be applicable to a single combination.*

Number/symbol : # % 4 6 * 5 2 ! 7 $ 3 + 9 & 1

Letter Code   : K M T L P S C V A R E H J F D

Conditions :

(*i*) If the second element is an odd number and the last element is a symbol, the odd number is to be coded as the code for the symbol.

(*ii*) If the group of elements contains a perfect square, that number is to be coded as the code for the element preceding it. (one is also a perfect square)

(*iii*) If both the second and third elements are symbols, the codes for these symbols are to be interchanged.

61. 7%&53#

A. AMFESK   B. AMFSEK

C. AMMSEK   D. AFFSEK

E. AFMSEK

62. %5&74!

A. MVFATV   B. MFVATV

C. MSFATV   D. MVFAAV

E. MVVAFT

63. #$9*3%

A. KRRPEM   B. KRPPEM

C. KRJPEM   D. KJREPM

E. RKJPEM

64. 6$1+#5

A. LRDDKS   B. LDRKHS

C. LRHDKS   D. LRRHKS

E. LRDHKS

65. +3!47&

A. HFVAAF   B. HFVTAF

C. HFVVAF   D. HFTVAF

E. HVVFAF

Quantitative Aptitude

Directions (Qs. 66–80): *What will come in place of question mark (?) in the following questions?*

66. ? % of 150 + 250 = 280

A. 30   B. 10

C. 20   D. 40

E. None of these

67. 25% of 40 ÷ 4 % of 25 = ?

A. 10   B. 1

C. 0   D. 2

E. None of these

68. 75% of 96 = ? × 12

A. 72   B. 6

C. 12   D. 96

E. None of these

69. 73.85 + 215.345 – 167.2134 = ?

A. 456.4084   B. 121.2166

C. 120.8296   D. 121.6711

E. None of these

70. 30% of 270 + 5/8 of 64 = ?

A. 121   B. 81

C. 40   D. 242

E. None of these

71. $\sqrt{3.61 / 102.4} = ?$

A. 29/32   B. 19/72

C. 19/32   D. 29/62

E. None of these

72. $\dfrac{\sqrt{32} + \sqrt{48}}{\sqrt{8} + \sqrt{12}} = ?$

A. $\sqrt{2}$ B. 2

C. 4   D. 8

E. None of these

73. $\dfrac{1}{\sqrt{9} - \sqrt{8}} = ?$

    A. $1/2\ (3 - \sqrt{2}\ )$ B. $1/3 + 2\sqrt{2}$

    C. $(3 - 2\sqrt{2}\ )$ D. $(3 + 2\sqrt{2}\ )$

    E. None of these

74. The prices of scooter and a moped are in the ratio of 9 : 5. If a scooter costs ₹ 4200 more than a moped, find the price of the moped.

    A. ₹ 5052   B. ₹ 5250

    C. ₹ 5053   D. ₹ 5060

    E. None of these

75. A sum of money is divided between two persons in the ratio of 3 : 5. If the share of one person is ₹ 20 less than that of the other, find the sum.

    A. ₹ 75   B. ₹ 90

    C. ₹ 80   D. ₹ 85

    E. None of these

76. The ratio between two numbers is 3 : 4. If each number be increased by 2, the ratio becomes 7 : 9. Find the numbers.

    A. 12, 16   B. 16, 12

    C. 12, 15   D. 13, 14

    E. None of these

77. A's capital is twice that of B's capital and B's capital is thrice that of C's capital. What is the ratio of the capitals of A, B and C ?

    A. 1 : 2 : 3   B. 2 : 1 : 3

    C. 1 : 3 : 6   D. 6 : 3 : 1

    E. None of these

78. Madan and Sunil are partners in a business. Madan invests ₹ 5,000 for 5 months and Sunil invests ₹ 6,000 for 6 months. If the Profit is ₹ 610, then Sunil's share in the profit is

    A. ₹ 250   B. ₹ 360

    C. ₹ 520   D. ₹ 630

    E. None of these

79. 67% of 89 ÷ 89 % of 67 = ?

    A. 5163   B. 5963

    C. 0   D. 1

    E. None of these

80. 80 % of 1200 + 40 % of 20 = ?

    A. 960   B. 1760

    C. 968   D. 96,800

    E. None of these

Directions (Qs. 81–85): *Insert the missing number:*

81. 4, –8, 16, –32, 64, (....)

    A. 128   B. –128

    C. 192   D. –192

    E. None of these

82. 5, 10, 13, 26, 29, 58, 61, (....)

    A. 122   B. 64

    C. 125   D. 128

    E. None of these

83. 1, 4, 9, 16, 25, 36, 49, (....)

    A. 54   B. 56

    C. 64   D. 81

    E. None of these

84. 1, 8, 27, 64, 125, 216, (....)

    A. 354   B. 343

    C. 392   D. 245

    E. None of these

85. 11, 13, 17, 19, 23, 29, 31, 37, 41, (....)

    A. 43   B. 47

    C. 53   D. 51

    E. None of these

86. The average score of a cricket for 10 matches is 49.9 runs. If the average for the first six matches is 49, then what is average score for the last 4 matches?

    A. 48.7   B. 49.8

    C. 46.4   D. 50

    E. None of these

87. The present age difference between father and son is 14 years. The ratio of their age will be 4 : 3 after 11 years. How old is son now?

    A. 25 years   B. 31 years

    C. 30 years   D. 28 years

    E. None of these

88. An article is marked for sale at ₹ 275. The shopkeeper allows a discount of 5% on the marked price. His net profit is 4.5%. What did the shopkeeper pay for the article?

    A. ₹ 250   B. ₹ 300

    C. ₹ 350   D. ₹ 225

    E. None of these

89. A shopkeeper bought 15 kg rice at the rate of ₹ 9.50 per kg and 25 kg rice at the rate of ₹ 7.25 per kg. He sold mixture of both types of rice at the rate of ₹ 10.50 per kg. In this transaction his profit is

A. ₹ 96.25   B. ₹ 105.20
C. ₹ 95.00   D. ₹ 108.45
E. None of these

90. At what rate per cent, a sum of money doubles itself in 15 Years?
A. 25%   B. 6%
C. 6.66%   D. 8%
E. None of these

91. A sum becomes 28/25 of itself in 5 years, find the rate of interest.
A. 3%   B. 5%
C. 12%   D. 2.40%
E. None of these

92. The compound interest on a certain sum for 2 years is ₹ 41 and the simple interest is ₹ 40. What is the rate per cent?
A. 4%   B. 5%
C. 6%   D. 8%
E. Data is insufficient

93. A sum of money at compound interest amounts to thrice itself in 3 years. In how many years will it be 9 times itself?

A. 18   B. 12
C. 9   D. 6
E. None of these

94. A can do a piece of work in 25 days and B can finish it in 20 days. They work together for 5 days and then A goes away. In how many days will B finish the work?
A. 10 days   B. 11 days
C. 20 days   D. $33\frac{1}{11}$ days
E. None of these

95. A can do a piece of work in 25 days which B alone can do in 20 days. A started the work and was joined by B after 10 days. The work lasted for

A. 15 days   B. $12\frac{1}{2}$ days
C. $16\frac{1}{2}$ days   D. $14\frac{2}{9}$ days
E. None of these

Directions (Qs. 96–100): *Study the following graph and the table and answer the questions given below.*

DATA OF DIFFERENT STATES REGARDING POPULATION OF STATES IN THE YEAR 2012

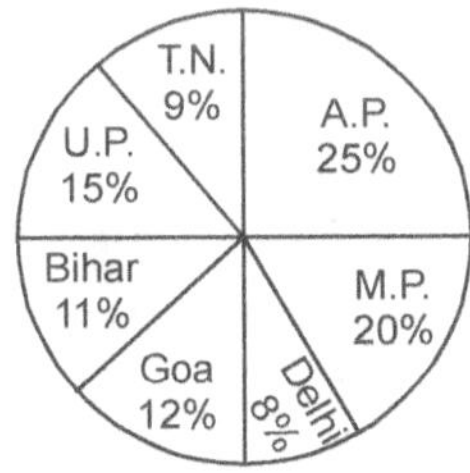

Total Population of the given States = 32,76,000

States	Sex and Literacy wise Population Ratio					
	Sex			Literacy		
	M	—	F	Literate	—	Illiterate
A.P.	5	:	3	2	:	7
M.P.	3	:	1	1	:	4
Delhi	2	:	3	2	:	1
Goa	3	:	5	3	:	2
Bihar	3	:	4	5	:	1
U.P.	3	:	2	7	:	2
T.N.	3	:	4	9	:	4

96. What was the number of males in U.P. in the year 1912?
A. 254650   B. 294840
C. 321470   D. 341200
E. None of these

97. What was the total number of illiterate people in A.P. and M.P. in 1912?
A. 876040   B. 932170
C. 981550   D. 1161160
E. None of these

98. What is the ratio of the number of females in T.N. to the number of females in Delhi?
A. 7 : 5   B. 9 : 7
C. 13 : 11   D. 15 : 14
E. None of these

99. What will be the percentage of total number of males in U.P., M.P. and Goa together to the total population of all the given states?
A. 25%   B. 27.5%
C. 28.5%   D. 31.5%
E. None of these

100. If in the year 1912, there was an increase of 10% in the population of U.P. and 12% in the population of M.P. compared to the previous year, then what was the ratio of population of U.P. and M.P. in 1911?
A. 42 : 55
B. 48 : 55
C. 7 : 11
D. 4 : 5
E. None of these

ANSWERS

1	2	3	4	5	6	7	8	9	10
D	D	C	D	D	D	A	E	B	A

11	12	13	14	15	16	17	18	19	20
C	D	B	E	C	C	E	D	A	D

21	22	23	24	25	26	27	28	29	30
C	D	C	E	C	B	D	B	B	C

31	32	33	34	35	36	37	38	39	40
B	A	E	D	C	D	B	E	A	A

41	42	43	44	45	46	47	48	49	50
A	D	C	B	E	D	B	C	C	A

51	52	53	54	55	56	57	58	59	60
C	C	E	B	C	E	C	A	B	B

61	62	63	64	65	66	67	68	69	70
E	D	A	D	C	C	A	B	E	A

71	72	73	74	75	76	77	78	79	80
C	B	D	B	C	A	D	B	D	C

81	82	83	84	85	86	87	88	89	90
B	A	C	B	A	E	B	A	A	C

91	92	93	94	95	96	97	98	99	100
D	B	D	B	C	B	D	D	C	A

Some Selected Explanatory Answers

31. P ★ Q → P ≥ Q, Q $ R → Q > R,
Q % S → Q = S
From all these three we get,

P ≥ Q = S > R
(*i*) P @ S → P < S (False)
(*ii*) R @ P → R < P (True)

32. T # V → T ≤ V, V \$ X → V > X,

X ★ Y → X ≥ Y

From all these three, we get

T ≤ V > X ≥ Y

(*i*) V \$ Y → V > Y (True)

(*ii*) X # T → X ≤ T (False)

33. C % E → C = E, E # W → E ≤ W,

W @ Z → W @ Z

From all these three, we get

C = E ≤ W < Z

(*i*) W ★ C → W ≥ C (True)

(*ii*) C @ Z → C < Z (True)

34. L # M → L ≤ M, M @ N → M < N, N \$ P →

N > P

From all these three, we get

L ≤ M < N > P

(*i*) L # N → L ≤ N (False)

(*ii*) M ★ P → M ≥ P (False)

35. F ★ G → F ≥ G, G % H → G = H,

H \$ K → H > K

From all these three, we get,

F ≥ G = H > K

(*i*) H @ F → H < F

(*ii*) F % H → F = H

37. Only one such type of combination, *i.e.*,

7 @ 4

39. 4 G @ © U 3 9 K I 7 4 B # 3 6

For Qs. (41–45)

Their sitting arrangement is shown below:

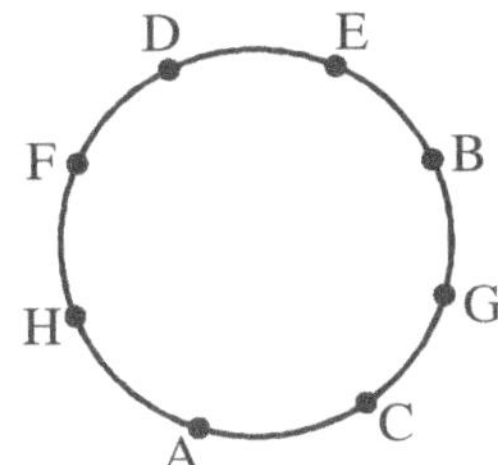

47. Here, 64 is a perfect square number as well as perfect cube also but all other are only perfect square number.

48. In TU first letter is consonant and second letter is vowel, while in all other pair first letter is vowel and second is consonant.

49. As,

Similarly,

50. 7 2 1 4 6 5 8

1 2 4 5 6 7 8

51.

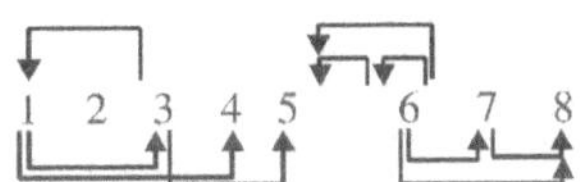

3 15 14 19 21 13 5 18

C O N S U M E R

52. Meaningful word ⇒ NONE, NEON

53.

5 1 3 4   8 7 6

1 2 3 4 5   6 7 8

54. 40 B 8 T 6 M 3 K 4 = ?

⇒ ? = 40 ÷ 8 − 6 + 3 × 4

⇒ ? = 5 − 6 + 12 = 11

55. ABCD, ABCDE, ABCDEF

PQRS, PQRST, PQRST U

56. W $\xrightarrow{-6}$ Q

T $\xrightarrow{-6}$ N

Similarly,

F $\xrightarrow{+6}$ L

C $\xrightarrow{+6}$ I

57. R I S E   M E A L

↓ ↓ ↓ ↓   ↓ ↓ ↓ ↓

8 4 1 9   5 9 2 7

Therefore,

R A I L

↓ ↓ ↓ ↓

8 2 4 7

58.

9	4	2	7	6	1	5	3
1	2	3	4	5	6	7	9

59. Grand father —son→ father —daughter→ Laxmi (Herself)
Grand father —son→ uncle —daughter→ Cousin

60. B > D, E > C > A

61.

7	%	&	5	3	#
↓	↓	↓	↓	↓	↓
A	F	M	S	E	K

Condition (iii) follows.

62.

%	5	&	7	4	!
↓	↓	↓	↓	↓	↓
M	V	F	A	A	V

Condition (i) and (ii) follows.

66. X% of 150 + 250 = 280

$$\therefore \ \frac{X \times 150}{100} = 30$$

$$\therefore \ X = \frac{30 \times 100}{150} = 20.$$

67. $\dfrac{25 \times 40}{100} \times \dfrac{100}{25 \times 4} = 10.$

68. $75/100 \times 96 = 12\,X$

$$\therefore \ X = \frac{96 \times 75}{12 \times 100} = 6.$$

69. 121.9816.

70. 81 + 40 = 121.

71. $\sqrt{36.1/102.4} = \sqrt{361/1024}$

$$\frac{\sqrt{19} \times \sqrt{19}}{32 \times 32} = 19/32.$$

72. $\dfrac{\sqrt{32} + \sqrt{48}}{\sqrt{8} + \sqrt{32}} = \dfrac{\sqrt{16} \times 2 + \sqrt{16} \times 3}{\sqrt{4} \times 2 + \sqrt{4} \times 3}$

$$= \frac{4\sqrt{2} + 4\sqrt{3}}{2\sqrt{2} + 2\sqrt{3}} = \frac{4\left(\sqrt{2} + \sqrt{3}\right)}{2\left(\sqrt{2} + \sqrt{3}\right)}$$

$$= 4/2 = 2.$$

73. $\dfrac{1}{\sqrt{9} - \sqrt{8}} = \dfrac{1}{\sqrt{9} - \sqrt{8}} \times \dfrac{\sqrt{9} + \sqrt{8}}{\sqrt{9} + \sqrt{8}}$

$$= \frac{3 + 2\sqrt{2}}{9 - 8} = 3 + 2\sqrt{2}.$$

74. We have, 9 − 5 = ₹ 4,200

$$\text{So, } 5 = \frac{4{,}200 \times 5}{9 - 5} = ₹\ 5{,}250.$$

75. $\dfrac{\text{Sum}}{\text{Difference}} = \dfrac{\text{Sum}}{20} = \dfrac{3 + 5}{5 - 3}$

$$\text{So, Sum } \frac{8}{2} \times 20 = ₹\ 80.$$

76. Following the above – said theorem the numbers are

$$\frac{2 \times 3\,(7 - 9)}{3 \times 9 - 4 \times 7} \text{ and } \frac{2 \times 4\,(7 - 9)}{3 \times 9 - 4 \times 7}$$

or, 12 and 16.

77. Trick :   A : B : C
          6 : 3 : 1.

78. Madan : Sunil

5 × 5 : 6 × 6 = 25 : 36

So, Share = 36/61 × 610 = ₹ 360.

79. The given expression can be written as

? = 89 × 67/100 ÷ 67 × 89/100

= 89 × 67/100 × 100/67 × 89 (Remove ÷)

= 1

80. The given expression

? = 1200 × 80/100 + 20 × 40/100

('of' is done)

= 960 + 8 = 968.

81. Each number is the preceding number multiplied by −2.

So, the required number is −128.

82. Numbers are alternately multiplied by 2 and increased by 3.

So, the missing number

= 61 × 2 = 122.

83. Numbers are $1^2, 2^2, 3^2, 4^2, 5^2, 6^2, 7^2$. So the next missing number is $8^2 = 64$.

84. Numbers are $1^3, 2^3, 3^3, 4^3, 5^3, 6^3$. So, the missing number is $7^3 = 343$.

85. Numbers are all primes. The next prime is 43.

86. Average Score $= (10 \times 49.9 - 6 \times 49)/4$
$$= 51.25 \text{ runs.}$$

87. The age of the son after 11 years
$$= 3 \times 14 = 42 \text{ years}$$
So, The present age of the son
$$= (42 - 11) \text{ years} = 31 \text{ years.}$$

88. We know that if the shopkeeper marked X% higher then
$$4.5 = X - 5 - 5X/100 \Rightarrow X = 10\%$$

Therefore, cost price $= 275\left(\dfrac{100}{100 + 10}\right) = ₹\ 250.$

89. **Trick:** Profit = S.P. – C.P.
$$= (15 \text{ kg} + 25 \text{ kg})\ 10.50$$
$$- (15 \times 9.50 + 25 \times 7.25)$$
$$= 420.00 - 323.75 = ₹\ 96.25.$$

90. Suppose Principal = P, $\qquad \therefore$ Amount = 2P
So, Interest $= 2P - P = P$, $P = P \times 15 \times r$
Where r = rate
So, $r = 100/15 = 20/3 = 6.66\%$
Trick: Rate = 100/ time $= 100/15 = 6.66\%$.

91. Suppose, Principal = P
So, $\qquad$ Amount = 28/25 P
So, $\qquad$ Interest $= P - 28/25\ P = 3\ P/25$
So, $\qquad 3P/25 = \dfrac{P \times 5 \times \text{rate}}{100}$

92. **Trick :**
$$\text{Rate } \% = \frac{41 - 40}{20} \times 100 = 5\%$$

Note : 40/2 = 20.

93. Because $3P = P(1 + r/100)^3$
So, $\qquad 3 = (1 + r/100)^3$
$$3^2 = 9 = (1 + r/100)^{3 \times 2}$$
$$= (1 + r/100)^6 = 6 \text{ years.}$$

94. $A + B = (1/25 + 1/20) \times 5 = 9/20$
So Remaining work $= 1 - 9/20 = 11/20$
B will finish it in $= 11/20 \times 20 = 11$ days.

95. A's 10 days' work $= 10/25 = 2/5$
Remaining work $= 1 - 2/5 = 3/5$
$$A + B = 1/25 + 1/20 = 9/100$$
So, (A + B), 3/5 of the work
$$= 100/9 \times 3/5 = 6\frac{2}{3} \text{ days}$$
So, work lasted for $= 10 + 6\dfrac{2}{3} = 16\dfrac{2}{3}$ days.

96. Number of males in U.P.
$$= \left[\frac{3}{5} \text{ of (15\% of 3276000)}\right]$$
$$= \frac{3}{5} \times \frac{15}{100} \times 3276000 = 294840$$

97. No. of illiterate people in A.P.
$$= \left[\frac{7}{9} \text{ of (25\% of 3276000)}\right] = 637000$$

No. of illiterate people in M.P.
$$= \left[\frac{4}{5} \text{ of (20\% of 3276000)}\right] = 524160$$

Total number $= (637000 + 524160)$
$$= 1161160$$

98. Required ratio
$$= \frac{\dfrac{4}{7} \text{ of (9\% of 3276000)}}{\dfrac{3}{5} \text{ of (8\% of 3276000)}} = \frac{\left(\dfrac{4}{7} \times 9\right)}{\left(\dfrac{3}{5} \times 8\right)}$$

$$= \left(\frac{4}{7} \times 9 \times \frac{5}{3} \times \frac{1}{8}\right) = \frac{15}{14}.$$

99. Number of males in U.P.
$$= \left[\frac{3}{5} \text{ of (15\% of N)}\right]$$
$$= \frac{3}{5} \times \frac{15}{100} \times N = 9 \times \frac{N}{100}$$

Where, $N = 3276000$

Number of males in M.P.

$$= \left[\frac{3}{4} \text{ of } (20\% \text{ of N}) \right]$$

$$= \frac{3}{4} \times \frac{20}{100} \times N = 15 \times \frac{N}{100}.$$

Number of males in Goa

$$= \left[\frac{3}{8} \text{ of } (12\% \text{ of N}) \right]$$

$$= \frac{3}{8} \times \frac{12}{100} \times N = 4.5 \times \frac{N}{100}.$$

$\therefore$ Total number of males in these three states

$$= (9 + 15 + 4.5) \times \frac{N}{100} = \left(28.5 \times \frac{N}{100} \right).$$

$\therefore$ Required Percentage

$$= \left[\frac{\left(28.5 \times \dfrac{N}{100} \right)}{N} \times 100 \right] \% = 28.5\%.$$

100. Let, x be the population of U.P. in 2011. Then, Population of U.P. in 2012

$$= 110\% \text{ of } x = \frac{110}{100} \times x .$$

Also, let y be the population of M.P. in 2011. Then,

Population of M.P. in 2012

$$= 112\% \text{ of } y = \frac{112}{100} \times y .$$

Ratio of population of U.P. and M.P. in 2012

$$= \frac{\left(\dfrac{110}{100} \times x \right)}{\left(\dfrac{112}{100} \times y \right)} = \frac{110x}{112y} .$$

From the pie-chart, this ratio is $\dfrac{15}{20}$.

$$\therefore \frac{110x}{112y} = \frac{15}{20} \Rightarrow \frac{x}{y} = \frac{15}{20} \times \frac{112}{110} = \frac{42}{55}.$$

Thus, ratio of populations of U.P. and M.P. in 2011 $= x : y = 42 : 55$.

SBI Junior Associates & Junior Agricultural Associates
(Clerical Cadre Exam)

General English

Directions (Qs. 1–15): *Read the following passage carefully and answer the questions given below it. Certain words have been printed in* **bold** *to help you locate them while answering some of the question.*

Political **ploys** initially hailed as master-strokes often end up as flops. The ₹ 60,000 crore farm loan waiver announced in the budget writes off 100% of overdues of small and marginal farmers holding upto two hectares, and 25% of overdues of larger farmers. While India has enjoyed 8%-9% GDP growth for the past few years, the boom has bypassed many rural areas and farmer distress and suicides have made newspaper headlines. Various attempts to provide relief (employment guarantee scheme, public distribution system) have made little impact, thanks to huge leakages from the government's lousy delivery systems. So, many economists think the loan waiver is a worthwhile alternative to provide relief.

However the poorest rural folk are landless labourers, who get neither farm loans nor waivers. Half of the small and marginal farmers get no loans from banks and depend entirely on moneylenders, and will not benefit. Besides, rural India is full of the family holdings rather than individual holdings and family holdings will typically be much larger than two hectares even for dirt-poor farmers, who will, therefore, be denied the 100% waiver. It will thus fail in both economic and political objectives. IRDP loans to the rural poor in the 1980s demonstrated that crooked bank officials demand bribes amounting to one-third the intended benefits. Very few of the intended beneficiaries who **merited** relief received it. After the last farm loan waiver will similarly slow down fresh loans to deserving farmers. While overdues to co-operatives may be higher, economist Surjit Bhalla says less than 5% of farmer loans to banks are overdue *i.e.* overdues exist for only 2.25 million out of 90 million farmers. If so, then the 95% who have repaid loans will not benefit. They will be angry at being penalised for honesty.

The budget thus grossly overestimates the number of beneficiaries, it also underestimates the negative effects of the waiver-encouraging wilful default in the future and discouraging fresh bank lending for some years. Instead of trying to reach the needy, through a **plethora** of leaky schemes we should transfer cash directly to the needy using new technology like biometric smart cards, which are now being used in many countries, and mobile phones bank accounts. Then benefits can go directly to phone accounts operable only by those with biometric cards, ending the massive leakages of current schemes.

The political benefits of the loan waiver have also been exaggerated since if only a small fraction of farm families benefit, and many of these have to pay bribes to get the actual benefit, will the waiver really be a massive vote-winner? Members of joint families will feel **aggrieved** that, despite having less than one hectare per head, their family holding is too large, to qualify for the 100% waiver. All finance ministers, of central or state governments,

177

give away freebies in their last budgets, hoping to win electroal regards. Yet, four-fifth of all **incumbent** governments are voted out. This shows that beneficiaries of favours are not notably grateful, while those not so favoured may feel aggrieved, and vote for the opposition. That seems to be why election budgets constantly fail to win elections in India and the loan waiver will not change that pattern.

1. Why do economists feel that loan waivers will benefit farmers in distress?
A. It will improve the standard of living of those farmers who can afford to repay their loans but are exempted.
B. Other government relief measures have proved ineffective.
C. Suicide rates of farmers have declined after the announce-ment of the waiver.
D. Farmers will be motivated to increase the size of their family holdings not individual holdings.
E. The government will be forced to reexamine and improve the public distribution system.

2. What message will the loan waiver send to farmers who have repaid loans?
A. The Government will readily provide them with loans in the future.
B. As opposed to moneylenders banks are a safer and more reliable sources of credit.
C. Honesty is the best policy.
D. It is beneficial to take loans from co-operatives since their rates of interest are lower.
E. They will be angry at being penalised for honesty.

3. What is the author's suggestion to provide aid to farmers?
A. Families should split their joint holding to take advantage of the loan waiver.
B. The government should increase the reach of the employment guarantee scheme.
C. Loans should be disbursed directly into bank accounts of the farmers using the latest technology.

D. Government should ensure that loans waivers can be implemented over the number of years.
E. Rural infrastructure can be improved using schemes which were successful abroad.

4. What was the outcome of IRDP loans to the rural poor?
A. The percentage of bank loan sanctioned to family owned farms increased.
B. The loans benefited dishonest moneylenders not landless labourers.
C. Corrupt bank officials were the unintended beneficiaries of the loans.
D. It resulted in the Government sanctioning thrice the amount for the current loan waiver.
E. None of these

5. What are the terms of the loan waiver?
1. One-fourth of the overdue loans of landless labourers will be written off.
2. The ₹ 60,000 crore loan waiver has been sanctioned for 2.25 million marginal farmers.
3. Any farmer with between 26 per cent to 100 per cent of their loan repayments overdue will be penalised.
A. Only 1　　　　B. Only 2
C. Both 2 and 3　D. All 1, 2 and 3
E. None of these

6. What is the author's view of the loan waiver?
A. It will have an adverse psychological impact on those who cannot avail of the waiver.
B. It is a justified measure in view of the high suicide rate among landless labourers.
C. It makes sound economic and political sense in the existing scenario.
D. It will ensure that the benefits of India's high GDP are felt by the rural poor.
E. None of these

7. Which of the following **cannot** be said about loan waiver?
1. Small and marginal farmers will benefit the most.
2. The loan waiver penalises deserving farmers.

3. A large percentage *i.e.* ninety-five per cent of distressed farmers will benefit.
   A. Only 3   B. Both 1 and 3
   C. Only 1   D. Both 2 and 3
   E. None of these

8. Which of the following will **definitely** be an impact of loan waivers?
   1. Family holdings will be split into individual holdings not exceeding one hectare.
   2. The public distribution system will be revamped.
   3. Opposition will definitely win the election.
   A. None   B. Only 1
   C. Both 1 and 2   D. Only 3
   E. All 1, 2 and 3

9. What impact will the loan waiver have on banks?
   A. Banks have to bear the entire brunt of the write off.
   B. Loss of trust in banks by big farmers.
   C. Corruption among bank staff will increse.
   D. Farmers will make it a habit to default on loans.
   E. None of these

10. According to the author what is the government's motive in sanctioning the loan waiver?
    A. To encourage farmers to opt for bank loans from money-lenders.
    B. To raise 90 million farmers out of indebtedness.
    C. To provide relief to those marginal farmers who have the means to but have not repaid their loans
    D. To ensure they will be re-elected
    E. None of these

Directions (Qs. 11–13): *Choose the word which is most nearly the SAME in meaning to the word printed in* **bold** *as used in the passage.*

11. **INCUMBENT**
    A. mandatory   B. present
    C. incapable   D. lazy
    E. officious

12. **PLOYS**
    A. surveys   B. entreaties
    C. ruses   D. sliders
    E. assurances

13. **AGGRIEVED**
    A. vindicated   B. intimidated
    C. offensive   D. wronged
    E. disputed

Directions (Qs. 14 & 15): *Choose the word which is most OPPOSITE in meaning to the word printed in bold as used in the passage.*

14. **PLETHORA**
    A. dearth   B. missing
    C. superfluous D. sufficient
    E. least

15. **MERITED**
    A. ranked   B. unqualified for
    C. lacked   D. inept at
    E. unworthy of

Directions (Qs. 16–20): *Which of the phrases A, B, C and D given below should replace the phrase given in* **bold** *in the following sentences to make the sentence grammatically correct? If the sentence is correct as it is and there is no correction required mark E i.e. 'No correction required' as the answer.*

16. During the recession many companies will **be forced to** lay off workers.
    A. have the force to   B. be forced into
    C. forcibly have   D. forcefully
    E. No correction required

17. He wanted **nothing else expecting** to sleep after a stressful day at work.
    A. nothing better than
    B. anything else unless
    C. nothing but having
    D. nothing else than
    E. No correction required

18. Ramesh took charge of the project, within a few days of **having appointed**?
    A. having an appointment
    B. being appointed
    C. after being appointed
    D. appointing
    E. No correction required

19. It is difficult to work with him because he is one of those persons who **think he is always** right.
  A. think they are always
  B. always thinks he is
  C. is always thinking they are
  D. always think his
  E. No correction required

20. Foreign business in developing countries have **usually problems with** lack of infrastructure and rigid laws.
  A. usual problems as
  B. usually problems on
  C. as usual problems like
  D. the usual problems of
  E. No correction required

Directions (Qs. 21–25): *Read each sentence to find out whether there is any grammatical error in it. The error, if any, will be in one part of the sentence. The number of that part is the answer. If there is no error, the answer is (E). (Ignore errors of punctuation, if any)*

21. It is more better (A)/ if one of the parents (B)/ stays at home (C)/ to look after the children. (D)/ No error (E)

22. With a fresh coat (A)/ of paint (B)/ the school can (C)/ look much nice. (D)/ No error (E)

23. I asked the salesman (A)/ if I could exchange (B)/ the faulty camera (C)/ with another one. (D)/ No error (E)

24. It took me (A)/ almost a hour (B)/ to fill the (C)/ application form. (D)/ No error (E)

25. She insists (A)/ you stay (B)/ until her husband (C)/ comes home. (D)/ No error (E)

Directions (Qs. 26–30): *Pick out the most effective word from the given words to fill in the blank in each sentence to make the sentence meaningfully complete.*

26. They work hard not because of the ______, but because of their inner urge.
  A. desire   B. drive
  C. energy   D. incentive
  E. motivation

27. His ______ background has made him so docile.
  A. famous   B. lucrative
  C. rich   D. advanced
  E. humble

28. It is ______ for everyone to abide by the laws of the land.
  A. expected   B. obligatory
  C. meant   D. optional
  E. recommended

29. ______ he is a hard worker, his quality of work is not of a desirable level.
  A. Despite   B. Because
  C. Although   D. Somehow
  E. However

30. In spite of repeated instructions, he ______ the same mistakes.
  A. commits   B. detects
  C. corrects   D. imitates
  E. exhibits

Reasoning Ability

31. The positions of how many digits in the number 523169 will remain unchanged if the digits within the number are written in ascending order? (from left to right)
  A. One   B. Two
  C. Three   D. Four
  E. More than four

32. In a certain code 'BUILD' is written as '5#31@' and 'LIKES' is written as '13©★8'. How is 'SKID' written in that code?
  A. 8©★@   B. 8@3©
  C. 8©3@   D. 83©@
  E. None of these

33. How many such pairs of letters are there in the word 'DAREDEVIL' each of which has as many letters between them in the word as in the English alphabet? (in both forward and backward directions)
  A. None   B. One
  C. Two   D. Three
  E. More than three

34. If it is possible to make only one meaningful English word with the second, the third, the seventh and the eighth letters of the word STEADFAST, which of the following will be the second letter of that word? If no such word can be formed, give 'X' as the answer and if more than one such word can be formed, give 'Y' as the answer.

A. E   B. A
C. T   D. X
E. Y

35. In a certain code 'TASK' is written as 'BUJR' and 'BIND' is written as 'JCCM'. How is 'SUIT' written in that code?

A. VTSH   B. VSTH
C. TRUJ   D. TRJU
E. None of these

Directions (Qs. 36–40): *In the following questions, the symbols δ, ★, $, @ and © are used with the following meaning as illustrated below:*

'P $ Q' means 'P is neither smaller than nor greater than Q'.

'P © Q' means 'P is either smaller than or equal to Q'.

'P @ Q' means 'P is neither smaller than nor equal to Q'

'P ★ Q' means 'P is not smaller than Q'.

'P H Q' means 'P is smaller than Q'.

Now in each of the following questions assuming the given statements to be true, find which of the two conclusions I and II given below them is/are definitely true?

Give answer (A) if only Conclusion I is true.
Give answer (B) if only Conclusion II is true.
Give answer (C) if **either** Conclusion I or II is true.
Give answer (D) if **neither** Conclusion I nor II is true.
Give answer (E) if **both** Conclusions I and II are true.

36. Statements : W $ F,   F δ R,   R ★ M
     Conclusions : I. R ★ W
               II. R $ W

37. Statements : V δ T,   T @ N,   N $ J
     Conclusions : I. J ★ T
               II. N ★ V

38. Statements : K © R,   R δ M,   M ★ F
     Conclusions : I. F @ R
               II. K ★ M

39. Statements : B @ J,   J ★ H,   H © N
     Conclusions : I. N @ J
               II. N @ B

40. Statements : T ★ K,   K © M,   M δ D
     Conclusions : I. D ★ K
               II. M @ T

Directions (Qs. 41–45): *Study the following arrangement of numbers, letters and symbols carefully and answer the questions given below:*

R 4 $ M E 7 T # A 2 J @ U K 9 P I % 1 8 Q W 3 δ Z 5 ★ N 6 F © V G

41. Which of the following should come in place of the question mark (?) in the following series based on the elements in the above arrangement?

M $ 7   A # J K U P   ?
A. 1 % W   B. 1 I Q
C. 1 I W   D. 1 % Q
E. None of these

42. How many such symbols are there in the above arrangement, each of which is immediately preceded by a consonant and also immediately followed by a vowel?

A. None   B. One
C. Two   D. Three
E. Four

43. How many such numbers are there in the above arrangement, each of which is immediately followed by a consonant but **not** immediately preceded by a letter?

A. None   B. One
C. Two   D. Three
E. More than three

44. If the positions of twenty-five elements from the right end are reversed, which of the following will be the sixteenth element from the left end?

A. Z   B. P
C. W   D. Q
E. None of these

45. Which of the following is the eighth to the left of the twenty-third element from the left end of the above arrangement?

A. 9
B. 1
C. $
D. ©
E. None of these

Directions (Qs. 46–50): *Study the following information carefully and answer the questions given below:*

P, Q, A, B, D, R and F are sitting around a circular table facing the centre. R is not second to the left of D and D is not an immediate neighbour of B. A is third to the right of F. B is second to the left of F. Q is not an immediate neighbour of B or F.

46. Who is second to the right of P?

A. R   B. Q
C. D   D. A
E. Data inadequate

47. Who is to the immediate left of F?

A. R
B. P
C. D
D. Data inadequate
E. None of these

48. Who is to the immediate right of D?

A. Q   B. A
C. F   D. P
E. None of these

49. What is D's position with respect to B?

A. Second to the right
B. Third to the left
C. Second to the left
D. Fourth to the right
E. Third to the right

50. Who is to the immediate right of Q?

A. D   B. R
C. A   D. B
E. None of these

Directions (Qs. 51–55): *Each of the questions below consists of a question and two statements numbered I and II given below it. You have to decide whether the data provided in the statements are sufficient to answer the question. Read both the statements and* ____

Give answer (A)   if the data in statement **I alone** are sufficient to answer the question, while the data in statement **II alone** are not sufficient to answer the question.

Give answer (B)   if the data in statement II alone are sufficient to answer the question, while the data in statement I alone are not sufficient to answer the question.

Give answer (C)   if the data **either** in statement I alone or in statement II alone are sufficient to answer the question.

Give answer (D)   if the data **given** in both the statements I & II together are **not** sufficient to answer the question, and

Give answer (E)   if the data **given** in **both** the statements I & II together are necessary to answer the question.

51. Who among P, Q, R, S and T, each having a different age, is definitely the youngest?
  I. R is younger than only T and P.
  II. Q is younger than T but not the youngest.

52. Towards which direction was Q facing after he stopped walking?
  I. Q walked 30 metres towards West, took a left turn and walked 20 metres. He again took a left turn and stopped after walking 30 metres.
  II. Q walked 30 metres towards East, took a right turn and walked 20 metres and he took a left turn and stopped after walking 30 metres.

53. How is 'always' written in a code language?
  I. 'rain is always good' is written as '5 3 9 7' in that code language.
  II. 'he is always there' is written as '3 6 8 5' in that code language.

54. How is M related to D?
  I. M has only one son and two daughters.
  II. D's brother is son of M's wife.

55. On which date in April is definitely Pravin's mother's birthday?

    I. Pravin correctly remembers that his mother's birthday is after fourteenth but before nineteenth of April.

    II. Pravin's sister correctly remembers that their mother's birthday is after sixteenth but before twenty-first of April.

Directions (Qs. 56–60): *Study the following information carefully and answer the questions given below:*

Following are the conditions for selecting a marketing Manager in an organization:

The candidate must—

  (i) be at least 25 years and not more than 35 years old as on 1.12.2011.

  (ii) be a graduate in any discipline with at least 55% aggregate marks.

  (iii) have completed Post Graduate Degree/Diploma in Management with specialization in Marketing Management with at least 60% marks.

  (iv) have post qualification work experience of at least 5 years as Assistant Marketing Manager in an organization.

In the case of a candidate who fulfils all the conditions **except**—

  (a) at (ii) above, but has secured at least 50% in graduation and at least 65% in Post Graduate Degree/Diploma in Management with specialization in Marketing Management, his/her case is to be referred to Head-Marketing.

  (b) at (i) above, but is not more than 40 years old and has work experience of 8 years as Assistant Marketing Manager, his/her case is to be referred to Managing Director.

In each question below, details of one candidate are provided. You have to take one of the following courses of actions based on the conditions given above and the information provided in each question and mark the number of that course of action as your answer. You are not to assume anything other than the information provided in each question. All these cases are given to you as on 1.12.2011.

Mark answer (A) if the data provided are inadequate to take a decision.

Mark answer (B) if the candidate is not to be selected.

Mark answer (C) if the candidate is to be selected.

Mark answer (D) if the case is to be referred to Head-Marketing.

Mark answer (E) if the case is to be referred to Managing Director.

Now read the information provided in each question and mark your answer accordingly.

56. Megha Gosavi was born on 8th March 1982. She has been working as Assistant Marketing Manager in an organisation for the past six years after completing her Post Graduate Degree in Management with specialization in Marketing Management with 70% marks. She has secured 53% marks in B.Com.

57. Mihir Sengupta was born on 24th July 1980. He has been working as Assistant Marketing Manager in an organizaton for the past seven years after completing his post graduate diploma in marketing management with 60% marks. He has secured 54% marks in graduation.

58. Arup Pathak has secured 59% marks in graduation and has been working as Assistant Marekting Manager in an organization for the past seven years after completing his Post Graduate Diploma in Management with specialization in Marketing Management. He was born on 15th February 1981.

59. Manish Agrawal was born on 2nd January 1978. He has secured 58% marks in B.Sc. and 65% marks in Post Graduate Degree in Marketing Management. He has been working as Assistant Marketing Manager in an organization for the past six years after completing his post graduation.

60. Nilima Patkar has secured 60% marks in graduation. She has been working as Assistant Marketing Manager in an organization for the past nine years after completing her post graduate degree in marketing management with 65% marks. She was born on 18th August 1972.

Directions (Qs. No. 61–65): *Study the following information carefully and answer the questions given below:*

P, Q, R, S, T, V and W study in Std. IV, V and VI with at least two in any of these standards. Each one of them has a favourite (likes) colour, viz. black, red, yellow, green, white, blue and pink not necessarily in the same order.

Q likes yellow and does not study in Std. VI. The one who likes black studies in the same Std. as T. R likes blue and studies in the same Std. as W. S studies in Std. V only with the one who likes pink. W does not study either in Std. V or VI. V does not like black. W does not like either green or white. S does not like green. T does not like pink.

61. Who likes white?
A. P B. W
C. S D. V
E. None of these

62. Which of the following combinations is **correct**?
A. P – Black – V B. S – White – IV
C. Q – Red – IV D. R – Blue – IV
E. All are correct

63. What is P's favourite colour?
A. Red B. Black
C. White D. Black or White
E. None of these

64. Which of the following students study in Std. IV?
A. QR B. QW
C. QRS D. QRW
E. None of these

65. Who likes red?
A. W B. S
C. P D. Data inadequate
E. None of these

Quantitative Aptitude

66. There are four red and three blue balls in a bag. If two balls are taken out randomly then what is the probability of no any balls of red colour?
A. 2/7 B. 4/7
C. 1/7 D. 3/7
E. None of these

67. On the occasion of the annual function of a school, some chocolates were to be distributed equally among 420 children, but, due to some reason 140 extra children were included on that very occasion. So, each child got one chocolate less. How many chocolates were to be distributed among the children originally?
A. 1640
B. 1680
C. 1690
D. 1600
E. None of these

68. Rajkumar got result of class eight. Maximum marks of each subject out of five subjects is 140. If he gets 98 marks in Science, 129 marks in Sanskrit, 131 marks in Mathematics, 110 marks in English and 120 marks in Hindi, then, what was his percentage aggregate in these five subjects?
A. 84% B. 82%
C. 77% D. 79%
E. None of these

69. If Suresh sells a good on ₹ 9300, then he earns a profit of ₹ 3100. On which price he should sell the good so that his gain will be 25% ?
A. ₹ 7250 B. ₹ 7350
C. ₹ 7650 D. ₹ 7750
E. None of these

70. Area of a circular field is 246400 square metre. How much time will take a person to complete a round of the field if he runs with a speed of 14.08 metre/second?
A. 125 second
B. 130 second
C. 100 second
D. 120 second
E. None of these

Directions (Qs. 71-75): *What will come in place of question mark (?) in the following number series?*

71. 2   4   16   96   768   ?   92160
- A. 7680
- B. 7580
- C. 7608
- D. 7090
- E. 7860

72. 14   36   ?   300   894   2676   8022
- A. 101
- B. 102
- C. 103
- D. 104
- E. None of these

73. 5   8   13   20   ?   44   61
- A. 29
- B. 30
- C. 31
- D. 32
- E. 37

74. 11   16   31   56   91   136   ?
- A. 171
- B. 181
- C. 185
- D. 191
- E. 197

75. 3   4   12   45   196   ?
- A. 985
- B. 990
- C. 995
- D. 1000
- E. 1005

76. Simple interest incurred on a sum of ₹ 24000 in 2 years is 1/8 of the principal. What is rate of interest per annum?
- A. 5
- B. 4.5
- C. 6.25
- D. 7.25
- E. None of these

77. If a person covers a total distance of 14.35 km in five weeks covering equal distances daily, then how much distance does he cover daily?
- A. 400 metre
- B. 410 metre
- C. 405 metre
- D. 415 metre
- E. None of these

78. If a 280 metre-long train runs with a speed of 7.4 metre/second then how much time it will take to cross a 460 metre long platform?
- A. 95 second
- B. 96 second
- C. 98 second
- D. 99 second
- E. 100 second

79. A trader sells apple's stock on ₹ 18270 and makes a profit of 45 per cent. What is the cost price of apple's stock?
- A. ₹ 12600
- B. ₹ 13600
- C. ₹ 12650
- D. ₹ 13650
- E. None of these

80. If numerator of a fraction is increased by 20% and denominator by 25%, then the resultant fraction is 3/5. What is original fraction?
- A. 3/5
- B. 3/8
- C. 5/8
- D. 7/11
- E. None of these

Directions (Qs. 81-85): *What will come in place of question mark (?) in the following questions?*

81. $\dfrac{12}{13} + \dfrac{1}{26} + 1\dfrac{1}{13} = ?$

- A. $1\dfrac{1}{26}$
- B. $2\dfrac{1}{26}$
- C. $1\dfrac{3}{26}$
- D. $\dfrac{11}{26}$
- E. None of these

82. $4 \times 566 \div 5 + 24.2 - 36 = (?)^2$
- A. 20
- B. 21
- C. 22
- D. 23
- E. 25

83. $5252 + 2525 = ? \times 25$
- A. 310.8
- B. 311.8
- C. 311.08
- D. 312.8
- E. 312.08

84. $8 \times ? = 4888 \div 4$
- A. 150.75
- B. 125.75
- C. 125.05
- D. 152.75
- E. None of these

85. $39254 + 5217 - 2286 = ? \times 50$
- A. 813.7
- B. 843.7
- C. 834.7
- D. 943.77
- E. None of these

86. $(62.5 \times 14 \times 5) \div 25 + 41 = (?)^3$
- A. 4
- B. 5
- C. 9
- D. 8
- E. 6

87. $(23 \times 23 \times 23 \times 23 \times 23 \times 23)^5 \times (23 \times 23)^2$
$\div (23)^2 = (23)^?$
A. 32　　　　　B. 30
C. 9　　　　　D. 7
E. 11

88. 27% of 510 + ? = 266.3
A. 182.6　　　　B. 122.6
C. 123.6　　　　D. 128.6
E. None of these

89. $2\sqrt{2} \times 3\sqrt{3} \times 7\sqrt{2} \times 4\sqrt{3} = ?$
A. 1080　　　　B. 1008
C. 1800　　　　D. $40\sqrt{3}$
E. $168\sqrt{6}$

90. $\dfrac{5}{8}$ of $\dfrac{4}{9}$ of $\dfrac{3}{5}$ of $222 = ?$
A. 42　　　　　B. 33
C. 39　　　　　D. 37
E. None of these

91. A car covers a distance between city A and city B with a speed of 58 km/hour and the distance between city B and city A with a speed of 52 km/hour. What is the average speed of the car?
A. 55 km/hr　　　B. 52 km/hr
C. 48 km/hr　　　D. 50 km/hr
E. 60 km/hr

92. Mr. Rohit invests a sum of ₹ 24200 on simple interest at a rate of 4% per annum for 6 years. After that he invests the principal and the received simple interest at the same interest rate for next 4 years. How much interest will he get at the end of 4 years?
A. ₹ 4800　　　　B. ₹ 4850.32
C. ₹ 4801.28　　　D. ₹ 4700
E. None of these

93. At a sale centre, perfumes are available at a discount of 25% on selling price. If the cost of a perfume is ₹ 5895 at the sale, then what is its selling price?
A. ₹ 6,020　　　　B. ₹ 7,860
C. ₹ 7,680　　　　D. Can't be determined
E. None of these

94. What will the nearest value come in place of question mark (?) in the following question?
$754 \div \sqrt{4136} \times 24 = ?$
A. 294　　　　　B. 276
C. 265　　　　　D. 300
E. 288

95. The cost of 15 digital cameras and 21 handy cameras is ₹ 354900. What will be cost of 5 digital cameras and 7 handy cameras?
A. ₹ 1,25,500　　　B. ₹ 1,18,300
C. ₹ 2,15,100　　　D. Can't be determined
E. None of these

96. In a canteen 56 kg rice is required for 7 days. How much rice will be required in the month of April and May together?
A. 496　　　　　B. 480
C. 498　　　　　D. 488
E. None of these

97. What fraction is 45 minute of a day?
A. $\dfrac{1}{42}$　　　　B. $\dfrac{1}{24}$
C. $\dfrac{1}{32}$　　　　D. $\dfrac{1}{48}$
E. None of these

98. There are 31700 students in a school. If the ratio of boys and girls is 743 : 842 respectively, then what is number of girls in the school?
A. 14860　　　　B. 16480
C. 15340　　　　D. Can't be determined
E. None of these

99. Sum of five consecutive even numbers A, B, C, D and E is 130. What will be product of A and E?
A. 720　　　　　B. 616
C. 660　　　　　D. 672
E. None of these

100. If a square of a number is subtracted from 4052 and the difference is multiplied by 15 then the resultant answer is 41340. What is that number?
A. 36　　　　　B. 1024
C. 32　　　　　D. 1296
E. None of these

ANSWERS

1	2	3	4	5	6	7	8	9	10
B	E	C	C	B	A	B	D	D	D

11	12	13	14	15	16	17	18	19	20
E	C	C	A	B	E	A	C	A	D

21	22	23	24	25	26	27	28	29	30
A	D	D	B	B	D	E	B	C	A

31	32	33	34	35	36	37	38	39	40
D	C	E	E	A	C	E	D	A	B

41	42	43	44	45	46	47	48	49	50
D	C	B	E	A	C	B	A	E	C

51	52	53	54	55	56	57	58	59	60
E	C	D	B	D	D	B	A	C	E

61	62	63	64	65	66	67	68	69	70
C	D	B	D	A	C	B	A	D	A

71	72	73	74	75	76	77	78	79	80
A	B	C	D	E	C	B	E	A	C

81	82	83	84	85	86	87	88	89	90
B	B	C	D	B	E	A	D	B	D

91	92	93	94	95	96	97	98	99	100
A	C	B	E	B	D	C	E	C	A

Some Selected Explanatory Answers

31.

```
5 [2] [3] 1 [6] [9]
1 [2] [3] 5 [6] [9]
```

32.

```
B    U    I    L    D
↓    ↓    ↓    ↓    ↓
5    #    3    1    @

L    I    K    E    S
↓    ↓    ↓    ↓    ↓
1    3    @    ★    8
```

Therefore,

```
S    K    I    D
↓    ↓    ↓    ↓
8    ©    3    @
```

33.

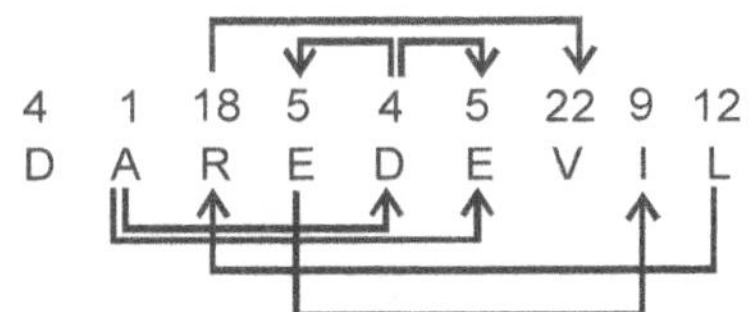

```
4   1  18  5   4   5  22  9  12
D   A   R  E   D   E   V  I   L
```

34.

```
1 [2] [3] 4 5 6 [7] [8] 9
S [T] [E] A D F [A] [S] T
```

Meaningful Words ⇒ SEAT, EAST

35.

```
T  A        S  K
 +1 ✕        −1 ✕
B  U        J  R

B  I        N  D
 +1 ✕        −1 ✕
J  C        C  M
```

Similarly,

```
S  U        I  T
 +1 ✕        −1 ✕
V  T        S  H
```

36-40.

$ ⇒ =	δ ⇒ ≥	© ⇒ ≤
℘ ⇒ <	@ ⇒ >	

36. W $ F ⇒ W = F
F δ R ⇒ F ≥ R
R ★ M ⇒ R < M
Therefore, W = F ≥ R < M
Conclusions:
I. R ★ W ⇒ R < W : Partialy True
II. R $ W ⇒ R = W : Partialy True

37. V δ T ⇒ V ≥ T
T @ N ⇒ T > N
N $ J ⇒ N = J
Therefore, V ≥ T > N = J
Conclusions:
I. J ★ T ⇒ J < T : True
II. N ★ V ⇒ N < V : True

38. K © R ⇒ K ≤ R
R δ M ⇒ R ≥ M
M ★ F ⇒ M < F
Therefore, K ≤ R ≥ M < F
Conclusions:
I. F @ R ⇒ F > R : Not True
II. K ★ M ⇒ K < M : Not True

39. B @ J ⇒ B > J
J ★ H ⇒ J < H
H © N ⇒ H ≤ N
Therefore, B > J < H ≤ N
Conclusions:
I. N @ J ⇒ N > J : True
II. N @ B ⇒ N > B : Not True

40. T ★ K ⇒ T < K
K © M ⇒ K ≤ M
M δ D ⇒ M ≥ D
Therefore, T < K ≤ M ≥ D
Conclusions:
I. D ★ K ⇒ D < K : Not True
II. M @ T ⇒ M > T : True

41.

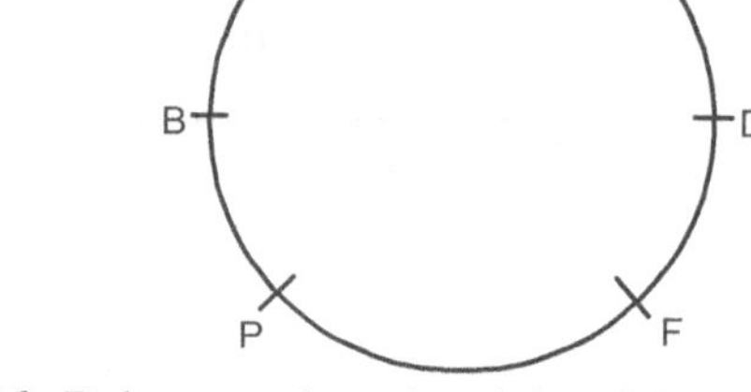

42.

Consonant	Symbol	Vowel

Such combinations are

T #A ; J @U

43.

Number/symbol	Number	Consonant

There is only one such combination : 1 8Q

44. Altogether there are 33 elements. If the positions of 25 elements from the right end are reversed, the 8 elements from the left will remain unchanged.
Now, 16th element from the left would be (16-8) = 8th element from the right end in the original sequence, i.e. 5.

45. 8th to the left of 23rd from the left end means 15th from the left, i.e. 9.

46-50.

46. D is second to the right of P.

47. P is to the immediate left of F.

48. Q is to the immediate right of D.

49. D is third to the right of B. D is fourth to the left of B.

50. A is to the immediate right of Q.

51. From both the statements,

T P R Q S

52. From statement I,

Q was facing towards East.

From statement II,

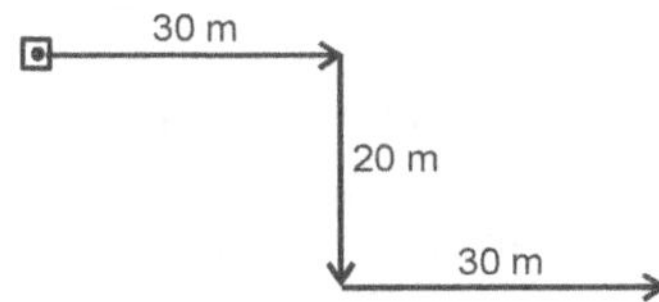

Q was facing towards East.

53. From both the statements,

rain $\boxed{\text{is always}}$ good $\rightarrow$ $\boxed{5\ 3}$ 9 7

he $\boxed{\text{is always}}$ there $\rightarrow$ $\boxed{3}$ 6 8 $\boxed{5}$

54. From statement II,
M is father of D.

55. From both the statements,

According to Pravin, the birthday of his mother $\Rightarrow$ 15th, 16th, 17th or 18th April

According to his sister, the birthday of Pravin's mother

$\Rightarrow$ 17th, 18th, 19th or 20th April.

For Qs. (56–60)

Candidate	Conditions				
	(i) or (b)	(ii) or (a)	(iii)	(iv)	
Megha Gosavi	✓	—	—	✓	✓	✓
Mihir Sengupta	✓	—	✗	✗	✓	✓
Arup Pathak	✓	—	✓	—	NG	✓
Manish Agarwal	✓	—	✓	—	✓	✓
Nilima Patkar	—	✓	✓	—	✓	✓

56. Megha Gosavi satisfies conditions (i), (a), (iii) and (iv).

Therefore, her case should be referred to Head-Marketing.

57. Mihir Sengupta does not satisfy condition (ii) or (a).

58. Marks in Management are not given.

59. Manish Agarwal satisfies all the conditions.

60. Nilima Patkar satisfies conditions (b), (ii), (iii) and (iv). Therefore, her case should be referred to Managing Director.

For Qs. (61–65)

Student	*Class*	*Favourite colour*
P	VI	Black
Q	IV	Yellow
R	IV	Blue
S	V	White
T	VI	Green
V	V	Pink
W	IV	Red

61. S likes white colour.

62. The Combination R-Blue-IV is correct.

63. P's favourited colour is Black.

64. Q, R and W study in Standard IV.

65. W likes red.

66. Total number of balls

$$= 4 + 3 = 7$$

Total number of ways of selecting any two balls

$$= {}^7C_2 = \frac{7!}{2! \times 5!}$$

$$= \frac{7 \times 6 \times 5!}{2 \times 5!} = 21$$

Again total no. of ways of selecting any two balls

$$= {}^3C_2 = \frac{3!}{2! \times 1!}$$

$$= \frac{3 \times 2!}{2!} = 3$$

Hence, required probability

$$= \frac{3}{21} = \frac{1}{7}$$

67. $420 + 140 = 560$

Let, total no. of chocolates $= x$

According to the question,

$$\frac{x}{420} - \frac{x}{560} = 1$$

$$\frac{4x - 3x}{1680} = 1$$

$$\Rightarrow \qquad x = 1680$$

Hence, number of chocolates = 1680

68. Maximum marks = 140 × 5 = 700

Obtained total marks

= 98 + 129 + 131 + 110 + 120 = 588

$$\% \text{ marks} = \frac{588}{700} \times 100 = \frac{588}{7} = 84\%$$

69. Cost price = 9300 – 3100 = ₹ 6200

100 + 25 = 125

when CP is ₹ 100 then SP = ₹ 125

when CP is ₹ 6200 then SP

$$= \frac{125}{100} \times 6200 = ₹ 7750$$

70. Area of circle = πr^2

According to the question,

$$\pi r^2 = 24600$$

$$\Rightarrow \qquad \frac{22}{7} \times r^2 = 24600$$

$$\Rightarrow \qquad r^2 = \frac{7 \times 24600}{22} = 78400$$

$$\Rightarrow \qquad r = \sqrt{78400} = 280 \text{ m}$$

$$C = 2\pi r = 2 \times \frac{22}{7} \times 280$$

$$= 1760 \text{ m}$$

$$\text{Required time} = \frac{1760}{14.08} = 125 \text{ seconds}$$

71. 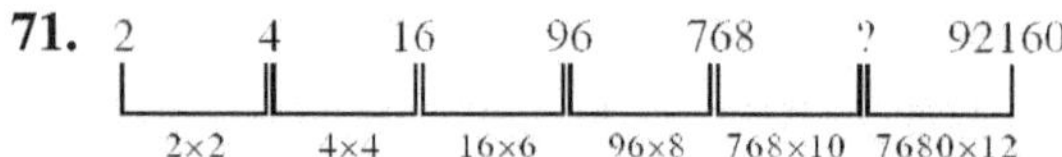

Hence, 7680 will come in place of question mark (?).

72. 14 36 ? 300 894 2678 8022

14×3–6 36×3–6 102×3–6 300×3–6 894×3–6 2676×3–6

Hence, 102 will come in place of question mark (?).

73. 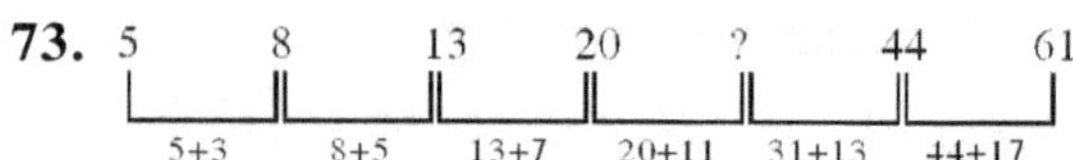

Added all consecutive prime numbers as 3, 5, 7, 11, 13 and 17.

Hence, 31 will come in place of question mark (?).

74. 11 16 31 56 91 136 ?

11+5 16+15 31+25 56+35 91+45 136+55

Added 5, 15, 25, 35, 45 and 55.

Hence, 191 will come in place of question mark (?).

75. 3 4 12 45 196 ?

$3×1+1^2$ $4×2+2^2$ $12×3+3^2$ $45×4+4^2$ $196×5+5^2$

Hence, 1005 will come in place of question mark (?).

76. $$\text{SI} = \frac{24000}{8} = ₹ 3000$$

$$\text{rate} = \frac{\text{SI} \times 100}{P \times t} = \frac{3000 \times 100}{24000 \times 2} = \frac{25}{4} = 6.25\%$$

77. In 35 days distance travelled = 14350 m

In one day distance travelled

$$= \frac{14350}{35} = 410 \text{ m}$$

78. Total distance = 280 + 460 = 740 m

Speed = 7.4 m/s

$$\text{time} = \frac{\text{distance}}{\text{speed}} = \frac{740}{7.4}$$

$$= \frac{740 \times 10}{74} = 10 \times 10 = 100 \text{ s.}$$

79. 100 + 45 = 145

when SP is ₹ 145 then CP = ₹100

when SP is ₹ 18270 then CP

$$= \frac{100}{145} \times 18270$$

$$= ₹ 12600$$

80. Let, the original fraction $= \dfrac{x}{y}$

According to the question,

$$\dfrac{x + \dfrac{20}{100}x}{y + \dfrac{25}{100}y} = \dfrac{3}{5}$$

$$\Rightarrow \quad \dfrac{x + \dfrac{x}{5}}{y + \dfrac{y}{4}} = \dfrac{3}{5}$$

$$\Rightarrow \quad \dfrac{\dfrac{6x}{5}}{\dfrac{5y}{4}} = \dfrac{3}{5}$$

$$\Rightarrow \quad \dfrac{6x}{5} \times \dfrac{4}{5y} = \dfrac{3}{5}$$

$$\Rightarrow \quad \dfrac{24x}{25y} = \dfrac{3}{5}$$

$$\Rightarrow \quad \dfrac{8x}{5y} = \dfrac{1}{1}$$

$$\Rightarrow \quad \dfrac{x}{y} = \dfrac{5}{8}$$

81. $\quad \dfrac{12}{13} + \dfrac{1}{26} + \dfrac{14}{13} = x$

$$\Rightarrow \quad \dfrac{24 + 1 + 28}{26} = x$$

$$\Rightarrow \quad \dfrac{53}{26} = x$$

$$\Rightarrow \quad x = \dfrac{53}{26}$$

$$\Rightarrow \quad x = 2\dfrac{1}{26}$$

82. $4 \times 566 \div 5 + 24.2 - 36 \qquad = x^2$

$$\Rightarrow \quad \dfrac{4 \times 566}{5} + \dfrac{242}{10} - 36 = x^2$$

$$\Rightarrow \quad \dfrac{4528 + 242 - 360}{10} = x^2$$

$$\Rightarrow \quad \dfrac{4770 - 360}{10} = x^2$$

$$\Rightarrow \quad \dfrac{4410}{10} = x^2$$

$$\Rightarrow \quad 441 = x^2$$

$$\Rightarrow \quad x = \sqrt{441} = 21.$$

83. $5252 + 2525 = x \times 25$

$$\Rightarrow \quad 7777 = x \times 25$$

$$\Rightarrow \quad x = \dfrac{7777 \times 4}{25 \times 4}$$

$$= \dfrac{31108}{100}$$

$$= 311.08$$

84. $\qquad 8 \times x = 4888 \div 4$

$$8x = 1222$$

$$x = \dfrac{1222}{8} = 152.75$$

85. $39254 + 5217 - 2286 = x \times 50$

$$\Rightarrow \quad 44471 - 2286 = 50x$$

$$\Rightarrow \quad 42185 = 50x$$

$$\Rightarrow \quad x = \dfrac{42185}{50}$$

$$= \dfrac{8437}{10} = 843.7$$

86. $(62.5 \times 14 \times 5) \div 25 + 41 = x^3$

$$\Rightarrow \quad \left(\dfrac{625}{10} \times 70\right) \div 25 + 41 = x^3$$

$$\Rightarrow \quad \dfrac{625 \times 7}{25} + 41 = x^3$$

$\Rightarrow \quad 25 \times 7 + 41 = x^3$

$\Rightarrow \quad\quad 175 + 41 = x^3$

$\Rightarrow \quad\quad\quad 216 = x^3$

$\Rightarrow \quad\quad\quad x = \sqrt[3]{216} = 6$

87. $(23 \times 23 \times 23 \times 23 \times 23 \times 23)^5 \times (23 \times 23)^2 \div (23)^2 = 23^x$

$\Rightarrow \quad \left(23^6\right)^5 \times \left(23^2\right)^2 \div \left(23\right)^2 = 23^x$

$\Rightarrow \quad\quad\quad 23^{30+4-2} = 23^x$

$\Rightarrow \quad\quad\quad 23^{32} = 23^x$

$\Rightarrow \quad\quad\quad x = 32$

88. 27% of $510 + x = 266.3$

$\Rightarrow \quad \dfrac{27}{100} \times 510 + x = 266.3$

$\Rightarrow \quad 137.7 + x = 266.3$

$\Rightarrow \quad x = 266.3 - 137.7$

$\quad\quad\quad = 128.6$

89. $2\sqrt{2} \times 3\sqrt{3} \times 7\sqrt{2} \times 4\sqrt{3} = x$

$\Rightarrow \left(2\sqrt{2} \times 7\sqrt{2}\right) \times \left(3\sqrt{3} \times 4\sqrt{3}\right) = x$

$\Rightarrow \quad\quad 28 \times 36 = x$

$\Rightarrow \quad\quad\quad x = 1008$

90. $\dfrac{3}{5}$ of $\dfrac{4}{9}$ of $\dfrac{5}{8}$ of $222 = x$

$\Rightarrow \dfrac{3}{5} \times \dfrac{4}{9} \times \dfrac{5}{8} \times 222 = x$

$\Rightarrow \quad\quad \dfrac{111}{3} = x$

$\Rightarrow \quad\quad x = 37$

91. Average speed $= \dfrac{2xy}{x+y}$

$= \dfrac{2 \times 58 \times 52}{58 + 52}$

$= \dfrac{2 \times 58 \times 52}{110}$

$= \dfrac{58 \times 52}{55}$

$= 54.83 \simeq 55$ km/hr

92. After 6 years,

$$\text{S.I.} = \dfrac{24200 \times 4 \times 6}{100}$$

$= 242 \times 24 = ₹\ 5808$

Amount $= 24200 + 5808$

$= ₹\ 30008$

Again after 4 years

$$\text{S.I.} = \dfrac{30008 \times 4 \times 4}{100}$$

$= ₹\ 4801.28$

93. $100 - 25 = 75$

when CP is ₹ 75 then SP = ₹ 100

when CP is ₹ 5895 then SP $= \dfrac{100}{75} \times 5895$

$\text{SP} = \dfrac{4}{3} \times 5895 = 4 \times 1965 = ₹\ 7860$

94. $754 \div \sqrt{4136} \times 24 = x$

$\Rightarrow 754 \div 64.3 \times 24 = x$

$\Rightarrow \quad\quad x = \dfrac{754}{64} \times 24$

$= 94.25 \times 3$

$= 282.75 \simeq 288$

95. Let, cost of 1 digital camera $= ₹\ x$ and

Cost of 1 handi camera $= ₹\ y$

$15x + 21y = 354900$

$5x + 7y = \dfrac{354900}{3}$

$= 118300$

Hence, cost of 5 digital and 7 handi cameras $= ₹\ 118300$

96. Total no. of days in April and May

$= 30 + 31 = 61$ days

For 7 days required rice = 56 kg

For 61 days required rice

$$= \frac{56 \times 61}{7}$$

$$= 8 \times 61$$

$$= 488 \text{ kg}$$

97. 1 day $= 24$ hrs $= 24 \times 60$ min.

$$= \frac{45}{24 \times 60} = \frac{3}{24 \times 4} = \frac{1}{8 \times 4} = \frac{1}{32}$$

Hence, 45 min. $= \dfrac{1}{32}$ part of a day.

98. Number of girls $= \dfrac{842}{(743 + 842)} \times 31700$

$$= \frac{842}{1585} \times 31700$$

$$= 842 \times 20 = 16840$$

99. Let, x, $x + 2$, $x + 4$, $x + 6$, $x + 8$ are five consecutive even numbers as A, B, C, D and E,

$x + x + 2 + x + 4 + x + 6 + x + 8 = 130$

$\Rightarrow 5x + 20 = 130$

$\Rightarrow 5x = 110 \Rightarrow x = 22$

Product of A and E $= 22 \times 30 = 660$.

100. Let, numbers be x

According to the question,

$$(4052 - x^2) \times 15 = 41340$$

$$\Rightarrow \quad (4052 - x^2) = \frac{41340}{15} = 2756$$

$$\Rightarrow \quad 4052 - 2756 = x^2$$

$$\Rightarrow \quad 1296 = x^2$$

$$\Rightarrow \quad x = \sqrt{1296} = 36$$

$$\therefore \quad \text{number} = 36$$

SBI Junior Associates & Junior Agricultural Associates
(Clerical Cadre Exam)

General English

Directions (Qs. 1–5): *In the following questions, each sentence has two blanks: each blank indicating that something has been omitted. Choose the set of words for the blanks which best fits the meaning of the sentence as a whole.*

1. After carefully .... the situation, the farmer sympathised .... the mule.
   A. scrutinising, on B. assessing, with
   C. observing, through D. fighting, by
   E. ignoring, for

2. Once there lived a cunning fox who always .... to .... others with his awful acts.
   A. wished, cheating B. desired, betrayed
   C. thought, fooling D. tried, deceive
   E. longed, between

3. I .... a friend named Raj who .... a horse ranch in the city.
   A. has, buys B. need, holds
   C. possess, run D. have, owns
   E. got, sells

4. As night .... in the heights of the mountains, Ramesh could not .... anything.
   A. fell, see B. darkened, view
   C. rose, advice D. dive, perceive
   E. become, get

5. Survival of mankind .... is in danger due to .... of atomic weapons.
   A. himself, prepetuation
   B. themselves, regularisation
   C. only, provocation
   D. itself, proliferation
   E. self, invention

Directions (Qs. 6–10): *Read the following passage carefully and answer the questions given below it. Certain words/phrases have been printed in **bold** to help you locate them while answering some of the questions.*

Akbar was the son of humble parents. His father was a school master. There was never very much money in the house so he didn't enjoy any luxuries. All he wanted was to learn more and more. Books were not easily available then as they were handwritten and very expensive. Akbar read all the books he could lay his hands on. In due course, he mastered Arabic, Persian, Philosophy and Astronomy and dreamt of getting a position at court. But for this one had to really excel in some field. Also one needed a patron **close** enough to the Emperor to recommend a newcomer. It was a few months before he could find a patron and a few more months before he could find a suitable opportunity to recommend him to the Emperor who asked what he had learnt and what work he could do. On hearing the same, he said, "We are pleased to give the young man a chance. Let him take charge of the royal poultry house!" When he heard the news Akbar was heartbroken. He, a scholar, capable of debating with the most learned men was asked to look after chicking hens! All the same he got down to work with great determination. His only concern was hens. He saw to it that they were well fed and had clean water, that their living quarters were clean and if a fowl took ill that it was separated from the others and given proper treatment. Meanwhile, the Emperor had forgotten about the scholar he had packed off to mind the hens. But one day while his Finance Minister was reading out the palace accounts to tell the Emperor how much money had been spent on the royal household, he mentioned such a **low** figure that the Emperor sat up.

"Have most of the hens died?" he asked 'No your Majesty', was the reply— "The hens are not only alive but are plump and fit." Send for the scholar! the Emperor demanded.

When Akbar came to the palace the Emperor demanded, "Aren't you feeding them properly?" I am sire, only the food is different? I'm feeding them what cannot be used in the royal kitchen, vegetable peels and dough used to seal the vessels while cooking for your Majesty. The hens not only enjoy it, but it is also very good for them. "Good work, we hereby promote you to the rank of royal librarian." Akbar was **bitterly** disappointed. He had spent the first thirty years of his life gaining knowledge. How he wished to gain that knowledge and help people. Instead as head of the royal library he would be seeing only books and no people. But he buckled down to organising the library.

A year later the Emperor came to visit the library. He was surprised to find each book covered with a packet of silk, velvet or brocade. There were hundreds of books and not one without a cover. "You have used expensive material to cover the books but have not charged us. Surely you are not spending your own money?" Akbar bowed low, Your Majesty these covers did not cost anything. Everyday dozens of people come to the court with humble grievances on sheets of paper which are folded and placed inside a bag of the most expensive material that they can afford. I have used them. The emperor was very pleased and gave him a bigger responsibility.

6. Which of the following can be said about Akbar's family?
1. They were poor and uneducated.
2. They discouraged him from becoming courtier.
3. He was ashamed of them and did not introduce them at Court.
A. None   B. Only 1
C. 2 and 3   D. Only 3
E. All of these

7. Which of the following is TRUE in the context of the passage?
1. Akbar was aged when he was finally made a courtier.
2. Akbar excelled at whatever job the Emperor assigned him.
3. The Emperor did not value a person's education but his family background.
A. All of these
B. Only 2
C. 1 and 2
D. 2 and 3
E. Only 1

8. How many years of Akbar's life were spent gaining knowledge?
A. 50   B. 20
C. 10   D. 30
E. None of these

9. Choose the word which is OPPOSITE in meaning to the word BITTERLY given in bold as used in the passage.
A. Sweetly   B. Angrily
C. Sourly   D. Freezing
E. Gladly

10. How did Akbar handle his appointment as royal librarian?
A. He was angry and was waiting for an opportunity to tell the King so
B. He was thrilled since he loved books
C. He was disappointed but put his best efforts into the job
D. He considered it a good opportunity to learn more
E. He was very happy since he preferred reading to interacting with people

11. How did Akbar manage the cover for books?
A. He used the used-sheets of papers
B. He spent his own money for this
C. He borrowed covers for books
D. He was not aware of it
E. None of the above

12. Why did the Emperor send for Akbar when he was in charge of poultry?
- A. To test Akbar's knowledge of poultry
- B. To see if Akbar was worthy of higher responsibility
- C. To understand why the poultry was thriving despite reduced expenditure on them
- D. To scold him for feeding the poultry leftovers instead of healthy food
- E. To demand an explanation for the poultry being overweight and unfit

13. What lesson can be learnt from the story?
- A. Patience and hard work will help one achieve success
- B. Pursuit of riches and wealth is all that matters
- C. One should use any means and possibility to attain a promotion
- D. One should be satisfied with whatever job one gets and not much more
- E. It is very difficult to get something in life without bribing

14. Choose the word which is most nearly the SAME in meaning as the word LOW given in **bold** as used in the passage.
- A. Small
- B. Gentle
- C. Unhappy
- D. Short
- E. Soft

15. Choose the word which is most nearly the SAME in meaning as the word CLOSE given in **bold** as used in the passage.
- A. Shut
- B. End
- C. Neighbouring
- D. Dear
- E. Careful

Directions (Qs. 16–20): *Rearrange the following six sentences/group of sentences 1, 2, 3, 4, 5 and 6 in the proper sequence to from a meaningful paragraph; then answer the questions given below them.*

1. He did whatever work was assigned to him and soon the lion became so fond of him that he promised to give him a cart full of almonds as pension when he (the squirrel) retired.

2. Once a squirrel joined the service of the king of the forest, the lion.

3. The squirrel had waited so long for this day but when he saw the almonds, he was seized with sadness as he realised that they were of no use to him now when he had lost all his teeth.

4. However, he envied other squirrels in the forest because of their carefree life which he could not enjoy as he had to be by the king's side all the time.

5. He consoled himself with the thought that at the end of his career, he would receive a cart full of almonds, a food that only a few squirrels got to taste in their lifetime.

6. Finally, the day came when it was time for him to retire and as promised the king gave a grand banquet in his honour and presented him with a cart full of almonds.

16. Which of the following should be the SECOND sentence after the rearrangement?
- A. 1
- B. 2
- C. 6
- D. 4
- E. 5

17. Which of the following should be the FIRST sentence after the rearrangement?
- A. 1
- B. 3
- C. 2
- D. 4
- E. 5

18. Which of the following should be the FIFTH sentence after the rearrangement?
- A. 5
- B. 4
- C. 2
- D. 6
- E. 1

19. Which of the following should be the FOURTH sentence after the rearrangement?
- A. 1
- B. 2
- C. 3
- D. 6
- E. 5

20. Which of the following should be the SIXTH (LAST) sentence after the rearrangement?
- A. 3
- B. 4
- C. 1
- D. 2
- E. 5

Directions (Qs. 21–25): *Read each sentence to find out whether there is any grammatical error or idiomatic error in it. The error, if any, will be in one part of the sentence. The number of the part is the answer. If there is 'No error' the answer is (E). (Ignore errors of punctuation if any)*

21. The oak tree always (A) / thought that (B) / he was strong (C) / than the other trees. (D)/ No error (E).

22. It was strange (A) / when people started (B)/ congratulating me (C)/ on completion of my dissertation. (D)/ No error (E).

23. Though Chandresh is known (A) / of his playful style, we admire him (B) / for his ability to shape a world clearly (C) / from few and carefully chosen words. (D) / No error (E).

24. A good employee (A) / is one which (B) / is always willing (C) / to go the extra mile. (D)/ No error (E).

25. Through her efforts (A) / she manage to (B)/ open several institutions to (C) / help the downtrodden. (D) / No error (E).

Directions (Qs. 26–30): *In following questions, which of the phrases given against the sentence should replace the word/phrase given in bold in the sentence to make it grammatically correct? If the sentence is correct as it is given and no correction is required. Select 'No correction' required as the answer.*

26. In a field one summer's day a grasshopper was hopping about, chirping and singing to its **heartfelt content.**

A. hearty content
B. hearts contention
C. heart's content
D. heart contents
E. No correction required

27. The donkey's master came up from behind him and gave him a **soundly thrashing** for the fright he had caused.
A. sounding thrash
B. sound thrash
C. sound thrashing
D. sounding thrashing
E. No correction required

28. You should accustom yourself, **for walking** straight forward without twisting from side-to-side.
A. At walks that are
B. for walking that is
C. for walk of
D. to walking
E. No correction required

29. When the crow put its beak into the mouth of the pitcher he found that **very little** water was left in it.
A. none of   B. so little
C. so much less   D. some few
E. No correction required

30. Inspite scoring very high in the exam. Arun failed to secure admission in the college of his choice.
A. Since   B. Despite
C. But   D. Even
E. No correction required

Reasoning Ability

31. The positions of first and the fourth letters of the word WORTHY are interchanged, similarly, the positions of second and fifth letters and third and sixth letters are interchanged. In the new arrangement thus formed, how many letters are there between the letter which is third from the right and the letter which is third from the left, in the English alphabetical order?

A. None   B. One
C. Two   D. Three
E. More than three

32. How many meaningful English words can be formed with the letters UOT using each letter only once in each word?
A. None   B. One
C. Two   D. Three
E. More than three

33. If each of the alphabets of the word COMPARE is arranged in alphabetical order from left to right and then each vowel in the new word thus formed is changed to the next letter in the English alphabetical series and each consonant is changed to the previous letter in the English alphabetical series which of the following will be fifth from the right?
A. F   B. P
C. L   D. E
E. O

34. How many such pairs of letters are there in the word FORCES, each of which has as many letters between them in the word (in both forward and backward directions) as they have between them in the English alphabetical order?
A. None   B. One
C. Two   D. Three
E. More than three

35. In a certain code language 'Siberia is a cold place' is written as 'a cold is place Siberia', in the same code, 'water freezes to ice here' is coded as 'freezes here ice to water'. How will 'covers ten percent of earth' be written in the same code?
A. covers earth percent ten of
B. earth of covers percent ten
C. covers earth percent of ten
D. covers earth of percent ten
E. covers earth ten of percent

36. Which of the following will come in the place of question mark?
HIZ   JYK   XLM   NOW   ?
A. PQV   B. QRV
C. QWR   D. VQP
E. PVQ

37. Sneha, Avni, Dhruv and Parth participated in a game-show and each earned a different amount. Avni earned more than Parth but not more than Sneha. Dhruv earned less money than Sneha but more than Avni. Who amongst them earned the most?
A. Parth   B. Sneha
C. Dhruv   D. Avni
E. Cannot be determined

38. Four of the following five are alike in a certain way and so form a group. Which is the one that **does not** belong to that group?
A. Swimming   B. Diving
C. Fishing   D. Driving
E. Bathing

Directions (Qs. 39–43) : *Each of the questions given below is based on the given diagram. The diagram shows students studying either Physics, Chemistry, Biology or combinations of these subjects.*

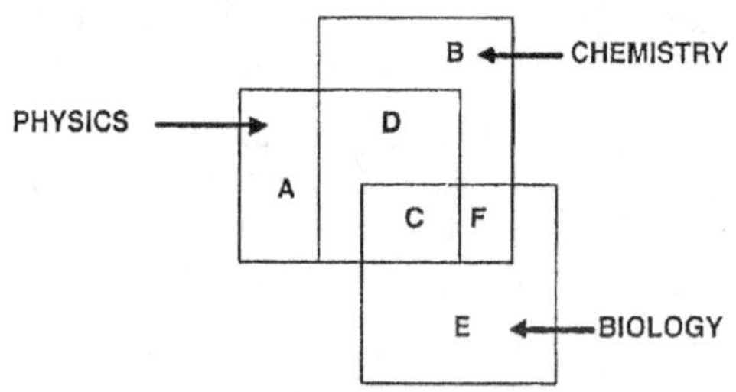

39. In which of the following groups are the students studying all the three subjects included?
A. A   B. B
C. C   D. D
E. None of these

40. Which of the following is **not** represented in the above diagram?
A. The students who study Biology, Chemistry as well as Physics.
B. The students who study Chemistry and Biology but not Physics
C. The students who do not study any of the three subjects.
D. The students who study Biology but not Physics and Chemistry.
E. The students who study Physics and Chemistry but not Biology

41. If a lecture is being attended by students from group B and group F together, on which of the following subjects could the lecture be?
A. Chemistry or Biology
B. Only Chemistry
C. Only Biology
D. Physics, Chemistry or Biology
E. Only Physics

42. Which of the following correctly represents the students studying both Physics and Chemistry but not biology?
A. Only C
B. C and D
C. C, D and F
D. Only D
E. Only F

43. Which of the following groups represents the students who do not study Chemistry?
A. E and F
B. Only A
C. A, C and E
D. D, C and F
E. A and E

Directions (Q. 44-48): *Study the following information carefully and answer the given questions.*

P, Q, R, S, T, V, W and Y are sitting around a circular table facing the centre.
(*a*) P sits second to left of T.
(*b*) Only two people sit between T and W.
(*c*) Q sits third to the left of W.
(*d*) V and Y are immediate neighbours of each other.
(*e*) Only one person sits between Y and R.

44. What is the position of R with respect to P?
A. Third to the left
B. Immediately to the right
C. Second to the left
D. Third to the right
E. Immediately to the left

45. If all the persons are made to sit in alphabetical order in clockwise direction, starting from P, the positions of how many (excluding P) will remain unchanged as compared to their original seating positions?
A. None
B. One
C. Two
D. Three
E. Four

46. Who sits between Y and R?
A. W
B. Q
C. T
D. P
E. None of these

47. How many persons sit between S and V when counted in clockwise direction from S?
A. None
B. One
C. Two
D. Three
E. Four

48. Four of the following five are alike in a certain way based on their seating positions in the above arrangement and so form a group. Which is the one that **does not** belong to that group?
A. QT
B. YW
C. SR
D. WS
E. VP

Directions (Q. 49-53): *Study the following arrangement carefully and answer the questions given below:*

7 6 1 7 9 2 4 1 5 6 4 9 2 3 4 1 2 5 8 5
8 4 8 3 1 2 7 5 2 6 7 2 9 5 3

49. How many 2s are there in the above arrangement, each of which is immediately followed by a digit which has a numerical value of more than four?
A. None
B. One
C. Two
D. Three
E. More than three

50. How many such 1s are there in the above arrangement, each of which is immediately preceded by a perfect square?
A. None
B. One
C. Two
D. Three
E. More than three

51. How many such 5s are there in the above arrangement each of which is immediately preceded and followed by an odd digit?
A. None
B. One
C. Two
D. Three
E. More than three

52. Which of the following is third to the left of the eighteenth digit from the left end of the above arrangement?
A. 8
B. 3
C. 4
D. 5
E. 1

53. If all the even digits are deleted from the above arrangement, which of the following will be ninth from the right end of the arrangement?
A. 9
B. 3
C. 1
D. 5
E. 7

Directions (Qs. 54 & 55): *Read the following information carefully and answer the questions which follow:*

If 'A × B' means 'A is wife of B'.
If 'A + B' means 'A is brother of B'.
If 'A ÷ B' means 'A is daughter of B'.
If 'A – B' means 'A is son of B'.

54. Which of the following means 'D is father of A'?
A. A – B × C + D   B. D ÷ C – B × A
C. A + B ÷ C × D   D. D + B × C – A
E. None of these

55. How is F related to J if 'F – G ÷ H × J' ?
A. Son   B. Grandson
C. Son-in-law   D. Father
E. Grandfather

Directions (Qs. 56–60) : *In each question below is given a group of letters followed by the combinations of number/symbol codes numbered (A), (B), (C), (D) and (E). You have to find out which of the combinations correctly represents the group of letters based on the following coding system and the conditions and mark the number of that combination as your answer.*

Letters : R B F C P Q A I H K U T E W M

Number /Symbol Code : $ β 6 8 ★ # % 2 © 4 7 9 @ 5 3

Conditions:

(*i*) If both the second and the fifth elements are vowels, the codes for both these are to be interchanged.

(*ii*) If the third element is a vowel and the fourth a consonant, the fourth element is to be coded as the code for the first element.

(*iii*) If the group of letters contains no vowel, the codes for the first and the last elements are to be interchanged.

56. FAWUCI
A. 6%5782   B. 2%5786
C. 6857%2   D. 6%5872
E. 6%5682

57. UECTAP
A. ★%89@7   B. 7@89%★
C. 7%89@★   D. 7%98@★
E. 789%@★

58. TFAQIM
A. 96%923   B. 96%239
C. 96%#23   D. #6%#23
E. #6%923

59. BWAFET
A. β5%6@9   B. b5%β@9
C. 65%6@9   D. b5%β9@
E. 65%β@9

60. HPKTMQ
A. ©★493#   B. #★349©
C. ©★943#   D. #★394©
E. #★493©

Directions (Qs. 61–65): *Study the information carefully and answer the given questions.*
A, C, D, I, L, P and M are sitting in a straight line facing North.

(a) P sits fourth to the right of A and C sits second to the left of P. D sits in the middle and is second to the right of M.

(b) I sits at the farthest possible distance from P (five persons sits between I and P)

61. If all the seven persons are made to sit in alphabetical order from left to right, the positions of how many will remain unchanged as compared to the original seating positions?
A. None   B. One
C. Two   D. Three
E. More than three

62. Four of the following are alike in a certain way based on their seating positions in the above arrangement and so form a group. Which pair does not belong to that group?
A. MA   B. DC
C. LP   D. AC
E. IM

63. What is the position of C with respect to M?
A. Second to the right
B. Immediate to the right
C. Immediate to the left

D. Third to the right
E. Fourth to the right

64. How many persons sit between A and L?
A. One   B. Two
C. Three   D. Four
E. More than Four

65. Which of the following pairs represents the persons sitting at the extreme ends of the line?
A. IC   B. DP
C. IP   D. AP
E. None of these

Quantitative Aptitude

Directions (Qs. 66-80): *What should come in place of the question mark (?) in the following questions?*

66. $120 \div 24 \times 36 + 8 = ?$
A. 188   B. 180
C. 184   D. 182
E. None of these

67. $6850 \div 25 \div ? - 24 = 30.8$
A. 4   B. 10
C. 6   D. 5
E. None of these

68. $39851 + 42305 = 122678 - ?$
A. 82156   B. 40522
C. 45022   D. 60256
E. None of these

69. $98 \times 64 - 3504 = ?$
A. 2572   B. 2768
C. 2964   D. 2732
E. None of these

70. $113698 - 105697 - 3058 = ?$
A. 4493   B. 4934
C. 4943   D. 4953
E. None of these

71. $(25 \times 6000) \div 150 \times 45 = ?$
A. 4500   B. 50000
C. 5000   D. 450000
E. None of these

72. $\sqrt[3]{2197} \times \sqrt[3]{729} = ?$
A. 117   B. 91
C. 126   D. 99
E. None of these

73. $(6)^2 + (8)^2 \times (2)^2 - (9)^2 = ?$
A. 215   B. 209
C. 221   D. 211
E. None of these

74. $7008 \div 24 + 6208 \div 16 = ?$
A. 640   B. 720
C. 700   D. 690
E. None of these

75. $\dfrac{3}{4}$ th of $\dfrac{3}{5}$ th of $\dfrac{2}{3}$ rd of ? $= 3174$
A. 10550   B. 10540
C. 10580   D. 10500
E. None of these

76. $8\dfrac{1}{3} + 7\dfrac{1}{2} - \dfrac{1}{3} = ?$
A. $10\dfrac{2}{3}$ B. $15\dfrac{1}{3}$
C. $10\dfrac{1}{2}$ D. $16\dfrac{1}{2}$
E. None of these

77. $648 \times 263 = ?$
A. 170424   B. 169128
C. 169372   D. 171072
E. None of these

78. $(408 + 220 + 102) \div (240 - ? - 57) = 29.2$
A. 156   B. 154
C. 158   D. 152
E. None of these

79. $\dfrac{52 \times 0.4 \times 4.5}{2 \times 3 \times 4} = ?$
A. 3.6   B. 4.2
C. 9.3   D. 8.3
E. None of these

80. $74 \times 25 - 33 \times 45 = ?$
A. 385   B. 365
C. 345   D. 325
E. None of these

81. The respective ratio of the number of boys to the number of girls studying in a School is 25 : 29. The total number of students studying in the School is 270. If 15 boys and 15 girls take admission in the School, what will be the new respective ratio of the boys and girls studying in the School?
A. 6 : 7
B. 8 : 9
C. 7 : 8
D. 7 : 9
E. None of these

82. The profit earned after selling T-shirt for ₹ 575 is the same as loss incurred after selling the same T-shirt ₹ 295. What is the cost price of the T-shirt?
A. ₹ 425
B. ₹ 445
C. ₹ 430
D. ₹ 450
E. None of these

83. In a class of 125 students 20% of the students can dance. $\frac{2}{5}$ th of the total number of students in the class can sing and $\frac{2}{5}$ th of the remaining number of students in the class are good at sports. What is the respective ratio of the number of students who can dance to the number of students who are good at sports?
A. 5 : 4
B. 4 : 3
C. 5 : 3
D. 6 : 2
E. None of these

84. Amrita took a loan of ₹ 50,600 at a certain rate of simple interest for 5 years. At the end of 5 years she repaid an amount of ₹ 65,780. What is the rate of interest at which Amrita took the loan?
A. 5 p.c.p.a.
B. 4 p.c.p.a.
C. 8 p.c.p.a.
D. 6 p.c.p.a.
E. None of these

85. What should come in place of the question mark (?) in the following number series?
3   5   13   43   177   ?   5353
A. 891
B. 713
C. 885
D. 899
E. None of these

86. What approximate value should come in place of the question mark (?) in the following question?
5040 ÷ 33 − 45 = ?
A. 115
B. 102
C. 120
D. 108
E. 125

87. The population of a town two years ago was 45,000. It increased by 12% in the first year and decreased by 15% in the second year. What was the population of the town at the end of two years?
A. 57,960
B. 42,840
C. 44,820
D. 50,400
E. None of these

88. Find the average of the following set of scores:
157, 348, 443, 221, 360, 795, 841, 101
A. 443
B. 368.50
C. 408.25
D. 348
E. None of these

89. If an amount ₹ 93,470 is distributed equally amongst 75 people, how much approximate amount would each person get?
A. ₹ 1,230
B. ₹ 1,240
C. ₹ 1,242
D. ₹ 1,246
E. ₹ 1,254

90. Samir scored a total of 455 marks out of 800 marks in an examination. What was his approximate percentage in the examination?
A. 60
B. 52
C. 54
D. 62
E. 57

Directions (Qs. 91-95): *Study the following table carefully and answer the questions given below:*

Number of Graduates and Post Graduates living in various Towns

Towns	Graduates	Post-Graduates
A	10,200	8,000
B	25,250	18,000
C	15,150	10,500
D	20,200	16,250
E	24,000	20,000
F	16,500	18,450

91. What is the difference between the number of graduates and the number of post-graduates in town C?
A. 4650
B. 4500
C. 4560
D. 4600
E. None of these

92. What is the average number of post graduates in all the towns together?
A. 16,250
B. 15,500
C. 15,200
D. 16,000
E. None of these

93. What is the respective ratio of the number of the graduates from towns A and B together to the number of post graduates from A and E together?

A. 709 : 535
B. 709 : 560
C. 540 : 709
D. 769 : 709
E. None of these

94. What is the total number of graduates and post graduates in towns A, D and F together?
A. 84,500
B. 90,200
C. 88,500
D. 89,600
E. None of these

95. The number of graduates in town F is approximately what per cent of the number of post graduates in the same town?
A. 84
B. 92
C. 95
D. 83
E. 89

Directions (Qs. 96-100): *Study the following graph carefully and answer the questions given below:*

Profit Earned by a company During Various Years (Profit earned in lakhs)

Profit = Income − Expenditure

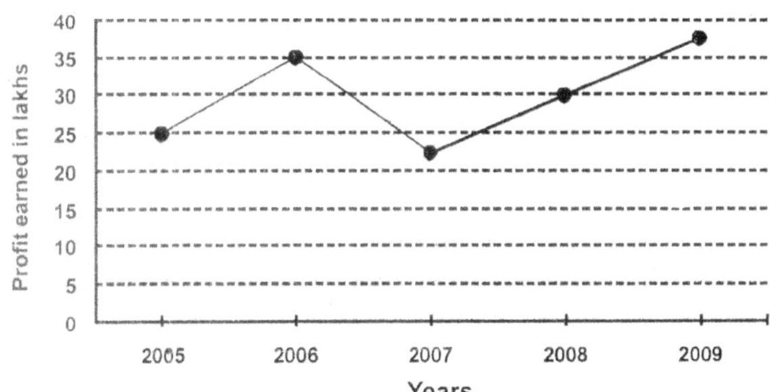

96. What is the average profit earned by the company over the years?
A. ₹ 35 lakhs
B. ₹ 40 lakhs
C. ₹ 25 lakhs
D. ₹ 30 lakhs
E. None of these

97. If the expenditure of the company in the year 2009 was ₹ 28 lakhs, what was the income of the company in that year?
A. ₹ 60 lakhs
B. ₹ 65.5 lakhs
C. ₹ 68.5 lakhs
D. ₹ 70 lakhs
E. None of these

98. What is the approximate per cent increase in the profit of the company in the year 2008 from the previous year?
A. 38
B. 28
C. 26
D. 33
E. 36

99. What is the respective ratio of the profit earned by the company in the year 2005 to the profit earned by the company in the year 2009?
A. 3 : 4
B. 4 : 5
C. 2 : 3
D. 2 : 5
E. None of these

100. If the income of the company in the year 2007 was ₹ 45 lakhs, what was the expenditure of the company in that year?
A. ₹ 22,00,000
B. ₹ 21,50,000
C. ₹ 20,00,000
D. Cannot be determined
E. None of these

ANSWERS

1	2	3	4	5	6	7	8	9	10
B	D	D	A	D	A	A	D	E	C

11	12	13	14	15	16	17	18	19	20
E	C	A	A	D	A	C	D	E	A

21	22	23	24	25	26	27	28	29	30
C	E	B	B	B	C	C	D	E	B

31	32	33	34	35	36	37	38	39	40
B	B	A	C	D	E	B	D	C	C

41	42	43	44	45	46	47	48	49	50
B	D	E	D	A	B	C	A	E	C

51	52	53	54	55	56	57	58	59	60
B	C	D	C	B	A	C	A	B	E

61	62	63	64	65	66	67	68	69	70
B	D	D	B	C	A	D	B	B	C

71	72	73	74	75	76	77	78	79	80
E	A	D	E	C	E	A	C	E	B

81	82	83	84	85	86	87	88	89	90
C	E	A	D	A	D	B	C	D	E

91	92	93	94	95	96	97	98	99	100
A	C	B	D	E	D	B	D	C	E

Some Selected Explanatory Answers

31. From question,

```
W   O R   T     H     Y
T   H Y   W     O     R
W   X Y
```

32. Meaningful word is OUT

33.

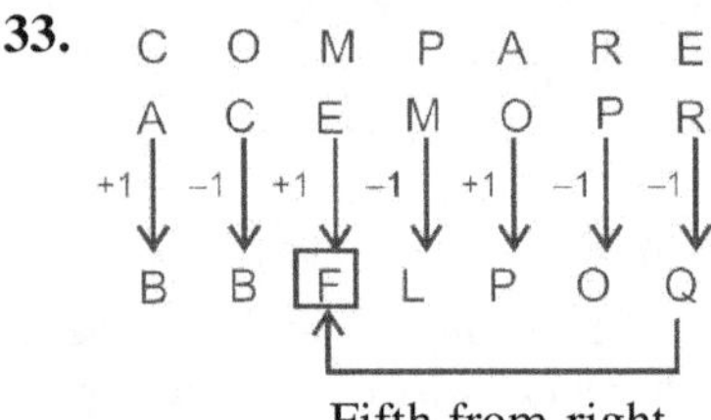

Fifth from right

34.

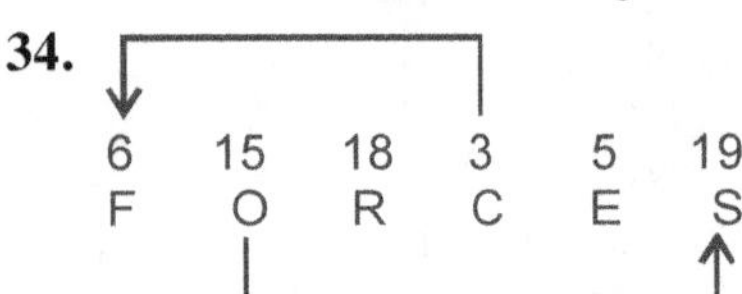

35.

Active	Passive
Siberia is a cold place	A cold place is Siberia
Water freezes to ice here	Freezes here ice to water
Cover ten percent of earth	Covers earth of percent ten

36.

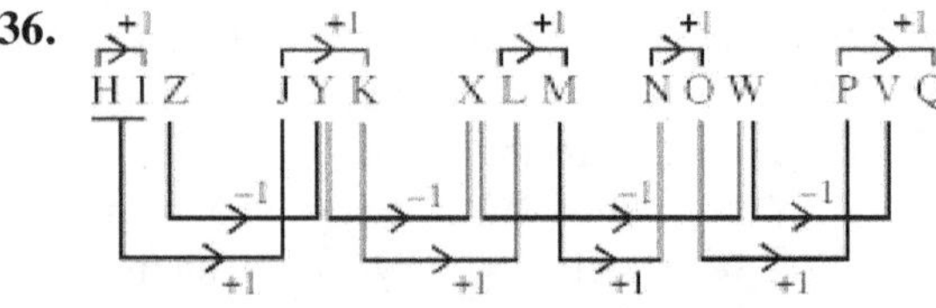

37. Sneha > Avani > Parth

Sneha > Dhruv > Avani

Therefore,

Sneha > Dhruv > Avani > Parth

For Qs. (44-48): Sitting arrangement

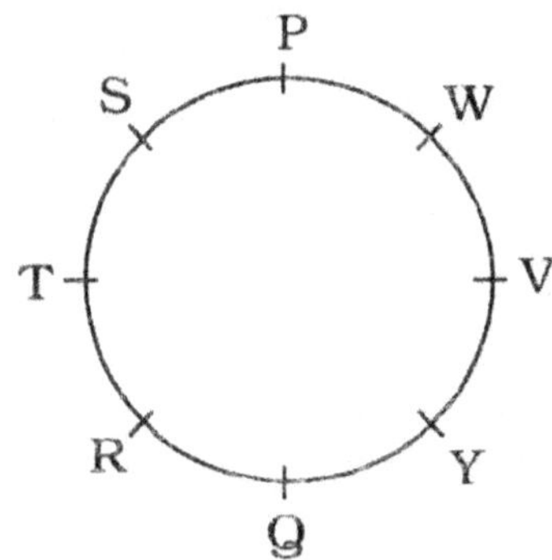

45.

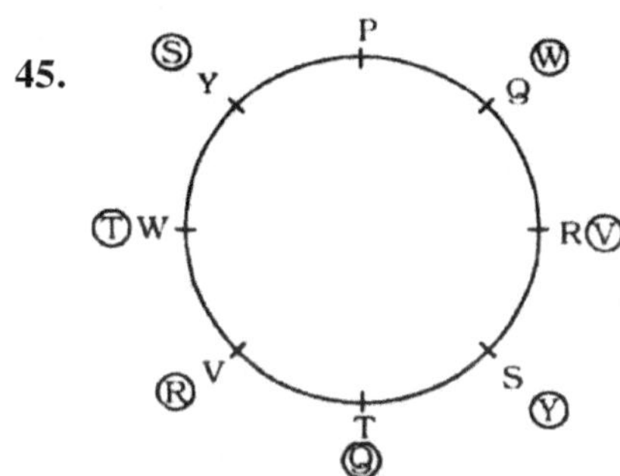

52. 3rd to the left of the 18th digit from the left means 15th from the left, i.e., 4.

54. A.A − B × C + D

⇒(−) B ⟷ C (+) —— D (?)

A (+)

Here, Gender of D is not given.

B.D ÷ C − B × A

⇒(−) B ⟷ A (+)

C (+)

D (−)

Here, A is Grand father of D.

C.A + B ÷ C × D

⇒(−) C ⟷ D (+)

(−) B —— A (+)

Here, D is Father of A.

Hence, Correct option is (C).

55. F − G ÷ H × J

⇒(−) H ⟷ J (+)

(−) G

(+) F

Hence, F is Grand Son of J.

61-65:

61.

62. Except in AC, the first person in sitting immidiately left to the second person.

63. C is third right to M.

64. Two persons are sitting between A and L.

65. I and P are sitting at the ends.

66. 120 ÷ 24 × 36 + 8

$$= \frac{120}{24} \times 36 + 8$$

$$= 5 \times 36 + 8$$

$$= 180 + 8 = 188.$$

67. $6850 \times \dfrac{1}{25} \times \dfrac{1}{x}$ = 54.8

$$\Rightarrow \qquad x = \frac{274}{54.8}$$

$$= \frac{2740}{548} = 5$$

68. 39851 + 42305 = 122678 − x

$$x = 122678 - 39851 - 42305$$

$$= 40522.$$

69. 98 × 64 − 3504 = 6272 − 3504

$$= 2768.$$

70. (25 × 6000) ÷ 150 × 45

$$= (150000) \div 150 \times 45$$

$$= \frac{150000}{150} \times 45$$

$$= 1000 \times 45$$

$$= 45000.$$

72. $\sqrt[3]{13^3} \times \sqrt[3]{9^3} = 13 \times 9 = 117$

73. $(6)^2 + (8)^2 \times (2)^2 - (9)^2$

$$= (6)^2 + (2^3)^2 \times (2)^2 - (9)^2$$

$$= (6)^2 + (2)^6 \times (2)^2 - (9)^2$$

$$= (6)^2 + (2)^8 - (9)^2$$

$$= 36 + 256 - 81$$

$$= 211.$$

74. $7008 \div 24 + 6208 \div 16$

$$= \frac{7008}{24} + \frac{6208}{16}$$

$$= 292 + 388$$

$$= 680.$$

75. Let, $\dfrac{3}{4} \times \dfrac{3}{5} \times \dfrac{2}{3} \times x = 3174$

$$\therefore \qquad x = 3174 \times \frac{3}{2} \times \frac{5}{3} \times \frac{4}{3}$$

$$= 1058 \times 10$$

$$= 10580.$$

76. $8\dfrac{1}{3} + 7\dfrac{1}{2} - \dfrac{1}{3}$

$$= (8 + 7 - 0) + \left(\frac{1}{3} + \frac{1}{2} - \frac{1}{3}\right)$$

$$= 15 + \frac{1}{2}$$

$$= 15\frac{1}{2}.$$

78. $730 \div (183 - x) = 29.2$

$$\therefore \qquad 183 - x = \frac{7300}{292} = 25$$

$$\Rightarrow \qquad x = 158.$$

79. $\dfrac{52 \times 0.4 \times 4.5}{2 \times 3 \times 4}$

$$= 13 \times 0.2 \times 1.5$$

$$= 13 \times 0.3$$

$$= 3.9.$$

81. Let, number of boys $= 25x$

And, number of girls $= 29x$

Then, from question

$$25x + 29x = 270$$

$$\Rightarrow \qquad x = 5$$

$\therefore$ when 15 boys are added the total number of boys

$$= 140$$

And that of girls $= 160$

$\therefore \qquad$ Ratio $= 7 : 8$.

82. Let, the Cost price of the T-Shirt is ₹ x.

Profit earned by selling it in ₹ 575

$$= 575 - x$$

Loss earned by selling it in ₹ 295

$$= x - 295$$

From question,

$$\text{Loss} = \text{Profit}$$

$$x - 295 = 575 - x$$

$$2x = 575 + 295$$

$$2x = 870$$

$$x = 435$$

Hence, Cost price of the T-Shirt is ₹ 435.

83. Number of students who can dance

$$= \frac{125 \times 20}{100} = 25$$

Number of students who can sing

$$= \frac{2}{5} \times 125 = 50$$

Remaining students

$$= 125 - 75 = 50$$

Now number of students who are good at sports

$$= 50 \times \frac{2}{5} = 20.$$

$\therefore$ Respective ratio

$$= \frac{25}{20} = 5 : 4.$$

84. Principal = ₹ 50,600

Amount repayed after 5 years

$$= 65780$$

$\therefore \quad$ S.I = 65780 − 50600 = 15180

Now let rate = r%

then, $\quad$ S.I. $= \dfrac{p \times r \times t}{100}$

$$15180 = \frac{50600 \times r \times 5}{100}$$

$\therefore \quad r = 6\%.$

85. The pettern follows

$$5 = 3 \times 1 + 2$$
$$13 = 5 \times 2 + 3$$
$$43 = 13 \times 3 + 4$$
$$177 = 43 \times 4 + 5$$
$$\boxed{891} = 177 \times 5 + 6.$$

86. $5040 \div 33 - 45$

$$= \frac{5040}{33} - 45$$
$$= 152.73 - 45$$
$$= 153 - 45$$
$$= 108.$$

87. Population of town at the end of 2 years

$$= 45000 \left(1 + \frac{12}{100}\right)^{1} \left(1 - \frac{15}{100}\right)^{1}$$

$$= 45000 \times \frac{28}{25} \times \frac{17}{20} = 42840.$$

88. Average $= \dfrac{\sum\limits_{i=1}^{n} x_i}{n}$

$$= \frac{157 + 348 + 443 + 221 + 360 + 795 + 841 + 101}{8}$$

$$= \frac{3266}{8}$$

$$= 408.25.$$

89. Let, each person get ₹ x

Then, 75 person get 75 x

From question,

$$75 \times x = 93470$$

$$x = \frac{93470}{75}$$

$$\cong ₹ \ 1246.$$

90. Percentage Score of Samir

$$= \frac{\text{Mark's Score}}{\text{Total marks}} \times 100$$

$$= \frac{455}{800} \times 100$$

$$= 56.875\%$$

$$\cong 57\%.$$

91. Difference between number of Graduate and Post-Graduates

$$= 15150 - 10500$$
$$= 4650.$$

92. Required average

$$= \frac{\begin{array}{c}8000 + 18000 + 10500 + 16250 \\ + 20000 + 18450\end{array}}{6}$$

$$= \frac{91200}{6} = 15200.$$

93. Required ratio $= \dfrac{35450}{28000} = 709 : 560$

94.

Town	Number of Graduates	Number of Post-graduates
A	10,200	8,000
D	20,200	16,250
F	16,500	18,450
Total	46,900	42,700

Total number of students together

$$= 46900 + 42700$$

$$= 89600.$$

95. Required percentage $= \dfrac{16500 \times 100}{18450}$

$$= 89.4\%$$

$$= 89\% \text{ (Approx.)}$$

96. Average profit earned by the Company

$$= \dfrac{\text{Total Profit earned}}{\text{No. of years}}$$

$$= \dfrac{25 + 35 + 22.5 + 30 + 37.5}{5}$$

$$= ₹\ 30 \text{ lakhs.}$$

97. Income of the company in the year 2009

$$= 28 + 37.5 = ₹\ 65.5 \text{ lakh.}$$

98. Increase in profit $= ₹\ 7.5$ lakhs

$$\therefore \text{ Increase } \% = \dfrac{7.5}{22.5} \times 100$$

$$= 33.3 = 33\% \text{ (Approx.)}$$

99. $\dfrac{\text{Profit earned by the Company in 2005}}{\text{Profit earned by the Company in 2009}}$

$$= \dfrac{25}{37.5} = \dfrac{2}{3}.$$

100. Required expenditure

$$= ₹\ (45 - 22.5) \text{ lakhs}$$

$$= 22.5 \text{ lakhs.}$$

www.ingramcontent.com/pod-product-compliance
Lightning Source LLC
Chambersburg PA
CBHW081935160726
47999CB00008B/2398